INDUSTRIAL RELATIONS IN IRELAND

Fifth Edition

Joseph Wallace, Patrick Gunnigle, Michelle O'Sullivan

IPA
INSTITUTE OF PUBLIC ADMINISTRATION

Published in 2020
by the Institute of Public Administration
57–61 Lansdowne Road
Dublin D04 TC62
Ireland
www.ipa.ie

British Library Cataloguing in Publication Data
A catalogue record for this book is available from the British Library.

ISBN: 978-1-910393-29-1

Cover design by Identikit Design Consultants
Typeset by Computertype
Printed by W & G Baird, Antrim

Contents

Chapter 3 Trade Unions

Chapter 12 Employee Participation, Employee Involvement and Workplace Partnership

Chapter 13 Collective Bargaining in Ireland

Acknowledgements

- Brian Sheehan, Colman Higgins and Andy Prendergast, *Industrial Relations News*
- Jane Brophy and Paula Butler, Local Government Management Agency
- Cedric Chau, James Connington, Edwin Maguire, Richard Boyle, John Paul Owens and Hannah Ryan, Institute of Public Administration
- Professor Bill Roche, University College Dublin
- Professor Jimmy Donaghey, University of South Australia
- Dr Brian Harney, Dublin City University
- Mary Connaughton, Director, Chartered Institute of Personnel and Development (CIPD) Ireland
- Mike Crowley, HR Director, Pfizer Ireland Pharmaceuticals
- Dr Gerard McMahon, Dublin Institute of Technology
- Alan O'Leary, Services Industrial Professional Technical Union (SIPTU)
- Ruth Gill, Gill & Macmillan
- Gillian Chamberlain and Barbara Nestor, Irish Business and Employers Confederation (IBEC)
- Michael McDonnell, chairman, UTS HR Group, and former managing director of CIPD Ireland
- Professor Aidan Kelly, University College Dublin and Shenzhen Business School
- Martina O'Callaghan and Gordon Cavanagh, Central Statistics Office
- Anna Perry, Workplace Relations Commission
- Liam Berney, Irish Congress of Trade Unions
- Professor Anthony Kerr, Sutherland School of Law, University College Dublin
- Professor John Coakley, University College Dublin
- Fintan O'Mahony
- Pat Ennis, General Secretary, Garda Representative Association
- Dr Daryl D'Art, Lecturer in Industrial Relations Emeritus, University of Limerick
- Verona Stellet
- Marian Geoghegan, Financial Services Union

Various colleagues at the University of Limerick (UL) were most helpful and supportive of our efforts: Drs Christine Cross, Sarah Kiernan, Juliette MacMahon, Sarah MacCurtain, Caroline Murphy, Lorraine Ryan; Professor Tony Dundon. We also wish to thank our Business Studies Librarian, Peter Reilly, and all the Library staff at UL.

List of Figures and Tables

Chapter 1

Industrial Relations: A Contextual and Theoretical Overview

THE SCOPE OF INDUSTRIAL RELATIONS

The term 'industrial relations' is one of a number of terms used to describe the subject, with others being 'employee relations', 'employment relations' and 'labour relations', as it is referred to in the US. As a subject matter, industrial relations has connotations with the traditional unionised blue-collar working environment in the manufacturing sector, while the term 'employee relations' conjures up images of the non-union or less unionised white-collar services sector. In recent years, the term 'employment relations' – which merges the more individualist 'employee relations' with the collectivist 'industrial relations' – has gained currency. This text retains the term 'industrial relations', not least because it is the one most commonly used by Irish practitioners but also because it is the term used in Irish legislation. However, the text considers not just collective *but* also individual aspects of the employment relationship, although there is naturally a concentration on the former. Accordingly, the terms 'employee relations' and 'employment relations' are also used in the text where they seem appropriate.

Industrial relations can be best understood in the wider context of the historical, political, social and economic processes that have shaped the regulation of working lives. That is, the subject draws upon a range of disciplines to facilitate an understanding of both individual and collective relationships, in white- and blue-collar work environments, at plant, office, sectoral, national and international levels. The multifaceted nature of the subject necessitates consideration of contributions from an array of other specialisms in order to accommodate a comprehensive analysis, including labour law, history, sociology, political science, economics and organisational psychology. Too often in the past Irish industrial relations was viewed through a narrow Irish lens without placing it in the context of international movements, developments and ideas. While this text is focused on Irish industrial relations, and that context has primacy, we have been conscious to have regard to international developments.

Traditionally, the subject of industrial relations has had a preoccupation with trade unions, and these remain a continuing source of interest. This emphasis, while understandable, needs to be accompanied by an appreciation of the importance of contextual matters and contrasting (non-union) perspectives. In so far as is possible, the text attempts to adopt an unbiased approach to the study of the subject matter. However, the study of collectivism inevitably gives the subject a certain aura no less than individualised approaches, rooted in organisational behaviour and management disciplines, in their own way engender a different aura.

By its very nature, industrial relations deals with contentious and controversial issues and debates, and it is essential to engage with these. The subject also throws up a plethora of factual data but dealing simply in 'facts', or for that matter common sense, is insufficient to understand the subject or processes involved. As Jackson (1982) pertinently pointed out, facts do not speak for themselves! They are open to a multitude of interpretations in the light of underlying ideas, ideologies, perceptions, competing interests and changing social mores. Accordingly, the text takes a scholarly approach to outlining the central strands of research and the views of authors from differing viewpoints and to interrogating these. The intention is not to provide definitive answers to issues raised but to provoke critical reflection and debate, as advocated by Ackers (2019).

There are a number of competing definitions of the study of industrial relations. Flanders defined it as the study of the institutions and rules of job regulation. This definition has a strong resonance with Dunlop's (1958) systems approach, which similarly placed a strong emphasis on rules and institutions. The focus on institutions and rules has been criticised by radical writers who draw attention to the relative neglect of power and control in these pluralist approaches. Recognising these objections, Flanders advanced a shorter, less value-driven definition of industrial relations as simply 'job regulation'. Salomon (2000: 3) offers a more expanded description, defining industrial relations as encompassing 'a set of phenomena, both inside and outside the workplace, concerned with determining and regulating the employment relationship'. This latter definition is useful in that it directs attention at a need for familiarity with a wide range of phenomena in order to understand the working of any industrial relations system. These are explored in the second part of this chapter under the interrelated headings of history, politics and economics.

Figure 1.1 presents a working model or overview of the Irish system of industrial relations. Elements of this model are explored throughout the text and critically evaluated. In this chapter, the main theoretical perspectives and contextual factors that form the shape of the industrial relations system are introduced. The system itself can be viewed from many perspectives. No single perspective yields a full understanding but each can add to our insights. The location of five theoretical perspectives on the outer perimeter of Figure 1.1 is designed to convey the potential of each of these theories to provide their own insights. That is, these theoretical perspectives or frames of reference offer contrasting explanations of the same phenomena or features of the industrial relations system.

The prevalence of dual-direction arrows depicts the relationship between the various components of the system. This may be reflected in a vast array of exchanges, such as:

- trade union opposition to legal intervention on grounds of history or tradition;
- the nature of third-party dispute-settling agencies;

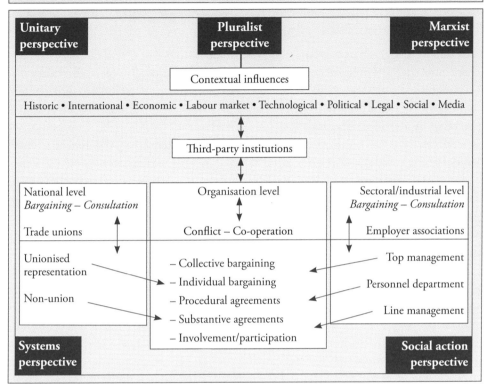

Figure 1.1
Model of the Irish System of Industrial Relations

- the impact of the economy on the terms of a collective agreement reached at national, industrial or organisational level by employees and employer(s) (or their representative organisations);
- the influence of international factors such as membership of the EU;
- the extreme openness of the Irish economy, which means international competitiveness is a major factor.

INDUSTRIAL RELATIONS THEORY

The role of theory is to develop conceptual understanding and facilitate the analysis and appraisal of the processes, structures and institutions of industrial relations. This section of the text outlines and evaluates the main academic theories that have been developed, in efforts to provide a means of understanding and interpreting industrial relations realities. As each theory originates from conceptual frameworks that embody differing assumptions, there is not a single 'best' theory of industrial relations. Each provides insights and has its relative strengths. It would be remiss not to acknowledge the centrality of the pluralist analysis in Irish industrial relations practices and debates, not least because the legislative and institutional framework is based, at least implicitly, on pluralist principles and ideas.

Pluralist Analysis

The pluralist model is based upon the premise of the existence of a 'post-capitalist' society, where industrial and political conflicts have become institutionally separated, ownership is distinguished from management, and authority and power in society are more widely distributed. A central feature of this post-capitalist perspective is that the class conflict generated by the Industrial Revolution is considered to have abated. Contemporary society, it is argued, is more open and mobile, with the extension of the franchise (vote) democratising politics and the advent of the welfare state serving to alleviate the worst extremes of deprivation and inequality. The spread and diffusion of property ownership, status and authority in the post-capitalist society have removed the sharp divisions between those who were once industrially and politically powerful and their counterparts, who were weak and powerless. Added to this is the growth of educational opportunity opening up hitherto closed occupational routes.

Pluralism acknowledges that society is comprised of a range of individuals, and interest and social groups, each in pursuit of their own objectives. Just as the political system is institutionalised and regulated through a party political and parliamentary process, so too is it desirable that the industrial system is institutionalised and regulated through representative organisations and appropriately structured processes. Management's job is to balance the competing organisational values and interests in order to maintain a viable collaborative structure (Fox 1973). Collective bargaining is the main process which engenders industrial relations stability and adaptability (Clegg 1975). Structured and representative organisations on both sides of industry are seen as necessary to address the tensions and conflicts between sectional interest groups. Pluralists approve of the establishment of third-party institutions to provide a generally acceptable route for selecting between contrasting objectives and for the mitigation and resolution of conflict (Dahrendorf 1959). In summary, pluralists acknowledge the inevitability of conflict but point to the relative stability of a society that institutionalises, manages and contains differences via structures that allow for negotiated compromises, conciliation, adjudication and collaboration.

Unitary Analysis

The basic premise of the unitary analysis is that all employment units are, or at least should be, cohesive and harmonious with a total commitment to the attainment of a common goal. Consequently, all staff members are expected to agree unreservedly with the aspirations of the organisation and the means deployed to give effect to them. Through this team or complementary partnership approach, it is assumed that both sides can satisfy their common goals of high profitability and pay levels, job security and efficiency. Members of staff are expected to give effect to organisational instructions and to show loyalty to the entity for the realisation of common goals.

The unitary philosophy, or framework, is predominantly managerialist and acts to legitimise management authority under the heading of commonality and serves as a means of justifying managerial decisions to any interested parties, while explaining opposition to same as either ill-informed or perverse. Management, of course, has responsibilities in the unitarist framework. It must provide appropriate communications structure to alert staff to organisational priorities and to manage their expectations. Indeed, a notable feature of unitarist thinking is that when differences or conflict do arise, these are often ascribed to 'communications' rather than any issues fundamental to the employment relationship. It is implicitly accepted that competent and effective leadership (or management) is a prerequisite to the pursuit of organisational effectiveness. If this is not in place, the remedy is to change the leadership (management) as necessary.

In practice this unitary view can give rise to widely differing outcomes. At one end it can lead to an employee-centred paternalism while at the other end it can embody authoritarianism and gross exploitation. During the nineteenth century, many employers adopted an aggressive unitary stance, actively excluding unions while employing women and children on low pay for long hours in unsanitary working conditions. In contrast, historical paternalism saw some employers, such as the Guinness brewing company, providing working conditions and benefits that went beyond those provided by modern companies, such as lifetime employment and housing for their workers. These different outcomes from a unitarist approach are still evident today in the practices of soft and hard versions of human resource management (HRM), respectively.

Radical and Neo-Marxist Approaches

These perspectives see a continuing relevance to the Marxist view of capitalist societies as being divided into antagonistic class forces. Although original Marxist analysis is a theory of capitalist society and social change, rather than industrial relations per se, it also provides a framework for the interpretation of the relationship between capital and labour at the workplace. Classical Marxism saw capitalism as an advanced stage in societal development, with class conflict over the distribution of the 'surplus value' of workers' efforts giving rise to irreconcilable antagonism between capital and labour.

In essence, Marxism is based upon the premise that class (i.e. capital and labour) conflict is at the root of societal change. This conflict is the product of the inequitable distribution of power and wealth in wider society. Therefore, social and political conflict (and social change) are the consequences of economic inequity within society, between the owners/capitalists and the labouring classes. Class and political conflict are linked to industrial conflict with struggles at the workplace over work organisation and the distribution of rewards, i.e. over 'surplus value' created by workers. Hence, the industrial relations system is viewed as a marginal arena for the conduct of this class war.

While based on the premise that economic and political issues cannot be separated, neo-Marxist and radical approaches do not share the extremes of the classical Marxist analysis. They do, however, regard the concepts that Marx explored as having explanatory value. They place emphasis on the continuing antagonistic interests of capital and labour and consider it essential to have regard to this in analysing the world of work and industrial relations. The neo-Marxist and radical frame of reference uses the prisms of power and control to analyse industrial relations. Put simply, employers are seen as possessing greater power sources and they use this greater power to try to control the labour process with workers contesting such efforts from time to time.

The focus on power and control offers a valuable insight into the operation of the industrial relations system and provides a critical research perspective on management practices, such as scientific management, human relations and HRM high-performance work systems. It also allows for an interrogation of the role of technology. In the modern labour process school, which has its roots in Marxist theory, technology is not seen as a neutral force but is viewed as a means for management to gain control of skill and knowledge that would otherwise reside in workers, and this results in deskilling.

In criticising the nature of work organisation under capitalism, it is important to appreciate that neither capitalists nor managers are considered 'bad' by Marxists. They may act against workers' interests but they are driven by the imperatives of competition. Of course, it is this competition which is at the root of economic progress and social development, and which state socialist systems, based on Marxist ideology, were unable to deliver in Eastern Europe from the 1950s onwards.

Systems Analysis

The essence of a systems theory approach to industrial relations is that individuals are constrained by systems factors which largely determine the possible range of actions and the nature of industrial relations. Systems theory owes its origin to the work of the American scholar John Dunlop (1958). Dunlop's construction of an integrated model is based on the view that, though overlapping and interacting with the economic and political decision-making systems, industrial relations should be considered as a societal subsystem in its own right. This subsystem's output or product is a set of rules pertaining to the employment relationship, which govern the actors at the workplace and in industry. The term 'actors' is used in social science to indicate that individuals act in a representative capacity filling the various roles allotted to them. It also implies that the actors are constrained, to a greater or lesser extent, by these roles.

Dunlop's model is best considered as a conceptual one, rather than applying to any specific system. It is based on a standard *input–process–output* model, which he argued may be applied regardless of the prevailing economic or political system. Under *input*, Dunlop identified three sets of influences: *actors*, *environmental contexts* and *ideology*. These combine in the bargaining, conciliation and legislative processes, yielding a body, network or web of *rules*. The *actors* include the different worker categories (whether organised or unorganised), various layers of management (together with their respective representatives) and the range of third-party agencies. Outputs primarily involve two types of rules: (i) substantive rules covering matters such as pay and condition of employment; (ii) procedural rules prescribing how substantive rules are to be made.

The *environmental context* impinging on the system is comprised of technological, market/budgetary and power variables in the wider society. Technology is seen as impacting on the nature of industrial relations and, unlike in Marxist analysis, its impact is independent of the capitalist nature of production. The market or budgetary constraints, whether applied locally, nationally or internationally, affect all enterprise types – not just the entity's management but also, ultimately, all of the system's role players.

Power in Dunlop's model refers to power in the wider society and is given expression in the degree of autonomy afforded to the industrial relations system. Power in the workplace is not part of Dunlop's model and this omission has been criticised by radical writers. Dunlop's system approach is inherently pluralist as the *ideological* input recognises that while each group of actors in the system may have their own set of ideas and values, these have to be sufficiently congruent for a level of ideological compatibility to prevail.

Social Action Approach

The social action perspective on industrial relations is at the opposite end of the continuum to systems theory. It 'stresses that individuals retain at least some freedom of action and ability to influence events' (Jackson 1982). This approach is rooted in a well-developed sociological school of thought which argues that just as 'society makes man … man makes society' (Silverman 1970). A social action perspective is concerned with individuals and the interpretation and meanings that they give to their lived work experience. Thus, individuals' definitions and perceptions are accorded a high degree of significance. It is these definitions and perceptions that determine, in part, relationships, behaviours and actions. As a result, social and industrial relations actions can only be fully understood by considering subjective meanings. Qualitative case study research is often used to explore meanings and intents that would otherwise not be amenable to discovery. Such research also needs to take account of influences outside the workplace. This is because individuals' actions and decisions are determined not just by the specific work situations they find themselves in but by a wider range of underlying influences such as attitudes, values, experiences and expectations.

Social action concentrates on the capacity of actors to influence outputs and does not see events solely determined by system structures. Historically, the impact of people like James Larkin and William Martin Murphy, arguably, provides support for the social action view that individuals have a capacity to influence and shape events. More recently, a small number of union leaders, known colloquially as the 'PESPI generation', changed the face of Irish industrial relations when they embraced a consensus and partnership approach in the late 1980s and 1990s. However, Larkin and James Connolly were parts of larger social movements of the time and the PESPI union leaders were influenced by the trade union defeats in the early and middle part of that decade in Ireland and by events in the UK.

Commentary on the Theories

The pluralist analysis has been criticised for its inherent conservatism through a ready acceptance of the social and political status quo (Fox 1973; Goldthorpe 1974). Furthermore, it tends to ignore the decision-making powers available to capital beyond the collective bargaining process. In this regard, radical theorists point out that power is also about the ability to prevent matters becoming the subject of negotiation. Yet, unlike both the unitary and Marxist theories, pluralism offers mechanisms for democratic societies to temper the excesses of capitalism without the paternalist control or the extremes of state socialism. Although it favours prescriptions advocating the constant negotiation of conflicts based on compromise, this can be seen as a practical strength (Clegg 1975). Indeed, it is difficult to conceive of how democratic societies could order their affairs other than in a way influenced by pluralism.

The unitary perspective, in its many guises, has been widely critiqued for its unrealistically utopian outlook and restricted applicability (e.g. to non-union entities), for being manipulative and for offering at best a paternalistic management orientation that assumes a generally accepted value system. However, the unitary approach is now arguably the dominant approach globally to the management of the employment relationship. In this regard, it appeals to mainstream management approaches and has informed conceptual and operational management from the time of the early human relations school through to the latest iterations of HRM.

In drawing attention to the nature of power and control in the workplace and society, the neo-Marxist and radical analyses present a valuable intellectual challenge to unitarist-based management approaches and to pluralist thinking (Ackers 2019). Neo-Marxist and radical approaches are at their strongest when interrogating and critically evaluating capitalist developments and conventional management approaches, such as human relations and HRM. They are at their weakest in providing practical prescriptions for regulating the world of work and labour markets. While Marxists have been critical of systems theory, it is important to acknowledge that Marxist approaches are inherently systems-based since they seek to explain the operation of capitalism as a functional system.

Harney (2019: 120) defends the systems theory approach and points out that systems theory need not necessarily 'direct attention from issues of power and control', and has defended it as having the potential to offer a useful 'heuristic device' to aid understanding of employment relations. However, to date, system theory has not been in any way as influential as the conceptual frameworks approach.

Critics of a social action approach point to its neglect of those structural features that influence individuals and actors. However, as the social action approach does not aim to address wider explanations, it is arguably unfair to dwell on this limitation. Social action makes its contribution in terms of allowing for an exploration of the experienced world of work and its subjective meaning to individuals. In this way, it supplements, rather than supplants, system-based approaches.

HISTORY AND INDUSTRIAL RELATIONS

The earliest identified trade union was an association of London hatters in the reign of Charles II (Boyd 1984). The first Irish combination (or trade union as they became known later) to be identified by name was the Regular Carpenters of Dublin, which, it is estimated, was founded in 1764. There is also evidence that there were several combinations active in the Cork area in the middle of the eighteenth century. Their activities included organising strikes, picketing, destroying tools, materials and machinery, and ostracising employers who would not give in to their demands. Eventually, Parliament declared that anyone in Cork City found guilty of being a member of an unlawful combination should be 'imprisoned not above six months, whipped in public and released only on giving recognisance of good behaviour for seven years' (Boyd 1972: 14). By the beginning of the nineteenth century, a series of statutory and judicial decisions (dating back to 1729) had served to make combinations illegal. In 1780 the Irish Parliament passed further legislation for the suppression of combinations, while members of the Irish clergy had condemned unions as 'iniquitous extortions' (Boyd 1972: 10).

The official hostility towards combinations can primarily be attributed to the dominant laissez-faire or liberal economic doctrine. This orthodoxy was informed by the belief that the market was the only means by which all prices, including wages, profits and economic priorities, should be determined (Barrow 2013). Labour was a factor of production – no more, no less – and there should be no interference with the laws of supply and demand in the marketplace. Combinations represented an attempt by workers to preserve their trade but also an effort to redress the imbalance wrought by the private enterprise system and the prevalent economic order.

As revolutionary and republican ideas spread throughout Europe, unions were at times blamed. They were wrongly identified as a factor in the French Revolution of 1798, which was largely a revolution by the emerging bourgeois class against the ruling order. In effect, unions were identified as a threat to the prevalent economic, social and political order, with the result being the introduction of the Anti-Combination Acts 1799–1800. While the law applied to all combinations, it was brought to bear much more stringently on collectivities of workers than on employer combinations. Thus, employer combinations that blacklisted workers were ignored. Despite the legal and social pressures, unions maintained their influence, as individual employers frequently disregarded the legal option and engaged with them. Eventually, in 1824 the Anti-Combination Acts were repealed, although unions only enjoyed a quasi-legal existence thereafter.

As the Industrial Revolution swept Britain in the nineteenth century, with the advent of factory-cum-machine production and the concentration of population in the large industrial cities and towns, trade unions grew in importance. It made little sense for a nation in the middle of colonial and industrial expansion to be at war with its skilled workers (Pelling 1976). The term 'trade union' only entered common usage around this time, following the founding of the nationally organised model unions that represented workers in the skilled trades that had grown out of the Industrial Revolution. They were careful in the use of the strike weapon but, because they were financially strong, were able to survive long strikes when ones occurred.

Industrial militancy was not a *raison d'être* of the earlier craft or later model unions, and they were reformist in orientation, wishing to have some of the benefits of industrial development. Collective bargaining as a concept and practice dates from the 1850s and, in time, it would become the mechanism for resolving disputes between employer and workers. Thus, Sidney and Beatrice Webb (1897: 1) came to define a trade union as a 'continuous association of wage earners for the purpose of maintaining and improving the conditions of their working lives'. This definition has continuing relevance despite its neglect of political and wider organisational issues in which trade unions engage.

The 'responsible' nature of the model unions was to lead to significant changes in political parties' attitude towards trade unionism – from one of hostility to one of accommodation and the according of certain rights and immunities. Their relative wealth enabled them to become owners of small properties (workers' cottages) and qualified them under the extension of the franchise to (male only) smallholders in 1867. At a time when the electorate was restricted, this gave them political clout, which they used astutely to gain political support for reform of the law on trade unions, first from the Liberals in the 1868 general election and then the Tories in 1874. Between 1871 and 1876, and then again in 1906, the UK Parliament passed laws serving to grant legality to trade unions, protect union funds from court action, recognise collective bargaining, grant immunities to strikes (and other forms of industrial action) and legalise peaceful picketing. In this way, trade unions grew up with liberal democracy. However, while the UK Parliament was granting liberties to trade unions, the judiciary limited and even, on occasion, reversed these. It is this historical experience that led to trade unions' traditional antipathy towards the law and the judiciary.

Irish Trade Union Development

In the nineteenth century Irish craft unions continued to surface, to a large extent as a branch of equivalent British model unions, which was facilitated by Ireland being part of the UK at that time. According to Ó Gráda (1994), by the earlier part of the nineteenth century, most crafts in Irish towns and cities appear to have been highly unionised. In a society plagued by unemployment, destitution, illness and emigration, the skilled tradesmen enjoyed a relatively privileged place in society by virtue of their comparatively high wages and greater security of employment – they were what Marxists referred to as the 'aristocracy of labour'. To sustain that position, they sought to maintain the value of their trade by protecting the apprenticeship system.

Apprenticeship systems dated back to the guild system and had benefits for employers and workers – employers were guaranteed a trained, skilled worker and workers were protected from 'the dilution of the trade' by unscrupulous employers. Where strong enough, the craft unions frequently unilaterally determined the rate for the job – employers had to pay the going rate or skilled workers would not work for them. The unions also controlled entry to the trade, often confining membership to relatives of members, and sought to prevent deskilling, sometimes by resisting technical innovations. The craft unions usually provided some minimal 'friendly society' insurance-type benefits against unemployment, sickness and death. These were important in the absence of any state welfare system.

Inter-union cooperation in Ireland formally emerged for the first time in the shape of trades councils (i.e. organisations representing trade unionists in individual towns and cities). Such councils were founded in Belfast in 1881 and in Dublin in 1884. Though primarily concerned with the interests of craft workers, their formation was a significant step in the overall development of the Irish trade union movement. The Irish branches of British unions were affiliated to the Trade Union Congress, which had been founded in 1868. However, Irish affairs were given minimal attention at annual conferences, being left until the afternoon of the last day when many delegates had departed, and this led to the growing disenchantment of Irish representatives. As a result, in 1894 a separate Irish Trade Union Congress (ITUC) was established and by 1900 a total of 60,000 workers were members of unions affiliated to ITUC. Most of those were skilled workers, with Boyle (1988) noting that unionisation amongst unskilled workers was extremely limited. He estimated that the total membership of Irish labourers' unions did not exceed 4,000 at any one time over the 1889–1906 period (Boyle 1988: 105).

Permanent widespread unionisation of unskilled workers dates from the end of the 1880s in Britain but it was a further twenty years before it was established in Ireland, in the first decade of the twentieth century. Unlike the craft unions, the general workers' unions were open to all, charged low subscription rates, provided no mutual benefits, had no control over access to work, were more inclined towards frequent and aggressive industrial action to gain recognition, and had explicit and radical political links. The extension of union membership and recognition beyond the relatively privileged craft workers was a bitter and sometimes bloody affair, on occasion involving the police and army in a series of repressive measures.

Major confrontations occurred in Belfast in 1907, Dublin in 1908, Cork in 1909 and Wexford in 1911 (McNamara et al. 1994). Directly related to these events was the establishment of the Irish Transport and General Workers' Union (ITGWU) in 1909 by James Larkin. The most renowned confrontation that this union became involved in was the 1913 Dublin Lockout (Nevin 1994; Yeates 2000). The lockout was sparked by the dismissal of 200 tramway workers who had refused to leave the union as a condition of keeping their jobs. A bitter five-month conflict ensued between the ITGWU, led by Larkin, and the Dublin Employers' Federation, established by the prominent businessman William Martin Murphy. Within one month of the start of the lockout, over 400 employers and 25,000 workers were in the throes of a violent confrontation.

In the face of police assaults, the workers established a self-defence group called the Irish Citizens' Army. A tactic of the employer grouping was effectively to starve the strikers and their families into submission – a tactic that proved successful as workers returned to work defeated. However, it was a pyrrhic victory for the employers, not least in the court of public opinion. Yeats' poem 'September 1913', which was, in part, written as a response to the lockout, damned the new Irish bourgeois class, which William Martin Murphy represented, as 'fumbling in a greasy till'. In the strike's immediate aftermath, the ITGWU reorganised and, in the social dislocation of the War of Independence, grew to become the country's largest trade union (Larkin 1965). Affiliation levels to the ITUC jumped from 110,000 in 1914 to 300,000 by 1921, although union membership declined dramatically again in the 1920s, notably in the ITGWU (Roche and Larragy 1986).

As the radical conflicts of the second decade of the twentieth century subsided, the nature of Irish industrial relations changed. Although employers reserved the right under the voluntarist system not to deal with unions, they no longer sought to smash them or prescribe the union that workers might join. The Dublin Employers' Federation that was involved in the lockout had been established in 1911, two years after its Cork counterpart, on which it was modelled. It subsequently played a major role in the founding in 1942 of the Federated Union of Employers, which later changed its name to the Federation of Irish Employers. In 1992 it merged with the Confederation of Irish Industry to become the foremost Irish employers' representative organisation, the Irish Business and Employers Confederation (IBEC). Employers engaged with trade unions but sought to limit their influence and impact on their business, again through collective bargaining. As a result of the historical developments, the nature of collective bargaining was to be largely adversarial.

By the early 1930s, the central objectives of trade unionism (including unskilled ones) had, as in the 1850s, again been reaffirmed as being about reform, not revolution. They aimed to secure recognition; procure collective agreements covering the terms and conditions of employment of their members; and influence the state's legislative and policymaking process in such areas as employment conditions, housing, healthcare, social welfare and education. In this way, and in common with labour movements in other European democracies, Irish trade unions accepted the emerging industrial (capitalist) society while exerting efforts to mould it to its advantage.

POLITICS AND IRISH INDUSTRIAL RELATIONS

The role of the state, first as part of the UK, then as an independent free state from 1922 and eventually a republic from 1949, has moulded the nature of Irish industrial relations over the past two centuries. Although the modern Irish state aspires to the role of independent referee and regulator of labour relations matters, as it addresses the worst excesses of liberal capitalism, it would be inappropriate to evaluate its role as only that of an impartial facilitator. Even in democratic societies, the state reflects the differences in power between capital and labour, and successive Irish governments have upheld the established norms, values and culture of liberal capitalism.

With the above caveat in mind, the Irish state has generally adopted a benign and even, at times, supportive approach to trade unions. This benign approach was given expression through an early 'auxiliary' or accommodative strategy to industrial relations. This can be seen by its willingness to retain the legal immunities inherited under UK legislation, which have remained largely intact, unlike in the UK. It has supported the voluntarist principle in labour relations, by the provision of robust dispute resolution institutions, initially in 1946 in the form of the Labour Court, then the addition of the Labour Relations Commission in 1990, which became the Workplace Relations Commission in 2015. Provision was also made for the right of Freedom of Association in the 1937 Constitution, although that was to prove problematic from a union perspective, with the courts interpreting a collective right in individualist terms.

While voluntarism has long been viewed as a bedrock of Irish industrial relations, it is a somewhat slippery concept (D'Art forthcoming). It is taken to mean that there is minimal intervention by the law and that the parties to industrial relations remain largely free to regulate the terms of the employment relationship without state intervention (D'Art forthcoming; von Prondzynski and McCarthy 1984). However, there are open questions: what is meant by state intervention and what degree of intervention is to be considered minimal? Individual employment law is now highly legalistic but even collective industrial relations has seen a growth in legalism. Legislative provisions have been accompanied by judicial activism, as in the 2007 Ryanair case and others, and even the Labour Court, which previously enjoyed considerable discretion, has also found its modus operandi come under much more judicial scrutiny where it is interpreting and applying legislative provisions. After over sixty years in existence, legislation providing for joint labour committees (sectoral minimum pay) and joint industrial councils (industry-wide pay agreements) were both struck down by judicial decisions in the last ten years. Government reconstituted these in revised legislative provisions in 2015 but legal challenges to these new provisions are not unlikely.

The non-intervention by the state in the area of pay negotiations proved illusory with the introduction of the Financial Emergency Measures in the Public Interest (FEMPI) legislation to counter the recent financial crisis. Trade unions may, of course, have preferred that such reductions would be accomplished through legislation rather than negotiations, as exemplified by teachers' unions repeatedly pointing out that two-tier pay was introduced on the floor of the Dáil and not agreed by them.

Given these developments, even in collective industrial relations the concept of voluntarism as 'minimal legal intervention' is much attenuated. Indeed, Kerr (2017: 894) questions the extent to which the labour relations process in Ireland can still be regarded as 'voluntarist'. He identifies it as now boiling down to: (i) no obligation to use the dispute resolution machinery of the state, (ii) not to be bound by any recommendations of such bodies, (iii) no compulsion on employers to recognise and negotiate with a trade union, and (iv) collective agreements not being considered legally binding (even this last point is not settled – see Chapter 7) (Kerr 2017: 894).

Political Party Influences on Industrial Relations

In the early part of the twentieth century, Irish trade unions, in common with other labour movements in Europe, sought to develop a political wing. The Irish Labour Party was established at the initiative of James Connolly, James Larkin and William O'Brien by the ITUC in Clonmel in 1912. Unlike in Britain and many continental European countries, the left–right divisions did not come to define political life in Ireland. Instead, the capital/labour divisions were masked by nationalism and the struggle for independence. Of relevance in this regard was the decision of the newly founded Labour Party and the ITUC not to contest the 1918 general election – expressed in the catch-all of the time, 'Labour must wait'. According to Kavanagh (1987), this policy of abstention removed Labour from centre stage in Irish politics for many years, although it is questionable if the Labour Party could have successfully campaigned in that election such was the heightened fervour surrounding the national question. Besides, a narrow industrial base (at least until the 1960s) limited the scope for the development of strong working-class communities and culture. In any case, a working class consumed by relativities and occupational status was unlikely to fill the ranks of a vibrant left-wing movement along the lines of some western European countries.

As a result of the War of Independence (1919–1921) and the Civil War (1922–1923), nationalism came to pervade Irish political life for generations. Two political parties dominated – Fine Gael (formerly Cumann na nGaedheal) and Fianna Fáil, based on the Treaty and anti-Treaty sides, respectively. A striking consequence of the absence of a large left-wing party was that there was little substantial difference in policy stances between successive Irish governments on social issues. Many working-class voters, who would have supported labour, social democratic or communist parties in other countries, voted for one of the two civil war parties. The absorption of working-class demands into the existing industrial and political structures facilitated the maintenance of widespread support for those parties. There was a tendency for the working class to favour Fianna Fáil, in part because of that party's promotion of industrialisation in the 1930s but also because Fine Gael came to be associated more with large farmers and small businesses.

Still, union activists were to be found in all political parties and all parties drew support from working-class voters at election time (Cunningham and Marsh 2018).

Into this party-political framework, the Labour Party formed part of what has been referred to as a 'two-and-a-half party system'. While Fianna Fáil was capable of forming a government on its own, from the 1930s to the 1980s Fine Gael was only able to enter government as part of a coalition with Labour (and sometimes others). The structure of the political system goes a long way to explaining the state's benign approach to trade unions, which stands in stark contrast to political approaches to trade unions in the UK since the early 1980s. As it attracted substantial working-class support, the Fianna Fáil Party had little to gain, and much to lose, if it alienated trade unions or pursued a too interventionist approach to industrial relations. As a result, it sought, with some exceptions (such as the restrictions on British union under the Trade Union Act 1941), to pursue a consensus approach. There were few ideological distinctions between Fianna Fáil and Fine Gael on industrial relations issues. Had the latter party wished to take a tougher line against trade unions militancy, it was restricted when in government by the presence of the Labour Party, with the Ministry for Labour traditionally being allocated to that party.

Wider Political Developments and Industrial Relations

The creation of a welfare state in the decades succeeding World War II reflected a belief within society that the state should accept responsibility for the provision of education, health and related social services. The gradual creation of a welfare state facilitated the maintenance of political consensus, stability and legitimacy. In the 1970s a more interventionist, corporatist ideology developed and this was accompanied by an integration of political, economic and social decision-making. Corporatist influences can be seen emerging from the 1960s as trade union representatives were invited on to consultative bodies with a role in economic planning, notably the National Industrial and Economic Council.

Entry to the European Economic Community (EEC) in 1973 was a hugely important political development for industrial relations. An immediate impact was felt in areas of industrial development as markets opened up to international competition. The influx of multinational enterprises attracted by access to European markets is commonly accredited with a greater level of professionalism in the area of personnel or HRM, together with an initial increase in trade union membership through preproduction agreements which provided for union recognition in advance of employees being recruited. These fell into disrepute after a number of major disputes, notably the inter-union dispute and strike in Ferenka in 1977. The long-run effect on the new multinational companies was the emergence of large non-union establishments (McMahon 1990). Entry to the EEC had a major impact on individual employment law, such that today EU law pervades many aspects of individual workplace relations.

Over the 1970s, government intervention in industrial relations increased, notably in the area of pay bargaining. National wage agreements replaced industry and establishment bargaining as governments sought to address growing inflation and high strike levels. These were known as corporatist-type arrangements and over the decade they expanded in scope to accommodate a range of economic and social affairs. This national-level approach suffered a temporary demise during the 1980s, primarily due to disinterest by employers and the Fine Gael/Labour coalition. The 1987 general election resulted in the election of a government led by Fianna Fáil, and with it a return to national agreements. These involved employers and unions in a wide range of economic and social issues under the rubric of social partnership. However, it is pertinent that neoliberal economic policies now prevailed in tandem with this neo-corporatist approach. The choice for the Irish unions, in an era of declining membership and rising unemployment, was between futile industrial action or participation in the nation's key decision-making forums. They chose the latter.

At a political level, it is apparent that the social partnership model effectively constituted a 'new form of governance' or a parallel political system within the state in this era (Roche 2007b). Some even complained that the agreements were supplanting the role of elected representatives and weakening democracy. However, all governments supported social partnership in the years 1987–2008. Fine Gael criticised it while in opposition, but when in government between 1994 and 1997 (as the lead party in the rainbow coalition with the Labour Party and the Workers' Party) it embraced the process with the same support (even enthusiasm) as the previous Fianna Fáil/Labour coalition. It is salutary to note that the positive view of social partnership changed almost overnight after the financial crisis of 2008. In a repeat of the disaffection with national wage agreements in the early 1980s, social partnership was seen as contributing to the crash, with its successes being disregarded by hostile commentators. In particular, critics claimed it contributed to the excess in state spending, especially through the benchmarking process within the public sector.

Industrial Relations and Contemporary Political Events

Following the onset of the economic crisis in 2009, the consensus approach to social and economic policymaking by political parties faded. However, it did not disappear altogether, with Enda Kenny, the Taoiseach of the new Fine Gael/Labour coalition government elected in 2011, labelling the shift as one from 'social partnership' to 'social dialogue' (Sheehan 2011c). This diluted form of consensus policymaking was part of the state's armoury used to navigate a period of severe austerity, which it achieved without major industrial relations conflict.

While widescale industrial relations conflict was avoided, the traditional party system was to be shattered by the financial crisis of 2008 and subsequent austerity policies. That system had already been fraying at the edges from the entry into government in 1989 of the newly founded Progressive Democrat Party, when coalition government became established as the new norm. That party pursued a more active neoliberal policy aimed at reductions in taxes and promotion of business. Its policies exerted as much influence on certain aspects of social partnership as trade unions, notably in the area of tax cuts. The entry of the Green Party into a coalition government with Fianna Fáil in 2007 further emphasised the weakening of the traditional party-political configurations.

The Fianna Fáil/Green coalition was swept from power in the general election of 2011 and replaced by a Fine Gael/Labour Party coalition. However, that coalition government pursued not dissimilar policies to its predecessors of austerity and retrenchment. As a consequence, both parties suffered in the 2016 general election but with the Labour Party paying the much higher price. The electoral fallout continued in the general election of February 2020, which saw Fine Gael lose power and Sinn Féin receive the highest popular vote. As a result, commentators claimed the traditional two-party-and-a-half party system was now 'dead'. The Sinn Féin Party stood for election on left-wing socialist policies, many of them anathema to Fine Gael and Fianna Fáil, especially in the areas of business and proposed tax increases. The long-run effects of the 2020 election remain to be determined, not least any industrial relations implications. Both Sinn Féin and the Labour Party support strengthening bargaining rights and providing for union recognition. However, even if these parties were to enter a government, giving effect to such proposals would have to take account of apparent constitutional impediments.

In the wider international sphere, social dislocation has been expressed in the resurgence of right-wing protest movements, the rise of populist politicians, attacks on international institutions, such as the EU and the UN, and a questioning of the free trade foundations of the neoliberal order. Whether, and to what extent, such developments may affect Ireland remains to be seen but, to date, they have had minimal domestic impact. The rise of Sinn Féin support in 2020 is akin to traditional political left–right divides. Democratic societies have found effective ways of dealing with these conflicts, not least because of their sophisticated and developed industrial relations systems. They have proved more vulnerable to right-wing extremist populist movements, which, in the form of 1920s and 1930s fascism, overthrew democracies and reduced industrial relations to a corporatist, state-controlled process under repressive dictatorships, with Mazower (2018) providing illuminating insights into how the subverting of independent trade unions and the capture of industrial relations systems by fascist states facilitated dictatorial control.

ECONOMICS AND INDUSTRIAL RELATIONS

In the context of the economic framework, developments in the labour market exert a significant influence on industrial relations and HRM policies and practices. Many of the main influences on such policies and practices are summarised in Table 1.1.

Table 1.1
Key Changes in the Irish Labour Market, 1922–2011

• After a lethargic forty-year period subsequent to the foundation of the state (characterised by a predominantly agricultural economy with high emigration rates) pursuant to modest industrial development in the 1960s, in the following decade a boom in the economy transpired, facilitating high levels of employment. In the 1980s a contraction in the domestic economy led to an employment crisis. In the 1990s employment improved in the export and international services sector but unemployment rates remained persistently high. In the 2000s a construction boom occurred in the domestic economy, facilitating full employment. In the 2008–2015 period a contraction of the domestic economy led to an employment crisis, although the export economy remained relatively stable throughout the boom–bust period. The period from 2015 has been categorised by economic recovery but substantial social issues, notably a housing crisis.

• Up to 2008 the size of the (better educated, more skilled) labour force had increased over a period of forty years. Reflecting the change in Ireland's economic fortunes over the 1971–2008 period, there was an increase of nearly 90 per cent in the size of the labour force. By 2011, out of a population of almost 4.5 million, 1.8 million were in the labour force, of which 86 per cent were employed. This is attributable to a combination of the underlying growth in the population aged fifteen years and over, increased female participation rates and immigration. The level of female participation in the labour force escalated from 28 per cent in 1971 to approximately 52 per cent by 2011. This increased participation level is particularly evident in retail distribution, insurance, financial/business, professional and personal services. Immigration more than doubled from 21,000 in 2004 (when EU enlargement took place) to 48,000 in 2007. However, as a consequence of the aforementioned recession, emigration returned, increasing sharply before declining again with the economic recovery.

• A salient feature of the changing composition of the labour force has been a substantial shift in employment levels from the agricultural to the services sector. The period since 1926 has witnessed major changes in the relative employment shares of the three broad sectors of economic activity: agriculture, industry and services. The diminishing importance of agriculture is clearly evident, as is the growth of the services sector since 1971. The composition of industrial types of employment has altered significantly, with contractions in many of the older, labour-intensive, indigenous sub-sectors (e.g. textiles, clothing and footwear) and expansions in technology-related, export-oriented and foreign-owned employments. A notable characteristic of the changing sectoral composition of the labour force is the decline in male manual jobs in the manufacturing sector, alongside a sizeable increase in the number of (predominantly female) part-time jobs, posing practical problems for trade union organisers. Alongside increased immigration levels, these changes also have implications for a host of areas related to industrial relations and HRM. These include labour market segmentation, 'atypical' work patterns, gig self-employment, zero-hours and 'if and when' work, trade union recognition, working methods, job content, wage differentials, skill protection practices, the incidence and extent of low pay, job security, downsizing, subcontracting, outsourcing, job displacement, 'race to the bottom', the management of diversity, equal opportunities, decreased union density and collective bargaining strength, and the protection of collectively agreed pay and employment standards (above legally fixed minima) and initiatives in respect of (and arising from) protective labour laws.

- Technological advances generally accompany (if not prompt) major waves of economic and social change, e.g. the Industrial Revolution. New technologies energising post-industrial societies are rooted in information technology (IT). The IT revolution is not confined to the economic sphere of production: it is changing the social, cultural and political arenas of society at an accelerating rate. The technological impact on matters such as the size, spread, location and duration of employment is sizeable (e.g. the electronics/IT revolution). The quickening pace of technological change has a dramatic impact on the structure and nature of the labour market and numerous job types therein. A notable impact of this trend is the aforementioned move away from manual work together with the ease of workplace relocation. Technology also affects cost structure and consequently impacts upon key aspects of industrial relations, e.g. job security, deskilling, demarcation lines, reward systems and relative bargaining power positions.

Source: Adapted and updated from Ahearne (2010).

In the nineteenth century industrial development in Ireland lagged greatly behind the rest of the UK. The absence of high-grade coal and iron ore was a contributory factor; however, one cannot disregard the historical determinants, such as the Great Famine and the colonisation of Ireland. Ireland was perceived as not just a political but also an economic threat to Britain. Restrictions were imposed on trade, which included a spell of tariff impositions and export restrictions. Consequently, throughout the nineteenth and early twentieth century, Ireland remained primarily an agricultural economy outside of Belfast. The Cumann na nGaedheal government of 1922 had no industrial policy, believing agriculture to be the mainstay of the economy. Half the workforce was in agriculture, food and drink made up most exports, and there was a huge market 'next door' in Britain, the overwhelmingly main destination of exports. Given this background, the transition to a modern industrial economy was a hesitant and slow process. In the 1930s Fianna Fáil governments made significant moves towards economic development under protectionist economic policies. These were designed to promote greater national economic self-sufficiency and proved effective in the short run, securing the development of new industries and the expansion of older ones. Notable from this period was the establishment of a number of semi-state enterprises such as Aer Lingus and Bord na Móna.

The onset of World War II led to a decline of over a quarter of industrial output during 'the emergency', as the war period was known in neutral Ireland. As late as 1946 agriculture accounted for 47 per cent of total employment, services for 36 per cent and manufacturing for just 17 per cent. Even that 17 per cent was predominantly characterised by small establishments so that by 1958 only forty concerns outside the public service employed more than 500 workers (Lee 1980). Over the 1945–1950 period a short post-war recovery was experienced, which was accompanied by an increase of about 70 per cent in both strike frequency and union membership, as workers sought to regain ground after the lifting of a wages standstill order introduced during the war years.

The recovery of the late 1940s concealed the limitations of the protectionist strategy. In contrast with the rest of Europe, the 1950s proved to be a miserable decade for the Irish economy and society. The decade was marked by emigration, unemployment, balance of payments difficulties and virtual stagnation – with an actual decline in national output occurring in the second half of the decade. O'Hagan (1987) points to a lack of quality economic policymaking and effective leadership in both government and civil service at this time. While the level of trade union membership increased marginally during the 1950s, under the influence of economic stagnation, strike frequency dropped significantly.

Such was the stagnant nature of society and the related lack of vision amongst the nation's leadership that considerable trade union energy was devoted to the establishment and maintenance of wage differentials, rather than the attainment of any wider economic and social goals. It could be said that status, rather than a class, consciousness prevailed. The fact that by 1960 there were 123 operating trade unions – of whom 84 had an enrolled membership of less than 1,000 – offers some insight into the priority accorded to status or relativity factors by the Irish worker, in preference to class consciousness or solidarity considerations (Lee 1980).

Uneven Economic Performance, 1960–1987

From the early 1960s onwards Ireland commenced a period of sustained economic growth arising from the adoption of a new development strategy set out in the highly influential Programme for Economic Expansion – the Whitaker report (Department of Industry and Commerce 1958). The programme was influenced by the prevailing Keynesian idea of state intervention in the economy, which trade unions tended to support. Economic isolationism and aspirations for self-sufficiency were abandoned in favour of free trade as 'Ireland opened a wider window on the world' (MacSharry and White 2000: 357). The policy switch involved inviting foreign companies, progressively dismantling tariffs and quotas, and seeking membership of the Common Market or EEC. These measures had a significant impact on Irish industry, which faced stiff competition and a consequent need to adapt. This adaptation placed pressure on industrial relations, with Kelly and Brannick (1988) demonstrating that it led to a significant increase in strike levels in British companies which had previously had stable relations (see Chapter 10).

Consequent to this economic development – with 1,000 foreign operations comprising a labour force of 87,600 established in Ireland – trade union membership levels rose to some 60 per cent of the employed workforce by the early 1980s and collective industrial relations was the dominant method governing the determination of pay and conditions of employment. Strike levels increased during the 1960s and up to the late 1970s to levels unprecedented since the first two decades of the 1900s. The barriers of pay relativity which had been established were now being reinforced, as both white- and blue-collar workers engaged in some of the most notorious industrial actions in Irish industrial relations history (McCarthy 1973).

Commenting upon the changing social climate of the 1960s, McCarthy (1973) suggested that it was 'a decade of upheaval' or period of national adolescence, with the old authoritarian societal structures facing unprecedented challenges. The demise of 'the deferential worker' transpired, as previously accepted values, attitudes and institutions came under challenge. Media influences increased awareness of the outside world and facilitated a greater preparedness to question previously sacrosanct practices and institutions. The surge in economic confidence brought with it a drift of power to the workplace, with shop stewards (workplace representatives) dominating the collective bargaining scene at workplace level. An upsurge in unofficial strike action (action without official trade union authorisation) also materialised.

Over the 1960s and 1970s, following in the path of its main trading partners, the Irish government was influenced by a Keynesian approach to economic growth management and planning. This involved successive governments stimulating demand through budgetary deficits and increased expenditure. These yielded higher levels of economic activity and reduced levels of unemployment. However, this brought with it a new set of ills. Chief amongst these was the spiralling level of inflation, which was driven by two oil crises in 1973 and 1979. A more enduring problem was the influence of dysfunctional, pro-cyclical economic policies which have characterised the Irish economy for much of the state's existence. Notable in this regard was the expansion of the public sector based on the 1997 Fianna Fáil general election manifesto.

The 1980s saw a deep recession, with government cutbacks. In industrial relations, there was an advent of this 'new realism'. Underlying the recession was a crisis in state finances and by 1986 the Irish economy was under severe pressure from an explosive national debt, increases in taxation on PAYE workers, large-scale redundancies, high emigration and rising unemployment. There was a concern amongst policy-makers and analysts that the International Monetary Fund would step in to impose the economic stringency that the politicians had failed to apply (MacSharry and White 2000). The government opted for 'fiscal rectitude', designed to tackle the budgetary deficit, reduce the growing national debt/GDP ratio and promote international competitiveness. The policies of particular relevance in the industrial relations context included moderate pay rises via 'consensus agreements' that were to transmute into 'social partnership'.

The Economy under Social Partnership

The economic performance during the period of social partnership is dealt with in detail in Chapter 13 and so will only be briefly reviewed here. It was a period characterised by four phases, with an uncertain early period up to 1993 followed by a solid productivity phase from about 1994 to 2000. No economic model had predicted the reversal of fortune that occurred in the second phase. Many sources accord social partnership a fundamental role in the economic miracle (Auer 2000; MacSharry and White 2000; National Economic and Social Council various years; O'Donnell and O'Reardon 1996, 2000). This view is not unchallenged, however, as Baccaro and Simoni (2004) point out that although the economic transformation began in 1987 and overlapped in time with the institutionalisation of social partnership, much of the economic literature discounts this overlap as sheer coincidence.

After 2000 the economy was booming but it was based on a property bubble and ever-increasing public spending. By 2007 the housing market had entered into decline, leaving the banking system in a perilous state. By September 2008 the government felt forced to intervene in order to save the banks, and the controversial bank guarantee was introduced. There was a dramatic downturn in 2008, as national economic weaknesses magnified the international recession caused by the collapse of the sub-prime property market in America and threatened the international banking system. The Irish property bubble collapsed and the economy officially entered into recession in the first half of the year.

Recession and Recovery

By the third quarter of 2010, the economy had contracted under the impact of what has been termed the 'Great Recession'. Although out of favour, social partnership still had an 'informal or depleted influence on employment relations in Ireland' (Roche *et al.* 2011: 245). This depleted influence was to prove significant as the state saw a period of austerity and recovery navigated without a return to high levels of industrial conflict. In 2010 IBEC and the Irish Congress of Trade Unions agreed to a protocol on private sector industrial relations and, although it largely atrophied in that sector during the period 2010–2012, collective bargaining quickly re-established itself (Roche and Gormley 2017a). In response to the near economic collapse, the government initiated public sector pay and pension reforms over the 2009–2015 period through the FEMPI legislation. However, it also entered into the Croke Park Agreement (CPA) 2010–2014 with public sector unions. This agreement served to secure agreement on pay cuts, public sector redundancies (on a voluntary basis) and related work practice reforms. The CPA was followed by the Haddington Road Agreement and two Lansdowne Road Agreements, which provided for public sector pay restoration and continuing public sector reform.

The Growth in Inequality

Industrial relations practice has in the past been concerned with subjective concepts of equity and fairness, and these are not just determined in a national context. Ireland now operates in a world economy and is greatly affected by international developments, not least the nature of contemporary global capitalism. At a macro level, modern capitalism has shown its transformative power and has led to economic development in parts of the globe, which has greatly reduced global poverty, notably in Asia. Simultaneously, it has presided over a huge increase in income and wealth inequality since the early 1980s. This inequality has been drawn to the world's attention by the work of Thomas Piketty, who, like a latter-day Karl Marx, has documented the explosive growth in inequality in his magnum opus *Capital in the Twenty-First Century* (Piketty 2014). Wilkinson and Pickett (2009) have shown that inequality has negative social consequences, irrespective of the wealth of a country (see Chapter 9).

Neither Piketty nor Wilkinson and Pickett are Marxists and their analysis is not grounded in class conflict. Piketty decries Soviet communism as a disaster that undermined the appeal of left-wing thought generally (Anthony 2020: 47). His thesis is that because the returns on private investment outstrip economic growth, the wealthy will get richer and leave the rest of society behind (Piketty 2014). This can only be avoided by redistribution of wealth and income through progressive taxation, with his latest work calling for more radical redistributive taxation (Piketty 2020). Piketty's 2014 work has garnered the attention of the world's elite who assemble annually in Davos and who have expressed concern at the growth in inequality. However, the nostrums emanating from Davos have seemed little more than hand-wringing.

Nation states can seem powerless to act in the face of modern corporations, largely because they compete to attract them to locate in their countries. In this scenario effective taxation, let alone substantial redistribution of wealth and income, is difficult. The Organisation for Economic Co-operation and Development is examining the hollowing out of that tax base by multinational companies through transfer pricing and other sophisticated tax avoidance practices and, while remedial action has been slow, new tax arrangements are due to take effect in 2022. As Ireland benefited from the existing taxation rules, it will lose corporation tax revenue – an estimated €500 million annually – as a result of the new arrangements.

In their 2019 Countess Markievicz Memorial Lecture, Wilkinson and Pickett (2019) count Ireland among the countries with the very highest gross levels of income inequality in Europe. Although that is redressed by social welfare and other redistributive measures, which leave Ireland in the middle of European countries for net equality. This indicates that the legacy of social partnership lags well behind the legacy left by Scandinavian neo-corporatism, the countries which still have the least inequality. Historically, of course, trade unions acted to redress inequality in income redistribution but their role in this regard has been greatly weakened. The Nobel Prize-winning economist Robert Solow has drawn attention to 'the decay of unions' as promoting inequality and the need 'to give wage earners more power within firms'. He sees union decline as rooted in structural change in labour markets and globalisation but, despite what he considers the desirability of reversing their decline, Solow confesses to having no real sense of how this can be done (Dizikes 2019). Into this gap, growing legislation, non-traditional actors (such as Social Justice Ireland) and the campaign for a living wage have now augmented and, in some cases, supplanted the functions of collective bargaining.

Concluding Comments

Many influences have shaped Irish industrial relations but the most significant have arisen from the ebb and flow of economic developments. Coming out of the Great Recession, the Irish economy had made a remarkable economic recovery but it also had a large overhang in public debt. The Covid-19 pandemic which emerged in early 2020 presented Irish society and the economy with another existential crisis – the second in twelve years. The state adopted an active interventionist policy and committed to borrowing to provide the necessary funds to combat the disease and its effects. The immediate economic impact of the measures to control the infection was dramatic, with unemployment rising to 18 per cent by the end of March 2020 and the Central Bank (2020) predicting a negative growth rate of 8.3 per cent for 2020. The medium-term economic impact of Covid-19 at both a national and global level will take time to emerge. The Taoiseach recognised in his St Patrick's Day speech in 2020 that borrowing would have to be repaid and this will place budgetary constraints on future governments. As in the past, Irish industrial relations will have to respond to the economic effects of Covid-19 and other events, not least the longer-term impact of measures to combat climate change.

Chapter 2

Collective Labour Law in a Historical, Social and Political Context

INTRODUCTION

This chapter examines the role of common law, legislation, the 1937 Irish Constitution (Bunreacht na hÉireann) and international developments via the International Labour Organisation (ILO), the Council of Europe, the EU and case law derived from the European Court of Human Rights (ECtHR). It is essential to examine in some more detail the historical origins of the law and industrial relations, and in their political and social contexts, for several reasons. First, the laws enacted prior to the foundation of the state in 1922 remain in place except where they have been repealed or found to be repugnant to the Constitution (Kerr 1989). Second, much of the recent legislation is based on legislative principles developed prior to 1922, and an understanding of the conceptual basis of these legal principles is essential. Third, the law cannot be understood in the absence of its social and institutional context. In this regard, the impact of trade union activism on the development of industrial relations legislation has been especially important. Fourth, historical experience can mark the boundaries of what is practicable and possible in legislating for industrial relations and for those considering resort to legal remedies. Finally, an understanding of the evolution of collective legislation is essential to critically evaluate contemporary debates on the role of the law in industrial relations.

OVERVIEW

There was early legal and political hostility to the emergent trade unions (or combinations), dating back to the sixteenth century when 'combinations of workmen were made illegal' (Boyle 1988: 7). Prior to the rise of capitalism, the skilled trades were regulated by the medieval guilds. Although the guilds were organisations of masters (employers), they fulfilled an indirect function of protecting labour standards. With the growth of capitalism in the eighteenth century the regulatory power of the medieval guilds progressively weakened, and the skilled trades were exposed to competition. Shorn of the indirect protection provided by the guilds, workers in the skilled trades formed trade clubs for protection. In time, these trade clubs became known as 'combinations' and later trade unions. Thus, the origin of trade unions in Britain and Ireland was in the skilled trades and among relatively privileged workers – not the deprived and exploited semi-skilled and unskilled workers of the Industrial Revolution.

In contrast, semi-skilled and unskilled workers were involved in the formation of early trade unions in many Western European countries. Because of later industrialisation, such unions only emerged over a century after the early British and Irish unions – from the mid nineteenth century onwards. A point of similarity is that the civil law systems applying in those countries were, like the common law system, frequently used as an instrument to suppress unions, again largely without success in the long run.

The restrictive approach adopted under common law has been ascribed to two factors. One is that the judiciary, which was drawn from the ruling class, lacked any understanding or empathy with working men and was biased against working-class organisations. The second, and probably more important, factor is that the legal judgments arose out of the logic of the individually based 'common law' system, which was at odds with the collective values embodied in trade unionism. Common law is judge-made law. It is based on the notion that rights are vested in individuals. A key principle of common law is that 'restraint of trade' is illegal. This means that interference with the right of individuals or businesses to pursue their own ends, including commercial ones, is contrary to the underlying principles of common law.

As trade unions sought to *collectively* regulate the terms and conditions of employment (to restrain trade), they inevitably came into conflict with common law. However, common law arose from liberal ideas that embodied competing principles. The first liberal principle is that individuals should be free to maximise their own welfare and that collective interference with this right is in restraint of trade and illegal. The second is that individuals should be free to combine to promote their own interests. This latter principle implies a right of association that would, if adopted, vindicate workers' entitlement to collectively organise in trade unions.

The evolution of state policy towards trade unions in the UK (including Ireland) during the eighteenth and early nineteenth centuries involved a recurring conflict between these two competing liberal principles – restraint of trade and freedom of association. In this conflict, the political system tended to deliver ever greater liberties to trade unions, while the common law legal system restricted and rowed back on these liberties. This meant that trade unions developed in conjunction with liberal democracy and, in time, became a key component of the democracy that gradually emerged. Most notably, they played a vital role in the foundation of the British and Irish Labour Parties.

EARLY LEGAL RESTRICTIONS

In Great Britain and Ireland, prior to 1824, the approach of both politics and the law to trade unions – or 'combinations' as they were then known – was one of trenchant opposition. Combinations were banned under a range of legislation in the eighteenth century, culminating in the Anti-Combinations Acts of 1799–1800. In 1803 the 1800 Act was extended to Ireland but with provision for the maximum jail sentence of six months, compared to three months on the British mainland (D'Arcy 1994: 9). Despite their coercive intent, the various legal attempts to suppress combinations failed, as evidenced by their growth in the skilled trades (Boyd 1972; Boyle 1988).

Legal suppression failed for several reasons. First, the laws were difficult to enforce because of the secrecy of the combinations. Second, social pressure was sometimes brought to bear on owners, and intimidation (even violence) was used against 'masters' (employers). Intimidation and violence were, however, more evident among non-union workers. This is demonstrated by the non-unionised Luddites, who opposed the introduction of new technology in textiles in the period 1811–1813. Third, the law was not enforced against combinations of employers in the same way as trade unions despite these also being conspiracies under common law. By far the most important reason for the failure of the Anti-Combination Acts was the scarcity of the skills possessed by craftsmen, which made employers reluctant to use the law. There was no reluctance among employers in opposing unionisation among unskilled or semi-skilled workers. It is important to note that resort to the law was not the main weapon of employers in resisting unionisation of unskilled and semi-skilled workers. In the case of these workers, simply replacing workers who joined unions, or went on strike, was the most common and effective tactic. Some employers required workers, as a condition of their continued employment, to sign an undertaking not to join unions – this was the so-called document at the root of the 1913 Dublin Lockout. In the US such documents were known as 'yellow dog' contracts, with the implication being that only a yellow dog would sign one.

In 1824 the Anti-Combination Acts 1799–1800 and other provisions banning unions were repealed following the campaigning work of Francis Place (a master tailor and an employer) and David Hume, MP. Among the key arguments used to support the case for repeal was the ineffectiveness of the Acts and evidence that they worsened relations between master and workmen. Boyle (1988: xi) notes that while the repeal of the combination laws gave trade unions a legal existence, this had only limited effect. There are two reasons for this. First, an 1825 Act created crimes of intimidation, obstruction and molestation, which resulted in 'criminal prosecution of workers engaged in industrial action' (Kerr and Whyte 1985: 214). Second, trade unions were vulnerable to arcane laws on the taking of oaths.

In 1834 the significance of the illegality of taking oaths became apparent in the celebrated Tolpuddle Martyrs case, which was the subject of the 1986 film *Comrades*. The martyrs were six Dorset farm labourers who had formed the Friendly Society of Agricultural Labourers to resist wage cuts: they refused to work for less than ten shillings per week. The oath of secrecy they had taken to protect their identity was found to be illegal and seditious. The six were sentenced to seven years' transportation to Australia. There was outrage at the sentence. Although the men were transported, they were eventually pardoned and repatriated following a campaign led (surprisingly) by the establishment newspaper *The Times* of London.

More long-lasting than repressive legislation was the doctrine of common law conspiracy. This doctrine meant that otherwise legal action was made illegal if two or more workers combined in that action. This doctrine placed the primary purpose of unions – the improvement of terms and conditions of employment through *collective* action – outside the law. In 1859 the UK Parliament moved to allow a limited use of industrial action in the Molestation of Workmen Act of that year. However, the intentions of Parliament were frustrated by judicial interpretations which found that the Act provided no protection for a breach of contract (a common-law offence), which a strike was said to involve. As seen in Chapter 1, by the 1850s a growing number of employers had begun to deal with the first nationally organised craft-based 'model unions' in the UK.

The Criminal Law and Collective Industrial Relations

By 1870 a growing acceptance of trade unions in the skilled trades had set the groundwork for change to the doctrine of *criminal* conspiracy. This was aided by the extension of the franchise (vote) to smallholders (those who owned small houses), many of whom were skilled workers and members of the model unions. In the 1870 elections the unions delivered support to the Liberal Party under Gladstone. That party in turn introduced reforming legislation – the Trade Union Act of 1871. This Act, as subsequently amended, still governs the legal status of trade unions in Ireland today. It legalised the existence of trade unions but, in order to prevent them being sued under the law of tort, carefully sought to refrain from giving them corporate status, i.e. entities capable of suing and being sued in their own name.

While legitimising the existence of unions, the 1871 Act did not protect the underlying common law concept of a criminal conspiracy. In *Regina* v. *Bunn* (1872) the judiciary found that the existence of a combination (two or more people acting together) converted an otherwise non-criminal act into a crime. The employer had a right to employ whomever he wished and any union (collective) interference with this was a criminal offence (O'Hara 1981: 16). It was 'unjustifiable annoyance and interference with the masters in the course of their business' (Kerr and Whyte 1985: 215). Furthermore, picketing was also held to be a criminal offence and even minor expressions of opinion were sufficient to lead to a jail sentence. Picketing is the congregation of workers (usually outside a place of work) to communicate a grievance and persuade other workers not to work. It is viewed as central to an entitlement to strike since it limits the possibility of striking workers being replaced by substitute labour.

The effect of *Regina* v. *Bunn* and other judicial decisions around this time was to frustrate the operation of trade unions and they again looked to politics for relief. In the election of 1874 the model unions switched their allegiance to the Conservative Party, led by Benjamin Disraeli, in return for a promise of favourable legislation. The Conservatives won the election and there followed a period of legislative activity. The main Act passed by Parliament was the Conspiracy and Protection of Property Act 1875, which restricted the remit of the criminal law. It decriminalised peaceful picketing and specified that no one is liable for any act committed *in contemplation or furtherance of a trade dispute* unless the act would also be a crime if committed by one person. In effect, it removed the notion of a criminal conspiracy from a peaceful trade dispute. Although the Act was repealed in the UK in 2008, it is still on the statute books in Ireland and continues to serve to limit the role of the criminal law in industrial disputes. The Employers and Workmen Act 1875 followed. It removed criminal liability from employees for breach of their employment contract and confined the penalty to civil damages. Since there was little point in employers suing individual workers, the practical effect of that Act was to nullify the doctrine that a strike was a breach of contract.

The broad effect of legislative changes in the 1870s was to establish a *voluntarist* system of industrial relations (or 'legal abstentionism') in which the law was designed to play a minor role. In the criminal law area this voluntarism represented a resolution of the conflict between a social movement seeking *collective* regulation of industrial relations and the *individually based* common law system. Trade unions were granted *immunities* from acts that would otherwise have been criminal offences, but they were not given rights. The net effect of the legislative provisions of this time is that the criminal law today applies to industrial relations only insofar as actions are in themselves criminal acts.

THE CIVIL LAW AND INDUSTRIAL RELATIONS

The legislation introduced by Parliament did not go unchallenged. Denied the use of criminal liabilities, employers challenged the legality of picketing and had resort to the notion of civil conspiracy under the law of tort (Kerr and Whyte 1985). A tort is a civil wrong arising from a breach of a duty of care, and it gives rise to an entitlement to damages. A series of cases in the 1890s meant the law on picketing was unclear; however, two cases in the early 1900s were to prove crucial. In the Belfast case of *Quinn* v. *Leathem* (1901) an inducement to breach a third-party contract was found to be a civil offence not protected by the 1875 Act.

The second case is the celebrated *Taff Vale* case, the full name of which is *Taff Vale Railway Company* v. *Amalgamated Society of Railway Servants* (1901). In this case a union official, Bell, had persuaded substitute workers hired by the employer (Taff Vale) to undermine a strike, not to pass pickets. This persuasion, although peaceful, was deemed to have induced a breach of a third-party contract – that between Taff Vale and the replacement workers. More significantly, it was found that, contrary to the prevailing belief, a trade union could be sued in its *own* name despite the 1871 Act provisions, which had been carefully drafted to avoid that possibility. The union was found liable for some £32,000 in damages and a further £19,000 in legal costs – a very substantial sum at the time, which translates into some €2.5 million in today's terms. The *Taff Vale* judgment threatened the very existence of trade unions since they could quickly become insolvent if they pursued industrial action.

Yet again, the trade union movement turned to the political system for relief (Boyle 1988; Saville 1967). Following the 1906 elections, a Liberal government was able to assume office only with the support of fifty-four Lib–Lab deputies. These were MPs who supported the trade unions: The Lib MPs were members of the Liberal Party and the Lab MPs were members of the Labour Representation Committee. Neither the Irish nor UK Labour Party existed at this stage but the campaign over *Taff Vale* is credited with leading to the establishment of the British Labour Party. In return for the support of the fifty-four Lib–Lab MPs in forming a government, the Liberal government enacted the Trade Disputes Act 1906.

The 1906 Act granted trade unions, and their members, immunity from the tort of civil conspiracy, reinforced the protection for peaceful picketing and granted immunities from defined common law liabilities. The immunities in the Act were available to union members and union officials only where they were *acting in contemplation or furtherance of a trade dispute* – the so-called golden formula, a phrase coined by the noted labour lawyer Lord Wedderburn (1965: 222). Trade unions themselves enjoyed stronger immunities since they were granted *total* immunity from being sued under the law of tort. This immunity reversed in its entirety the *Taff Vale* decision that unions could be sued in their own name. Von Prondzynski (1989: 214) notes that the Trade Disputes Act 1906 adopted a very simple technique: it identified the main judicial decisions that had disabled trade unions and gave them immunities from these judicial precedents.

Known as a 'Bill of Rights for Workers', the 1906 Act actually provided no legal rights and specifically did not confer a right to strike. It met a demand of unions that is encapsulated in Wedderburn's (1965: 9) celebrated remark that: 'they wanted nothing more from the law than it should leave them alone'. Kerr and Whyte (1985) report that the trade unions opposed the enactment of a comprehensive labour law code with positive rights and obligations. They opted instead for the pragmatic immunities approach that had been employed in the 1870s. This 'legal abstentionism' contrasts with the approaches adopted in some continental European countries where, although initially subject to severe legal restrictions, positive rights to union organisation, collective bargaining and industrial action were progressively made available during the twentieth century.

In northern Europe today, such positive rights systems normally distinguish between *disputes of rights* and *disputes of interest*. Disputes of rights involve situations where a pre-existing rule can be used to decide on the rights and wrongs of a dispute. In legally based systems, employment legislation or a collective agreement constitutes such a rule. Such disputes are said to be justiciable (capable of being decided by a legal authority) and strikes are not legally protected in such cases (Commission of Inquiry on Industrial Relations 1981). In contrast, strikes involving disputes of interest *are* protected. An example of such a dispute is where on the termination of a collective agreement, a trade union makes a claim for a 5 per cent pay increase and an employer responds with a demand for a pay freeze because of competitive pressures. There is no pre-existing rule that can be used to decide between these two positions and, as a result, strikes in pursuit of such issues are legal.

While it arose from the demands of trade unions, it is important to stress that voluntarism also had advantages for employers. In the collective arena no requirements were placed on employers to recognise or negotiate with trade unions. It left management free to decide on a pragmatic basis if they would, or would not, engage in collective bargaining. Legal abstentionism also extended to the area of individual employment law, leaving employers with few obligations. Notably, there was no prohibition on discrimination, no general right to minimum pay or maximum working time (Hepple 2002), and no protection against unfair dismissal as an employer could dismiss for 'any reason or none' – the so-called employment at will system.

The final piece of collective legislation enacted prior to 1922 (which remains on the statute books) was the Trade Union Act 1913. This Act allows trade union funds to be applied to political purposes, provided that political purposes are included in the union's objectives and a separate political fund is set up. As a result, unions in Ireland may operate a political fund but they must offer members an easy way of opting out of paying the political contribution. The issue of whether trade unions should be allowed to contribute to political parties has arisen again in recent years with the debate framed in the context of limiting or abolishing corporate donations. Some have argued that any restrictions on corporate donations should equally apply to trade unions. As of 2017 only three unions are noted by the Registry of Friendly Societies as operating a political fund in Ireland. These are the Services Industrial Professional and Technical Union (SIPTU), the Association of Secondary Teachers, Ireland and the Irish National Teachers' Organisation (Registry of Friendly Societies 2019a).

COLLECTIVE LEGISLATION, 1922–1990

The trade union movement in the newly independent Irish state was concerned with preserving the legacy embodied in the acts of the UK Parliament and it did not seek positive rights (McGinley 1990). Table 2.1 lists the main legislative developments in Irish collective labour law since 1922.

The first major piece of legislation post 1922 was the Trade Union Act of 1941. That Act sought to regulate collective bargaining. It established a requirement that in order to engage in collective bargaining, organisations had to possess a negotiation licence or be deemed an excepted body. Any organisation granted such a licence, including an employer organisation, would then be an 'authorised trade union'. The immunities in the Trade Disputes Act 1906 were then confined to authorised trade unions. The Trade Union Act 1941 led to conflict within the trade union movement over limitations on the granting of negotiation licences to UK unions. Following a constitutional challenge, Part III of the Act was struck down in 1947 (McCarthy 1977). This is examined further in the section on the Constitution.

Table 2.1

Collective Labour Legislation Enacted by the Oireachtas, 1922–2019

Statute	Provisions
Trade Union Act 1935	Trade unions allowed to own unlimited amount of land
Trade Union Act 1941	Negotiation licences, sole representation rights
Trade Union Act 1942	Exemptions from negotiation licences, appeals in sole rights situations
Industrial Relations Act 1946	Establishment of the Labour Court
Trade Union Acts 1947–1952	Six Acts extending power to reduce deposits to be maintained with Registry of Friendly Societies Irish unions by 75 per cent
Industrial Relations Act 1969	Enlargement of the Labour Court, establishment of Office of Rights Commissioners
Trade Union Act 1971	New negotiation licence rules: £5000 deposit, 500 members, 18-month wait
Trade Union Act 1975	Encouraged the amalgamation of trade unions by providing funding for expenses for successful mergers
Industrial Relations Act 1976	Established a joint labour committee (JLC) for agricultural workers and allowed them access to the Labour Court
Worker Participation (State Enterprises) Act 1977–1988	Elected worker directors in state enterprises
Trade Disputes (Amendment) Act 1982	Extended immunities of the 1906 Act to public servants except the Defence Forces and Gardaí
Industrial Relations Act 1990	Established the Labour Relations Commission (LRC), repealed 1906 and 1982 Trade Disputes Acts, pre-strike secret ballots, immunities restricted, injunctions curbed, funding for trade union rationalisation even if unsuccessful
Industrial Relations (Amendment) Acts 2001 and 2004	Allows for legal determination of terms and conditions of employment but not statutory union recognition
Industrial Relations (Amendment) Act 2012	Amendments to joint industrial council (JIC) and JLC institutions
Industrial Relations (Amendment) Act 2015	Amends the 2001–2004 Acts and also provisions for JICs and JLCs
Workplace Relations Act 2015	Provides for new institutional arrangements, establishing the Workplace Relations Commission (WRC), abolishing the Employment Appeals Tribunal and transferring its functions to the WRC
The Employment (Miscellaneous) Provisions) Act 2018	Amends a number of Acts to provide for banded hours, the provision of written terms and *within 5 days of commencing employment and compellability of witnesses in dismissals cases*
The Industrial Relations (Amendment) Act 2019	Provides Gardaí access to the WRC and Labour Court

Source: Adapted and extended from McGinley (1990).

Controversy also dogged the proposed Trade Union Bill 1966, which sought to legislate for secret ballots prior to industrial action and to remove the immunities in the 1906 Act from those engaged in unofficial industrial action. Although initially supported by the Irish Congress of Trade Unions (ICTU), the Bill was strongly opposed by individual trade unions and union activists. The jailing of strikers in the Electricity Supply Board (ESB) in a 1968 strike backfired since taxis had to be sent by the authorities late at night to Mountjoy Jail in order to facilitate the strikers' release (the strikers had refused to leave until this was done.) For the government of the day, the embarrassment seemed to reinforce the limitations of the law; and the incident was instrumental in the 1966 Bill being allowed to lapse subsequently. These experiences emphasised the need for consensus as a requirement for successful industrial relations legislation. The institutional provisions in the Industrial Relations Acts of 1946 (establishing the Labour Court) and 1969 (establishing rights commissioners) enjoyed such a consensus, as did the Trade Union Act 1971, which limited the formation of new unions, and the Trade Union Act 1975, which encouraged union mergers. However, amending trade disputes law remained a highly charged issue.

The Operation of Trade Disputes Law in Ireland

In the 1950s trade disputes law was not subject to any major controversy, which was a manifestation of the low strike levels in that decade. With the growth in strikes in the 1960s, it became common to find commentators decrying the imperfections of the Irish system, especially the Trade Disputes Act 1906. Among some of the readily identifiable defects of the 1906 Act, from an employer perspective, was the availability of protection for unofficial strikes, strikes by a minority of workers and strikes in breach of collective agreements. The most famous denunciation of the Act was made by Justice Parke in *Goulding Chemicals Ltd* v. *Bolger* (1977):

> The Trade Disputes Act 1906 was a child of political expediency hastily conceived and prematurely delivered. It has now survived more than the allotted span of life with all its inbred imperfections still uncorrected. (quoted in Commission of Inquiry on Industrial Relations 1981: 222)

Parke's views were seen by critics as evidence of continuing judicial bias against workers, and they have not gone unchallenged. Far from being a rushed response to a political situation, Kidner (1982) notes that factually the 1906 Act had been the subject of great care and consideration. It has also been pointed out that the imperfections had largely been used to restrict the intended effect of the Act (Kerr and Whyte 1985; von Prondzynski and McCarthy 1984). The most serious of these restrictions related to the granting of injunctions – restraining orders preventing named individuals from engaging in certain actions. An injunction may be granted on an interim, interlocutory or permanent basis. An interim injunction is one granted pending a hearing on the application for an injunction. An interlocutory injunction is one granted pending a full hearing of the case, with a permanent injunction only available following a full hearing of a case.

Prior to 1990 an interim or interlocutory injunction was available to an employer if they met the following two criteria:
- there was a fair case that there was a legal problem with the union action; and
- the balance of convenience was in favour of granting the injunction.

The 'fair case' criterion is a very low threshold and, once established, the court would proceed to consider where the 'balance of convenience' lay. An employer could easily demonstrate that they would incur a financial loss that could not be recovered from the union since unions possess immunity under the law of tort. This almost invariably led to an employer being granted an injunction against picketing. This might suggest that employers had frequent resort to injunctions but this was not so.

Injunctions were not without their problems. Employers were reluctant to enforce injunctions if employees disregarded them since this could lead to the jailing of strikers. In order to enforce the injunction, an employer would need to have employees cited for contempt of court, with jailing being likely if workers continued to picket in defiance of the injunction. This risked creating public sympathy for those workers and greater difficulty in resolving a dispute. While it is rare, if not unknown, nowadays for union members not to abide by injunctions, the difficulties that can arise were demonstrated during the dispute over cattle prices in 2019. In this instance, injunctions created sympathy for farmers and all the injunctions (and threats of farmers being sued) had to be lifted to allow a Department of Agriculture taskforce to be convened to address issues (McNulty 2019).

The Debate on Legal Reform

By the mid 1970s calls for reform had become common and, in response, the Fianna Fáil government in 1978 established a Commission of Inquiry on Industrial Relations (Duffy 1993). The commission, from which ICTU withdrew shortly after it was established, recommended the repeal of the legislation on trade disputes and its replacement by new consolidated legislation (Commission of Inquiry on Industrial Relations 1981). This legislation would place procedural requirements on trade unions and would make them again liable to be sued in tort if the procedures were not observed. The commission, however, favoured the retention of the immunities-based approach to the criminal law in the Conspiracy and Protection of Property Act 1875.

The commission's report, while generally welcomed by employers, drew a negative reaction from trade unionists and academics. For trade unions, the recommendations were totally unacceptable, since they would have reversed the gains of the 1906 Act.

Academics also pointed to both methodological and practical flaws in the report. They highlighted the absence of any original research, the selective and misleading use of secondary research, and the recommendations that were not congruent with the voluntarist tradition of Irish industrial relations (Kelly and Roche 1983; von Prondzynski and McCarthy 1984). Subsequently, a study by Wallace and O'Shea (1987) covering the years 1978–1986 undermined a claim by the commission that unofficial strikes – a major concern of the commission – were associated with small unions. The study found that unofficial strike action was actually overwhelmingly associated with members of larger unions – the direct opposite of the commission's assertion.

In 1986 the Department of Labour, with Ruairí Quinn TD as minister, published proposals for a 'positive right to strike' (Department of Labour 1986). This was an apparent total rejection of the commission's recommendations; however, the unions soon became concerned at restrictions that were to be placed on the positive rights. As a result of the unenthusiastic response of the unions and ICTU, the proposals were dropped (Bonner 1989). In 1988 revised departmental proposals were presented, which retained the voluntarist approach with modifications. It quickly became clear that, even if the proposals did not enjoy total agreement, there was enough consensus for their acceptance – notably by trade unions and ICTU (Kerr 1991a). One reason for this ready acceptance was a suggestion that the total immunity unions enjoyed under the 1906 Act would not survive a legal challenge based on Article 34 of the Constitution, which guarantees access to the courts (Wallace and O'Sullivan 2002).

THE INDUSTRIAL RELATIONS ACT 1990

The Industrial Relations Act 1990 is the most significant piece of collective industrial relations legislation in Ireland. Its stated purpose is 'to put in place an improved framework for the conduct of industrial relations and for the resolution of trade disputes [with] the overall aim ... to maintain a stable and orderly industrial relations climate' (Department of Labour 1991: 1). When the Bill was presented to the Dáil, there were some sharp criticisms from Pat Rabbitte TD and Eamon Gilmore TD of the Workers' Party. They criticised the provisions on the grounds that the Section 9 requirements (see below) would make the position of shop stewards vulnerable and that there would be more, not less, intervention into industrial relations by the courts – in effect a dilution of voluntarism (Rabbitte and Gilmore 1990).

Despite these objections, and because the Bill was based on consensus, not compulsion, it was passed into law with only one significant amendment. That was to provide protection for the all-out picketing provision of ICTU. An all-out picket is an ICTU-sanctioned picket that requires members of all unions in an employment to observe it during a strike. It was introduced by ICTU in 1970 to regulate picketing in companies with multi-union representation and it requires consultation with all unions prior to sanction for an all-out picket being granted by ICTU.

Trade Disputes and Trade Union Provisions of the 1990 Act

The following is a summary of the main trade disputes provisions, with a more complete treatment available in Kerr (2015).

1   Section 8 contains definitions of an employer, a trade dispute, a trade union, a worker, industrial action and a strike. Some key points from the definitions are as follows:
    • A worker does not include a member of the Defence Forces or of the Garda Síochána – this means their representative associations do not enjoy the immunities in the Act.
    • A trade dispute only covers disputes between employers and workers or former workers. This has the effect of withdrawing the previous protection from worker versus worker (inter-union) disputes.
    • The purpose of a strike must be to compel an employer to accept or not accept certain terms or conditions affecting employment.

2   Section 9 withdraws immunities from any form of industrial action in individual disputes that are in breach of agreed procedures contained either *in writing, in custom or in practice*. Should an employer not observe procedures, or should there be no procedures in place, workers are free to engage in industrial action in individual disputes.

3   Section 11 sets down provisions for picketing as follows:
    • Picketing is lawful at a place where an employee works or where an employer carries on business or, where this is not practical, at the approaches to the place of work.
    • Workers may only picket *their* employer or, in the case of secondary action, picket another employer if that (secondary) employer is seeking to frustrate the industrial action by directly assisting the primary employer.
    • Normal commercial activity does not meet the criterion for frustration of industrial action. Sympathy action in support of workers in one company by workers in other companies is not protected.
    • All-out strikes and pickets and secondary action involving more than one union are required to be sanctioned by ICTU.

4   Section 12 provides the same immunities against civil conspiracy and combination as in the 1906 Act, namely immunity is provided to persons when they are 'acting in contemplation or furtherance of a trade dispute'.

5   Under Section 13, the previous total immunity that trade unions enjoyed from being sued under the law of tort is withdrawn. Immunity is now only available where a union can show it is 'acting in contemplation or furtherance of a trade dispute'.

6   Section 14 requires that a secret ballot be conducted in the event of *any form of industrial action* and that prescribed rules on this be incorporated in union rule books. Immunities are withdrawn from any industrial action where a majority of workers vote against such action in a secret ballot. A union which persistently disregards the balloting provisions may have its negotiation licence withdrawn.

7   Section 19 places limitations on the granting of *ex parte* injunctions. An interim injunction will not be granted where all the following conditions have been met:
   • a secret ballot has been held;
   • a majority has voted in favour of industrial action; and
   • seven days' notice of such action has been given to an employer.
   Interlocutory injunctions (injunctions pending a full trial) are not available to an employer where, in addition to the previous requirements, the union establishes a fair case that it is acting in contemplation or furtherance of a trade dispute.

Continuity and Change

There is considerable continuity between the 1906 and 1990 Acts, most notably the retention of the immunities approach and the absence of any right to strike. The provisions in Section 11 largely confirm previous case law on secondary and sympathy picketing and clarify the law on picketing. For example, it allows for picketing on the premises of a shopping centre with multiple owners where employees are only in dispute with one company. Section 12 is unchanged from the 1906 Act, and Kerr (1991a) makes it clear that unofficial industrial action (action not sanctioned by the relevant union) is not outlawed per se. Thus, unofficial action does not necessarily lose immunity, as is sometimes suggested. Unofficial action that complied with the balloting provisions and where seven days' notice had been served (perhaps an unlikely situation) would continue to enjoy immunities.

Major changes include the withdrawal of immunities from individual disputes where procedures have not been exhausted. This departure seems to represent a step on the road to distinguishing between disputes of rights and disputes of interest. It is noteworthy that strikes over individual issues are nowadays a rarity, although this development predated the 1990 Act. The requirement that trade unions be able to prove they are acting in contemplation or furtherance of a trade dispute when engaging in industrial action places a new onus on them. A union that cannot show it is acting within those boundaries risks being held liable for damages under the law of tort. The requirement to incorporate balloting provisions in union rules represented a substantial change. This was not just because of the requirement to ballot members but because the exact rules that unions should incorporate in their rule books were specified in the 1990 Act. Unions had previously resisted any intrusion into their internal affairs since the 1870s. The requirement that a strike must be over terms or conditions affecting employment means there is no longer protection for unions in the case of political strikes over such matters as a general strike over taxation, or over a protest at the imprisonment of an individual (Kerr 1991a; Meenan 1999). However, it must be questionable whether the state would ever use the option to sue in these cases.

THE OPERATION OF THE INDUSTRIAL RELATIONS ACT 1990

The 1990 Act was presented as an adaptation of existing trade disputes law, allowing trade disputes to be brought back within the legal system without compromising the principles of voluntarism. However, doing this opened up a range of issues. Within a short time trade unions found themselves again involved in legal disputes and these cases indicated that judicial interpretation was going to be a key factor in the operation of the 1990 Act (Kerr 2010). The *G&T Crampton* and *Nolan Transport* cases are particularly important as they set precedents that established how the Act was going to be interpreted and applied.

In *G&T Crampton* v. *BATU* (1997), the Supreme Court found that the onus lay on the party resisting an application for an interlocutory injunction (the union) to prove the requirements had been met:
- a secret ballot had been held;
- it had been properly conducted;
- the outcome was in favour of the action taken; and
- the required notice (a minimum of one week) had been given.

Failure to be able to provide this proof would lead to the granting of the injunction. If the requirements were met, then the union also needed 'to establish a fair case that it was acting in contemplation or furtherance of a trade dispute' for an employer's application for an injunction to be refused.

The Nolan Transport Cases, 1993–1998

The series of cases running from 1993 to 1998 between Nolan Transport and SIPTU have been the most important under the 1990 Act. The dispute revolved around the issue of union recognition and the claimed dismissal of two employees (members of SIPTU) for union activism, with an interlocutory injunction being granted against the picket in 1993. The central legal issues revolved around the conduct of the ballot for strike action and the existence of a trade dispute. In the High Court case in 1994, Justice Barron found that the employees were not dismissed, the ballot for strike action was fraudulent and there was not a valid trade dispute because the dispute was really an attempt by the union to gain recognition. He determined that union recognition did not constitute a trade dispute and, as a result, concluded that the immunities were not available to either SIPTU or union members. As a result, damages in the amount of

IR£600,000 and costs were awarded against the union. The judgment led to accusations of judicial bias being made at union conferences and parallels being drawn with the Taff Vale case. A survey found that 73 per cent of union officials thought that 'the 1990 Act was a mistake which should not have been accepted in its current form' (Wallace and Delany 1997: 114).

The High Court decision was appealed to the Supreme Court, and this led to the judgment being overturned in 1998. The Supreme Court found that the employees 'at the very least, had good grounds for thinking themselves dismissed' and that, as a result, a trade dispute existed on that basis. In addition, the Supreme Court disagreed with the High Court decision in key areas, as follows:

- a union recognition dispute did constitute a trade dispute;
- union liability in tort did not follow from an improperly conducted ballot;
- the prescribed penalty for an improper ballot was the loss of a union's negotiating licence, not loss of immunity;
- the penalty for an improper ballot only applied if there was a persistent disregard of the 1990 Act's balloting provisions.

The outcome of the Supreme Court appeal was greeted with a sigh of relief from trade unions (O'Keeffe 1998). While the decision has seen controversy over the Act largely disappear, this does not mean that the Act is without potential difficulties for trade unions. Kerr (1991a) had suggested that the effectiveness of the restrictions on injunctions would be limited 'unless there is a radical change in the judiciary's attitude'. The experience of the Act is that, despite the restrictions in Section 19, injunctions that impede industrial action continue to be granted. Kerr (2010) notes three leading cases that were successful at full trial but where the industrial action had been injuncted. The courts have placed strict requirements on balloting, with not just union members entitled to challenge the conduct of ballots but employers also being so entitled. Given their importance, the balloting requirements in Section 14 are reproduced in Table 2.2. Even observing the requirements in Table 2.2 is not enough to ensure compliance. The key issue is not whether a secret ballot has been held but whether a union can prove this to be the case. Kerr (2010) notes that issues arising under case law indicate that the standard of proof that is to be applied is unclear and that this leaves unions somewhat in limbo. Finally, it should be noted that in the debate on reform in the 1980s the focus had been on tackling unofficial action (action not sanctioned by a union), but it is largely the union as an organisation that has been exposed by the greater access to the courts brought about by the Act.

An Employer View on the Law and Industrial Action

While much legal action has involved issues of concern to unions, notably the right to bargain, there are indications of some employers wishing for further legal requirements

Table 2.2

Balloting Requirements Applying to Any Industrial Action

1   The union shall not organise, participate in, sanction or support a strike or other industrial action without a secret ballot, entitlement to vote on which shall be accorded equally to all members whom it is reasonable to believe will be called upon to engage in the strike or other industrial action.

2   The union shall take reasonable steps to ensure that every member entitled to vote in the ballot votes without interference from, or constraint imposed by, the union or any of its members, officials or employees and, so far as is reasonably possible, that such members shall be given a fair opportunity of voting.

3   The committee or management or other controlling authority of a trade union shall have full discretion in relation to organising, participating in, sanctioning or supporting a strike or other industrial action notwithstanding that the majority of those voting in the ballot, including an aggregate ballot, are in favour of such strike or industrial action.

4   The committee or management or other controlling authority of a trade union shall have full discretion in relation to organising, participating in, sanctioning or supporting a strike or other industrial action against the wishes of a majority of those voting in a secret ballot, except where, in the case of ballots by more than one trade union, an aggregate majority of all votes cast favours such strike or other industrial action.

5   Where the outcome of a secret ballot conducted by a trade union which is affiliated to ICTU or, in the case of ballots by more than one such trade union, an aggregate majority of all the votes cast is in favour of supporting a strike organised by another trade union, a decision to take such supportive action shall not be implemented unless the action has been sanctioned by ICTU.

6   As soon as practicable after the conduct of a secret ballot the trade union shall take reasonable steps to make known to its members entitled to vote in the ballot (i) the number of ballot papers issued, (ii) the number of votes cast, (iii) the number of votes in favour of the proposal, (iv) the number of votes cast against the proposal and (v) the number of spoilt votes.

Source: Adapted from the Industrial Relations Act 1990.

to be placed on industrial action beyond those in the Industrial Relations Act 1990. Stratis Consulting, which is headed by Brendan McGinty, former director of industrial relations at the Irish Business and Employers Confederation (IBEC), has proposed wide-ranging changes to trade disputes law. In essential services these cover a requirement to exhaust procedures and a requirement to maintain a minimum level of service in the event of a strike, a substantial cooling-off period following a Labour Court recommendation and a ballot on that recommendation, and binding arbitration and a no-strike policy in essential services which are of strategic importance to the public (Stratis Consulting 2019). In the event of industrial action generally, changes to balloting requirements are proposed to require seven days' notice of a ballot, a requirement for a 50 per cent turnout of those entitled to vote, independent oversight of all ballots and an extension of the notice period for a strike from seven to fourteen days, with the availability of immunities contingent on a statutory requirement to exhaust procedures (Stratis Consulting 2019). Sheehan (2019c) observed that these were likely to 'provoke the ire of trade unionists' and Patricia King, general secretary of ICTU, subsequently rejected a need for change (Sheehan 2019d). Thus, any large-scale movement in the direction proposed in the Stratis document could only be envisaged in the context of an abandonment of the previous consensus approach to legislating on trade disputes.

THE CONSTITUTION AND INDUSTRIAL RELATIONS

As noted earlier, nineteenth-century liberal ideas supported the right of individuals to combine to promote their own interests. Such a right is known as a 'right of association' and is incorporated in the 1937 Irish Constitution in the following Articles:

- Article 40.6.1 (iii) guarantees 'the right of citizens to form associations and unions. Laws, however, may be enacted for the regulation and control in the public interest of the foregoing right'.
- Article 40.6.2 specifies that the laws regulating this right 'shall contain no political, religious or class discrimination'.

Part III of the Trade Union Act 1941 provided for the establishment of a tribunal that could grant 'a determination that a specified union (or unions) alone should have the sole right to organise workers of a particular class'. In effect, this was an exclusive right to organise, which encouraged 'sole negotiating rights' (Forde 1991: 29). It was aimed at curbing the operation of British-based unions in Ireland since they could not be granted the sole right to organise. Part III was highly controversial and within a short time the provision was tested as a result of an inter-union dispute. In 1945 the Irish Transport and General Workers' Union (ITGWU) applied to the tribunal for the sole right to organise workers in the road passenger service of Córas Iompair Éireann (CIÉ). A British-based union, the National Union of Railwaymen (NUR), and a number of its members initiated a constitutional challenge against Sullivan (the chairman of the tribunal). Regarding it as merely a regulation of the right to form a union, the High Court found the provision to be constitutional. This judgment was overturned in the Supreme Court, which found 'the denial of a person's choice of which union he can join is not a control of the exercise of the right of freedom of association but a denial of it altogether' (Forde 1991: 18).

The right to join unions does not automatically create a right to be accepted into membership by a trade union, as indicated in the case of *Tierney* v. *Amalgamated Society of Woodworkers (ASW)* (1995). Tierney had sought to join the ASW in pursuit of a right to work but his application was refused because he had not served an apprenticeship and the union did not accept that he was a genuine carpenter. Tierney failed in both the High Court and the Supreme Court on a number of grounds, including that the

Constitution provided no support for the case as the union had acted fairly within their rules (Forde 1991).

The most significant interpretation of the right of association in the 1937 Constitution is that it has been found to imply an equal and opposite right of disassociation. The *Educational Company of Ireland* v. *Fitzpatrick* (1961) case involved thirty-six members of the Irish Union of Distributive Workers and Clerks who went on strike and picketed in pursuit of enforcing a closed shop. A closed shop arises where all employees in a particular class of employee are required to be union members. In this case, the Supreme Court granted an injunction against the picket but not against the strike. The picketing was found not to be protected by the immunities in the 1906 Act as these were subordinate to the right of disassociation of the non-union members. In relation to the strike, the court suggested that there was a pre-existing 'higher order' right to strike that was not contradicted by anything in the Constitution. This claimed 'higher order' right to strike has not subsequently been developed or legislated for and, as a result, there is not considered to be an established right to strike in Ireland. Although no injunction was granted against the strike, it collapsed without the protection for picketing being available.

The existence of a right of disassociation was confirmed in the case of *Meskell* v. *CIÉ* (1973). John Meskell, a bus conductor with fifteen years' service, was dismissed for failure to give an undertaking to 'at all times' remain a member of one of four named unions. He lost his appeal against dismissal in the High Court but was successful in the Supreme Court. The company argued that it was entitled in common law to dismiss. However, the entitlement to dismiss in common law was found to provide no justification for the dismissal because of the superior position of the employee's constitutional right of disassociation as established in the *Educational Company* case.

The above two cases do not limit the right of employers to require workers to join specified unions prior to them commencing employment (Kerr and Whyte 1985). Thus, while the post-entry closed shop is unconstitutional, the pre-entry (prior to employment) closed shop may well be constitutional. This is because, while it guarantees the right to work, the Constitution does not guarantee a right to employment and generally employers can employ whoever they wish – see *Becton Dickinson* v. *Lee* (1973).

The right of association does not place a requirement on an employer to recognise or negotiate with any trade union. The leading case in this regard is that of *Abbott and Whelan* v. *the Southern Health Board and ITGWU* (1982). About half of a category of workers in the Southern Health Board (SHB) left the ITGWU and joined the Amalgamated Transport and General Workers' Union (ATGWU). The SHB refused to recognise their new union and continued to negotiate with the ITGWU. Two employees, Abbott and Whelan, initiated a High Court case requiring the SHB to recognise and negotiate with the ATGWU and to prevent the ITGWU from purporting to negotiate with the SHB on their behalf. They lost on both grounds. The High Court found that as the SHB was not required to recognise any union, it did not have to recognise the ATGWU. Neither was there any constitutional right for an employee to have negotiations conducted by a union of one's choice. The SHB could not be prevented from negotiating with the ITGWU on behalf of Abbott and Whelan even if they did not wish this.

The principles in the *Abbott and Whelan* case have been subsequently confirmed in the more complex series of cases taken by the Irish Locomotive Drivers' Association (Higgins 2000). These judgments make it clear that, although the Constitution provides for a right to form unions, this right does not have as a corollary the rights to recognition, negotiation or representation. In effect, under the 1937 Constitution these are voluntary options for an employer.

The Constitution in Context

A number of the above decisions have given rise to controversy. For example, the *NUR v. Sullivan* decision restricted government's capacity to regulate trade unions. It is, of course, an open question to what extent government regulation of independent unions is desirable in a free society. On the other hand, the decisions establishing an implied right of disassociation have been criticised for converting a collective right into an individual one. Kerr and Whyte (1985: 12) write that 'the right to *form* unions is of its very nature a collective right, so it is difficult to see how its corollary can be a right not to join unions, which is an individual right'. Seen in this way, this is an example of common law individualism affecting the exercise of a collective right.

The controversy over the *Educational Company* case largely petered out in the twenty-five years following the decision. Although procedure agreements that require employees to be union members may still exist, newer agreements tend to deal with the issue of union recognition in a different fashion. These make it a matter for the union involved to recruit employees if the employees wish to join, and they require the union to take into membership all such eligible employees. The growth in union density to over 60 per cent by the early 1980s demonstrated the capacity of trade unions to grow their membership irrespective of the Supreme Court's individualist interpretation of the right of association. This demonstrates that the restrictive constitutional interpretations had little practical effect on the fortunes of unions. It also hints that favourable legal provisions for union recognition may have only a limited impact if other factors, notably structural ones, work against unionisation – a point also alluded to by former chairman of the Labour Court Kevin Duffy (2019).

THE RIGHT TO BARGAIN DILEMMA AND THE LAW

With the reversal of the historical growth in union density in the 1980s and 1990s, recognition and negotiation rights appeared back on the union movement's agenda. For unions, there was a manifest contradiction between their involvement in social partnership at the national level and the growing inability to gain recognition from employers at a company level. However, trade unions had some reservations about reversing the voluntary approach and lobbying for a legal right to union recognition, as had been introduced in the UK in 1999. There was a fear that a law prescribing union recognition could lead to union derecognition, just as the right of association had led to a right of disassociation. A high-level group set up under the national agreement Partnership 2000 considered the issue and its conclusions led to the Industrial Relations (Amendment) Act 2001 (Kerr 2017).

The Industrial Relations Acts 2001–2004

The Industrial Relations (Amendment) Act 2001 represented an attempt by the government to resolve trade union complaints about anti-union employers without interfering in the principle of voluntary union recognition. The Act gave the Labour Court the power to set legally binding wages and conditions of employment in an organisation where collective bargaining was not in place and dispute resolution procedures had failed to resolve the dispute. It gave no right to union recognition with an impediment being judicial comments in the previous Supreme Court decisions suggesting this would be unconstitutional. The Industrial Relations (Miscellaneous Provisions) Act 2004 aimed to strengthen the provisions of the 2001 Act, most notably setting time limits for Labour Court determinations as there had been complaints at the length of time cases were taking. Cullinane and Dobbins (2014) consider that the legislation was moderately successful although the cases taken were largely confined to small to medium enterprises. It had little impact on larger non-union multinational companies where pay rates were generally comparable with collectively agreed terms. This focus on smaller employers changed in 2004 when the Irish Municipal, Public and Civil Trade Union (and its branch, the Irish Airline Pilots Association (IALPA)) requested a Labour Court investigation under the 2001–2004 Acts on behalf of a number of pilots in the Irish multinational Ryanair, which at the time did not negotiate with unions.

IALPA sought an investigation about a number of issues, including conditions attached to an offer by Ryanair to retrain pilots on a new aircraft. One issue was that the pilots would have to repay training costs to the company if it was forced to recognise the union (O'Sullivan and Gunnigle 2009). Ryanair argued that the Labour Court could not hear the case, with one of the reasons being that collective bargaining took place through the company's employee representative committees (ERCs). The Labour Court rejected this argument and found that the conditions in the Acts had been met. Ryanair challenged that decision in the High Court, which upheld the Labour Court's decision. However, Ryanair appealed to the Supreme Court and it overturned the High Court's decision in 2007. It found that the Labour Court erred in:

- finding that a trade dispute within the terms of the 2001 Act existed; and
- in dismissing Ryanair's claim that collective bargaining existed without hearing direct oral evidence from at least one of Ryanair's pilots.

The Supreme Court also found that the internal machinery of ERCs had not been exhausted. It concluded that the ERCs were excepted bodies within the meaning of the Trade Union Act 1941 and they could have conducted collective bargaining; but the Labour Court had not investigated properly whether this was the case or not and no evidence had been presented to support its conclusions. It also criticised the Labour Court's use of an industrial relations definition of collective bargaining, preferring a dictionary definition, although, as Kerr (2017) notes, the court did not identify what dictionary it used, and he quotes several leading dictionaries as incorporating trade unions in their definitions. The Supreme Court's judgment undermined the intent of the 2001–2004 Acts and cases fell away to a trickle (Cullinane and Dobbins 2014; Duffy 2019).

Ryanair – The International Labour Organisation Dimension

D'Art and Turner (2007) were highly critical of the Supreme Court judgment. They pointed out that it appeared to sanction 'company' or 'house' unions that are not independent of the employers and that the definition of collective bargaining adopted by the Supreme Court differed from that in Article 91 of the ILO, of which Ireland is a member. These, and other aspects of the judgment, they suggested opened up the option for unions to initiate a complaint against Ireland to the ILO, and such a complaint was made by ICTU in 2010.

In reporting on the complaint in 2012 the ILO reaffirmed the voluntary nature of the ILO provisions on union recognition. However, it was highly critical of the possibility that inducements (not having to pay retraining costs) might have been offered to Ryanair pilots not to unionise. The report said this would, if true, 'be tantamount to employer interference in the right of workers to form and join the organisation of their own choosing' (ILO 2012: 228). Attention was also drawn to ILO Recommendation 91, which provides that representatives of unorganised workers are only to be granted a 'role in collective bargaining solely when no workers' organisation exists', i.e. in the absence of a trade union (ILO 2012: 230). In conclusion, the Irish government was requested to review the existing framework and give consideration to appropriate measures (including legislative ones) 'to ensure respect for the freedom of association and collective bargaining principles' (ILO 2012: 231).

The Industrial Relations (Amendment) Act 2015

The Industrial Relations (Amendment) Act 2015 represents a response to the ILO report, trade union representations and consultations with employer groups. It provides for a hybrid, two-stage process where the Labour Court can first issue a non-binding industrial relations recommendation on terms and conditions and, only if that is disregarded by the employer, can it then issue a legally binding determination. The Act's provisions are quite extensive, reflecting an attempt to insulate it from legal challenge (Duffy 2019). In summary, the 2001–2004 Acts addressed union complaints to (i) strengthen the role of trade unions versus that of excepted bodies, (ii) require excepted bodies to be independent of the employer and employer bodies (iii), provide protection against victimisation of workers who are party to a case, (iv) allow the chief officer of a union to make a statutory declaration as to the number of union members, (v) provide protection against the Labour Court disclosing names of union members, and (vi), most importantly, provide a definition of collective bargaining consistent with the ILO one. That definition reads as follows:

> 'collective bargaining' comprises voluntary engagements or negotiations between any employer or employers' organisation on the one hand and a trade union of workers or excepted body to which this Act applies on the other, with the object of reaching agreement regarding working conditions or terms of employment, or non-employment, of workers. (Industrial Relations (Amendment) Act 2015: 23)

The above changes served to redress the complaints made of the Supreme Court judgment in the Ryanair case; however, as by early 2020, only five cases have proceeded to the Labour Court. Of these two were not found eligible for consideration and recommendations have been issued in two cases.

The low usage reflects trade unions' waning enthusiasm for the Act and their 'general hesitancy' to use it (Prendergast 2019c). Duffy (2019) has identified the reason for union reluctance to use the 2015 Act as being due to the amendments designed to insulate the Act from further legal challenge. He identifies the following: (i) meeting the 'insignificant' membership threshold for claims, (ii) a burdensome requirement to establish that the 'grade group or category', on whose behalf a claim is taken, is appropriate, and (iii) that comparisons must be made with the prevailing terms and conditions of employment in the totality of a sector. He points out also that the 2015 Act had effectively reversed the decision of the High Court in *Ashford Castle* v. *SIPTU* (2006) and, as a result, 'the Labour Court could no longer attach particular weight to collectively bargained terms and conditions over those in non-union comparable employment' (Duffy 2019).

There has also been a return of the complaints about undue delay made originally against the 2001 Act, with cases taking a very long time to pass through the Labour Court process – twenty months in one case. Reflecting the difficulties, ICTU has now sought further amendments to the legislation. In contrast, Brendan McGinty, the former director of industrial relations for IBEC, has argued that such calls require '"robust challenge" by employers' (Sheehan 2018c). On the political front, Sinn Féin had proposed a Trade Union Representation (Miscellaneous Provisions) Bill 2017, which is moribund, and the Labour Party also now supports a right of employees to be represented by a trade union, and that employers 'be required to negotiate with their employee's representatives' (Labour Party 2020: 7). Given previous judicial comments, there seem to be constitutional impediments to union recognition or negotiation rights (D'Art forthcoming). The Labour Party acknowledges that an amendment of the Constitution may be required. The questions arise as to what the specifics of any amendment would involve and whether it would pass in a referendum.

Unions have displayed a preference for invoking the voluntarist provision in Section 20(1) of the Industrial Relations Act 1969 to seek a Labour Court recommendation in favour of union recognition. Section 20(1) of that Act allows for a trade union to refer a case on its own to the Labour Court provided it agrees to accept the Labour Court's recommendation. In pursuit of its mandate to promote collective bargaining, the Labour Court normally recommends recognition. In the years 2015–2019, some twenty-five cases were referred under section 20(1), with the Labour Court recommending in favour of union recognition in twenty-four cases (Sheehan *et al.* 2020). This compares with sixty-seven referrals in the years 1985–1991, with fifty-nine (87 per cent) leading a recommendation for recognition, of which sixteen (27 per cent) were accepted by employers (D'Art and Turner 2003). While there is no obligation on an employer to attend a hearing or accept a recommendation, the moral suasion attached to a positive Labour Court recommendation is considered useful by trade unions and can form the basis for a campaign for recognition, even if rejected initially.

FURTHER INTERNATIONAL DEVELOPMENTS

Apart from membership of the ILO, Ireland has obligations under several other international treaties and conventions. These can come in the nature of the soft law arising from our membership of the ILO and the rights conferred by the Social Charter of the Council of Europe, or hard law as with EU membership or obligations under the European Convention on Human Rights (ECHR). In recent years there have been significant developments arising from these sources that have implications for Irish industrial relations.

Council of Europe

Ireland's membership of the Council of Europe imposes obligations under that body's Social Charter. The original Social Charter dates from 1961, with a revised and extended version coming into force in 1999. The Charter is an international treaty intended to guarantee fundamental social and economic rights, which are designed to complement the civil and political rights provided for in the ECHR. The Charter contains several provisions dealing with industrial relations issues, including those on collective bargaining, representation and the right to strike. Trade unions or employer organisations may make complaints and these are heard by the European Committee of Social Rights (ECSR). As with the ILO, enforcement is by way of reports made by states on action taken to address complaints that have been upheld. In 2016 ICTU successfully complained to the ECSR about a decision of the Irish Competition Authority preventing certain workers – deemed self-employed – from concluding collective agreements setting minimum pay rates and other working conditions. While the ECSR found in favour of the ICTU complaint in 2018, it noted that the Competition (Amendment) Act of 2017 had brought Irish law in line with its obligations under the Social Charter (Committee of Ministers of Council of Europe 2018).

In 2014 the ECSR found Ireland in breach of its treaty obligations in denying the Association of Garda Sergeants and Inspectors (AGSI) direct access to negotiations and in the absolute prohibition in Ireland on Gardaí striking (see Table 2.3). Despite the Irish legislative framework on industrial action being based on a system of immunities, not rights, the ECSR framed its decision in terms of a 'right to strike'. While the framing of the decision in this way is anomalous, there is no suggestion that the ECSR was critical of the system of immunities or that the decision would require a change to a rights-based approach. Instead, the ECSR decision criticised a lack of proportionality attaching to the Irish state's absolute prohibition on strike action by members of An Garda Síochaná. The main point of the decision was that while a right to strike should be available, it could be subject to regulation to ensure continuity of policing during a strike.

The decision in the European Confederation of Police (EuroCOP) case stands in contrast to that in the 2018 case *European Organisation of Military Associations (EUROMIL)* v. *Ireland Complaint No. 112/2014* – the EUROMIL case – which was taken on behalf of the Permanent Defence Force Other Ranks Representative Association (PDFORRA). The complaint dealt with restrictions on joining ICTU, access to national public sector bargaining and a prohibition on strike action. The ECSR determined that the prohibition against the defence forces engaging in industrial action was allowed under the terms of the Social Charter. However, it found against the restriction placed on the representative associations joining ICTU and 'the nearly total exclusion of the representative military organisations from direct negotiations concerning pay' (Committee of Ministers of Council of Europe 2018). In responding to that finding Ireland reported that in negotiations leading to a new public sector stability agreement in 2017, 'the Permanent Defence Force Representative Associations had attended and participated at all plenary sessions and … were afforded equal standing with members of ICTU throughout the process' (Committee of Ministers of Council of Europe 2018). It is unclear if that meets the requirement of the ECSR's determination in relation to ICTU membership, and PDFORRA continues to campaign to be allowed to join that body.

EU Developments

Two important cases have dealt with industrial action and the regulation of employment in organisations operating on a transnational basis within the EU. The first is the *International Transport Workers' Federation* v. *Viking Line ABP* (2008). This case concerned

Table 2.3
The Garda Case Study Part 1
A 'Right to Strike' and Right to Union Status?

At its annual conference in 1993 the Garda Representative Association (GRA) sought the right to trade union status. Over the period 2000–2009 the conciliation and arbitration scheme for An Garda Síochaná was effectively supplanted by national social partnership negotiations to which the garda representative bodies did not have direct access. Both the GRA and the AGSI complained at this exclusion and eventually came to seek a right of access to the LRC and Labour Court from which they were also excluded. In 2012 EuroCOP, acting on behalf of the AGSI, made a complaint under the provisions of the Social Charter to the Council of Europe. The complaint centred on Gardaí being denied the following: (i) trade union rights, (ii) direct involvement in national collective bargaining arrangements, (iii) membership of ICTU, and (iv) the prohibition on Gardaí (and their representative associations) from engaging in strike action. In 2014 the ECSR found Ireland in breach of its obligations on the collective bargaining and right to strike complaints but not on the trade union one. It was found that the garda representative associations effectively met the requirement for collective representation. A review was subsequently conducted into these and other matters by John Horgan, former Labour Court chairman. The Horgan (2016) report recommended that the garda associations should become trade unions and have the rights and obligations of trade unions, but with a five-year ban on pension accrual in the event of industrial action. Subsequently, the Department of Justice and Equality established a working group to consider Horgan's report. In submissions to the working group, both the GRA and the AGSI sought legislative access to the WRC and Labour Court, an entitlement to strike and the option to become a trade union. The working group recommended in favour of granting access to the WRC and Labour Court but against trade union status or an entitlement to strike. In 2018 the ECSR noted that the garda associations had now been granted access to national negotiations but that the Irish state had not reported on the right to strike recommendation. It indicated that it expected this to be dealt with in a subsequent report. Under the terms of the Industrial Relations (Amendment) Act 2019, Gardaí and their representative associations now have legislative access to the WRC and Labour Court but trade union status and immunity for industrial action have not been granted.

Discussion Points
1. Should Gardaí be prevented or allowed to engage in industrial action?
2. To what extent is the ECSR decision involving the Gardaí above consistent with the ECSR decision involving the defence forces outlined in Table 3.5 in Chapter 3?
See http://hudoc.esc.coe.int/eng/?i=reschs-2014-12-en;
http://hudoc.esc.coe.int/eng/?i=reschs-2018-2-en.

a Finnish shipping company, Viking Line, that was reflagged to Estonia and employed Estonians at lower wages than in Finland. The Finnish Seamen's Union threatened industrial action and sought International Transport Workers' Federation support by requiring affiliate unions not to negotiate with Viking. The case was referred to the Court of Justice of the European Union (CJEU), which recognised that the right to strike was

a fundamental right but considered it was to be strictly circumscribed. The court identified the following four conditions that strike action would have to meet. It must:
- be justified and have a legitimate aim;
- be for overriding reasons of public interest;
- be suitable for securing the attainment of the objective pursued; and
- not go beyond what is necessary in order to attain it.

In effect, the decision of the court established a strong proportionality test that any strike involving the provision of cross-national services would have to meet. The court determined that the union, in this case, had not met these conditions.

Judgment in the second important case was issued a week after the Viking case: *Laval Un Partneri Ltd* v. *Svenska Byggnadsarbetareförbundet*. This case involved 'posted workers' (workers sent to another country) who were sent by Laval from Latvia to Sweden. The Swedish unions sought to conclude a collective agreement on wages and working conditions covering them. To avoid this, Laval signed a collective agreement in Latvia for lower wages and conditions. In return, Swedish electrical unions blockaded the worksite and engaged in 'solidarity or secondary action', which, unlike in Ireland, is legal in Sweden. The CJEU found that the strike, although legal under Swedish law, was illegal under EU law and was secondary to the right of businesses to supply cross-border services.

Hug and Tudor (2012: 16) claim that the CJEU 'identified the right to strike as a fundamental right' and then 'appeared to strangle that right at birth'. Responding to these judgments, Barnard (2012: 264) pointed out that the CJEU adopted an asymmetrical approach in which once it considered that an 'economic right has been infringed by the exercise of the social right … the onus is on the trade union to justify this breach and show that it is proportionate'. She argued that this 'asymmetrical approach' meant that 'economic rights were likely to prevail' and warned of the dangers this has for a social Europe (Barnard 2012: 124). She noted that the proportionality test creates many practical difficulties for trade unions that place their funds at risk in the event of strike action since they cannot know whether they have met a proportionality test in advance of a court case.

The trade union response to their difficulties with the Industrial Relations Acts 2001–2015 has now moved beyond the national level to EU level. At its 2019 biennial conference ICTU launched a policy document that commits it to working through the European Trade Union Confederation 'in seeking to have the laws of the EU Member States on collective bargaining harmonised' by way of a European Union Directive (ICTU 2019: 17). General Secretary Patricia King noted that the 'supremacy of EU law would overcome any lingering doubt around the Constitutionality of any legislative initiative in this sphere' (Sheehan 2019b). However, the ICTU policy document recognises that there are challenges to achieving an EU directive, including strong opposition by employer groups at EU level and the current requirement for unanimity across all twenty-seven EU countries (ICTU 2019). Tom Hayes, of the Brussels European Employee Relations Group, has pointed out further issues in that a directive could take decades and, even if achieved, it might, as with the EU's Company Statute, deliver 'a much watered-down version' of what unions want (*Industrial Relations News* 2019). There could also be unintended consequences if a directive were achieved. If the benefits of unionisation were widely available, through extending the provisions of collective agreements, that could reduce the incentive to join a union and depress union density.

European Court of Human Rights Developments

In contrast to the *Viking* and *Laval* cases, two separate leading cases under the ECHR have suggested that priority must be given to the right to bargain and to engage in strike action. Like the Irish Constitution, the ECHR incorporates a right to freedom of association. Article 11 of the Convention states that 'everyone has the right to freedom of peaceful assembly and association, including the right to form and join trade unions for the protection of his interests'. Because the ECHR has been incorporated into EU law (as a result of the Lisbon Treaty), its provisions are especially important for all member states, including Ireland.

Article 11 had long been interpreted as not implying a right to union recognition or negotiation rights – still less a right to strike (Ewing 2012). Only a very limited individual right to representation had previously been recognised, in the case *National Belgian Police Union* v. *Belgium* (1975). The unanimous reversal of this approach by the seventeen-member ECtHR in the case of *Demir and Baykara* v. *Turkey* (2008) was a major surprise. In that case the court found that Article 11 of the ECHR had to be seen as involving a right to bargain collectively. It considered that restrictions on this right could only apply insofar as they met the requirements of ILO conventions. In effect, the 'soft law' of the ILO was influencing the hard law of the ECHR. In 2009 this decision was further expanded in *Enerji Yapi-Yol Sen* v. *Turkey*, in which it was found that a right to strike was required as part of a trade union's right to defend their members' interests.

Ewing (2012) considers that the ECtHR decisions provide a basis for rolling back the restrictive interpretations of the rights to strike under EU (and UK) law. Others are sceptical of human rights legislation when applied to the industrial relations arena. Hepple (2010) has doubts about courts in common law countries embracing ILO jurisprudence. He also argues that judicial involvement in deciding on abstract principles 'hardly seems a suitable way to settle labour disputes in the modern globalised economy' (Hepple 2010: 15). EU proposals to deal with the decisions of the CJEU and the ECtHR do not give primacy to either economic freedoms or fundamental social rights. Ewing is highly critical of this approach, claiming it to be 'either naïve or disingenuous'. He points out that it is fundamental in 'disputes between economic freedoms and social rights that both cannot prevail simultaneously' (Ewing 2012: 14).

CONCLUDING COMMENTS

Irish industrial relations legislation is based on an immunities approach that dates back 145 years in the criminal area and over 110 years in the civil area. Nearly 20 years after the legislation was introduced to allow for pay and conditions to be set by the Labour Court where a collectively bargained arrangement was not in place, that legislative approach seems of limited relevance. It is unclear what will happen now. Suggestions for a right to union recognition are likely to run up against the Constitution. At a European level, systems of rights have not prevented tensions between commercial and collective rights, most notably in contrasting decisions of the EU and the requirements of the ECHR. These international developments demonstrate that problems with the role of the law in industrial relations are not confined to common law systems. Neither are they just of historical interest. They are evidence of continuing underlying tensions that apply to legal systems and industrial relations generally, whether these be characterised by systems based on immunities or rights.

Chapter 3

Trade Unions

INTRODUCTION

Trade unions are the most common form of worker representation across the world. The chances of students having contact with unions depend very much on where they work. They are less likely to come across unions if they work in part-time jobs in bars, restaurants, hotels and small businesses, but later in their careers they may be more likely to have contact with them in teaching, medical fields, universities, the civil service, construction, transport and banking. Some people argue that unions are archaic organisations of a bygone era. Yet surveys across Europe indicate that the vast majority of people believe trade unions are necessary. In addition, while working conditions for many are much better than when unions developed in the late nineteenth and early twentieth centuries, an ongoing concern for unions are precarious jobs where people have insecure hours and income. For example, in recent years, unions have been involved in representing people over zero-hours contracts in Sports Direct in the UK, professional soccer players in Limerick FC over unpaid wages, and the Ireland national women's soccer team over pay and conditions. In much the same way that students' unions were created by students for students, trade unions were created by workers to give a collective voice to workers. Workers believed that they would have more bargaining power to improve their conditions by acting together than by acting individually. Even in organisations with no unions, we have seen the emergence of collectivism and worker activism to express dissatisfaction, such as the mass walkout of Google workers over sexual harassment issues and strikes by Deliveroo workers over changes to contracts and safety issues. In fact, a survey of large companies globally found that 81 per cent expect a rise in employee activism in the future over artificial intelligence, company surveillance of employees, pay and benefits, corporate social responsibility and diversity, and 55 per cent view workforce activism as a risk to their reputation (Herbert Smith Freehills 2019). Unions have had a lasting impact on workers' lives and their influence has pervaded popular culture in television shows and films like *Peaky Blinders*, *The Crown*, *The Good Wife*, *The Irishman* and *Made in Dagenham*.

In this chapter we examine the multiple factors that influence why union membership might go up or down, the trend of declining unionisation amongst workers, how unions are responding to this major challenge, and whether there are alternative bodies which can adequately represent workers. First, we will explain what trade unions do, examine how and why they emerged, and outline the trade unions that operate in Ireland.

WHAT ARE TRADE UNIONS?

Trade unions are organisations present in most countries in the world. Their primary goal is to represent the interests of workers by 'improving or maintaining conditions of employment' (Webb and Webb 1920: 1). The employment relationship consists of an imbalance of power between the employer and individual worker. The employer has financial resources and legal authority in an employment relationship while a worker has only their labour to offer and is therefore in a weaker position. Trade unions have traditionally been seen as the most effective means of countering employer power and achieving satisfactory pay and working conditions for workers. Unions' greatest source of power is uniting workers and they use this collectivism to get 'a seat at the table' with employers and engage in collective bargaining (Table 3.1). If needed, this collectivism can be used to engage in industrial action, such as a strike, as a way of exerting pressure on an employer to accept terms or conditions of employment or resist terms and conditions being imposed by the employer. In other words, industrial action and the threat of it are sources of negotiating power for workers.

Table 3.1
What is Collective Bargaining?

The International Labour Organisation defines collective bargaining as all negotiations which take place between an employer(s) or an employer organisation(s), on the one hand, and workers' organisation(s) on the other, for
(a)   determining working conditions and terms of employment;
(b)   regulating relations between employers and workers;
(c)   regulating relations between employer(s) or employer organisations and workers' organisations. (Convention No. 154 1981)

In general, trade unions perform three overarching functions (Crouch 2017):
1.   they secure wage rises for workers through collective bargaining;
2.   they represent members' grievances and try to ensure managerial fairness in how workers are treated;
3.   'they are part of wider political movements seeking social and fiscal policies that reduce inequality and provide security for the lives of workers and their families' (Crouch 2017: 53).

In the pursuit of these functions, unions offer a range of services like giving information and advice to workers on their rights, representing workers in the workplace in disciplinary and grievance processes, representing members in legal cases and disputes referred to the Workplace Relations Commission and Labour Court, sanctioning industrial action like strikes during disputes with employers, and providing education and training to members. Trade unions have also, over time, increasingly sought to influence public policies and members' attitudes on non-employment issues (Table 3.2).

Table 3.2
Trade Unions and Members' Attitudes

It has been argued that trade unions encourage more liberal views in their members on economic and cultural issues (Kitschelt 2013; Pateman 1970). In recent years the umbrella body for unions, the Irish Congress of Trade Unions (ICTU), called for support of gay marriage in 2015 and of repealing the Eighth Amendment on abortion in 2018. It has also organised protests calling for more state provision of housing. In this way, trade unions expand their influence beyond work-specific issues. There can also be a 'chicken and egg' scenario when it comes to union members' attitudes, in that while unions influence members' views, it is also the case that people with more left-wing political attitudes tend to join unions more than people with right-wing attitudes (Toubøl and Strøby Jensen 2014). So people who join unions may already be predisposed to more liberal views.

THE ORIGINS OF TRADE UNIONS

The early 'combinations' of workers were almost exclusively composed of skilled craftsmen, or 'journeymen' as they were known. They were purely local bodies and their existence was often tenuous. The historical development of trade unions is inextricably linked to the development of industrial relations. The current nature of the trade union movement in Ireland has its origins in the dramatic changes brought about by the Industrial Revolution, beginning in Britain in the eighteenth century and later spreading to Europe and North America. There was a gradual change from a largely peasant society based on agriculture and craft production to an industry-based society with new social divisions, where greater numbers of people worked in the 'factory system' and relied on wages for their existence.

In this new order, people now worked together in much larger numbers and on much more tightly defined tasks. This scenario led to the emergence of modern management as a result of the need to plan, control, direct and organise the use of equipment, capital, materials and people in the factory system. By and large, early factory owners adopted authoritarian approaches to workers. Working conditions were poor, working hours were long and 'sweated labour' was common. Workers themselves could do little about this situation, since they had little or no economic or political power. It was only the skilled workers who were successful in establishing any significant permanent unionisation in Ireland up to the early twentieth century. Until 1850 even the trade unions of skilled workers were modest and local in terms of their organisation. A new type of trade union was prompted by the foundation of the Amalgamated Society of Engineers in the UK in the 1850–1851 period.

In Ireland in the early 1900s the growth in influence and power of the 'new unionism', which primarily sought to organise unskilled workers, was most obviously manifested in the leadership skills of Jim Larkin, who founded the Irish Transport and General Workers' Union (ITGWU) in 1909. Many employers refused to engage with this trade union, and since the workers were unskilled, they had little power as individuals and they could easily be replaced. Therefore, unions such as the ITGWU frequently engaged in industrial action in the form of strikes in order to force employers to recognise and negotiate with them and to improve the pay and conditions of members. The festering conflict between employer and worker interests came to a head in the Dublin Lockout of 1913 (Table 3.3). The fallout from this bitter dispute initially dealt a severe blow to

---

Table 3.3
Three Snapshots of Trade Union Actions in History

Dublin Lockout, 1913
In August 1913 Jim Larkin, a union organiser, organised 200 union members in the Dublin Tramway Company to abandon their tramways on O'Connell Street after the chairman, William Martin Murphy (who also had business interests in Clerys department store and the *Irish Independent* and *Evening Herald* newspapers), refused to allow workers join the ITGWU. Murphy had replacement workers operating the tramways within one hour and persuaded other employers to lock most of Dublin's ITGWU workers out of their jobs until they signed a document renouncing the ITGWU. The lockout lasted six months and saw violent riots, thousands of people evicted from their homes, an unknown number killed, thousands living in poverty and severe increases in infant mortality. Workers eventually succumbed, renounced the ITGWU and returned to work.
Source: Yeates (2000; 2003).

The Anti-Conscription Campaign, 1918
In 1918 the British government passed legislation providing for conscription (compulsory recruitment into the army) in Ireland for men up to fifty-one years of age. Trade unions in Ireland opposed the legislation and began an anti-conscription campaign. During April and May 1918 unions organised strike rallies around the country, including in Dublin, Cork, Derry, Limerick, Sligo and Waterford. The conscription crisis gave a clear illustration of the power of organised labour and trade unions.
Source: Hanley (2018).

The Limerick Soviet, 1919
In April 1919, 14,000 workers in Limerick joined a general strike called for by the Limerick United Trades and Labour Council, which had thirty-five affiliated trade unions. The strike was a response to British authorities proclaiming the city as a Special Military Area. The council's Strike Committee, known as the Soviet, took control of the city by regulating the price and distribution of food, publishing its own newspaper and printing its own currency. The strike, which lasted two weeks, 'was the first workers' Soviet in Britain or Ireland and it brought the Irish Labour movement to the brink of a revolutionary confrontation with British power in Ireland'.
Source: Cahill (2019).

the ITGWU: their membership declined from 45,000 in 1913 (prior to the lockout) to 5,000 afterwards. However, by 1919 membership had recovered to 100,000 (Boyd 1972; McNamara *et al.* 1988).

An important effect of this turbulent period was that it served to accelerate the organisation of employees into trade unions and employers into employer associations, thus placing an ever-increasing emphasis on industrial relations. After the difficulties and confrontation of 1913, labour relations slowly moved towards a more constructive approach based on negotiations and bargained agreement. The union movement had arrived and employers had to take steps to accommodate it. This was done through multi-employer bargaining via employer associations and through the employment of labour relations officers to deal with personnel and industrial relations matters at organisation level. The period 1914–1920 has been described as the 'first phase of rapid mass union membership growth in Ireland', when union membership rose from 110,000 in 1914 to 250,000 in 1920 (Roche 1997: 54; Roche and Larragy 1986).

Types of Trade Unions

Not all employees have the same interests and it is for this reason that multiple trade unions have been established to cater for differing needs. Trade unions in Ireland have traditionally been grouped into three broad categories: craft unions, general unions and white-collar unions. It should be noted that it is extremely difficult to categorise unions as 'pure' craft, general or white-collar, so the categorisation should be interpreted as broadly indicative of union types.

Craft unions represent the first form of union organisation. They have their origins in the early unions that emerged in Britain in the eighteenth century. Craft unions catered for workers who possessed a particular skill in a trade where entry was restricted to workers who had completed a prescribed apprenticeship programme or equivalent. Craft unions no longer control entry to the trade and the relative influence of them has decreased over time in accordance with increased mechanisation and consequent deskilling. Some craft unions have struggled with recruiting new members since the recession of 2008, given the significant job losses and changing employment patterns such as increased self-employment and agency work. In this context, a number of craft unions have recently rationalised to form Connect, now the largest of the craft-related unions, representing workers in engineering, electrical and technical jobs. Craft unions remain an important part of Ireland's industrial relations system, particularly as they negotiate with employer organisations to set pay and conditions for large groups of workers in construction, mechanical engineering and electrical contracting (Table 3.4 and Chapter 5).

General unions adopt an open approach, taking into membership all categories of workers regardless of skill or industry. The origins of general trade unions lie in the organisation of semi-skilled and unskilled workers employed in the large factories in the late nineteenth and early twentieth centuries in Britain and Ireland. They initially organised general labourers and dockworkers, and were noted for both their aggressive bargaining style in attempting to improve pay and working conditions of their members and their greater political consciousness in attempting to advance working-class interests. Their development in Ireland is especially associated with the arrival of Jim Larkin in 1907. He arrived as an organiser for the National Union of Dock Labourers but fell out with that union and formed the ITGWU. He was general secretary of the ITGWU and later became general secretary of the Workers' Union of Ireland, which was a breakaway union from the ITGWU formed in 1924. The largest union in the country is the Services, Industrial, Professional and Technical Union (SIPTU), which was formed in 1990 following the merger of the ITGWU and the Federated Workers' Union of Ireland (FWUI). The FWUI was a descendent of the Workers' Union of Ireland. SIPTU has many other organisations affiliated to it or in receipt of support from it, e.g. Professional Footballers' Association of Ireland and the National Union of Journalists.

White-collar unions normally cater for professional, supervisory, technical, clerical and managerial jobs. Such workers have long-established unions: the Irish National Teachers' Organisation, formed in 1868; the Teachers' Union of Ireland, formed in 1899; and the Financial Services Union, which was originally established as the Irish Banks Officials' Association in 1918 (Logan 1999). There was significant growth in white-collar union membership in the period from the late 1960s until the early 1980s. The dramatic growth in the services sector, particularly in the public sector, was a major factor facilitating the growth of white-collar unionisation. While some white-collar workers were reluctant to join trade unions, Kelly (1975) notes that poor job design and general quality of working life were important factors encouraging white-collar unionisation. Another significant aspect in white-collar unionisation was the large advances in pay and conditions secured by blue-collar unions representing manufacturing and craft workers, which encouraged more conservative white-collar workers to unionise. Today, most of the largest white-collar unions are in the public sector, representing civil servants, teachers and nurses, and they have high proportions of female membership (Table 3.4).

THE IRISH CONGRESS OF TRADE UNIONS

ICTU is a union confederation and acts as the national umbrella body for the trade union movement. Unlike the unions affiliated to it, ICTU does not represent individuals in negotiations with an individual employer. Instead, its functions are:
- to voice the common interests of unions to government, state bodies, employer organisations and the media. They do this through research, lobbying, communication and negotiation;
- to nominate union representatives to participate on national institutions or agencies (e.g. the Labour Court and the Low Pay Commission);

Table 3.4
Largest Trade Unions Affiliated to ICTU, 2018

Trade Union	Membership	Female Members as a % of Membership
Services, Industrial, Professional and Technical Union (SIPTU)	180,000	40
Fórsa	89,401	69
Irish Nurses and Midwives Organisation (INMO)	39,150	99
Connect	39,000	3
Irish National Teachers' Organisation (INTO)	45,682	84
Mandate (The Union of Retail, Bar and Administrative Workers)	33,462	65
UNITE	54,778	27
Teachers' Union of Ireland (TUI)	18,352	63
Association of Secondary Teachers, Ireland (ASTI)	16,849	70
Communications Workers' Union (CWU)	15,003	23
Financial Services Union (FSU)	11,089	69

Source: ICTU.
Note: Membership figures include Republic of Ireland and Northern Ireland.

- to represent Irish unions at the EU level through membership of the European Trade Union Confederation;
- to manage disputes between affiliated trade unions over who should represent particular groups of workers.

Another key function of ICTU between the years 1987 and 2009 was to represent member unions in the negotiation of national wage agreements (also called social partnership), along with the government, employer associations, and farming and voluntary sector representatives. Since 2012 the Public Services Committee of Congress has been involved in all except one of the Public Sector Stability Agreements (see Chapter 13).

ICTU was established in 1959 as a result of a merger between the Irish Trade Union Congress (ITUC) and the Congress of Irish Unions (CIU). This merger served to heal a longstanding rift in the Irish union movement, which was partially related to personality differences but also resulted from ideological differences between Irish and British unions (Incomes Data Service/Institute of Personnel and Development 1996). The CIU was founded in 1945 and had primarily represented some ten Irish-based unions (most notably the ITGWU), while the ITUC, which was founded in 1894, was composed of the remaining Irish- and British-based unions. In 1958, the year prior to the merger, the CIU had unions with 188,969 affiliated members, while the figure for the ITUC was 226,333 (McCarthy 1977). At the end of 2018 ICTU had 44 unions and 6 associate organisations affiliated to it, totalling 714,685 members, 72 per cent of whom were in the Republic of Ireland and the remainder in Northern Ireland (data provided by ICTU). Most trade unions in the country are affiliated to ICTU and they retain a large degree of autonomy over their activities. ICTU also has associate members, who can attend ICTU conferences but do not have voting rights. Associate members include organisations that are not legally defined as trade unions but do represent workers' interests (Table 3.5). Finally, there are a small group of worker representative bodies which are neither full nor associate members of ICTU, including those representing An Garda Síochána (police), which are not legally allowed to be trade unions.

Table 3.5
The Defence Forces and Unionisation

An example of an organisation which has applied for associate status with ICTU is the Permanent Defence Force Other Ranks Representative Association (PDFORRA), which represents personnel in the defence forces. Legislation prohibits the defence forces from joining a trade union or taking industrial action and, in the past, governments refused PDFORRA's attempts to join ICTU. PDFORRA initiated a complaint to the European Committee of Social Rights, which found in 2017 that Ireland was in violation of the European Social Charter in preventing military representative organisations from joining national employee organisations and in offering insufficient access to military representative organisations to pay-agreement discussions. However, the European Committee also stated that Ireland's ban on military organisations from striking was not in breach of the Charter. PDFORRA's application to become an associate of ICTU provides an avenue to correct these violations but they must also get the permission of the Minister for Defence to do so. Interestingly, the representative body for officers in the defence forces, the Representative Association of Commissioned Officers, has not sought associate membership of ICTU because it believes that trade unionism is incompatible with military service (Higgins 2019a).

TRADE UNION MEMBERSHIP AND DENSITY

Workers can derive power from a number of sources to help them advance their interests in their interactions with employers and government. A key source of power is associational power, which stems from the collective organisation of workers, particularly through unions. The performance of unions can be measured in many ways but common measures are union membership numbers and density (Table 3.6). Key historical and contemporary trends in union membership in Ireland are summarised in Table 3.7.

Table 3.6
Measures of Union Membership: Density

- **Workforce density:** The percentage of the total civilian workforce, i.e. including those employed and those seeking employment, who are trade union members.

- **Employment density:** The percentage of civilian employees who are trade union members. For the remainder of this chapter, 'union density' refers to employment density.

Table 3.7
Union Membership Trends, 1920s to 1970s

1920s: Membership fell in the face of economic recession and external competition, as the government pursued an open economy policy.

1930s: Union membership rose steadily, increasing from 99,500 in 1930 to 151,600 in 1940 (Roche 1997).

1940s: The rate of growth in union membership slowed during World War II while there was fast growth from 1945 until the early 1950s (by 80 per cent).

1950s: A continued but much less rapid increase in trade union density as the economic recession of the 1950s slowed union growth.

1960s: A steady growth in union membership and density.

1970s: A slowing of the pace of unionisation in the early 1970s attributed to a saturation effect, where there was almost full unionisation in those sectors of the economy where unionisation was easiest to achieve, like manufacturing (Roche 1997). After 1976 there was a further increase in unionisation due to the expansion of the public sector.

Below is a summary of some of the key contemporary trends in trade union membership and density in Ireland (Figure 3.1 and Table 3.8).

- There are stark differences in trends between union membership and density. In 2019 union membership was approximately only 6 per cent lower than the figure in 1980 but union density fell by 60 per cent over the same period. Union membership has not kept pace with the expansion in employment numbers.

- Density varies hugely across sectors. It has remained higher in the public sector than in the private sector. The share of union members who were public sector workers rose from 40 per cent to 55 per cent between 2004 and 2014 (Walsh 2019).

- However, density in the public sector has also declined over time. The category 'public administration and defence' in particular has seen a recent substantial drop in density, from 78 per cent to 65 per cent between 2007 and 2018.

- Private sectors that experienced substantial falls in density since the economic recession are 'industry', 'information and communication', and 'financial, insurance and real estate'.

- Union density remains lowest amongst young people. Between 2007 and 2018, union density fell by 25 per cent in the 15–34 age group, by 32 per cent in the

35–44 age group, by 30 per cent in the 45–54 age group, and by 16 per cent in the 55+ group. It should be noted, however, that analysis can be sensitive to the time period chosen. For example, if the period 2005–2018 is used, the 15–34 age group has the greatest reduction in union density. In any case, the common trend is that the 55+ age group has experienced the lowest fall in density.

- In line with trends in other countries, unionisation is lower amongst people in part-time jobs and amongst non-nationals.
- Trade unions have become increasingly feminised in terms of membership composition and this has occurred as more women have entered the workforce. In 2003, 39 per cent of men and 36 per cent of women were trade union members. By 2018, 27 per cent of women were union members compared to 22 per cent of men. The higher unionisation of women has been attributed to their employment in the public sector (Turner and D'Art 2003).
- Data suggest that there are substantial numbers of 'free riders' – that is, people who are not members of trade unions but who benefit from trade union presence in a workplace. Walsh (2019: 97) estimates from survey data that 'in workplaces where unions have quite a lot of influence almost 50 per cent of workers are non-members'.

Figure 3.1
Trade Union Membership and Density, 1925–2019

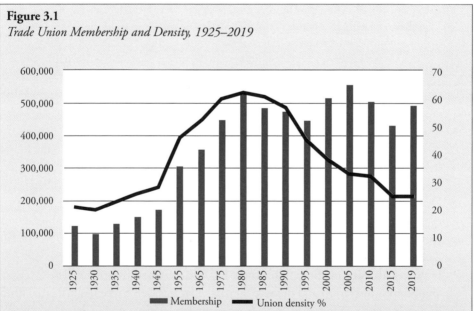

Membership ▬▬ Union density %

Source: Figures for 1925–1990 from DUES Data Series (Roche 2008); figures for 1995–2019 from CSO.
Note: These figures come from different sources so there are differences in the calculations of density. In addition, CSO data are drawn from Labour Force Surveys and there are variances between those data and union membership figures collected by ICTU. For further information, see Walsh (2019).

Table 3.8
Union Density by Demographics and Job Characteristics, 2007 and 2018 (%)

Characteristics	Union Density 2007	Union Density 2018
Sex		
Male	30	22
Female	32	27
Age group		
15–34	20	15
35–44	38	26
45–54	47	33
55+	42	35
Nationality		
Irish nationals	34	28
Non-Irish nationals	12	9
Working hours		
Full-time	34	28
Part-time	18	13
Industry		
Agriculture, forestry, fishing	9	4
Industry	32	19
Construction	21	17
Wholesale and retail	16	12
Transport and storage	45	39
Accommodation and food	7	3
Information and communication	22	9
Financial, insurance and real estate	30	18
Professional, scientific and technical	14	8
Administrative and support services	16	14
Public admin. and defence	78	65
Education	61	61
Health and social work	49	43
Other services	13	9
Occupational group		
Managerial/professional	40	32
Administrative/skilled trades	29	22
Service/manual	23	18

Source: CSO, personal communication; derived from Labour Force Survey data.

WHY DO PEOPLE JOIN TRADE UNIONS?

The process of union joining is not a straightforward one. There are a significant number of factors that can affect the process of union joining and we examine some of these in this section. There are two steps to union joining: (1) the availability of a union and (2) the decision to join a union (Green 1990). The Irish Constitution gives people the right to join trade unions but the reality is that an individual is more likely to join if a union has access to their workplace and it asks the individual to join (Kerr 1992). Traditionally, in some heavily unionised industries and companies, employees had no choice but to join a union. Unions operated a 'closed shop', whereby every employee was required to be a member, often with the approval of employers. When everyone was a union member, there was no 'free rider' problem. However, the closed shop practice has dwindled and most new members voluntarily choose to join. A key difficulty for unions is that many employers do not recognise or negotiate with them and therefore do not allow them access to workplaces so there is much less chance that a worker will be asked to join a union.

Generally, there are four categories of reasons for people joining unions.

1. Collectively based reasons, where people join because they want the benefits of collective strength and they want to address a perceived injustice, have support if they encounter a future problem, and improve pay and conditions (Wheeler and McClendon 1991). In other words, a union is often seen as a type of insurance policy. A number of international studies show that the collective category is the strongest motivation for people to join unions (Peetz 1997; Tolich and Harcourt 1999; Waddington and Whitson 1997).

2. Individual-based reasons, where people want the services offered by a union, e.g. legal advice and financial services. While legal advice can be a strong reason to join a union, studies indicate that the financial services offered by unions (e.g. cheaper car insurance) are rarely an attraction for potential members (Kerr 1992; Tolich and Harcourt 1999; Waddington and Whitson 1997).

3. Ideological reasons, where people join because they believe in trade unions.

4. Peer-related reasons, where people feel they should join because their relatives and colleagues are already members.

Factors Affecting Union Membership

Demographics

- Gender: Historically, men had higher unionisation rates than women, since women tended to work in jobs that were short-term and 'marginal to the main (male) labour force' (Turner *et al.* 2008: 481). However, women's share of union membership increased in twenty-five out of thirty-one countries between 2000 and 2016 and their share of union membership exceeded men's in fourteen countries in 2016 (Vandaele 2019).

- Age: Younger age groups (under thirty) have historically tended to have lower unionisation levels than older age groups, but this trend has deepened and the average age of union members in Europe has increased (Vandaele 2019). Research has not yet fully established why young people are less likely to join unions (Visser 2019a) but some point to their lack of knowledge about unions and their employment in precarious jobs which are difficult for unions to access (Simms *et al.* 2018; Tailby and Pollert 2011).

- Nationality: Migrant workers tend to have lower unionisation levels than local workers, partly because they are less likely to have a union available in their workplace (Turner *et al.* 2008).

Cyclical Factors

Another set of factors that can be important in determining union membership is that of *cyclical factors*, i.e. the impact of unemployment and inflation on unionisation (Ebbinghaus and Visser 1999). It might be expected that people will be less inclined to join trade unions when the economy is in recession and unemployment is high, and vice versa (Roche 1997). It has been argued that people will be more likely to join unions when wage levels rise, since unions receive credit for the increase (credit effect), and when inflation rises, since people seek to protect the value of their wages (threat effect) (Roche and Larragy 1989). If we examine union membership and density trends in Ireland, we can see that the business cycle was particularly influential in the 1980s. Union membership and employment density peaked in 1980 but then fell throughout the 1980s. This decline is principally attributed to the economic recession and increased unemployment.

The business cycle was again influential when the economy began to recover in the 1990s and boomed until the late 2000s. As employment increased, so too did the number of people joining unions. Between 1990 and 2007 the number of union members increased by 15 per cent, from 491,000 to 565,000. However, union density continued to fall throughout the economic boom. Why did this happen? As a hypothesis, let us say that the number of people in employment in a country is 100,000 and 50,000 of these are union members, i.e. the union density rate is 50 per cent. Let us imagine one year later: the number of people in employment increases to 150,000 and the number of union members grows to 55,000. Even though employment and union membership grows, the union density rate *falls* to 36.6 per cent. This is the type of scenario that occurred during Ireland's 'Celtic Tiger' years – even though more people were joining unions, the increase in union membership could not keep pace with the increase in employment, so union density actually fell. The opposite trend occurred during the economic recession that started in 2008. Between 2007 and 2011, union membership numbers fell but union density slightly increased from 30 per cent to 32 per cent. The fall in union membership did not keep pace with the fall in employment and it is likely that density was affected by the types of jobs which were lost during the recession. Union density amongst men fell but women's union density increased, suggesting that jobs where more women were employed had fewer redundancies, such as in the public sector, while more male-dominated jobs like construction experienced significant job losses. As the economy recovered and expanded following the recession, union density reverted to a pattern of decline, falling to 25 per cent by early 2019. Union membership fell also between 2007 and 2016, before rising again.

Structural Factors

Structural factors include the type of job or sector, change in the type of job, firm size, proportion of part-time workers, and the extent of a collectivist or individualist orientation (Beaumont and Harris 1991; Blanchflower 2006; Roche 1997). In certain types of jobs, industries and occupations, trade unions have a strong presence, and in others they have a weak presence. Structural factors 'emphasize shifts in employment away from occupations, industries, and regions where union density has traditionally been high toward sectors with lower density' (Hirsch 2008: 158). A key structural change internationally has been a shift in jobs from industry to services, and deindustrialisation is 'transforming trade unions' (Visser 2019a: 19). In Ireland and elsewhere manufacturing has been traditionally highly unionised while private services sector employments have been more difficult for unions to penetrate (Roche 1997; Roche and Ashmore 2001). The private services sector tends to have more jobs which are non-standard – e.g. part-time, temporary and casual – and unionisation rates amongst these types of jobs are lower than amongst permanent, full-time jobs. Visser (2019a: 21) argues that 'unless trade unions find ways to halt their decline in manufacturing employment, strengthen their position in commercial services or expand employment in public and social services (where density rates tend to be much higher than in manufacturing), they are in for further decline'.

Institutional Factors

Institutional factors include the 'legal environment in which unions organise, the role of management opposition, worker preferences toward unions, and government regulation of the labour market' (Hirsch 2008: 159). In terms of employer and manager attitudes to unions, Ireland is known as a liberal market economy in which employers have a lot of freedom to pursue their own employment practices (Roche *et al.* 2011). We noted earlier that Irish employers grew to accommodate and negotiate with unions, particularly after World War II. Unions that are recognised by employers are more likely to grow (Bain and Price 1983). However, trade unions have been finding it more difficult to gain recognition from employers, and union officials have reported an increase in the use of coercive tactics by employers who do not want to recognise unions (D'Art and Turner 2005, 2006b). A particular group of firms which oppose or avoid recognising unions are American multinationals. Evidence suggests that there is a 'country of origin' effect, with a trend of union avoidance among US-owned companies coming into Ireland since the mid 1980s due to the 'anti-union sentiment characteristic of the US national business system' (Geary and Roche 2001; Gunnigle *et al.* 1997; Lavelle 2008: 58).

In terms of government regulation of unions and the labour markets, historically, Irish governments have supported a voluntarist approach, letting trade unions and employers voluntarily regulate their own affairs. It could be argued that government/state agencies have been supportive of trade unions in the following ways:

- by setting up bodies like the Labour Court to help unions and employers resolve disputes and by having union nominees form part of the Labour Court;
- by state agencies recommending to incoming multinational companies (MNCs) in the 1960s and 1970s that they should recognise trade unions;
- by the government negotiating with unions on national wage agreements (or social partnership) between 1987 and 2009;
- by the government consulting with trade unions on issues relating to employment law;
- by introducing legislation, the Industrial Relations (Amendment) Acts 2001–2015; the legislation was the result of lobbying by unions and provides a way for them to take cases against organisations which do not have collective bargaining.

Despite these examples, some point to the 'paradoxes between espoused public policy, which supports a strong trade union role in industry, and actual practice, which contributes to an ongoing diminution in the role of organised labour' (Gunnigle *et al.* 2002: 224). Evidence of a lack of state support for trade unions include the following:

- The practice of state agencies recommending that MNCs recognise unions was abandoned by the 1990s.
- Government policy has allowed MNCs to avoid unions (McDonough and Dundon 2010). In particular, current and past governments have refused to introduce statutory union recognition legislation, i.e. a law that would compel employers to recognise and negotiate with a union. As noted in Chapter 2, this opposition has led ICTU to redirect its lobbying focus to the EU and start a campaign for the adoption of an EU directive on collective bargaining.
- The introduction of the Industrial Relations Act 1990 placed restrictions on union operations, such as on the process for deciding to take industrial action. The Act has been criticised, for example, by the retail union Mandate. It has called for the repeal of the Act, which it has said 'took large areas of control and decision making away from unions and handed them to employers and the legal system' (Mandate 2019).
- During the economic recession in 2011 the government discontinued a scheme which offered income tax relief to individuals who paid trade union membership fees. ICTU (2019) has argued that other countries with strong collective bargaining systems encourage union membership through tax incentives.

THE BIG CHALLENGE FOR UNIONS: DECLINING UNIONISATION

Visser (2019a: 47) notes the stark trend that 'since 2000, unionisation trends have declined in all but two world regions, North Africa and South America'. A study of union membership in thirty-two European countries between 2000 and 2017 found that union membership numbers had fallen in twenty-four of them and union density had declined overall in the thirty-two countries by six percentage points (Vandaele 2019). Only four countries experienced an increase in unionisation: Iceland, Italy, Spain and France (Vandaele 2019). Union density in a selection of OECD (Organisation for Economic Co-operation and Development) countries is presented in Table 3.9, and the long-term trend across them is one of decline, though there are still significant differences in unionisation levels. Various factors have contributed to the decline in unionisation, including unemployment or, conversely, unionisation not keeping pace with growing employment, lower unionisation amongst young people, greater power of employers to resist unions, changes in types of jobs and characteristics of employment, the changing nature of collective bargaining arrangements, digitalisation, internal union inadequacies and politics, and less union-friendly political environments and public policies (Pedersini 2010; Schmitt and Mitukiewicz 2011; Vandaele 2019; Visser 2019a; Waddington 2005). An example of the impact of public policy is evident in some Scandinavian countries. One of the reasons for high union density levels in Scandinavian countries is the so-called Ghent system in which individuals voluntarily register for earnings-related unemployment insurance and funds linked to trade unions administer the system, giving people a strong incentive to join unions. However, these countries have also experienced declines in density and this has been mainly attributed to government policy which reformed unemployment insurance and weakened unions' role in its provision (Visser 2019a). Despite the declines in union density internationally, 'it is hard to imagine any other member organisations, based on voluntary membership' with the sizes of membership that unions still have (Vandaele 2019: 11).

Caution is needed when interpreting the impact of union density rates in different countries, since the figures do not always give a full picture of union strength. Another measure of union strength or influence is collective bargaining coverage, i.e. the percentage of employees whose pay and conditions are governed by a collective bargaining agreement, whether or not they are members of a union (Figure 3.2). The coverage of collective bargaining is a major issue. If a country has an industrial relations system in which collective bargaining agreements can cover a large percentage of employees, then a decline in union density may not be as significant to workers. In many European countries there is provision for extending union–employer agreements reached at sector, industry or national level to all workers in an industry. This is referred to as the 'extension of collective bargaining' and is frequently done in legal systems where such agreements are legally binding. This extension of collective bargaining means that the proportion of workers covered by collective bargaining (coverage) is routinely greater than union density. For example, in France only 8 per cent of employees are in a union but 98 per cent of employees are covered by a collective bargaining agreement. Collective bargaining coverage has remained relatively stable in countries where collective bargaining involves multiple employers, thereby covering large groups of workers (Vandaele 2019). In Ireland collective bargaining coverage fell by 10 per cent between the periods 2000–2009 and 2010–2016 (Vandaele 2019).

Table 3.9

Union Density in Selected OECD Countries, 1980–2016

Country	1980 (%)	2000 (%)	2016 (%)
Australia	49.6	24.7**	14.5**
Austria	51.6	36.9	26.9
Canada	34.0	31.1	26.3**
Chile	12.2 (1986)	12.2	16.7
Denmark	77.9	73.6	65.4*
Finland	69.3	74.6	64.5
France	18.2	7.9	7.9***
Germany	34.8	24.5	17.0
Ireland	57.1	36.0	24.3**
Italy	49.5	34.3	35.7*
Japan	30.8	21.4	17.3
Netherlands	34.7	22.5	17.3
New Zealand	69.1	22.3	18.3**
Norway	57.8	54.1	52.4*
Poland	65.6 (1981)	17.5	11.7***
Spain	13.2	16.4	13.8*
Sweden	78.0	80.1	66.8*
Switzerland	27.4	20.1	23.5**
United Kingdom	52.1	29.7	23.5**
United States	22.0**	12.9**	10.2**

Source: https://stats.oecd.org/Index.aspx?DataSetCode=TUD#

Notes: Caution should be taken when comparing figures as some are from different sources. The majority of figures are from administrative sources in each country, such as trade union membership databases. Other data marked with ** are from surveys in each country, usually labour force surveys where samples of the population are asked to self-report if they are a union member. *2015 data; ** survey data; *** 2014 data.

THE CONSEQUENCES OF DECLINING UNIONISATION

In the Workplace

There are a number of consequences of falling unionisation. It means that a non-unionised individual may have to rely on their own individual bargaining power to defend or improve pay and conditions. However, if they do not have unique skills or if demand for their skills is not strong, they may have very limited negotiating power with employers. Research internationally shows that unions attract a wage premium, that is, that union-negotiated wages are on average higher than non-union wages (Turner *et al.* 2014). Part of a union's role within an organisation is a democratic one in which they challenge management decisions, try to ensure decision-making is fair through the

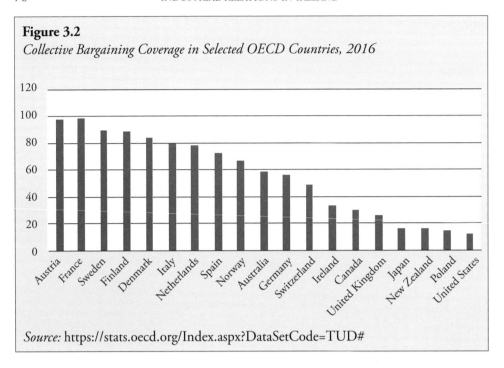

Figure 3.2

Collective Bargaining Coverage in Selected OECD Countries, 2016

Source: https://stats.oecd.org/Index.aspx?DataSetCode=TUD#

introduction of rules and procedures, and try to ensure workers have a say in workplace decision-making. If employees do not have access to a union, these benefits may be lost. In addition, disputes within an organisation may be less likely to be resolved collectively in the absence of a union, and disputes can become individualised, where an individual worker has to pursue vindication of their own rights. This phenomenon is already evident by the large number of employment law cases taken by individual workers against organisations (see Chapter 5). It could be argued that a decline in union density is not problematic if people do not want or need unions. However, survey data indicate workers, including young workers, have positive attitudes towards unions and believe trade unions are needed, which suggests there is a representation gap (Haynes *et al.* 2005; Turner and D'Art 2012). A representation gap refers to the proportion of employees who would join a union but are unable to (Freeman and Rogers 1999).

In Society: Income Inequality and Attitudes to Democracy

Declining unionisation and weaker collective bargaining at a societal level have contributed to rising income inequality. Widening income inequality is the gap between low- and high-income individuals and households and is widely regarded as a critical global problem. Unions reduce inequality principally through collective bargaining, which reduces the gap in wages within a firm and across firms (Freeman 2007). However, weakened unions reduce the power of workers and increase the power of employers, leading to lower wage rises and increases in the share of income going to capital (Bank for International Settlements 2019; Jaumotte and Buitron 2015; OECD 2018). In addition, weaker unions mean workers have less influence on corporate decisions such as the size of top executives' pay, which increases pay dispersion in firms (Jaumotte and Buitron 2015: 31). A study of advanced economies between 1980 and 2010 concluded that 'the decline in unionisation appears to be a key contributor to the rise of top income shares' and 'less redistribution of income' (Jaumotte and Buitron 2015: 31).

Declining unionisation can impact individuals' attitudes to democracy and participation in politics. Union members are more likely than non-members to engage in political activities such as voting and joining political parties, and to have positive attitudes towards democracy (Turner *et al.* 2019). This association is particularly strong amongst young people. Individuals aged between eighteen and twenty-four who are union members are much more likely to vote than non-members of the same age (Bryson *et al.* 2013). This is important because evidence from the US and Europe indicates that there is weakening support for democratic political systems and rising support for authoritarianism (Foa and Mounk 2016). So it has been argued that 'the decline in union density and the dilution of the collective bargaining effect is likely to increase the drift towards populist and authoritarian forms of government' (Turner *et al.* 2019: 14-15).

THE BIG RESPONSES TO DECLINING UNIONISATION

In the context of declining unionisation, Visser (2019a: 59-68) identifies four possible futures for unions:
1. marginalisation;
2. dualisation, where unions protect the job security of their 'insider' members potentially at the expense of 'outsiders', such as in casual jobs;
3. replacement by other forms of social action and representation;
4. revitalisation.

Trade unions in Ireland and internationally have engaged in six strategies to tackle lower unionisation and revitalise unions (Frege and Kelly 2003):
1. recruiting new members and organising them;
2. organisational restructuring;
3. building coalitions;
4. partnerships with employers;
5. political action;
6. international links.

Examples of these strategies in the Irish context are outlined in Table 3.10 while one strategy, recruiting and organising, is discussed further.

Table 3.10
Examples of Trade Union Revitalisation Strategies

Building coalitions
ICTU has joined with other civil society organisations to progress climate change policies in Coalition 2030 and has campaigned with the Migrant Rights Centre of Ireland on issues relating to migrant workers.

Organisational restructuring
Some unions have rationalised by ceasing to operate, transferring membership and finances to another union, or merging together to form a new union. For example, in 2018, the Union of Construction, Allied Trades and Technicians engaged in a transfer of engagement with the Technical Electrical and Engineering Union and formed Connect, while a number of public sector unions (the Public Services Executive Union, IMPACT and the Civil and Public Services Union) merged to establish Fórsa, now the largest union in the public sector. There have been mixed results for the success of union mergers, which are complex processes (Behrens and Pekarek 2016; Undy 2008).

Partnerships with employers
An example of this is the 'stability' agreement between SIPTU and the previously non-union company GE Healthcare in 2018 (Sheehan 2018a; 2018b).

International links
In 2018 and 2019 trade unions across EU countries cooperated with each other in representing pilots and cabin crew in a dispute over pay and conditions in Ryanair, resulting in strikes in multiple countries.

Political action
Political action by unions can partly compensate for lower unionisation and can lead to additional rights for workers. In recent years unions have lobbied the government with varying degrees of success to introduce laws on tipping practices in hospitality sectors, on protections for workers in low-hours or zero-hours jobs, on wage-setting mechanisms for low-paid sectors like hotels, and on workers' right to disconnect from technology after working hours.

Recruiting and Organising

Organising is the idea that workers are 'empowered' to define and pursue their own interests through the medium of collective organisation (Heery *et al.* 2000: 38). Instead of members being reliant on a full-time union official to serve their needs, they become more active and try to address their needs collectively themselves within an organisation. This emphasis on organising arose because union officials were spending too much time representing the problems of individual employees; they had very little time to recruit new members and members had an expectation of being 'serviced' by the union rather than being active in it. For example, in Ireland's largest union, SIPTU, employment rights issues of individual members are now dealt with by a unit called the Workers

Rights Centre, while union officials are responsible for organising workers in particular sectors and representing workers in negotiations with employers. Research has suggested that union efforts at organising have yielded mixed results, and challenges for unions include difficulties in gaining access to workplaces and union organisers relying on employees with previous union membership experience to become activists (Murphy and Turner 2016).

Unions in Ireland and other countries have made efforts to recruit young people, migrant workers and people in precarious jobs, and these groups overlap with each other. The need to recruit and organise young people has also become a key concern of unions because fewer young workers are joining unions, so that the 'rise of "never-membership" is considered a "demographic time bomb" for unions' (Vandaele 2019: 24). Trade union members tend to first join unions in their early working years and 'workers who do not join a union before the age of 30 or 35 will most probably never join' (Visser 2019a: 26). Strategies of Irish unions to recruit and organise young people and people in precarious jobs include developing young worker networks within their union structures, signing accords with the Union of Students in Ireland, publicising campaigns around precarious work and organising particular groups of workers such as health support workers, school secretaries, early years workers, retail workers and video games workers. Internationally, unions are engaging more in digital technologies (Table 3.11) and have engaged in high-profile organising campaigns such as the Fight for $15 movement in the US and organising of workers in 'gig' companies like Uber and Deliveroo across the EU. In some instances, new unions and organisations have emerged to specifically represent groups who felt underrepresented by traditional unions (Table 3.12).

Table 3.11
Trade Union Apps

Unions and worker representative bodies are developing apps as a way of connecting with workers, especially young workers and people in jobs outside of the traditional nine-to-five. Examples of apps are Action Builder in the US, which helps union organisers manage their interactions with members; WorkIt in the US, which gives information to workers about their rights and provides worker-to-worker support; and WorkSmart in the UK, which facilitates job and career advice targeted at workers in their twenties.

Source: UNI Global Union (2019).

ALTERNATIVES TO TRADE UNIONS? IN-COMPANY ASSOCIATIONS AND CIVIL SOCIETY ORGANISATIONS

In the absence of a trade union, employees in some companies may have no alternative mechanism for collective representation. In other organisations there are internal

Table 3.12
Examples of New Worker Representative Bodies

Game Workers Unite is not a trade union but describes itself as an international grassroots movement and organisation dedicated to unionising the game industry, and operates in the UK, France, Scotland and Finland. When it expanded into Ireland in 2019, however, it launched as a branch of an established trade union, the FSU, which historically represented banking employees. The Games Workers Unite branch in Ireland aims to improve conditions for games workers through increased pay, improved security of contracts, and ending of bullying and harassment.

The Independent Workers Union of Great Britain is a trade union which was established in 2012 to represent low-paid migrant workers, and has launched campaigns to improve conditions for cleaners, security workers and workers in gig companies like Deliveroo. It uses a range of pressure tactics, including social media use, employment law cases, loud and visible strikes and protests, flash occupations of buildings, as well as pressuring the clients of businesses it targets.

structures that have a representative function, including employee forums, works councils and employee associations. These in-company associations are often introduced by management either voluntarily or because of legal requirements, e.g. EU Works Council Directive and the EU Directive on Information and Consultation. Such structures can be used for information sharing or to allow employees to participate in decision-making, though the extent of this varies widely. Unlike trade unions, an employee association consists only of employees who work in the same organisation. Joining an employee association gives some of the benefits of collective organisation:

- by joining together, workers can present a united front to employers and redress some of the bargaining imbalance;
- they provide a collective voice for employees without the introduction of an 'outside' third party, and therefore management may be more likely to deal with them and less likely to engage in confrontation.

However, work-based associations have been criticised because:

- they lack independence, i.e. they are often established and resourced by management;
- they may also be at a serious disadvantage due to the absence of a structure external to the organisation and they lack access to bargaining expertise or legal advice available in trade unions;
- these factors may combine to limit the bargaining power of employee associations in their interactions with management.

Traditionally, trade unionists have taken a cynical view of employee associations, seeing them as a poor apology for a real trade union and responsible for inhibiting collective solidarity.

Other possible alternatives to trade unions and in-company employee associations are civil society organisations, also called 'non-worker organisations', 'community unions', 'quasi-unions', 'non-bargaining actors' and 'non-member organisations' (Williams *et al.* 2011). These include charities, voluntary associations, advocacy bodies, social movement organisations and non-governmental organisations such as citizens' advice bodies and migrant worker centres (Abbott *et al.* 2011). It has been suggested that the activities of these bodies partly fill the vacuum left by the decline in unionisation and that they challenge unions' 'alleged neglect of interests grounded in gender and minority status or in vulnerable labour market positions' (Heery *et al.* 2012: 156–77). Like trade unions, these civil society bodies are independent of management and are external to the organisation. They are not established with the objective of advancing workers' pay and conditions, like trade unions, but their activities can influence workers' conditions. They advise workers on their rights, try to persuade employers to act in a socially responsible way, such as through labour codes of conduct, engage in political lobbying and campaigns, try to influence legislation and sometimes represent workers when they have problems at work (O'Sullivan and Hartigan 2011; Williams *et al.* 2017). It has been argued that the legitimacy and non-adversarial approach of voluntary organisations allow them to influence employers (Heery 2010; Williams *et al.* 2011). While a strongly held view is that there is no viable alternative model of employee representation to trade unions (D'Art and Turner 2006b), others suggest that civil society organisations should cooperate more with trade unions to enhance the power of both (Abbott *et al.* 2011).

Concluding Comments

This chapter has reviewed the growth, operation and evolution of trade unions in Ireland. Unions have had a tumultuous history that has somewhat come full circle. They are lobbying the EU for measures to help them get recognition by employers and increase membership – key issues for unions a hundred years ago. The review of union joining indicated that union membership is not a simple process of a person deciding whether to join one. There are many factors that affect whether individuals have access to a union, and this is critical to the union joining process. A key influence on union stability across countries is the institutional environment – in particular, how supportive employers and political parties are of unions. The approach of employers to unions varies considerably from one of support, to acceptance to outright opposition. In Chapter 4 we will examine employer representative bodies, which have traditionally accepted and negotiated with unions.

Chapter 4

Employer Organisations

INTRODUCTION

As with organisations that represent workers (trade unions), employers also combine for purposes associated with employment and labour matters through employer organisations. The major impetus historically for the growth of employer organisations was the perceived need to counter growing union power. Employer organisations have had a much less complex and tumultuous history than trade unions. They represent a smaller number of members than trade unions and most represent employers from the same industry. While employer organisations in Ireland do not affiliate to a particular political party (as trade unions often do), their role is not just confined to workplace-level issues but extends to larger societal-level matters such as political control and economic and social policies.

The defining activity of employer organisations internationally has been collective bargaining with trade unions (Demougin *et al.* 2019). The collective organisation of employers is potentially more difficult than for workers because of the diversity of business interests based on their organisational size, market position, geographical location and competitive relationships (Thornthwaite and Sheldon 1997; Tolliday and Zeitlin 1991). Internationally, employer organisations have evolved and adapted to meet the needs of their members and in the context of declining unionisation. Employer organisations have offered more services in order to attract employers (particularly non-unionised employers) and they now have varying perspectives on the need for collective bargaining. This chapter considers the role of employer organisations by examining their operation, structure, membership and the services they provide. We begin by considering employers' objectives in industrial relations, which crystallises the reasons why employers join associations.

EMPLOYER OBJECTIVES IN INDUSTRIAL RELATIONS

The primary concern for organisations operating in a competitive environment is to maximise organisational effectiveness and generate satisfactory returns for the owners/stakeholders. Such returns are often expressed in terms of cost-effectiveness and, for commercial organisations, profitability. Management's primary role is to organise the factors of production, including labour, in order to achieve these objectives. It is difficult to assess the degree to which employers have specific industrial relations objectives because employing organisations vary so greatly. Indeed, it is clear that a particular organisation's industrial relations priorities and approach are heavily influenced by a combination of internal and external variables, such as product market conditions and business goals, and these differ considerably between organisations. Nevertheless, it is worth considering some general beliefs common among employers. Thomason (1984) identifies the following:

1. **Preservation and consolidation of the private enterprise system:** This has larger political overtones and relates to employer desires to develop and preserve a 'business-friendly' political and economic environment conducive to achieving business objectives at enterprise level. They will be particularly concerned that principles such as private ownership, the profit motive, and preservation of authority and control in decision-making are maintained and fostered.

2. **Achievement of satisfactory returns for the owners:** In order for commercial organisations to survive in the long term, satisfactory profit levels must be achieved. Managerial approaches and strategies will always be influenced by this primary concern. Non-profit-making organisations will also be concerned with cost-effectiveness and the quality of their product or service.

3. **Effective utilisation of human resources:** One of the challenges of the employment relationship is the indeterminate nature of employees' effort. When an employee is offered a job, they are told how much they will be paid, the benefits they will get and how many hours they will work. It is much more difficult for employers to predetermine the level of effort they will get from employees. Therefore, an objective of employers is to ensure that employees achieve the maximum level of effort and productivity. This can be done through a range of practices: positive ones, such as training and promotion; or negative ones, such as reduced bonuses or disciplinary procedures.

4. **Maintenance of control and authority in decision-making:** Employers/senior management are the prime decision-maker in the organisation. Even when organisations negotiate with trade unions, or devolve some decision-making power to employees, senior management will often ensure that they retain authority on major issues such as the company strategy and employee numbers. Employers may decide to share information but not necessarily share decision-making power with employees.

5. **Good employer–employee relations:** Employers will also strive to maintain good working relations with employees but within the operational constraints of the organisation. The scope to agree attractive remuneration levels and conditions of employment, for example, will vary according to the organisation's market position and profitability, as well as its human resource philosophy. Effective industrial relations will be a priority, since it constitutes an important ingredient in ensuring the organisation achieves its primary business goals (as well as being laudable in itself). To help achieve such objectives, particular employers have found it beneficial to combine with other employers into permanent organisations.

What are Employer Organisations?

Oechslin (1985) defines employer organisations as 'formal groups of employers set up to defend, represent or advise affiliated employers and to strengthen their position in society at large with respect to labour matters as distinct from commercial matters'. While trade unions have individual workers as members, employer organisations have firms as members (Ahrne and Brunsson 2005). Employer organisations defend the interests of capital as a whole and the specific interests of their members (Gardner and Palmer 1992). Employer organisations include those that specialise in labour market interests, and those that are concerned about both labour market and product market interests – 'dual associations' (Traxler 2004). For example, the Construction Industry Federation (CIF) represents employers in negotiating pay and conditions for the industry and it also lobbies government on policies that stimulate building activity. Employer organisations should not be confused with trade associations, which only represent the commercial and product market interests of an industry, and generally are not involved in industrial relations, e.g. the Retail Jewellers of Ireland and the Associated Craft Butchers of Ireland.

There are a number of reasons why employer organisations developed:

1. Employers wanted to counteract the growing power of trade unions. Employer organisations undoubtedly existed before the emergence of modern trade unionism and some possibly had connections with the guilds of the Middle Ages. Adam Smith observed as far back as 1776 that employers were likely to combine into associations for purposes related with employment and labour matters generally. However, employers began to coordinate with each other in a number of countries as a response to 'new unionism' in the late nineteenth and early twentieth centuries (Barry and Wilkinson 2011). Employer organisations 'protected individual employers faced with emerging trade unions, the threat of strike action, and pressure to raise wages' (Demougin *et al.* 2019: 4). Employer organisations responded to trade unions by trying to suppress them such as through lockouts, or by accepting and negotiating with them, sometimes at the direction of governments (Demougin *et al.* 2019; Silvia and Schroeder 2007), and these multiple strategies continue to exist.

2. Employers formed associations to prevent harmful economic competition with each other. In some countries it was employers who sought the regulation of wages in order to prevent their competitor employers from undercutting them on the basis of low wages (Barry and Wilkinson 2011).

3. Employer organisations have been a response to growing state regulation of employment, since governments began to introduce laws on health and safety, minimum wages and working hours (Barry and Wilkinson 2011; Howell 2005).

Employer organisations have essentially three roles: they are an industrial relations actor, a political actor and a service provider (Demougin *et al.* 2019). We examine each of these roles.

Industrial Relations Actor

Employer organisations represent their members in collective bargaining with trade unions.

The role of employer associations in representing members in collective bargaining is important at two levels: multi-employer bargaining at industrial, regional or national level; and enterprise-level bargaining. Enterprise-level bargaining involves an employer organisation representing a single employer in negotiations with employees and their trade union. Enterprise-level bargaining dominates during periods of decentralised bargaining or so-called free collective bargaining (1946–1969, 1982–1987 and 2009–present in Ireland), when much of the decision-making on workers' pay and conditions occurs at enterprise level. The role of employer organisations ranges from being the key employer actor in pay negotiations to a more supportive role in providing advice and assistance to individual enterprises and coordinating approaches to pay negotiations.

Multi-employer bargaining involves one or more employer organisations negotiating with one or more trade unions on the pay and conditions of groups of workers across multiple companies, and sometimes this covers a whole industry, region or country. The advantage of this type of collective bargaining for employers is that it directs 'union pressure away from individual businesses, thereby supporting management prerogative' (Demougin *et al.* 2019: 5). Multi-employer collective bargaining results in standardised pay for groups of workers across companies, which means those companies cannot use lower pay as a source of advantage amongst competitors, providing a 'cartelising function' (Barry and Wilkinson 2011: 152). In such negotiations individual companies delegate bargaining responsibilities to their employer organisations, thus making them, and not the individual employer, the main actor on the employer side in negotiations. In many EU countries the negotiation of pay for employees for a whole industry or sector is common through a so-called extension mechanism, whereby the pay and conditions contained in a collective agreement between employer organisations and trade unions will be extended to all employers in a particular sector. This type of industry-level bargaining is rare in Ireland but has occurred in the case of sectors like construction and security (see Chapter 5). Collective bargaining at the national level, covering large groups of workers across industries, was a key feature of Irish industrial relations during the late twentieth century. During these periods of centralised pay agreements (1970–1982, 1987–2009), employer organisations (particularly the Irish Business and Employers Confederation (IBEC)) played a pivotal role in representing employer views to the parties in negotiations, most importantly the government and trade unions. The agreements provided for pay increases over a period of time, usually three years, to all unionised employees. Employers who were not members of IBEC were not obliged to pay the increases but could do so if they wished.

In addition to representing employers in collective bargaining, employer organisations represent employer members in industrials relations disputes referred to the Workplace Relations Commission (WRC) and the Labour Court, and in employment law cases taken by workers against their member organisations to those same state bodies (see Chapter 5).

Political Actor

It has been argued that the measure of employer organisation influence includes their capacity as pressure groups to shape public policy to suit their preferred regulatory settings (Schmitter and Streeck 1999). A large proportion of non-union multinational companies (MNCs) are members of employer organisations in Ireland because of their political influence in economic and social policy, particularly during the period of national wage agreements between 1987 and 2009 (Lavelle *et al.* 2009). The interactions that employer organisations have with government is a two-way street – employer organisations lobby government and the government can invite employer organisations to present their business interests. Countries vary in the level of interaction between the state and employer organisations, with some governments/state bodies engaging them infrequently while others involve employer organisations in social and economic policy (Brandl and Lehr 2016). Employer organisations will generally support conservative economic policies which protect the interests of capital and they will attempt to prevent, or at least lessen, the effects of protective labour or social legislation. In Ireland, when government seeks employers' views on employment matters, it will generally approach the appropriate employer organisations who make written and oral submissions to the government and Oireachtas. The overall objective of employer organisations in responding to state intervention is to seek to defend managerial prerogative (Howell 2005). Employer organisations can also influence state policy by sitting on various state bodies and agencies, and they are usually invited to do so, along with trade unions, by government. For example, the largest employer organisation, IBEC, has membership on the board of the WRC, the board of the Health and Safety Authority and the Low Pay Commission, and IBEC nominates employer representatives to become full-time Labour Court officials.

Service Provider

Employer organisations are generally funded by subscription fees from member firms and they have increasingly sought to provide additional services as a way of making membership more attractive and to grow revenue. Employer organisations operate in an environment where there is competition between employer organisations and competition from other types of service providers like solicitors and management consultants, and where a decline in unionisation and collective bargaining can potentially remove the incentive for some firms to be members of employer organisations (Demougin *et al.* 2019; Sheldon *et al.* 2016). Employer organisations have sought to offer 'commercially priced, expert services marketed to non-members, and with discounts to members' (Sheldon *et al.* 2019: 18). Services include information and research on industry trends and regulatory compliance, education and training, consultancy on human resource management practices, and employment law advice (Thornthwaite and Sheldon 1997). The growth of collective industrial relations legislation and individual employment legislation since the early 1970s has led to a significant increase in employer demand for specialist legal advice. Employer organisations are expected to provide specialist legal advice and assistance to members in areas such as dismissal, redundancy, employment conditions, employment equality and industrial disputes. It is now usual for larger employer organisations to have a specialist legal section that provides such advice and assistance in addition to providing guidance on legislation for the general membership.

A more traditional service concerns the provision of information and advice on both basic wage rates and levels of pay increases to member firms. Some employer organisations carry out surveys and analyses of wage rates and fringe benefits for differing occupations, regions and sizes of organisation. Consequently, they are able to provide member firms with up-to-date information on local, regional and national pay trends and advise such firms on reward issues. It is common for larger employer organisations to provide training and development programmes for their membership in a variety of areas such as employment law, health and safety, management and industrial relations. Providing training has become a more important part of employer organisations' activity and it acts as a source of revenue for them, outside of membership fees.

Employer Organisations in Ireland

Employer organisations and trade associations are required to register with the Registry of Friendly Societies. Employer organisations that are involved in industrial relations must hold a negotiating licence under the terms of the Trade Union Act 1941. This distinguishes them from trade associations, which are not required to hold such a licence. Employer organisations are, in effect, trade unions of employers and fall within the same legal definition as a trade union. While this may not initially seem significant, it can have important implications for the role and membership of employer organisations. In particular, it suggests an approach to industrial relations which emphasises the role of collectives or combinations as opposed to individuals. In 2018 there were eleven employer organisations registered with the Registry of Friendly Societies (Table 4.1). While the number of employer organisations with negotiation licences is much less than their trade union counterparts, there is considerable diversity in membership composition. Ten of the eleven employer organisations are industry specific – for example, representing butchers and hotels. The only general employer organisation with membership across industries is IBEC, which has been the major employer force in both labour and trade matters.

Table 4.1
Registered Employer Organisations, 2018

Construction Industry Federation
Cork Master Butchers Association
Irish Business and Employers Confederation
Irish Commercial Horticultural Association
Irish Hotels Federation
Irish Pharmacy Union
Irish Printing Federation
Licensed Vintners Association
Regional Newspapers & Printers Association of Ireland
The Irish Dental Union
Society of the Irish Motor Industry

Source: Registry of Friendly Societies (2019b).

Irish Business and Employers Confederation (IBEC)

By far the largest employer organisation in Ireland is IBEC, which was formed in 1993 as a result of the merger of the Federation of Irish Employers (FIE, formerly the Federated Union of Employers) and the then dominant trade/commercial association, the Confederation of Irish Industry (CII). IBEC represents business and employers in all matters relating to industrial relations, labour and social affairs. In 2018 IBEC had 3,266 firms as members (Registry of Friendly Societies 2019b). It has a network of affiliated bodies which cater to the interests of specific types of employers. These include the Small Firms Association, which represents businesses with less than fifty employees, and industry-specific trade bodies like Retail Ireland, Irish MedTech, Dairy Industry Ireland and Financial Services Ireland. As the country's major representative of business and employers, IBEC seeks to shape national policies and influence decision-making in a manner that protects and promotes member employers' interests. IBEC's mission is to 'lead, shape and promote business policy to drive economic success and enhanced quality of life for all in Ireland' (IBEC 2019). In outlining its mission and values, IBEC notes its work in lobbying government and policymakers, undertaking research, holding business events and providing information and advice, but interestingly it does not mention its activities in collective bargaining (IBEC 2019). In its political actor role, IBEC lobbies government and state policy through written submissions, participating in Oireachtas hearings on issues relevant to employers, and having membership on bodies like the National Economic and Social Council (NESC). It also cooperates with other employer organisations internationally and seeks to influence EU-level policymaking (Table 4.3). IBEC's services include information and advice on human resource management and it has expanded its services into areas not traditionally associated with employer organisations, like developing a corporate well-being initiative, The KeepWell

Mark, and hosting a Diversity Forum. IBEC's emphasis on its role as a political actor and service provider is a strategy to market itself to as wide an employer audience as possible, especially to non-unionised firms which do not engage in collective bargaining with trade unions.

Yet its role as an industrial relations actor remains important and activities in this regard include representing member firms in collective bargaining and in disputes to the WRC and Labour Court. One of IBEC's most important functions was its participation in collective bargaining at the national level in so-called social partnership (or national wage) agreements between 1987 and 2009 along with the government and trade unions, and IBEC has more recently called for the introduction of a social-partnership-type system (Table 4.2). While a few other employer organisations were also involved in negotiations, IBEC was the significant employer player (see Chapter 12).

Table 4.2
IBEC and the Follow-Up to Social Partnership

After social partnership ended in 2009, IBEC and the Irish Congress of Trade Unions (ICTU, the primary trade union representative) negotiated a 'protocol' or set of commitments about the conduct of industrial relations in the private sector. This was done because during the period of social partnership, 1987–2009, unions and employers in enterprises had little experience of negotiating pay rates with each other since they were previously determined at the national level. In 2015 the chief executive of IBEC, Danny McCoy, indicated that 'there was no desire for national pay agreements in the foreseeable future' (Sheehan 2015). He stated IBEC was opposed to a return to social partnership but wanted a 'greater level of dialogue than currently exists' (Sheehan 2015). In 2019 Mr McCoy stated that a 'social partner-type moderate wage arrangement' should be considered, in which wage restraint by workers would be negotiated in return for improvements in social infrastructure (Sheehan 2019a). This, in Mr McCoy's view, would address employer concerns that workers were increasingly demanding pay rises because of a lack of social infrastructure such as housing (Sheehan 2019a). The largest trade union, the Services Industrial Professional Technical Union (SIPTU), rejected IBEC's proposal, arguing, 'why should workers take moderate pay increases through a centralised pay system and pay for social infrastructure?' (Sheehan 2019a). However, it did indicate support for social dialogue at a national level to deal with some issues.

There was much criticism of social partnership after it ended in 2009, with some partly blaming it for the economic recession. However, the absence of some level of coordination at national level between unions and employer organisations can make it challenging for parties to deal with industrial relations matters that are influenced by wider economic and social factors.

Construction Industry Federation (CIF)

Unlike IBEC, which represents employers from a range of industrial sectors, the CIF is essentially an industry-based association dealing with both trade/commercial and industrial relations matters affecting the construction industry. Some of the CIF's services include advice on construction, tendering and financial planning, training and education, and influencing public policy through, for example, being a member of the NESC. In the area of industrial relations, the CIF advises members on employee relations and employment law matters and represents members in negotiations with unions and in disputes/cases referred to the WRC and the Labour Court. The CIF's most important industrial relations function is representing employers in collective bargaining at an industry level. The CIF has generally supported the setting of legally binding pay and conditions for craft construction workers in the industry because it gives firms stability and they 'can tender for work on a level playing field with regard to labour costs' (CIF 2017: 3). In other words, when all firms are legally required to pay certain minimum pay rates, it prevents them undercutting each other and winning construction contracts on the basis of lowering pay (see Chapter 5, section on sectoral employment orders).

Irish Small and Medium Enterprises Association (ISME)

Thomason (1984) differentiates between entrepreneurs, who essentially own (at least partly) and run their businesses, and abstract corporate entities that are run by professional management. The corporate business firm has replaced the older entrepreneurial firm as the prevalent type of organisation in membership of employer organisations. Thomason suggests that this mix partly explains the diverse philosophies and roles of different employer organisations. Despite the existence of the Small Firms Association within IBEC, ISME argues that it is 'the only independent representative association for Small and Medium Enterprises (SME) … and … is independent of big business, big banks and government and gives voice to the issues facing SME owner-managers' (ISME 2019). ISME was established in 1993 by a group of SMEs that broke away when the FIE and CII amalgamated to form IBEC. While ISME does not hold a negotiating licence and thus does not meet the established definition of an employer organisation, it has been prominent in commenting on economic and social affairs,

---

Table 4.3
Employer Organisations at the EU Level

Given the importance of the EU in national issues such as employment law, Irish employer organisations have joined networks of international employer organisations to influence EU policymaking.

Business Europe is a Brussels-based organisation that represents the voice of business in European policymaking. It represents the national business federations of thirty-five European countries, including IBEC, and it offers services to sixty-nine individual companies, including Accenture, Facebook, Google, Microsoft and BMW (*Source:* www.businesseurope.eu).

SMEunited is the association of crafts and SMEs in Europe with around seventy member organisations from over thirty European countries, including ISME. It represents the interests of SMEs in European Institutions (*Source:* www.smeunited.eu).

including industrial relations. ISME's primary function is to represent the interests of its members to government, government bodies and other organisations impacting on business. It has lobbied for labour market deregulation, and was critical of the system of social partnership and of IBEC's role in it, which, O'Donnell and Thomas (2002: 180) argue, stems from ISME's resentment at not being offered a role in social partnership. Its services include offering information and advice on employment law, finance, entrepreneurship and other employment issues, and training and education. Like IBEC, it has branched out into offering services relating to contemporary issues like employee wellness.

Irish Hotels Federation (IHF) and Licensed Vintners Federation (LVF)

Historically, the main industrial relations activity of the IHF and the LVF has been to represent the voice of hotels and Dublin publicans, respectively, on the joint labour committees (JLCs) of hotels and catering. On these bodies, the IHF and LVF negotiated with trade unions on the pay and conditions for large groups of workers, which became legally binding. However, in recent years, these employer organisations have refused to participate on JLCs because they argue that the JLCs are outdated and that the pay and conditions they set threaten competitiveness and job creation. This means that workers in hotels and catering businesses have no general legal entitlements to pay or conditions above the national minimum wage and other employment legislation.

OTHER EMPLOYER BODIES IN IRELAND

A number of other organisations that represent employers do not have negotiating licences but have been influential in the area of industrial relations. One such body is the Quick Service Food Alliance (QSFA). It was established in 2008 to represent the interests of fast-food employers, including Supermac's, McDonald's and Subway, and it took a legal challenge against the JLC which set legally binding minimum pay and conditions for catering workers, resulting in the JLC being found unconstitutional (O'Sullivan and Royle 2014; further discussion in Chapter 5). Since the legal case, there has been no order setting legally binding pay and conditions for the catering sector, and the QSFA seems to have engaged in little further activity.

Like the QSFA, the National Electrical Contractors of Ireland (NECI) was set up to represent employers who opposed the setting of national legally binding pay and conditions in the electrical contracting sector. NECI opposed the pay and conditions set in registered employment agreements (REAs) and argued that other employer organisations which were involved in the pay setting did not represent their interests. NECI supported a group of individual employers who took a successful legal challenge in 2011 against the REA for electrical contracting (see Chapter 5). NECI remains active in opposing the current system of sectoral employment orders (that replaced REAs) which set legally binding pay and conditions in electrical contracting (see Chapter 5). In 2019 NECI initiated a judicial review against the 2019 sectoral employment order (SEO) for electrical contracting and obtained a High Court injunction, meaning employers will not have to abide by some aspects of the SEO until the full judicial review is heard in the courts. However, there are other employer organisations who support the principle of legally binding pay and conditions across the electrical contracting sector, namely the Electrical Contractors Association and the Association of Electrical Contractors Ireland. Because of the support of these large organisations, SEOs have been made but the process has been delayed and frustrated by NECI.

An employer representative body that has had a growing voice on public policy matters is the American Chamber of Commerce Ireland (Amcham). Amcham is the representative voice of American MNCs located in Ireland and its mission is 'to keep Ireland the global location of choice for US companies'. Amcham develops policy through its advocacy groups such as on taxation, employment law, cybersecurity, and research, development and innovation. An activity of the employment law group is to 'represent members' interest in the formulation stage of EU and Irish employment law' (www.amcham.ie). A study of MNCs in Ireland found that Amcham had a high level of access to senior government officials and that this had influenced the content of Irish laws that transposed EU directives (Collings *et al.* 2008). Collings *et al.* (2008: 258) argue that 'most of these directives have been enacted along lines which are broadly pro-business and tend to impose the minimal possible restrictions on business and management'. Amcham has lobbied the government to retain the 12.5 per cent corporation tax rate and it has consistently lobbied the government against introducing compulsory union recognition or collective bargaining involving unions. In 2011 the president of Amcham, Gerard Kilcommins, said that 'any dilution of the current voluntary model would create a barrier to job creation and could damage our capacity to attract and retain inward investment' (Higgins 2011).

MEMBERSHIP OF EMPLOYER ORGANISATIONS

While initially it might seem incompatible for public sector organisations to join an employer organisation (traditionally a bastion of free enterprise), some have taken up membership as a result of high levels of unionisation and the consequent need for expertise and advice on industrial relations issues. The amount spent by public sector organisations and semi-state bodies on employer organisation fees led to some controversy during the financial crisis (Sheehan 2011a). Local authorities can avail of the services of the Local Government Management Agency, which provides human resources and industrial relations research and advice, and negotiates with trade unions on behalf of the local authority sector.

There is some debate as to the impact of firm size on employer organisations. For example, it has been suggested that small firms have more to gain by joining employer organisations (International Labour Organisation 1975). Such firms are not generally in a position to employ HR specialists and owner/managers may not have either the necessary time or expertise to effectively handle such matters. However, subsequent research showed that employer organisations were not more frequently used by smaller organisations (Brown 1981; Daniel and Millward 1983). Small companies can be problematic for employer organisations because they are less committed to a collective identity and 'provide fewer membership resources relative to the demands they make on those resources' (Sheldon and Thornthwaite 2005: 20). Certainly, larger companies are important to associations' membership strength because of the number of employees they have and the fees they pay. Research on employer organisations suggests there are often tensions between satisfying the interests of larger and smaller employers (Grote *et al.* 2007). In Germany larger, export-oriented companies have increasingly influenced employer organisations and encouraged them to concede to trade union demands in order to avoid industrial action, while smaller companies have left the organisations (Thelen and van Wijnbergen 2003).

Membership of employer organisations is seen as a useful indicator of preferred management approaches to industrial relations (see also Chapter 8). Membership has traditionally been associated with the pluralist industrial relations model. Past research indicated that trade union recognition and formalised collective bargaining arrangements appeared to be key factors in determining membership of an employer organisation (Brown 1981). Therefore, it might be expected that companies which unilaterally determine pay and conditions and do not negotiate with trade unions would be less likely to be members of an employer organisation. This would be expected to be the case with non-union MNCs (such as Intel, Dell, Google and Microsoft), which are now an integral part of the industrial scene. Some of these firms have brought with them a particular corporate approach to industrial relations that emphasises dealing with employees on an individual basis rather than through trade unions. Some international research indicates that MNCs generally avoid being members of employer organisations in the country they invest in (Marginson *et al.* 2004). However, a large-scale survey of 260 MNCs in Ireland found that 92 per cent were members of an employer organisation, and most of these were members of IBEC (86 per cent) (Lavelle *et al.* 2009). Interestingly, there was not a significant difference in membership rates between unionised MNCs (92 per cent) and non-unionised MNCs (85 per cent) (Lavelle *et al.* 2009). This suggests that non-union companies here do not view membership of an employer organisation as a de facto acceptance of collectivism, and that they see other benefits of membership.

It is estimated that the employer density rate (the proportion of workers in firms organised in employer organisations as a proportion of all workers in employment) is 60 per cent in Ireland (Table 4.4). This is much higher than the employer density rate in the UK but similar to many other EU countries. On average, the employer union density rate in twenty-six OECD (Organisation for Economic Co-operation and

Development) countries is 51 per cent (OECD 2017). The OECD notes that employer organisation density partly mirrors trade union density. For example, Austria and Belgium have high densities in both while Central and Eastern European countries have low rates, though there are countries like France with high employer union density and low trade union density (OECD 2017). The institutional context can heavily influence employer union density, such as legal requirements, trade union density and collective bargaining practices. In Austria employers are legally required to be members of the principal employer peak organisation (the 'umbrella' organisation), the WKO. In Belgium, the Netherlands and Spain employers are not legally required to be members of employer organisations but they have to pay fees to a central fund for their sector, some of which goes towards funding employer organisations (Traxler 2004). Employers may be more likely to be members of an employer organisation where there are strong trade unions (Sheldon and Thornthwaite 2005: 20). This can be viewed as the continuing relevance of the key rationale for the creation of employer organisations, i.e. to deal with unions.

It might have been expected that employer organisation density would decline as trade union density and collective bargaining declined. The argument behind this is that employer organisations can become less relevant as companies are less incentivised to join for solidarity reasons and the needs of companies in industrial relations become more diverse (Sheldon and Thornthwaite 2005). It might also be expected that employer organisation density would decline because of pressures from globalisation (Brandl and Lehr 2016). For example, Silvia and Schroeder (2007) argue that for many firms in Germany, increased costs and quality pressures as a result of globalisation are the main explanations for a decline of membership in employer organisations. However, in general, employer organisation density has not declined as expected and has remained relatively stable across countries (Brandl and Lehr 2016; OECD 2017). Brandl and Lehr (2016: 18–19) argue that 'trade union density is no longer a significant predictor' of employer organisation density and that employer organisations have adapted their organisational structures and activities which 'allowed them to take advantage of changing socioeconomic circumstances'. Employer organisations have merged with each other, improved the range of services or conversely cut the range of services, charged on a fee-per-service basis for some services, focused more on the product market or commercial interests of employers, and increased political lobbying and opinion formation (Barry and Wilkinson 2011; Brandl and Lehr 2016; Traxler 2004).

Advantages and Disadvantages of Employer Organisation Membership

The potential advantages and disadvantages of employer organisation membership for individual organisations are summarised in Table 4.5. One of the disadvantages of employer organisation membership is a possible reduction of *autonomy* in decision-making for the individual organisation. Employer organisations will be keen that

Table 4.4
Employer Organisation Density

Country	Employer Organisation Density (%)
Austria	100
Belgium	82
Czech Republic	65
Denmark	62
Finland	70
France	75
Germany	60
Ireland	60
Italy	65
Luxembourg	80
Netherlands	85
Norway	73
Spain	75
Sweden	88
United Kingdom	33

Source: Visser (2019b); years of data vary.

members maintain a standard line in negotiations on pay and conditions of employment through the development of agreed policy guidelines. The individual organisation must decide if such norms are appropriate to its particular needs. This is less of an issue in Ireland since the breakdown of the social partnership wage agreements in 2009: companies now have greater autonomy to decide on pay and conditions. *Comparability* is also an important factor. By virtue of association membership, a particular organisation's pay and conditions will generally be compared to that pertaining in other member firms. A traditional negotiating tactic of trade unions is to use the terms of collective agreements (particularly wage increases) struck with some member firms as leverage to secure similar terms with other organisations.

The issues of autonomy and comparability reflect the difficulties employer organisations face in developing common policies for a diverse membership. They also highlight the difficulties employer organisations face in enforcing policy guidelines, and they raise the issue of control over affiliates. Breaches of agreed policy guidelines by individual member organisations can detrimentally affect the credibility of such guidelines and may incur the wrath of sections of the affiliated membership. This has occasionally resulted in firms withdrawing from membership or being disaffiliated by the association. Such breaches of discipline are almost inescapable in associations where membership is voluntary and general policies are laid down for a diverse membership. Employer organisations will often exercise only informal authority over members, relying on persuasion and peer pressure to secure adherence to common policies. They are generally reluctant to punish non-conforming members, particularly where expulsion is considered. Should a large number of enterprises (or even a few significant employers) decide not to join an employer organisation, its representativeness is clearly called into question. This has become an issue in some sectors where pay and conditions are set at a sectoral level through SEOs, and some employers, such as in electrical contracting, have set up break-away employer organisations like NECI in an attempt to resist such systems.

Table 4.5
Advantages and Disadvantages of Employer Association Membership

Advantages	Disadvantages
Collective approaches and uniform policy	Cost of membership
Advice on trade union matters	Potential loss of full autonomy
Technical advice and information	Potential loss of flexibility
Skilled negotiators	Comparisons with other firms
Expert advisory and consultancy services	Greater acceptance of role of trade
Standardised pay and employment conditions	unions
On par with regional/industry norms	Greater formalisation in industrial
Assistance in industrial relations difficulties	relations
Influence on government/national affairs	

An issue of concern for employers with regards to membership can be how association membership fits in with the *corporate personnel/HR philosophy*. As noted, employer organisations have traditionally sought to deal with their employee counterparts through collective bargaining. However, some firms have a clear preference for a non-union status and may view membership of an employer organisation as incompatible with their HR philosophy. Conversely, we noted earlier that many non-union MNCs have joined an employer organisation. A more pragmatic reason for non-membership is related to *cost*. An important issue here can be that firms pay the full cost of membership regardless of services used. By contrast, an organisation that uses management consultants normally pays on the basis of services rendered. Most employer organisation subscriptions are related to the size of the firm (number of employees) or to the companies' total salaries and wages or turnover in a financial year, so subscription costs can be substantial for larger organisations. Related to the issue of costs may be the perception among firms with a highly developed and well-resourced HR function that they do not need the services provided by an employer organisation. This is based on the premise that such services can be adequately provided by the company's own HR function. Reynaud (1978) suggests that larger firms with well-developed HR functions may not need many of the services provided by employer organisations. However, research evidence does not support this view and it seems that large firms use employer organisations more than small ones.

CONCLUDING COMMENTS

This chapter has reviewed the structure and functions of employer organisations. Employer organisations were generally created to deal with trade unions and their functions have broadened over time. Many are now heavily engaged in lobbying and presenting their positions on a variety of public policy issues. In the EU there is a strong tradition of employer organisations negotiating with unions at an industry level, and the function of employer organisations in this case is to coordinate the employers' negotiating position. In Ireland there is only limited industry bargaining, and employer organisations, including IBEC, have had to adjust to a changed industrial relations landscape in which pay bargaining has shifted from national to firm level.

Chapter 5

Dispute Resolution and Wage-Setting Institutions

INTRODUCTION

While employers and employees have a common interest in keeping companies open and creating employment, they can also have conflicting interests over a range of issues such as pay, workload and working hours. As well as organisations having their own internal dispute resolution mechanisms, governments recognise that some disputes can be difficult to resolve and employers and employees may need assistance. The need for dispute resolution bodies is driven by a need to promote social justice and also by political and economic imperatives. Political pressure can arise from a need for the state to act in the role of industrial peacemaker, especially in the case of disputes in essential services like electricity, water and police (Farnham and Pimlott 1990). The study of industrial relations has long been concerned with the role of institutions. Early industrial relations scholars such as Flanders (1965) and Dunlop (1958) gave institutions a central role in the study of industrial relations, while others from radical or Marxist perspectives criticised this institutional focus. Radical thinkers drew attention to the need to study industrial relations as a struggle for power and control (Edwards 2003; Fox 1973; Hyman 1975). Despite such differences of emphases, there is general agreement amongst scholars, practitioners and policymakers that institutions are an important part of industrial relations. Many countries have recognised the need for mechanisms/bodies to help employers and workers resolve disputes and conflicts through mediation, conciliation and adjudication, either through civil courts or through specialised bodies outside the civil courts system. Ireland has two state bodies that are not part of the civil courts system: The Workplace Relations Commission (WRC) and the Labour Court.

Cases which are referred to these bodies by workers and employers are generally of two types.

1. *Industrial relations disputes* occur between an employer(s) and usually a group of workers on a wide range of issues such as pay, work practices, staffing and pensions. These are disputes of interest, which may have nothing to do with employment law and therefore there may be no legal 'right' or 'wrong' solutions. Negotiation between representatives of the employers and employees may have failed to resolve the conflict and both sides may request the WRC or Labour Court to assist them in reaching a collective agreement. The role of the WRC and Labour Court is important because these industrial relations disputes can involve large numbers of workers and they

may involve industrial action like a strike, which results in loss of pay and lost productivity. For example, the WRC intervened in the health support workers' strike in 2019, and the WRC and Labour Court intervened in the threatened strike involving the Gardaí in 2016 and the nurses' strike in 2019. In general, the role of the WRC and Labour Court in these types of disputes is not to impose a solution but to help the parties resolve their issues.

2. *Employment rights cases* are cases taken by an individual worker against organisations for alleged breaches of employment legislation (see Chapter 6). Usually, the case involves the alleged infringement of the right of one employee though there have been instances where large numbers of employees each refer the same employment rights case over the same issue against the same employer, ostensibly using legal avenues to pressure an employer on a 'collective' issue. The WRC can try to help the parties come to a resolution but many employment rights cases involve adjudication, where a single adjudicator in the WRC or a panel in the Labour Court make a legally binding decision as to whether an individual's rights under employment law are breached or not. If rights are breached, each piece of employment law dictates what the WRC or Labour Court can award as a maximum level of compensation.

The WRC and Labour Court, which are generally free to users, are very important actors in the employment relations and HR landscape in Ireland, and this chapter examines in detail how they work. Some groups of workers in the public sector may not have access to the WRC and Labour Court but have their own separate mechanisms of dispute resolution known as C&A (conciliation and arbitration) schemes, which will also be reviewed in this chapter. Finally, the chapter examines dispute resolution in a second area of industrial relations in which the state is often involved, that of minimum wage setting. In some sectors, pay and conditions of employment are decided for large groups of workers collectively and involve bodies called joint industrial councils (JICs) or joint labour committees (JLCs). In some other EU countries, setting pay and conditions for a large part, or all, of a sector is commonplace and requires strong trade unions and employer organisations. However, in Ireland such sectoral wage setting is not common and only exists for a small number of sectors. First though, we begin by examining dispute resolution bodies.

HISTORY OF STATE DISPUTE RESOLUTION PROVISION

Since 1946, the state has established a number of bodies to deal with collective industrial relations disputes and employment rights cases:

- the Labour Court was established under the Industrial Relations Act 1946;
- the Office of Rights Commissioner was created under the Industrial Relations Act 1969;

- the Employment Appeals Tribunal (EAT) was originally established as the Redundancy Appeals Tribunal under the Redundancy Payments Act 1967;
- the Labour Relations Commission (LRC) was set up under the Industrial Relations Act 1990;
- the Equality Tribunal was created under the Employment Equality Act 1998;
- the National Employment Rights Authority (NERA), housing labour inspectors, was provided for in the social partnership agreement, Towards 2016.

These bodies were created to deal with an expanding list of employment laws and decide on employment rights, to offer a wider set of dispute resolution services to try to help employers and workers solve disputes, and to enforce employment rights. While the services offered by these bodies were accepted and praised by many users, they were also subject to criticism. Much of this related to operational inefficiencies of the overall system – employers and workers were confused by the multiplicity of bodies and they needed substantial knowledge to understand which body to use. In addition, the following criticisms were made of some bodies: duplication of work, significant time delays in getting a decision, and an overly legalistic approach in their operation (Bruton 2011; Sheehan 2011b; Teague and Doherty 2009). Various governments commissioned reports on reforming the institutions and reform eventually occurred under the Workplace Relations Act 2015. The stated objectives of reforming the bodies, according to the Department of Jobs, Enterprise and Innovation (2016), were:

- to deliver a world-class workplace relations service which is simple to use, independent, effective, impartial and cost-effective;
- to provide for workable means of redress and enforcement within a reasonable period; and
- to reduce costs.

The most significant elements of the Workplace Relations Act 2015 were:

- The functions of the Rights Commissioner, the EAT, the LRC, the Equality Tribunal and NERA were merged into two bodies: the WRC and Labour Court.
- A single route for cases was created whereby they would be referred in the first instance to the WRC and appeals would be referred to the Labour Court.
- Cases would have a common pathway and procedures.
- A standard time limit was set for cases. Cases must be referred within six months and could be extended if there is 'reasonable cause'. Appeals to the Labour Court must be made within forty-two days of a WRC adjudication unless there are 'exceptional circumstances'.
- Adjudication of cases in the WRC would be carried out by single officers while the make-up of a Labour Court hearing would remain the same, involving a panel of three members.
- Labour inspectors were given additional powers to penalise employers for contraventions of certain parts of employment laws.

The Workplace Relations Act 2015 provided for the dissolution of the former bodies, including the EAT, but it will only dissolve once it clears its 'legacy cases', that is, any cases referred to it before 1 October 2015. In 2018 the EAT disposed of forty cases, mostly under unfair dismissals legislation, and had sixty-seven cases remaining at the end of the year (EAT 2019).

THE WORKPLACE RELATIONS COMMISSION (WRC)

The WRC is the primary state dispute resolution body as it is generally the first port of call for employers and workers who need assistance to resolve disputes or for workers who refer employment law claims. The WRC has a tripartite advisory board with trade union, employer and independent representation, but its day-to-day operations are led by a director general, who is a public servant. The functions of the WRC under the Workplace Relations Act 2015 are to:
* promote the improvement of workplace relations, and maintenance of good workplace relations;
* promote and encourage compliance with employment legislation;
* provide guidance in relation to compliance with codes of practice;
* conduct reviews of, and monitor developments in respect of, workplace relations;
* conduct or commission research into matters pertaining to workplace relations;
* provide advice, information and the findings of research conducted by the WRC to JLCs and JICs;
* advise and apprise the Minister for Business, Enterprise and Innovation in relation to the application of, and compliance with, relevant legislation;
* provide information to members of the public in relation to employment legislation;
* attend meetings outside the state relating to employment law matters and industrial and workplace relations upon the request of the minister (Workplace Relations Act 2015).

The WRC offers a number of services to fulfil its objectives. Some services are used for industrial relations disputes and some cater for employment rights disputes.

Industrial Relations Disputes

Conciliation is the WRC's most important function, focused on industrial relations disputes between employers and groups of workers that do not generally involve 'legal rights and wrongs'. Conciliation is 'an advisory, consensual and confidential process, in which parties to the dispute select a neutral and independent third party to assist them in reaching a mutually acceptable negotiated agreement' (Law Reform Commission 2010: 17). Industrial relations officers (IROs) in the WRC provide conciliation which can involve meetings or 'conferences' between the disputing parties either jointly or separately, and the IRO steers the discussions and explores possible avenues of settlement in a non-prejudicial fashion. IROs have no power to compel the parties to reach agreement and it is this element of 'disputant control' that is the essential ingredient of conciliation which makes the process attractive to the parties. The outcomes of a resolved dispute are usually an agreement, not a legal decision. If the parties to the dispute do not resolve their differences in conciliation, they have a number of options such as:

- they can agree to request the WRC to refer their dispute to the Labour Court; or
- they can return to negotiations in the workplace; or
- they can take any other action that the employees or employers may deem suitable, e.g. engaging in industrial action.

Examples of companies which have used the conciliation service in recent years include GSK, MSD, Novartis, Pinewood Healthcare, Dairygold, Donegal Meat Processors, Independent News & Media, Smurfit Kappa New Press, Musgrave, Lufthansa Technik Shannon, Bord na Móna, Dublin Airport Authority, Kerry Ingredients, AIB and Bausch & Lomb. Settlement rates are high at conciliation, hovering between 75 per cent and 80 per cent since the late 1990s (Wallace and O'Sullivan 2002; Figure 5.1).

Employment Rights Cases

Pre-adjudication Mediation
There are a large number of employment laws granting rights to workers. If an individual believes their employment rights have been breached in an organisation, they can refer a complaint to the WRC through its website. The various pathways that a case might take after it is referred to the WRC is depicted in Figure 5.2. The director general may refer the complaint to 'pre-adjudication mediation' if they believe mediation would help resolve the issue without the need for adjudication. Mediation is 'a facilitative, consensual and confidential process, in which parties to the dispute select a neutral and independent third party to assist them in reaching a mutually acceptable negotiated agreement' (Law Reform Commission 2008: 48). Mediation, by its nature, is a voluntary form of dispute resolution and the parties must agree to use it and they can withdraw during the process. Mediation is undertaken by mediation officers and they may engage with both parties by telephone or through face-to-face meetings. If a resolution is reached between the parties, the mediation officer records the terms of the resolution, and it is signed by both parties and becomes binding. These binding agreements have legal force in that if either party breaches a term of the agreement, it is actionable in a civil court. The terms of a resolution and any communications between the mediation officer and the parties are confidential, except where there is a court action involving an alleged breach of the agreement. The WRC (2019) reported that 64 per cent of cases involving mediation in 2018 resulted in a resolution. If the parties do not reach a resolution through mediation, the case is referred to adjudication.

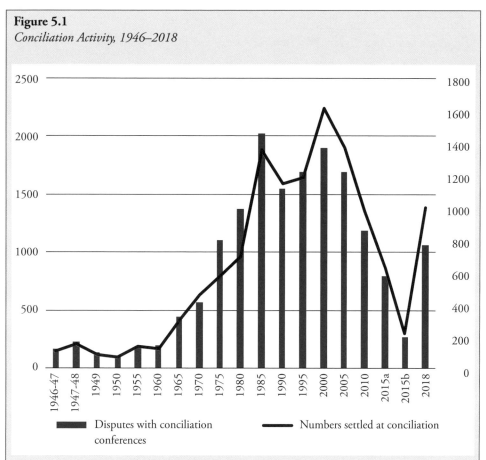

Figure 5.1
Conciliation Activity, 1946–2018

Source: WRC, LRC and Labour Court annual reports, various years.
Notes: (i) These figures have been calculated from the rounded percentage figure and as such are approximations. (ii) The year 2015 is split into two periods (2015a and 2015b): 2015a refers to the period 1 January to 1 October when conciliation figures were reported by the LRC, and 2015b refers to the period 1 October to 31 December when conciliation figures were reported by the WRC.

Adjudication

Referring a case to adjudication means that a WRC officer – adjudication officer – will decide if employment rights have been breached or not (Table 5.1). There are almost fifty adjudication officers, who are either full-time employees of the WRC (many are former rights commissioners or equality officers from the Equality Tribunal) or from a panel of external adjudicators who work in law, industrial relations or human resource management. Cases must be referred to the WRC within six months of the alleged breach of employment right taking place unless the individual has reasonable cause for not submitting their complaint within the time limit. In that case the adjudication officer

Figure 5.2
Routes for Complaints under Employment Law in the WRC

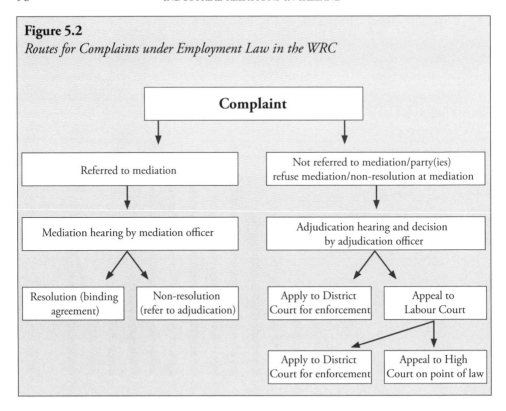

can grant a six-month extension. A worker's attempts to use internal procedures in an organisation about their complaint has not been an accepted reason for not complying with time limits (*Brothers of Charity Services Galway and Kieran O'Toole, Labour Court Determination* 2017 EDA177). Cases referred to adjudication can contain multiple complaints – for example, someone who claims they were unfairly dismissed might also claim that their rights to minimum notice or to annual leave were also breached. In 2018 there were 7,724 referrals to the WRC, containing 15,451 specific complaints. Almost 70 per cent of the specific complaints related to pay, unfair dismissals, equality and working hours.

Adjudication officers hold hearings for parties to present their arguments and they have powers to require a person to attend a hearing, to give evidence or to produce documents. It is an offence for non-compliance. They also have the power to throw out a case if they think it is frivolous or vexatious and this decision can be appealed to the Labour Court. The employer and worker in the case do not need to have representation but if they do, they can be represented by a trade union official, employer association official, solicitor, barrister or some other person permitted by the adjudication officer. Adjudication hearings are held in private and written decisions are published but generally anonymised. However, parties' names are published in decisions under the Employment Equality Acts, Equal Status Acts and Pensions Acts, unless an adjudication officer decides otherwise. Many cases heard in adjudication are relatively small, or at least they do not attain large awards. The director general of the WRC, Liam Kelly, noted that 44 per cent of adjudication decision awards between January and June 2019 were for amounts of less than €1,000 (Prendergast 2019a). A significant number of complaints do not reach an adjudicated decision. Fifty per cent of specific complaints in 2017 did not get a decision for a variety of reasons, including that they were withdrawn or not pursued by the parties, were dismissed by the WRC for being vexatious or out of time, or were settled by the parties (WRC 2018).

Table 5.1
Case Study
WRC Adjudication in Action

An employee began work as a trainee accountant on a salary of €22,500 with an accounting firm. During her employment, she completed many accounting exams and the company paid her exam fees. Three years later, she handed in her notice and claimed that her manager was not happy with her resignation and that they told her she would have to repay the company €9,000 in exam fees. She was due over €3,000 in her last pay cheque for wages, holiday pay and TOIL (time off in lieu), but instead she received just 3 cent, with the remainder deducted for exam fees. The employee took a case against the company to the WRC for unlawful deduction of wages under the Payment of Wages Act 1991. In defending the claim, the company argued that the employee had breached their training contract, which stated that they would have to repay education costs to the firm if they resigned before the expiry of the contract. The adjudication officer noted their role was to determine if the money deducted was lawful and not whether the employee owed other monies to the company, which would be a matter for the civil courts. They found in favour of the employee, noting that the deductions made were not 'fair and reasonable', as required by the legislation. They concluded that even if a contract permitted a deduction in pay, this could not over-ride the employee's entitlement to holiday pay under working time legislation, and the adjudication officer noted the company had accrued substantial benefit from the employee's success in passing exams by charging clients more for the employee's work. The company was ordered to pay the ex-employee €3,600, which included the amount owed to her and compensation for 'loss and inconvenience'.

Source: WRC Decision ADJ-00019646.

Although the majority of the adjudication service's work is on individual employment laws, it also deals with individual complaints submitted under Industrial Relations Acts 1969–2015. It might be appropriate for an employee to submit a claim under the Industrial Relations Acts where they believe they have been treated unfairly but not necessarily illegally under employment laws. A common type of case submitted under the legislation is unfair dismissals where the employee does not have the one year's service requirement needed to submit a case under the Unfair Dismissals Acts 1977–2015. Cases submitted under the industrial relations legislation do not have the same criteria or redress stipulated under employment laws and usually the adjudication officer issues a recommendation that is not legally binding.

Generally, appeals of a decision of the adjudicator to the Labour Court must be made within forty-two days (the date of the adjudication decision is day one) unless there are exceptional circumstances for not abiding by the time limit. There are different time limits for appeals of industrial relations cases. Sometimes both parties appeal an adjudication decision. For example, if an employee won a case, they might appeal the size of the award given by the adjudication officer while an employer might appeal the fact the decision favoured the employee. If the decision is not appealed, and the employer does not comply with an adjudication decision, the WRC, the employee, or a trade union/excepted body on their behalf can apply to the District Court to order the employer to carry out the decision, and it can also direct the employer to pay interest on any compensation previously awarded to the employee.

Inspection and Enforcement

The aims of the inspection and enforcement service of the WRC are to monitor employment conditions, ensure compliance with employment legislation and, if necessary, enforce employment rights legislation (WRC 2019). Labour inspectors (formerly part of NERA) make announced and unannounced visits to employments around the country and they ensure compliance of employment laws through information and awareness, issuing penalties and prosecuting employers. Some inspections are the result of complaints made by employees. Given the size of the workforce and number of employments, labour inspectors pay particular attention to sectors/jobs considered at high risk of breaches of minimum employment rights like minimum wages and working time rights (Table 5.2). They have undertaken targeted inspection campaigns in the accommodation and food sectors, the equine sector, fisheries, hand car washes, the market garden sector (vegetable/fruit picking) and nail bars. Some of these involve employments susceptible in Ireland and abroad to economic slavery (Clark and Colling 2018; Lally 2019). They can carry out enforcement operations in conjunction with other bodies such as the Gardaí and officers of the Department of Employment Affairs and Social Protection. The role of labour inspectors is important because workers who may be vulnerable to exploitation may not be aware of their rights or have the capacity to exercise them, and labour inspectors have considerable powers to pursue their rights on their behalf, including the following rights:
- to enter places of work (if necessary, using reasonable force);
- to inspect and take copies of documents and records;
- to require an employer or employee at the place of work to produce documents and require them to answer questions;
- to examine an employer or employee once they have been cautioned that the person is not obliged to say anything unless he or she wishes to do so but that whatever he or she says will be taken down in writing and may be given in evidence;

- either by consent of an owner, or by a District Court warrant, to enter a dwelling that has documents relevant to an inspection.

It is an offence for someone to obstruct, refuse or fail to comply with the work of an inspector. Table 5.2 shows the number of announced inspections across sectors and breaches of employment rights between 2016 and 2018. Food and drink and retail have higher numbers of inspections because of the high levels of employment and because half of all employees who are paid the national minimum wage work in these sectors (McGuinness *et al.* 2019). Many breaches found by labour inspectors relate to a lack of employment records held by employers. The retention of adequate employment records is critical for employers to show they have complied with employment laws. Yet, unpaid wages are a significant phenomenon, with almost €6.5 million recovered by the inspectorate for employees between 2016 and 2018 (WRC 2017–2019).

If a labour inspector is satisfied that an employer has breached certain sections of some employment laws, they have the power to issue compliance notices which can require the employer to take some action or stop certain practices. An employer can appeal a compliance notice to the Labour Court, the decision of which in turn can be appealed to the Circuit Court. In 2018 a total of 120 compliance notices were issued and 42 employers were prosecuted for not complying with a notice (WRC 2019).

In addition to compliance notices, an inspector can issue a fixed payment notice to a maximum of €2,000 where they have reasonable grounds for believing a person has committed an offence under certain sections of the Protection of Employment Act 1977, the Payment of Wages Act 1991 or the National Minimum Wage Act 2000. If the person pays the notice within forty-two days, they will not be prosecuted for the offence.

Labour inspectors attempt to work with employers to correct breaches of employment laws but, if needed, can pursue criminal prosecutions. Between 2016 and 2018 a total of 327 criminal prosecutions were concluded, though numbers fell progressively over that short period. That was expected by the inspectorate given their newly acquired powers to penalise employers through notices (WRC 2017–2019). Individuals and organisations that are convicted as a result of prosecution are named in WRC annual reports.

Other Workplace Relations Commission Services

Workplace Mediation Service
In addition to pre-adjudication mediation, the WRC also offers 'workplace mediation', which had been introduced by the former LRC in 2005. In practice, there is sometimes little difference between conciliation and mediation in terms of process but there is a distinction within the WRC as to the types of issues dealt with by each. While the conciliation service deals with collective industrial relations disputes involving issues such as pay, the workplace mediation service is aimed at relatively small-scale disputes

Table 5.2
WRC Inspection Activity, 2016–2018

Sector	No. of Announced Inspections	% Where Breaches Found
Agriculture	201	52
Construction	225	49
Contract cleaning	64	44
Domestic worker	47	36
Electrical	22	55
Equine	99	69
Fisheries	144	28
Food and drink	2,018	57
Hair and beauty	289	59
Health nursing and childcare	220	36
Hotel	208	46
Manufacturing	131	40
Other	851	46
Professional services	468	30
Security	55	38
Transport	175	51
Wholesale and retail	916	55
Total Announced Inspections	6,133	50
Additional Unannounced Inspections	9,197	36
Recovered unpaid wages	€6,429,000	

Source: WRC annual reports, 2016–2018.

involving individuals and small groups, provided such disputes have not already been referred to the conciliation service or the Labour Court. Typical issues referred to mediation may be interpersonal differences, a breakdown in working relationships, bullying, issues arising from a grievance and disciplinary procedure, and group dynamics (WRC 2019). The workplace mediation service received eighty-one cases in 2018, seventy cases in 2017 and thirty-seven cases in 2016 (WRC 2017–2019).

Advisory Service

The advisory service speaks to the role of the WRC to promote the improvement of workplace relations. It aims to 'promote good practice in the workplace by assisting and advising organisations on all aspects of industrial relations, and engages with employers, employees and their representatives to help them develop effective industrial relations practices, procedures and structures' (WRC 2019). The advisory service was originally part of the LRC's services. The reasoning behind its establishment, according to the Minister for Labour in 1990, Bertie Ahern TD, was that there were some organisations using the Labour Court's conciliation service regularly and it was clear that there were underlying problems that needed to be addressed in a more fundamental manner (Dáil Éireann 1990). Disputes may be merely a symptom of greater underlying problems in the workplace and such problems often remain after a dispute has been settled. To this end, the advisory service carries out industrial relations reviews. These involve an examination of an organisation's industrial relations procedures and practices by an advisory officer, followed by the issuing of a report containing recommendations for the parties involved and, if needed, by follow-up assistance through joint working parties (LRC 2001). Seven such reviews were carried out in 2018 (WRC 2019). Other areas of activity are facilitation and training, research, the development of codes of practice, and assistance in the resolution of disputes referred under Statutory Instrument (SI) 76/2004.

Codes of practice are sets of guidelines on particular employment situations/issues, which are developed by the WRC in consultation with employer and trade union organisations and other interested parties (Table 5.3). When approved by the WRC, the draft is then submitted to the Minister for Business, Enterprise and Innovation, who can make an SI. Codes of practice are not directly enforceable as a breach of the code and will not attract any civil or criminal sanction. However, they are 'admissible in evidence' in cases before the state third parties. One of the more controversial codes of practice in recent years has been SI Number 76/2004, the Code of Practice on Voluntary Dispute Resolution. Under the code, the WRC provides assistance in cases taken by workers/unions about pay and conditions of employment where there is no collective bargaining in a company, i.e. in generally non-unionised companies. The code of practice and the accompanying legislation (the Industrial Relations (Amendment) Acts 2001–2015) have been the subject of much debate; and since a Supreme Court case involving

---

Table 5.3
WRC Codes of Practice, 2019

- Dispute procedures, including procedures in essential services
- Duties and responsibilities of employee representatives
- Grievance and disciplinary procedures
- Compensatory rest periods
- Sunday working in the retail trade
- Employee involvement in the workplace
- Procedures to address bullying in the workplace
- Victimisation
- Voluntary dispute resolution
- Access to part-time work
- Protecting persons employed in other people's homes
- Protected disclosures
- Longer working
- Sexual harassment and harassment at work

Ryanair in 2007, the use of the Act and the code has diminished. Only six cases were referred to the WRC under the Code of Practice on Voluntary Dispute Resolution in 2018 compared with eighty-two in 2006 (LRC 2007; WRC 2019).

THE LABOUR COURT

The Labour Court was established under the Industrial Relations Act 1946 and at a time when there was very little by way of employment legislation. The original function of the court was to promote harmonious relations between workers and employers and 'for this purpose to establish machinery … for the prevention of trade disputes' (Industrial Relations Act 1946). Initially, it did not determine legal rights but over time the Labour Court's functions evolved and it now has a much greater role in deciding employment rights cases, either in the first instance or as an appellate body (hearing appeals of decisions from other bodies). Since the Workplace Relations Act 2015, the Labour Court continues to hear industrial relations cases but it only hears appeals of employment law cases, and none in the first instance. In dealing with industrial relations and employment rights cases, the chairman of the Labour Court (2019: 6) has called it an 'organisation with two faces'. The Labour Court treats industrial relations and employment rights cases differently and there are different outcomes for each. The Labour Court has been aptly described as 'a mix of arbitrator, facilitator and inquisitor. It is a tribunal with specialist expertise in a wide area including labour law, labour relations, social and political policy' (Duffy 2010: 69).

Despite its name, the Labour Court is not part of the civil courts system, it does not issue judgments and it is not staffed by judges but by people with extensive experience in industrial relations or employment law. The Labour Court currently consists of thirteen full-time members – a chairman, four deputy chairmen and eight ordinary members. The ordinary members are equally split between employers' members and workers' members. Employer members are nominated by the Irish Business and Employers Confederation (IBEC) and worker members are nominated by the Irish Congress of Trade Unions (ICTU) and then selected by the Minister for Business, Enterprise and Innovation. However, the ordinary members do not act as representatives of these bodies – while sitting on the Labour Court, they act independently. The Labour Court has four divisions and each division consists of three people: either the chairman or deputy chairman, and one employer member and one worker member. In special circumstances, all of the members of the court may sit on a case.

The Labour Court aims to carry out its functions in a fast, fair and inexpensive way. The Labour Court's services are free to users with one exception. Under the Workplace Relations Act 2015 (Fees) Regulations 2015, if someone fails or refuses to appear at a WRC adjudication hearing without a reasonable excuse, and subsequently wishes to appeal the adjudication officer's decision to the Labour Court, they must pay a fee of €300 to the court. The fee can be refunded if the Labour Court decides the appellant had good cause for not attending the WRC hearing.

Industrial Relations Cases and Functions

Most of the industrial cases which are referred to the Labour Court have already used the conciliation service of the WRC but the dispute remains unresolved. The WRC can refer the case to the Labour Court with the permission of both parties. These cases are usually trade disputes referred under the Industrial Relations Acts 1946–2015. In general, in industrial relations cases the parties are free to choose whether to use the court or not, and the outcome of such cases is usually a *recommendation,* which has no legal force and the parties are free to accept or reject the recommendation. In this respect, the Labour Court is very unlike a 'court of law'. This role of the court reflects the voluntarist nature of Irish industrial relations. This voluntarism means that parties are generally free to attempt to resolve disputes through the process of collective bargaining and the Labour Court. Though the parties to a dispute are generally free to reject Labour Court recommendations, there can be significant constraints to doing this, e.g. negative publicity and the prospect of a protracted dispute. Even where parties reject a recommendation, it may continue to have relevance as the basis for further negotiations between parties. In some industrial relations disputes, the parties can skip the WRC and refer their case directly to the Labour Court, usually under Section 20(1) or Section 20(2) of the Industrial Relations Act 1969, but in such circumstances either one or both agree in advance to be bound by the court's recommendation. Here again though, these recommendations do not have legal force.

The Labour Court has the following functions in relation to industrial relations. These are:

- investigate trade disputes under the Industrial Relations Acts 1946–2015;
- investigate (at the request of the Minister for Business, Enterprise and Innovation) trade disputes affecting the public interest or conduct an inquiry into a trade dispute of special importance and report on its findings;
- hear appeals of the recommendations of WRC adjudicators under the Industrial Relations Acts;
- establish JLCs and decide on questions concerning their operation;
- register, vary and interpret employment agreements;
- register JICs;
- investigate complaints of breaches of registered employment agreements (REAs);
- investigate complaints of breaches of codes of practice made under the Industrial Relations Act 1990;
- give its opinion as to the interpretation of a code of practice made under the Industrial Relations Act 1990;
- upon receipt of a request from a trade union and/or employer association, the Labour Court can initiate a review of the pay and pension and sick pay entitlements of workers in a particular sector and, if it deems it appropriate, make a recommendation to the minister on the matter (see section below on sectoral employment orders).

Under the Industrial Relations Acts 1946–2015 there are prescribed circumstances in which the Labour Court may investigate disputes. The court may investigate when:

- it receives a report from the WRC that no further efforts on its part will help to resolve the dispute (from conciliation);
- it is notified by the chairperson of the WRC that it has waived its function of conciliation in the dispute;
- it is hearing an appeal in relation to a recommendation of an adjudication officer;
- it decides after consultation with the WRC that exceptional circumstances of the case warrant a Labour Court investigation;
- there is a direct referral to the Labour Court and an advance acceptance of the court's recommendation under Sections 20(1) and 20(2) of the Industrial Relations Act 1969.

The court requires that each side make a written submission to it outlining the background to the dispute and their arguments. In industrial relations cases written submissions should reach the court no later than five days in advance of a hearing, and in many of the employment law cases written submissions must be made no later than seven days before a hearing. At the hearing a spokesperson from each side will read out the written submission to the court and the parties are free to make additional arguments and raise queries on each other's case. The members of the court may also seek clarification or elaboration on the arguments of the employer or the employee. A recommendation normally takes the form of a summary of the case submitted by each party to the dispute followed by a rationale for the court's recommended solution. Occasionally, the court may issue an oral recommendation. If any member of the court dissents from the recommendation (i.e. disagrees with it), the dissenting opinion is not issued. The Industrial Relations Act 1969 outlines that 'the Court having investigated a trade dispute may make a recommendation setting forth its opinions on the merits of the dispute and the terms on which it should be settled'. This marked a change from the Industrial Relations Act 1946, which required the court to have regard to a number of issues when making recommendations. This included the public interest, the promotion of industrial peace, the fairness of the terms to the parties concerned and the prospect of the terms being acceptable to them. This section was repealed in 1969, since it was clear to the court that it was almost impossible to reconcile all of the criteria (Kerr and Whyte 1985). R. J. Mortished, the first chairman of the court, highlighted this when he wrote that 'a settlement acceptable to the parties might be against the public interest and one which was not acceptable to the parties would not promote industrial peace' (Labour Court 1948). Yet in the Industrial Relations Acts 2001–2015 the Labour Court is required to take into account a number of criteria on varying issues under the Acts. These requirements were inserted as a result of increasing legalism in industrial relations and to ensure the court's recommendations would stand judicial reviews. In general though, the role of the court has been one of persuasion, cajoling and the promotion of accommodation amongst the parties before it. Its recommendations have been described as soft regulation instruments (Duffy, cited in Forde 1991; McCarthy 1984; Teague and Thomas 2008; von Prondzynski 1998). At times, the court has been accused of being anti-employer, anti-union or anti-government, but such criticisms generally relate to the perceived effectiveness of the court or the acceptability of its recommendations, not its role within the industrial relations institutional framework (see Forde 1991).

Table 5.4
Case Study
The Labour Court in Action

An industrial relations dispute between Primark and 5,000 retail staff was not resolved by the parties' own negotiations or by them using the conciliation service of the WRC, so it was referred to the Labour Court under the Industrial Relations Act 1990. In the Labour Court hearing Primark was represented by IBEC, and the retail staff by the trade union Mandate. The dispute centred on the union's demand for a 'no concession' pay increase of 3.4 per cent for one year, meaning the staff would not give anything in return, and the union argued the pay increase was to account for the cost of living and for productivity gains. The union also demanded an increase in annual leave of one day in service-related leave, arguing that the company was saving money on service-related leave because many workers left the company before they could get such leave. Primark argued that they had better wage rates than competitors, and it sought to change the timing of the unsocial hours premium. The court recommended that there should be no concessions in relation to the union's claim for additional leave nor in relation to the company's claim on the unsocial hours premium arrangements, so the status quo remained on those issues. In relation to pay, the court recommended a pay increase of 2.25 per cent over one year.

Source: Labour Court Recommendation LCR22120.

The Labour Court (2019) has commented that the vast majority of its industrial relations recommendations are accepted voluntarily by the parties, though there is no regularly collected information on this. Previous research suggests that acceptance of Labour Court recommendations is much lower in regard to union recognition. These are cases taken by a union against a non-unionised employer, seeking the Labour Court to recommend that the employer recognise and negotiate with the union. Between 1990 and 1999 only 30 per cent of employers actually recognised a union following a court recommendation (Gunnigle *et al.* 2002).

Table 5.5 presents a snapshot of industrial relations referrals to the Labour Court at three points in time. In 2018 the Labour Court had 399 referrals of industrial relations cases, which was much lower than in 2000 and 2010. While appeals of recommendations of adjudication officers under industrial relations legislation remained strong, there were much fewer referrals in 2018. The reduction in industrial relations cases has been offset by a rise in employment law referrals, which accounted for about a third of all cases in 2011 but two-thirds of cases in 2018 (Labour Court 2011; 2019). However, the chairman of the Labour Court has commented that 'the work of the Court in the area of industrial relations has the most widespread impact across the economy', given that industrial relations disputes involve groups of workers (Labour Court 2019: 5). The number of referrals to the court overall increased by 38 per cent between 2014 and 2018, and much of this is accounted for by its increased responsibilities since the Workplace Relations Act 2015.

Table 5.5
Industrial Relations Referrals to the Labour Court, 2000, 2010 and 2018

Activity	2000	2010	2018
Breach of REA	64	328	0
Appeals (from rights commissioners in 2000 and 2010 and from adjudication officers in 2018)	147	184	194
Cases referred directly by the workers or both parties under Industrial Relations Act 1969	130	130	70
Cases referred from conciliation	315	229	132
Cases referred directly under Industrial Relations Act 1990 (exceptional circumstances)	0	1	0
Industrial Relations (Amendment) Act 2001/2004	0	7	2
REA/JLC/Code of Practice/ERO/Agreement	5	114	1
Total	**661**	**993**	**399**

Source: Labour Court annual reports.

Employment Law Functions

Although it was initially established as an industrial relations body, the Labour Court now has a significant employment law remit, being the sole appellate body for employment law cases from the WRC adjudication service since the Workplace Relations Act 2015. Appeals must be made within forty-two days unless there are exceptional circumstances. The functions of the court in the area of employment law are to:

- determine appeals of adjudication officer decisions under employment legislation;
- determine complaints that adjudication officer decisions have not been implemented under certain employment laws – the Protection of Employees (Fixed-Term Work) Act 2003; the Protection of Employees (Part-Time Work) Act 2001; the National Minimum Wage Act 1997; and Safety, Health and Welfare at Work Act 2005;
- decide on applications for (temporary) exemptions from the obligation to pay employees their entitlements under the National Minimum Wage Act 2000;
- approve and vary collective agreements, as provided in some employment laws like the Organisation of Working Time Act 1997 and the Protection of Employees (Part-Time Work) Act 2001.

Each party is required to send copies of their written submission to the court and to the opposing party, and there are different time limits on these submissions depending on whether the case concerns unfair dismissal/employment equality or one of the other employment laws. Parties should consult the Labour Court Rules to ensure they satisfy procedural requirements. The Labour Court generally hears the case *de novo*, meaning it hears the case again in its entirety. It makes a legally binding decision, which can only be appealed to the High Court and only on a point of law, reinforcing the position of the Labour Court as a court of last resort. Ten per cent of WRC adjudication decisions in 2018 were appealed to the Labour Court. Over half of these concerned unfair dismissals, the organisation of working time or employment equality, and almost 70 per cent of appeals were made by workers (Labour Court 2019). A significant proportion of cases do not reach a decision because they are withdrawn or settled beforehand. This is not an unusual phenomenon as referrals to a state body often provide an incentive for parties to reach a settlement themselves rather than have an arbitrator make the decision for them.

A key difference between industrial relations and employment law cases concerns the outcomes. In industrial relations disputes the remit of the court is to 'resolve disputes', but in employment law cases the court has less discretion in regard to how it reaches its decisions and it must follow the legislation's provisions with regard to redress (actions it can take to award a successful claimant). The Labour Court can uphold, overturn or vary the decision of the WRC adjudication officer.

Challenges for the Workplace Relations Commission and Labour Court

Prior to the Workplace Relations Act 2015, there was general consensus that reform of the state bodies was necessary. While some of the reforms proposed by then Minister Richard Bruton TD were welcomed, other parts of the proposed changes were controversial – in particular, the provisions that (i) WRC adjudication hearings would be held in private, (ii) WRC adjudications would be held by a single officer rather than a panel, and (iii) adjudication officers and Labour Court officers would not be required to have a legal qualification. When these changes were proposed, they were criticised in a report approved by members of the former EAT and by the members of the Employment Bar Association (Sheehan 2012; Wall 2012). However, Minister Bruton proceeded with the changes, arguing that 'in any reform agenda you will have people who have done very well out of the existing system and they will throw up reasons why you should not change it' (Wall 2012).

While there has been general acceptance of the new institutions and processes, there have also been challenges. One challenge has been a judicial review pursued by someone who had used the WRC's adjudication service. He has argued that parts of the Workplace Relations Act 2015 contravene the Irish Constitution, which provides that justice shall be administered in courts established by law by judges and shall be administered in public (*Zalewski v Adjudication Officer & Ors* [2019] IESC 17). The case was heard by the Supreme Court in 2019 and the court concluded that Mr Zalewski had *locus standi* to pursue the constitutional challenge, meaning he has the status or qualification to take the action against the WRC. The full case is due to be heard again by the High Court in 2020. Should Mr Zalewski be successful, this will present significant challenges to the current legislation and will raise questions about how employment law cases should be dealt with by the state.

An additional challenge that relates to the powers of the WRC arose in a Court of Justice of the European Union (CJEU) decision in 2018. In a case concerning discrimination the CJEU considered the role of the WRC in enforcing EU equality law. It concluded that, as the WRC was conferred powers to enforce EU employment law, the principle of primacy of EU law requires the WRC, if needed, to disapply national employment legislation that may conflict with EU law (*Minister for Justice and Equality, Commissioner of An Garda Síochána* v. *WRC, Ronald Boyle and Others Case* C-378/17). Some have argued that the decision was 'wide ranging' and introduced 'radical change to the Irish legal framework for the resolution of disputes' (McDermott 2019), while the WRC has expressed scepticism that the impact will be as significant as suggested (Prendergast 2019a).

In terms of operational issues for the state bodies, the new structures may increase efficiencies but they are unlikely to change the trend of the state having to increasingly deal with large numbers of individual employment law cases. We have already noted that Ireland's legal system has an individualist orientation in contrast to other legal systems, which have a collective orientation (O'Sullivan *et al.* 2015a; Teague 2009). The high usage of the WRC and Labour Court emphasises the high degree of reliance on institutional usage, and this has been attributed to the growth in workplace procedures and the requirement in some procedures that parties refer an issue to the state bodies should a dispute remain unresolved (Wallace and McDonnell 2000; Wallace and O'Sullivan 2002). A further operational challenge for the WRC and Labour Court will be the likely increase in activity arising from additional groups of workers gaining access to its services who had previously been prohibited from using them. The Industrial Relations (Amendment) Act 2019 granted Garda representative bodies access to the WRC and Labour Court, and this has significantly widened the scope of workers who will come under the ambit of the state bodies in 2020.

DISPUTE RESOLUTION IN THE PUBLIC SECTOR

The state is the main employer in the country, with some 351,300 public service employees and a further 56,500 employed in semi-state bodies in 2019 (CSO 2019c).

Dealing with large groups of employees through collective (as distinct from individual) bargaining offers substantial advantages to state employers and governments. While public sector industrial relations have been of particular concern since the foundation of the state, the relative importance of public sector industrial relations has grown in recent years. Among the factors driving this are the diverging union density rates between public and private sectors, a concern with quality of the delivery of public services and increased efficiencies, the impact of privatisation of former state companies, the impact of austerity on public sector pay and services during the economic recession, resurgent industrial action in the public sector during the economic recovery, and the series of public sector agreements dealing with pay and conditions. While recognising the differences between the public and private sectors, Cox and Hughes (1989: 99) suggest it would be inappropriate to view public sector industrial relations as inherently different.

There is, however, one distinctive area – the provision for third-party institutions – embodied in a range of internal C&A schemes. McCarthy (1984: 35) writes that the exclusion of some public servants appeared to have been based on the grounds 'that their inclusion might lead them to take a view of their relationship with their employer, the government, which would be excessively and improperly adversarial in character'. The government eventually conceded a C&A for civil servants on a temporary basis in 1950, which was made permanent in 1955. This was followed by schemes for teachers, Gardaí and officers of local authorities, health boards and vocational educational committees. The 'conciliation' stage generally consists of a conciliation council, involving equal numbers of staff (employee) and official (employer) representatives. Issues that are not resolved may proceed to arbitration, provided they are arbitrable under the terms of the particular scheme. All of the schemes provide for an arbitration board with representatives of the official and staff sides. The boards are chaired by a jointly agreed independent chairperson appointed by government, usually eminent senior counsels (McGinley 1997). The finding of the board is sent to the Minister for Finance and the other appropriate ministers, who have one month to approve the report or submit it to the government. Under the local authority and health board schemes, the management or staff side have the option of rejecting the decision at arbitration. In the other schemes an award can only be refused by moving a Dáil motion to reject or amend it. This course of action is rare but it has happened on two occasions: in 1953 and 1986. Since the late 1990s, employers and unions in some areas of the public service have agreed to abandon their C&A or change their avenues for resolving claims and disputes in favour of using the WRC/Labour Court, e.g. the health service, local authorities, Teachers' Union of Ireland, academic staff of institutes of technology and Gardaí. These developments are hardly surprising given what Frawley (2002) notes as the more flexible and pragmatic approach of the state bodies compared to the inflexibility of C&A schemes.

Wage-Setting Institutions – Joint Industrial Councils (JICs) and Joint Labour Committees (JLCs)

While negotiation or collective bargaining at an industry level is common in many Western European countries (e.g. Germany), most private sector collective bargaining (negotiations on pay and conditions between an employer and employee representatives) in Ireland occurs at the level of the organisation. Collective bargaining at an industry level means that every employer in the same industry would pay the same wages, or at least same minimum wages, to its employees. In Ireland the only industry-type bargaining that occurs is through JICs, associations established under the Industrial Relations Act 1946 with the objective of promoting harmonious relations between workers and employers. They are made up of worker and employer representatives and an independent chairperson, and their primary activity has been to negotiate pay and conditions for groups of workers. JICs may be registered with the Labour Court and there were five registered JICs in 2018:

- Boot and Shoe Industry of Ireland;
- Dublin Wholesale Fruit and Vegetable Trade;
- Construction Industry;
- Security Industry;
- Contract Cleaning Industry.

There were also two unregistered JICs for Electrical Contracting and State Industrial Employees.

JLCs are statutory bodies established under the Industrial Relations Act 1946, which are generally created to protect vulnerable workers in employments where there is low pay and poor collective bargaining, typically as a result of low unionisation levels. The JLCs' function is to set legally binding minimum pay and conditions of employment for groups of workers in particular sectors through documents known as employment regulation orders (EROs). Like JICs, JLCs are comprised of employer and worker representatives and an independent chairperson. The following JLCs were in existence in 2019:

- Agricultural Workers;
- Catering;
- Contract Cleaning;
- Hairdressing;
- Hotels;
- Retail, Grocery and Allied Trades;
- Security.

In 2019 the Labour Court recommended the creation of a new JLC for the English language teaching sector, which has had a series of disputes over pay and conditions.

Some of the JLCs have been inactive, and in some cases (Hotels; Catering; Retail, Grocery and Allied Trades) the inactivity is due to employer associations not engaging with them. Without employer participation, the JLCs have not set any minimum pay and conditions so workers in those industries are not entitled to more than that already specified in employment legislation. The Security and Contract Cleaning JLCs are the most active.

Up until the late 2000s, JICs and JLCs existed with little public policy attention or controversy. Any criticisms of them were generally dealt with by negotiation between employer organisations and trade unions sitting on the bodies themselves. However, this pattern has changed with a series of legal cases taken against JLCs and JICs by employers and new employer organisations. An employer organisation for the fast-food industry, the Quick Service Food Alliance (QSFA), initiated a legal case in 2008 against the JLC for the catering industry, on the grounds that it was unconstitutional because it set legally binding regulations which, according to the Irish Constitution, only the Oireachtas has the authority to do (*John Grace and Quick Service Food Alliance Limited and the Catering Joint Labour Committee, the Labour Court, Ireland and the Attorney General* [2011] 3 IR 211). The motivation behind the legal case was that employers in the newly created QSFA were dissatisfied with the operational and structural aspects of JLCs, they were reacting to the improved enforcement of JLC pay and conditions by labour inspectors, and they believed the minimum pay rates they set were too high (O'Sullivan and Royle 2014; Turner and O'Sullivan 2013). In 2011 the High Court found in favour of the QSFA and deemed that the processes of setting EROs was unconstitutional, meaning that all the existing EROs became immediately invalid. In a similar case a group of electrical contracting employers successfully took a legal case, using the same constitutional arguments as the QSFA, against the REA wage mechanism. In *McGowan and others* v. *the Labour Court, Ireland and the Attorney General* [2013] IESC 21, the Supreme Court concluded that Part III of the Industrial Relations Act 1946, establishing REAs, was unconstitutional, and therefore they were struck down.

In another development, around the time of the legal cases, the government agreed in 2010 to review the JIC and JLC systems as part of an agreement with the International Monetary Fund/EU/European Central Bank for a financial bailout in the recession. The implication of undertaking such a review was that the JICs and JLCs might be acting as a barrier to employment. The subsequent review concluded that both systems should be retained but radically reformed (Duffy and Walsh 2011). Following this, the government introduced the Industrial Relations (Amendment) Act 2012 and the Industrial Relations (Amendment) Act 2015 to implement the review's conclusions and to satisfy the High Court and Supreme Court judgments in relation to wage-setting mechanisms. The current wage-setting mechanisms provided for under the 2012 and 2015 Acts are discussed below.

Registered Employment Agreements (REAs)

An REA is an agreement on the remuneration or the conditions of employment of workers made between a trade union(s) and employer(s) or employer association, and their agreement is registered in the Register of Employment Agreements. Historically, REAs were sector-wide agreements set by JICs but the Industrial Relations (Amendment) Act 2015 changed their focus. A REA is now only binding on the parties to the agreement, meaning they do not automatically extend to cover workers across an entire sector. Either party can apply to register an agreement with the Labour Court and it must be satisfied of a number of issues, including that:
- all parties agree that the agreement should be registered;
- the trade union involved is substantially representative of the relevant workers;
- the agreement provides that, if a trade dispute occurs between workers to whom the agreement relates and their employers, industrial action or a lockout shall not take place until the dispute has been submitted for settlement by negotiation;
- registering the agreement would promote harmonious relations between workers and employers and avoid industrial unrest.

In 2019 there were three REAs, covering workers in Dublin Bus and Bus Éireann, certain workers in Freshways Food Co. and temporary veterinary inspectors engaged by the Department of Agriculture, Food and the Marine.

Employment Regulation Orders (EROs)

An ERO is an SI setting out wages and conditions of employment applying to specified grades or categories of workers in a particular sector. The employer and worker representatives on a JLC can make proposals for an ERO but, in doing so, the JLC has to consider a range of factors such as the financial interests of employers, the desirability of maintaining fair and sustainable minimum rates of remuneration, competitiveness, and levels of employment and unemployment. The proposed ERO has to be considered by the Labour Court, and if it adopts the proposals, these must be approved by the minster and the Oireachtas. There are two EROs in existence – one for the contract cleaning industry and one for the security industry. The EROs set legally binding minimum pay rates for all contract cleaning and security workers covered by them, as well as conditions such as working hours, facilities, death-in-service benefit and sick pay. The sectors are characterised by low-paid work but the EROs raise the minimum pay rates to above the national minimum wage. In addition, the minimum conditions also cover areas not legislated for elsewhere in employment legislation, giving additional protections to workers. For example, the ERO for the security industry provides that workers who enter the industry have the right to a contract of employment with a minimum of twenty-four hours per week after six months' service, making security workers the only group in the country who are legally entitled to a minimum number of hours' work.

Sectoral Employment Orders (SEOs)

The Industrial Relations (Amendment) Act 2015 provided for the making of SEOs. These essentially replace the previous function of REAs in relation to standardised pay and conditions for large groups of workers in a sector. SEOs are documents setting legally binding minimum pay and conditions for a particular class, type or group in an economic sector. To set an SEO, a trade union and/or an employer organisation must make a request to the Labour Court to initiate a review of remuneration, sick pay and pension schemes of workers in an economic sector. The trade union or employer organisation making the request must show they are substantially representative of workers or employers in the relevant sector, respectively. In undertaking a review the Labour Court must consider a range of issues such as employment, competitiveness and remuneration in other sectors. Notably, it does not need the agreement of all trade unions and employer organisations to set an SEO. The Labour Court can make a recommendation to the minister about setting minimum pay and conditions for workers in a sector, and a proposed SEO must be approved by the minister and Houses of Oireachtas. In 2019 SEOs were in place for the electrical contracting sector, the construction sector, and the mechanical engineering and building services contracting sector. Other sectors where groups are considering applying for an SEO include the early years sector, meat processing and windfarms (Higgins 2019b).

In the case of EROs and SEOs the legislation includes 'inability to pay provisions', meaning that an employer who is in financial difficulty can apply to the Labour Court to get a temporary exemption from the remuneration and conditions set.

CHALLENGES TO WAGE-SETTING MECHANISMS

Despite the legal challenges by employers noted above, the continuing existence of EROs and the emergence of SEOs show that employers in some sectors see benefits to having standardised pay and conditions in a sector. SEOs can help to raise industry standards and prevent a so-called race to the bottom. This is of particular concern to some employers in industries like contract cleaning, security and construction that are characterised by tendering competitions, which can incentivise businesses to compete for tenders by paying lower wages. The EROs and SEOs try to create a level playing field in tendering where all employers must pay at least the same rates. For example, an employer body, the Mechanical Engineering and Building Services Contracts Association (MEBSCA), noted that when there was no sectoral pay mechanism between 2013 and 2018, 'contractors from outside the state, with a lower cost base, enjoyed a competitive advantage over Irish mechanical contractors' (MEBSCA/CIF 2019). Indeed, before an

SEO was introduced for the mechanical engineering sector in 2018, MEBSCA voluntarily agreed a pay deal with trade unions covering workers in all the firms affiliated to MEBSCA.

Some employer organisations continue to oppose sectoral-level pay and conditions. As noted earlier, some JLCs, like those in hotels and catering, are inactive and employers in these sectors do not have the same economic incentives to have legally binding pay and conditions that security, cleaning and construction employers do. Employer associations like the Irish Hotels Federation have argued that JLCs would negatively impact competitiveness and profitability while ICTU has argued that JLCs are needed to tackle exploitation of workers and the casualisation of jobs. In the case of SEOs there continues to be opposition to the electrical contracting SEO by an employer organisation, the National Electrical Contractors of Ireland. In 2019 it obtained a High Court injunction which prevents the application of certain parts of the 2019 SEO, relating to pensions and sick pay, from being applied until a judicial review is heard by the courts. Another employer organisation, the Association of Plumbing and Heating Contractors Ireland, has also suggested it might launch a legal challenge against the SEO for mechanical engineering (Higgins 2019c). These employer organisations represent smaller employers and their opposition to standardised pay rates reflects the tensions that exist between the different interests of small and large employers.

CONCLUDING COMMENTS

This chapter has reviewed the role of key institutions in employment relations. Bodies such as the WRC and Labour Court perform a necessary function of helping employers and employees to resolve disputes. The chapter also reviewed changes made to wage-setting mechanisms, which were introduced by government in response to new developments in Irish industrial relations, specifically the sustained efforts by some employers to abolish standardised wage setting and, somewhat unusually in the history of Irish industrial relations, employers using legal cases to pursue their objectives. In addition, these challenges have come from new employer bodies that have not had the experience (or perhaps the desire) to negotiate with trade unions.

Chapter 6

Individual Employment Law

INTRODUCTION

At the root of the employment relationship is the common law contract of employment, with its power to command and duty to obey. Although management still retain the power to 'hire and fire', this prerogative has been considerably restrained by a plethora of legislative initiatives. The principal purpose of labour law is to regulate, to support and to restrain the power of management and the power of organised labour (Kahn-Freund 1977). Employment legislation may be viewed as a countervailing force, attempting to redress the unequal bargaining power of the individual vis-à-vis the employing organisation. The process of legislative intervention in the employment relationship can be traced back as far as the 1349 Ordinance of Labourers, when wage ceilings were imposed on both artisans and labourers in the 'Black Death' era of severe labour shortages. Since the 1970s, there has been significant expansion of employee rights through employment legislation, often in response to Ireland's membership of the European Community or Union.

Legislation covers many aspects of the employment relationship but not everything. For example, many issues relating to bonuses, company car use, employees' use of the Internet at work, sick pay, and organisations' monitoring of employees are generally not regulated by employment legislation in Ireland. Many countries have established specialised fora for dealing with employment disputes and legal cases which are usually either part of the civil courts or, as in Ireland, are state bodies outside of the courts system. In Ireland the Workplace Relations Commission (WRC) and the Labour Court are the state dispute resolution and employment rights bodies. This chapter reviews a selection of the key employment laws which grant rights to individual workers from the beginning of the employment relationship until it ends, including in relation to terms of employment, minimum wages, equality, health and safety, dismissal and redundancy legislation (see Table 6.8 for a list of employment laws). The aim of the chapter is to give a brief overview of key pieces of legislation (see also Table 6.8 at the end of the chapter) but readers should consult legal texts for in-depth examinations of each piece of law.

The chapter begins with a discussion of two critical questions. First, how useful is employment law? The law is not a panacea for all workplace problems, and there are advantages and disadvantages to workers and also to trade unions in their representation of workers. Second, when is an employee not an employee? Determining the employment status of workers is fundamental to establishing individuals' rights, i.e. are they employees or independent contractors? A myriad of legal tests and cases have developed to help distinguish an employee from an independent contractor but the increasing complexity of employment relationships means employment status continues to be the subject of disputes.

Using Employment Law: The Advantages and Disadvantages

The critical benefits of employment law are that it counteracts the power imbalance in the employment relationship and promotes social justice (Heery 2011). Employment law sets a floor of rights for workers and provides an avenue for them to pursue those rights, which is arguably increasingly important given the decline in union density. There is generally no fee to pursue legal cases through the WRC and Labour Court, and both workers and employers can represent themselves, though many will choose to bring a representative like a union official, employer association official or solicitor/barrister. By pursuing legal cases, workers may highlight unfair practices in an organisation which can lead to changes in how organisations deal with people management issues. Even amongst organisations with no history of legal claims, many have established policies and procedures to avoid employees taking a case and to help them defend potential cases. For employers, legislation defines the boundaries of their obligations to workers and also workers' responsibilities, though of course much of the nature of the employment relationship cannot be set in stone. No employment legislation or employment contract can define exactly the amount of effort needed of workers, and many employers recognise that they must offer pay and conditions in excess of the legal minima to attract and motivate workers.

The growth in employment legislation and the decline in union density have contributed to changes in how workplace conflict is dealt with. Conflict has shifted from collective forms to individual forms, with people increasingly attempting to exercise their rights through employment law and legal cases rather than through industrial action. This has led to criticisms that there has been a 'juridification' (or legalisation) of the employment relationship, that conflict has become individualised, that the law is complex for individuals to understand and navigate, and that even if a worker wins a case, penalties may be low (Colling 2009). Even when employment law exists on an issue, it is not always the rational or optimal option for workers (Table 6.1), but if they do pursue a legal case, it can take take time to process, which leaves a period of uncertainty for workers and employers. In addition, and unlike collective bargaining, employment law by its nature generally imparts the same rules across an economy and therefore often cannot customise regulations to the needs of particular workers or organisations.

For trade unions, employment law represents somewhat of a 'catch-22'. On the one hand, unions can use employment law as a floor upon which to negotiate enhanced terms of employment, and employment law is most advantageous where strong worker organisation can enforce rights and incorporate them into collective agreements. A survey of Irish union officials found that over half had threatened the use of the law in negotiations with employers (O'Sullivan *et al.* 2015a). Trade union officials have identified employment law as useful in their work, particularly in protecting vulnerable groups in the labour market. For these reasons, unions have lobbied the government to introduce employment laws, most recently in relation to tipping practices in hospitality and to workers' 'right to disconnect' from work technology. On the other hand, the law can have some negative effects on trade unions. For example, almost 60 per cent of union officials in a survey believed that the law encourages people to use an individual route to protect their rights rather than a collective route (O'Sullivan *et al.* 2015a). In this vein, it has been argued that the law can to some extent supplant the role of unions.

Not all countries have experienced the same trend of increasing legalisation and individualisation of workplace conflict. For example, the number of people taking individual employment law cases against organisations is much lower in Sweden than in Ireland. Why is that? Swedish law places greater onus on trade unions and employer associations to resolve individual and collective conflicts in the workplace without going to a state body, and the law places greater obligations on employers to negotiate with unions (O'Sullivan *et al.* 2015a; Teague 2009). So workplace conflict in Sweden is addressed through collective means while Irish law has a more individual orientation.

Table 6.1
Case Study
The Limits of the Law

The economic recession which began in 2008 resulted in wide-scale redundancies. Employment legislation provides that employers must give workers a certain amount of notice when they are made redundant and that workers are entitled to redundancy pay after two years' service. However, some organisations announced full or partial closure of sites with little or no notice to workers, and while some offered statutory redundancy pay or more, others provided no redundancy pay and some owed wages to workers. This resulted in workers staging sit-ins and occupying premises – for example, in 4Home Superstores, Game, HMV, La Senza and Thomas Cook. The occupations were motivated by workers' perceptions of procedural and substantive injustice and they were angry about the unilateral and abrupt nature of employer actions (Cullinane and Dundon 2011). The limitations of employment law are evident in such cases. Exercising their rights under employment law would require each worker to submit an individual legal case to a state body but it could be months before a hearing and decision. In the meantime, workers would have no leverage to force the employers or liquidators to negotiate with them, especially since some company headquarters were based outside of the country. In addition, some workers were looking for redundancy payments higher than the minimum stated in legislation given their fears about future unemployment. Workers appeared to believe they had no alternative option to workplace occupation. The outcome of the occupations was 'the ability to change employer strategy away from unilateral action and force them back to the table for further negotiation, assisted by third-party mediation', and the relatively small number of occupations, it has been argued, sent signals to other organisations to handle redundancies with caution to avoid embarrassing publicity (Cullinane and Dundon 2011: 637).

THE START OF AN EMPLOYMENT RELATIONSHIP

Employment Status – When is Someone an Employee and Not an Employee?

In many countries, legal, tax and social welfare systems classify people in the labour market as either employees or self-employed, independent contractors and then apply different rules, rights and obligations on each. However, distinguishing between who is an employee and who is a self-employed person is not always clear-cut and for decades there have been disputes about the classification. These disputes generally centre on claims by workers that they have been misclassified by an employing organisation as a self-employed, independent contractor instead of being classified as an employee. Similarly, state bodies responsible for social welfare and tax can investigate relationships between workers and employers to ensure they are classified correctly. The deliberate misclassification by employing organisations of workers as self-employed instead of as employees is known as 'disguised', 'sham' or 'bogus' self-employment, and has been identified as prevalent in particular sectors such as construction, food processing, aviation and information technology. Bogus self-employment basically means that, on paper (a contract), a person is labelled as self-employed but the nature of their job, and their relationship with the employing organisation, would suggest they satisfy the criteria of an employee. The reasons for deliberate misclassification generally stem from the fact that it can be cheaper for employing organisations to classify workers as self-employed because of lower social insurance contributions (PRSI) and, in the area of employment law, employing organisations have much fewer legal obligations and responsibilities towards self-employed contractors than towards employees. The different outcomes from being classified as an employee or a self-employed person are outlined in Table 6.2.

Disputes around employment status are not unique to Ireland and many countries are grappling with such issues. In recent years a significant number of disputes over employment status have occurred in so-called gig companies in the transport and food delivery sectors. For example, workers with Uber and Deliveroo have undertaken protests, strikes or legal cases in the UK, France, Ireland, the Netherlands, the US, Australia and South Africa on the issue of employment status. The business model of gig companies is to act as an intermediary between workers and customers, and they seek to engage people on a self-employed basis but workers have claimed that the level of control the companies have over them means the companies should classify them as employees. There have been conflicting outcomes in legal cases taken by workers across countries, with some state bodies/courts deciding that the workers are employees or workers, while others have decided that they are self-employed contractors. Cases of this nature are likely to continue given the growth of gig companies.

The contract of employment is the legal basis of the employment relationship and is central to the interpretation and application of statutory rights. As with the basic law of contract, it requires that there be (1) an offer from the employer, which is accepted by the employee; (2) consideration (or remuneration) from the employer for work done;

Table 6.2
Differences in Outcomes Between an Employee and Self-Employed Worker

Employees	Self-Employed
PRSI: Employees earning at least €352 per week pay 4 per cent PRSI and employers pay 8.7–10.95 per cent PRSI for employees earning over €386 per week	Pay 4 per cent PRSI
Covered by all employment laws	Covered by very few employment laws, e.g. no legal entitlement to holidays, maternity/paternity leave, unfair dismissals protection, redundancy pay
Covered by employers' insurance	Responsible for their own insurance
The employer is responsible for processing the employees' tax/PRSI	Responsible for processing own tax and PRSI
Entitled to many social welfare benefits	Entitled to fewer social welfare benefits

and (3) an intention to create a legal relationship. The contract may be concluded on an oral or written basis.

Common law (judge-made law) has long distinguished between contract *of* service (i.e. with an employee) and a contract *for* service (i.e. with an independent contractor), and over time case law has developed tests to help differentiate between the two in disputes. These tests have examined issues such as:

- does mutuality of obligation exist, i.e. is there an obligation on one side to provide work and an obligation on other side to do work?
- how much control does the employing organisation have over the individual?
- how integrated is the individual in the business?
- what is the nature of the entire arrangement between the employer and the worker?

A Code of Practice for Determining Employment or Self-Employment Status of Individuals provides guidance on employment status. It sets out the common characteristics of someone who is an employee and someone who is self-employed (see Table 6.3). Though not legally binding, it is helpful and persuasive in distinguishing employees from independent contractors.

In Ireland the vast majority of employment legislation grants rights to employees who are individuals who enter into a contract of employment, which is a contract *of* service. However, a small number of laws have a slightly wider coverage, including contracts of service but also contracts whereby an individual agrees with another person to do or perform personally any work or service for that person or a third person. Laws which have this wider definition include the National Minimum Wage Act 2000, the

Table 6.3
Criteria Characterising an Employee and a Self-employed Worker

A Worker is Normally an Employee If They:	A Worker is Normally Self-Employed If They:
Are directed by someone how, when and where to work	Control how, when and where the work is done
Supply labour only; do not supply materials/equipment other than small tools of the trade	Provide the materials, equipment and machinery for the job
Receive a fixed wage; are entitled to extra pay or time off for overtime; receive payments to cover travel expenses	Control costs and pricing; provide their own insurance cover
Cannot subcontract/hire other people to do the work	Can hire other people to complete the job
Are not exposed to financial risk; do not assume any responsibility for investment in the business; do not have the opportunity to profit from sound management	Own a business; are exposed to financial risk; assume responsibility for investment and management in the enterprise; have the opportunity to profit from sound management
Work for one person or one business	Can provide the same services to more than one person or business at the same time
Work set hours	Control their working hours

Source: Code of Practice for Determining Employment or Self-Employment Status of Individuals.

Employment Equality Acts 1998–2015 and the Payment of Wages Act 1991. Legal cases about this wider definition are rare but a recent example is *Moyne Veterinary and Natasha Nowacki* (Determination No. EDA198 2019), where a veterinary practice claimed a vet was not covered by equality legislation because she was not an employee. However, the vet claimed she satisfied the definition of 'personally executing work', and the Labour Court agreed with her argument. The European Court of Justice has noted that, under EU law, a 'worker' is someone who satisfies 'the essential feature of an employment relationship', which is that 'a person performs services of some economic value for and under the direction of another person in return for which he receives remuneration' (*Lawrie-Blum* v. *Land Baden-Württemberg* (1986) Case 66/85). The EU has recently moved to enhance the minimum rights afforded to workers under the EU Directive on Transparent and Predictable Working Conditions 2019/1152.

Wedderburn (1986) argued that the variety of legal 'tests' to determine employment status had splintered in the hands of the judiciary and that it was 'not practicable to lay down precise tests' or a 'hard and fast list'. He suggested that most courts appeared to apply the 'elephant test' for the employee, i.e. an animal that is difficult to define but easy to recognise when you see it! However, in the landmark decision of *Henry Denny and Sons (Ireland)* v. *The Minister for Social Welfare* (1998), the Irish Supreme Court provided a measure of clarity on this issue and sent out a strong message to employers that, despite the stated nature of the relationship, a court will look at the reality of the arrangement. Indeed, the EU has recently noted that the issue of employment status should be determined 'by the facts relating to the actual performance of the work and not by the parties' description of the relationship' (EU Directive on Transparent and Predictable Working Conditions, para. 8). An interesting judgment was made in a 2006 case, *Murphy* v. *Grand Circle Travel*. Ms Murphy claimed she had been under duress when she signed an agreement with the company identifying her as an independent contractor. Despite the company having a significant level of control over Ms Murphy in her job, 'Moriarty J in the High Court said he found it difficult to believe that someone who had asserted herself so well before the court could have been pressurised in the way she claimed' (MacMahon 2019: 456). This is interesting because, as MacMahon (2019) notes, it diverges from many other cases in which judges have taken into account the inequality in bargaining power between the organisation and worker.

In recent years, there has been growing concern about the prevalence of bogus self-employment and trade unions have argued that the government needs stronger measures to address the issue. The Competition (Amendment) Act 2017 provided a definition of a 'false' self-employed worker and a 'fully dependent' self-employed worker, and in 2019 the government indicated it would introduce measures to tackle bogus self-employment, including revising the Code of Practice for Determining Employment or Self-Employment Status of Individuals.

Agency Work

In 2019 a total of 2.6 per cent of employees identified themselves as agency workers (CSO 2019b). The rights of agency workers are regulated by the Protection of Employees (Temporary Agency Work) Act 2012, introduced because of the EU Directive on Temporary Agency Work 2008/104/EC. The Act states that for the duration that an agency worker is on an assignment with a 'hirer', they are entitled to the same basic working and employment conditions as those of employees of the hirer doing the same or similar work to the agency worker. Basic working and employment conditions refer to pay, working time, rest periods and breaks, night work, overtime, annual leave or public holidays. The entitlement to equal pay does not generally apply to agency workers who have a permanent contract with the agency and are paid a particular rate between assignments, a provision known as the 'Swedish derogation'. In the UK it was announced that the 'Swedish derogation' would be abolished in 2020 after evidence of its potential abuse by some agencies.

DURING THE EMPLOYMENT RELATIONSHIP

Terms of Employment

There is no law which obliges employers to provide employees with a written contract about every aspect of the employment relationship. They are only obliged to provide employees with certain information about basic conditions of employment. When an employee starts a job, they are entitled to information about the terms of their employment, and two pieces of legislation cover this. Under the Employment (Miscellaneous Provisions) Act 2018, an employer is obliged to give a written statement to the employee with five 'core' terms of employment within five days of starting a job. These five terms are:

1. the full names of the employer and the employee;
2. the address of the employer;
3. the expected duration of a temporary contract or expiry date of a fixed-term contract;
4. the rate or method of calculation of the employees' remuneration and the pay reference period for the purposes of the national minimum wage (NMW);
5. the number of hours which the employer reasonably expects the employee to work per normal working day and week.

In addition to these five terms, the Terms of Employment (Information) Act 1994 obliges an employer to give an employee who has one month's service a written statement with an extended list of terms and conditions of employment. This statement must be provided within two months of the employee taking up employment.

Minimum Wages

The majority of countries in the EU have a statutory NMW, except Austria, Denmark, Finland, Italy and Sweden, which set minimum wages in collective agreements. Ireland introduced an NMW for the first time through the National Minimum Wage Act 2000. Up until 2000, Ireland had minimum hourly rates of pay for selected groups of workers such as in hotels and hairdressing but not a minimum wage for the whole country. The 2000 Act established an adult hourly minimum wage and also allowed for certain groups to be exempt from the full rate. These groups included trainees, young people with certain levels of work experience and disabled workers. The Employment (Miscellaneous Provisions) Act 2018 amended these provisions by abolishing the trainee minimum rate and simplifying the language around young people's minimum pay rates (Table 6.4). In addition, the Act has an 'ability to pay' clause, which allows an employer to apply to the Labour Court for a temporary exemption from the full NMW rate. The National Minimum Wage (Low Pay Commission) Act 2015 provided for the establishment of an independent Low Pay Commission, which makes recommendations to the government on the NMW, but the government retains decision-making power on any changes to the rate. Labour force data indicate that 8.1 per cent of employees earned the NMW or less in 2018 (McGuinness *et al.* 2019). A profile of minimum wage employees is shown in Table 6.5.

Table 6.4
National Minimum Wage Entitlements

Age of Worker	Entitlement
Below eighteen years of age	70 per cent of the NMW
Eighteen years of age	80 per cent of the NMW
Nineteen years of age	90 per cent of the NMW
Twenty years of age and up	Full NMW

Table 6.5
Who are Minimum Wage Employees?

- 54 per cent work in wholesale and retail or accommodation and food
- Average age is 31
- 55 per cent are female
- 59 per cent work part-time; 33 per cent are on temporary contracts
- 17 per cent have third-level education

Source: McGuinness *et al.* (2019).

The National Minimum Wage Act 2000 stipulated how employers can construct the NMW by noting which elements of pay are 'reckonable' or 'non-reckonable', that is, can be included or not included in the calculation of the hourly wage. The question of what should or should not be included in making up a worker's NMW has become controversial in recent years, with claims made that some employers have been using tips in their calculation of the NMW and that tips were being withheld from workers. The legislation is not very clear in this regard. It notes that tips or gratuities paid into a central fund managed by the employer and paid through the payroll are non-reckonable in calculating the NMW but it does not mention tips which are paid in cash. During 2019 trade unions called for greater regulation of tipping practices and a number of pieces of legislation were proposed by the government and opposition parties.

Certain groups of workers are legally entitled to different minimum wage rates, which are usually higher than the NMW, and these are set through employment regulation orders, registered employment agreements and sectoral employment orders (see Chapter 5).

EMPLOYMENT EQUALITY

The introduction of equality legislation was primarily prompted by Ireland's membership of the European Community (EC) and the necessity to comply with Community directives. Initial equality legislation was focused largely on gender. The Anti-Discrimination (Pay) Act 1974 and the Employment Equality Act 1977 were passed to implement the equal pay and equal treatment directives, respectively. The subsequent consolidation of these two measures into one Act – the Employment Equality Act 1998 – has significantly altered and broadened the law in this area. The purpose of the Employment Equality Acts 1998–2015 is to promote equality between employed persons, outlaw discrimination on nine grounds (Table 6.6), provide for equal pay and equal treatment between men and women, outlaw harassment, sexual harassment and victimisation, and place responsibilities on employers with regard to accommodating people with disabilities. The Acts are significant pieces of legislation because of the breadth of their scope in employment. The following reflect the substantial scope of the law:

- The legislation prohibits discrimination in relation to job advertising; access to employment, training, promotion or regrading; classification of posts; collective agreements; and conditions of employment, including in regard to shifts, dismissals, redundancies and disciplinary measures.
- It applies to employment agencies, vocational training and membership of bodies like trade unions and professional associations.
- It provides that employers have vicarious liability, meaning that anything done by a person in the course of his or her employment shall be treated as done also by that person's employer for the purposes of the Acts, whether or not it was done with the employer's knowledge or approval.

Table 6.6
The Nine Grounds

Gender, civil status, family status, sexual orientation, religious belief, age, disability, membership of the Travelling community, race.

Discrimination under the Acts occurs where, on any of the nine grounds, a person is treated less favourably than another is, has been or would be treated. Unlawful discrimination can take place on a direct or indirect basis. Direct discrimination occurs where a person is treated less favourably than the way in which a person with or without the relevant characteristic (gender, age, disability, etc.) is (or would be) treated in similar circumstances. For example, claims in relation to discrimination at the recruitment and selection stage are common and often revolve around alleged discriminatory questions or treatment at interview (McMahon 2001). A high-profile example of this occurred in 2017 when a government department was ordered by the WRC to pay €7,500 to a woman who was discriminated against on grounds of civil status and family status in a job interview. In the interview for a private secretary position, she was asked by a minister of state, 'I know I shouldn't be asking this, but are you a married woman? Do you have children? How old are your children?' The WRC adjudication officer was satisfied that the interview process was 'tainted by the fact that these questions were raised and allowed to be raised' (*A Government Employee and A Government Department* ADJ-00005366).

The definitions of indirect discrimination were reshaped in the 1998 Act to take into account the decision of the Supreme Court in the *Nathan* v. *Bailey Gibson Ltd* case and EU definitions (Moffatt 2006). Basically, indirect discrimination involves an apparently neutral practice or requirement that effectively serves to discriminate against a particular category because fewer of its members are able to comply with it. The practice or requirement must not be objectively justifiable for the employment in question. For example, a minimum height requirement for a job where height was not a relevant factor might operate to indirectly discriminate against women as a group as opposed to men.

For the purposes of an equal pay claim, pay is interpreted as basic wages, together with all direct and indirect financial benefits and incentives (excluding pension benefits). The person or persons claiming – group claims are common – must compare themselves with an actual comparator. The complainant must also satisfy the following conditions. He/she must be:

- working under a contract of service;
- working for the same or an associated employer; and
- performing 'like work' with the comparator, i.e. either (a) his/her work is identical, (b) job differences are insignificant in relation to the job as a whole or (c) his/her work is 'equal in value' in terms of criteria such as responsibility, skill, physical or mental effort.

Harassment refers to any form of unwanted conduct related to any of the discriminatory grounds while sexual harassment refers to any form of unwanted verbal, non-verbal or physical conduct of a sexual nature. In both cases the unwanted conduct has the purpose or effect of violating a person's dignity and creating an intimidating, hostile, degrading, humiliating or offensive environment for the person. Whether or not someone intended to violate a person's dignity may be irrelevant; it is the effect of their behaviour on someone that is important. Harassment can be verbal, physical or written, such as through text messages and Facebook posts, and can occur inside or outside the workplace, in the course of someone's employment (Irish Congress of Trade Unions 2018). Other forms of harassment include excessive monitoring of someone's work or excluding someone from social activities (Code of Practice on Harassment and Sexual Harassment at Work 2012).

Redress Routes

Between 1998 and 2015 the Equality Tribunal was the forum for mediating and adjudicating on employment equality cases but this was abolished under the Workplace Relations Act 2015. Since 2015, all equality cases can be referred to the WRC, though

gender-based complaints, or claims in relation to the infringement of the equal pay or
equal treatment directives, may be brought directly to the Circuit Court. The WRC
offers mediation and adjudication services in equality cases (see Chapter 5). If mediation
does not resolve issues or either party refuses mediation, the case will have an adjudication
hearing. During a hearing, the individual taking the case (the complainant) has to
establish a prima facie case of discrimination, i.e. show that the employer has a case to
answer. After doing so, the burden of proof shifts to the employer and they are required
to defend their actions in the claim. If discrimination or harassment is found, a WRC
adjudication officer can make an order for redress, including compensation, equal pay,
arrears for equal pay, equal treatment or an order for a particular course of action to be
taken. Either party may appeal a decision of the WRC adjudication officer to the Labour
Court and from there to the High Court on a point of law only. The number of equality
cases has expanded significantly since the introduction of the 1998 legislation. There
were only about 100 claims in 2000, while in 2018 almost 1,500 complaints were made
under the Employment Equality Acts to the WRC (WRC 2019).

The equality legislation is complex and detailed, and there are many additional
provisions not discussed here, including exemptions to discrimination protection,
employer responsibilities regarding employees with disabilities, as well as positive actions
employers can take to achieve workplace equality.

In addition to enforcement bodies, legislation has also provided for the creation of
equality promotion bodies. The Employment Equality Agency was established under
the Employment Equality Act 1977 and this was renamed as the Equality Authority
under the 1998 Act. The Equality Authority was subsequently merged with the Human
Rights Commission to form the Irish Human Rights and Equality Commission
(IHREC) under the Irish Human Rights and Equality Commission Act 2014. The
functions of the IHREC are:
- to protect and promote human rights and equality;
- to encourage the development of a culture of respect for human rights, equality
  and intercultural understanding in the state;
- to promote understanding and awareness of the importance of human rights and
  equality in the state;
- to encourage good practice in intercultural relations, and to promote tolerance and
  acceptance of diversity in the state and respect for the freedom and dignity of each
  person;
- to work towards the elimination of human rights abuses, discrimination and
  prohibited conduct.

LEAVE AVAILABLE TO PARENTS
Parents are entitled to a number of forms of leave – maternity, paternity, parental, parents
and adoptive. It is unfortunate that the labels are so similar, as this creates confusion for
employers and employees. With the exception of parental leave, the individual may be

entitled to paid benefit from the state while on leave. There is no legal obligation on employers to pay the employees during any of the forms of leave though some may voluntarily choose to provide some pay to 'top up' state benefits. The individual retains employment rights while on leave, they have the right to return to their position and it is illegal for organisations to penalise employees or dismiss them for exercising their leave rights. Each piece of legislation contains rules about how someone can apply for leave and the way in which leave can be accessed, so individual laws should be consulted.

The Maternity Protection Acts 1994–2004 grant a number of rights to pregnant employees regardless of their length of service, including:

- a right to twenty-six weeks' paid *maternity leave* and sixteen weeks' further unpaid leave;
- a right to time off – without loss of pay – for antenatal and postnatal medical visits;
- time off from work or reduced working hours for breastfeeding.

There is no qualifying service or minimum weekly working hours requirement to secure the right. The employee can choose the exact dates of the maternity leave but the period should cover the four weeks prior to and post confinement. While on paid maternity leave, the employee's employment rights are preserved. She is entitled to return to her job after the birth, provided she notifies the employer of her intentions in writing at least four working weeks in advance of the envisaged date of return. Pregnant workers and workers who are breastfeeding or who have recently given birth may also have a right to 'health and safety leave' if workplace conditions or tasks put the employee's or baby's health and safety at risk. In addition, if a doctor certifies that night work is unsuitable, and the worker cannot be moved to day work, she may become entitled to such leave. Employers who dismiss an employee while she is pregnant or after returning from pregnancy must be able to justify the dismissal on grounds unrelated to pregnancy. Employment rights bodies take such pregnancy-related dismissals very seriously and workers have won significant levels of compensation in unfair dismissal cases.

Other forms of leave for parents are as follows:

- *Paternity leave* rights have historically lagged well behind maternity leave in Ireland and paternity leave in other EU countries. The Paternity Leave and Benefit Act 2016 provides for fathers or spouse/civil partner/cohabitant of the mother of the child to statutory paternity leave of two weeks that can start within the first six months of the birth or adoption. This right extends to the employee regardless of how long they have worked for an employer.
- The Parent's Leave and Benefit Act 2019 entitles each parent of a child up to one year with the right to two weeks' *parent's leave* to enable them to care for the child.
- The Parental Leave Acts 1998–2019 provide the opportunity to parents to take unpaid *parental leave* from work to care for children. Since September 2019, parents can take up to twenty-two weeks' leave for each eligible child up to the age

of twelve or sixteen for a child with a disability and, in general, they must have one year's continuous service with an employer to be eligible for the entitlement. This entitlement to leave will increase to twenty-six weeks from September 2020. There is no entitlement to state benefits during the leave period.

- An adoptive mother or sole adoptive father is entitled to up to twenty-four weeks' paid *adoptive leave* and additional sixteen weeks' unpaid leave under the Adoptive Leave Acts 1995–2005.

In addition to leave for parents, the Carer's Leave Act 2001 entitles employees with one year's service to *carer's leave* of between 13 and 104 weeks should they need to provide full-time care to someone.

HEALTH AND SAFETY AT WORK

Over the past thirty years, the subject of health and safety has shot up the list of human resource management priorities in Ireland. This prioritisation has been propelled by the enactment of comprehensive and detailed health and safety legislation and extensively supplemented by case law precedents. Related to these facts is the reality that many Irish employers have awoken to the priority now accorded to health and safety matters as a result of a series of court awards in the area (Butler 2007). This dimension has become even more pronounced since 2004, with the establishment of the Personal Injuries Assessment Board (PIAB), whose role includes the assessment of compensation due to an injured person where those injuries arise from workplace accidents. Prior to the establishment of the PIAB, employees suffering personal injuries could issue proceedings (depending on the potential size of the claim) in the District Court, Circuit Court or High Court. Successful plaintiffs were awarded the majority (if not all) costs. In an attempt to reduce such costs (and employers' premium payments), the insurance industry and employers sought reform of the system, and this culminated in the establishment of the PIAB.

Garavan (2002) claims that with the eventual recognition of the immensity of such costs to employers – and the prospect of reduced costs through safer and healthier work environments and practices – it was apparent that more proactive safety management practices were emerging in many Irish workplaces. In this regard, the enactment of the Safety, Health and Welfare at Work Act 1989 was also relevant. However, health and safety issues remain problematic. While the rate of worker fatalities declined from almost 4 in 100,000 workers in 1998 to 1.9 in 100,000 workers in 2017, Ireland has a relatively poor comparative ranking within the EU for worker fatalities (Health and Safety Authority (HSA) 2018). In addition, an estimated 481,612 days were lost in 2016 due to work-related injury, though this was much lower than the 810,900 days lost in 2015 (HSA 2018). In terms of work injury and illness, high-risk sectors include agriculture, forestry and fishing; construction; health and social work; transport and storage; and industry (HSA 2018).

Under common law (judge-made law), the Irish courts have decided that employers are obliged to exercise reasonable care towards employees in relation to health and safety matters. The implications of common law are that employers must:

- provide a safe system of work;
- ensure the provision of competent fellow workers;
- provide safety equipment and effective supervision; and
- provide a safe place of work.

The provision of a safe system of work obliges the employer to show that the system provided is at least in accord with the general practice of that trade. Accordingly, an employer would not be responsible solely because an accident occurred in the course of the job; some element of negligence has to be involved. The failure to employ competent fellow workers (including subordinates and supervisors) may, but rarely does, constitute the basis of a claim. Nevertheless, the employer may be found liable for the careless action of one employee which causes injury to another employee (i.e. vicarious liability). The common law obligation to provide proper safety equipment (for the purpose of avoiding staff exposure to risk and injury) includes a requirement that management take reasonable steps (up to and including disciplinary action) to ensure the use of that equipment. The provision of a safe place of work requires that the workplace be organised in the interests of health and safety. This obligation also extends to a customer's premises. Consequently, if workers are injured while working on a customer's premises they may successfully claim against their own employer.

In recent years the employer's duty to provide a safe workplace (hitherto confined to reducing risks to the physical health of the employee) has been extended to one's psychological well-being. Several court decisions have established the obligation on employers to prevent foreseeable risk from stress in work and numerous successful claims have also been brought in relation to bullying and harassment at work (McMahon 2009). Notably, the aforementioned Employment Equality Acts 1998–2015 provide a redress route for those scenarios where harassment (under one or more of the nine grounds) is alleged.

The main legislation in this area is the Safety, Health and Welfare at Work Act 2005 and its large number of accompanying regulations, notably the Safety, Health and Welfare at Work (General Application) Regulations 2007. The legislation applies to all employers, employees (including fixed-term and temporary employees) and self-employed people at work. The Act sets out the rights and obligations of both employers and employees. The overarching obligation on employers is to ensure the safety, health and welfare at work of his or her employees through undertaking risk assessments, having a written safety statement, having a safety representative, and training and consulting of employees. Employees also have obligations, particularly to take reasonable care to protect the safety of themselves and others who might be affected by their acts and omissions. Directors and senior managers may be prosecuted for breaches of the legislation by the HSA in the District or Circuit Court, potentially resulting in large fines or imprisonment. Employees can also take legal cases to the WRC against an employer if they believe they were penalised or dismissed for exercising their rights under health and safety legislation.

The HSA is the statutory body responsible for ensuring workers are protected from work-related injury and ill health through conducting workplace investigations, inspections, enforcement, research, developing codes of practice and providing information. The HSA undertook over 9,000 inspections and investigations under safety, health and chemicals legislation in 2018 (HSA 2019). Between 2005 and 2015 there were 292 prosecutions for health and safety offences, 226 of which were corporate offences and 66 involved prosecutions against individuals. Courts tend to impose fines rather than imprisonment so that, up until 2017, 'no individual has been sent to prison following conviction for a health and safety offence' (Law Reform Commission 2017: 98).

WORKING TIME

Maximum Hours and Rest Breaks

The Organisation of Working Time Act 1997 was introduced to transpose into Irish law the EU Directive 93/104/EC on the organisation of working time and the directive viewed the regulation of working time as a health and safety issue for workers. The Act provides, amongst other things, for:

- A maximum average working week of forty-eight hours, over a reference period.
- Minimum rest breaks of fifteen minutes per 4.5 hours worked and thirty minutes per six hours worked. Shop employees, whose hours include hours between 11.30am and 2.30pm, are entitled to a minimum break of one hour during those hours (see Organisation of Working Time (Breaks at Work for Shop Employees) Regulations, 1998).
- Minimum daily and weekly rest periods.
- Minimum annual leave entitlements of four weeks for full-time workers and 8 per cent of hours worked in the case of part-time or casual employees.
- Entitlement to a premium payment or paid time off in lieu for Sunday work.
- Special restrictions on hours worked at night, in particular night work involving particular hazards.

The Protection of Employees (Part-Time Work) Act 2001 was introduced as a result of the EU Framework Directive on Part-Time Work. The Act extended the protection of employment legislation to all part-time workers regardless of the number of hours worked per week. It entitles part-time workers to pro rata treatment with comparable full-time colleagues in relation to conditions of employment such as pay and annual leave.

Zero-Hours and Low-Hours Work

While the Organisation of Working Time Act 1997 regulated maximum working hours, it provided no right to minimum working hours. There have been calls in Ireland and internationally to regulate work with no minimum hours or with unpredictable hours such as 'zero hours', 'on-call', 'on-demand', 'gig' or 'intermittent' work (O'Sullivan *et al.* 2019). The EU Directive on Transparent and Predictable Working Conditions 2019/1152 states that 'workers who have no guaranteed working time, including those on zero-hour and some on-demand contracts, are in a particularly vulnerable situation' (para. 12), and seeks to provide a number of new minimum rights aimed to promote security and predictability in employment relationships. In Ireland trade unions campaigned for legislation to regulate employments where workers were getting no hours or a low number of hours, and some industrial disputes have arisen over working hours, such as that between the Mandate trade union and Dunnes Stores in 2015 (Murphy *et al.* 2019).

The Irish government commissioned a study into zero-hours and low-hours work, and the study subsequently identified two types of contracts that involve zero-hours work (O'Sullivan *et al.* 2015b). One is a zero-hours contract which does not guarantee any hours of work to an individual but they are required by the employer to be available for work. The Organisation of Working Time Act 1997 provided that someone on this type of contract was entitled to be paid for 25 per cent of the hours for which they were expected to be available or fifteen hours, whichever was the lesser. For example, if someone was required to be available for four hours but they were never called into work, they were entitled to one hour's pay. Because the person was required to be available, this increased the likelihood of them being classified an employee. The second type of contract was labelled an 'if and when' contract, which does not guarantee any hours of work to an individual but they are not contractually required by the employer to be available for work. No legislation had regulated this type of contract and it was argued that someone on this contract may not satisfy the criteria of being an employee and therefore could be excluded from many employment rights (MacMahon 2019).

The government subsequently introduced the Employment (Miscellaneous Provisions) Act 2018. The legislation prohibits the use of zero-hours contracts except:

- where the work is of a casual nature; or
- where work is done in emergency circumstances; or
- where short-term relief work covers routine absences for the employer.

If an employer fails to require an employee to work 25 per cent of their contracted hours, the employee is entitled to a minimum payment (equivalent to 25 per cent of the contract hours or fifteen hours, whichever is lesser; this is a similar provision to the Organisation of Working Time Act). However, when an employer is calculating this payment, the minimum payment must be three times the national minimum wage or three times the minimum hourly rate of remuneration established by an employment regulation order (Chapter 5).

In addition, the legislation sought to regulate situations where an employee regularly works more hours than the number stated in their contract. The legislation provides that employees who regularly work more hours per week over a twelve-month period than is stated in their contract shall be entitled to be placed in a 'band' of weekly hours specified in the Act. The law provides for a scale of eight 'bands' of hours from band A with 3–6 hours, rising to band H with 36+ hours. The employer must move the employee to the new band of hours within four weeks of the written request by the employee unless:

- the employer has evidence that the employee's claim is unsupported;
- there has been significant adverse changes to the business or job during or after the twelve-month period; or
- the employee's higher level of working hours noted in their request was a temporary situation that no longer exists.

The legislation has been praised and criticised. It has been argued that the provision on 'banded hours' may provide additional protection to workers but the Act has been criticised for only regulating one type of zero-hours work and for not regulating 'if and when' contracts (MacMahon 2019; O'Sullivan *et al.* 2017).

Temporary Contracts

The Protection of Employees (Fixed-Term Work) Act 2003 seeks to protect fixed-term employees by ensuring that they cannot be treated less favourably than comparable permanent workers and that employers cannot continually renew fixed-term contracts. The law provides that workers cannot be given successive fixed-term or specific-purpose contracts that last longer than four years, after which they become entitled to a contract of indefinite duration, unless an employer has objective grounds to keep them on a temporary contract. Research indicates that the proportion of workers under the age of thirty-one on temporary contracts increased between 2004 and 2016 (Nugent *et al.* 2019), and temporary contracts are particularly prevalent in parts of the public sector (Cush 2016; Ward 2014). As a result of lobbying by education trade unions, the government introduced special protections for teachers in 2015 and third-level lecturers in 2016, and both groups are entitled to a contract of indefinite duration after two years of successive contracts.

Ending the Employment Relationship – Dismissals

Dismissals are one of the most contentious areas of the employment relationship and a source of significant conflict. Despite unfair dismissals law being in place since the 1970s, claims of unfair dismissals still account for a substantial proportion of employment law cases. In some EU countries legislation prevents employers from dismissing employees until certain actions take place, such as an employer getting approval from an external state body. This is not the case in Ireland. The Unfair Dismissals Acts 1977–2015 do not prevent an employer from dismissing someone. The purpose of the legislation is to provide redress (or reparation) for employees unfairly dismissed but this only happens if an employee pursues a legal case after a dismissal. An employee can only prevent a dismissal temporarily, or temporarily stop an employer from hiring someone else in their job, if they obtain a court injunction, which is a court order. Individuals who have sought such injunctions have tended to be in high-level positions, and examples include a chief financial officer with Easytrip in 2018, a commercial and risk advisor with the Electricity Supply Board (ESB) in 2018, a Munster Rugby fitness coach in 2012, a group buyer with Brown Thomas in 2011 and a general manager with Citywest Hotel in 2010. Individuals may also take legal proceedings in the civil courts against an employer for wrongful dismissal, which can involve significant cost and can be highly public.

The Unfair Dismissals Act 1977 was an important development in Irish labour law, with considerable consequences for the workplace. Under its provisions, once an employee has been continuously employed for one year, he/she has a right to claim unfair dismissal. Employees with less than one year's service can pursue a claim under the Industrial Relations Acts 1946–1990, but the disadvantage of this for the worker is that the outcomes are not legally binding on an employer. The Unfair Dismissals Acts do not cover everyone; for example, civil servants and persons employed in the defence forces and Gardaí are excluded. They cover an employee and someone hired through an employment agency. When an individual takes an unfair dismissals case to the WRC, they must first show that they are actually covered by the Act's provisions and also that a dismissal actually took place. Once an individual satisfies these issues, the burden of proof in dismissal cases normally resides with the employer, i.e. the employer must show that they acted reasonably. When a WRC adjudicator is deciding on whether an employer acted reasonably, they examine the events and behaviours of each side leading up to the dismissal. In particular, they assess two key areas: the substantive reason for the dismissal and the process of the dismissal.

Reasons for the Dismissal

The Act provides that a dismissal will automatically be deemed to be unfair if it can be attributed to:
- trade union membership or activities (including industrial action);
- involvement in civil or criminal legal proceedings against the employer;
- religious or political opinion, race/colour, sexual orientation, age, membership of the Travelling community;
- pregnancy or matters connected with pregnancy;

- the exercise of maternity, adoptive, carer's, parental, parent's or paternity leave; or holiday and minimum wage entitlements;
- making a protected disclosure under the Protected Disclosures Act 2014.

Those areas where a dismissal may be justified can largely (but not exclusively) be categorised under the following headings: (1) conduct, (2) capability/competence and (3) redundancy.

Conduct

This may take the form of a single act of gross misconduct or a series of such minor acts where the employee disregards relevant warnings. Dismissal arising out of alleged employee gross misconduct is one of the most common case types. A fair dismissal under this heading normally occurs where the essential employer–employee relationship of trust is undermined. It generally applies to matters of abuse of sick leave, substance or alcohol abuse, criminal convictions, dishonesty, disobedience, breach of the duty of loyalty and fidelity, and violence or intimidation (Madden and Kerr 1996). However, the WRC has not established any objective standard of 'unacceptable conduct' that justifies dismissal. Instead, it opts to evaluate the dismissal decision on the grounds of 'reasonableness' given the particular circumstances of each case. Consequently, one cannot construct a comprehensive and rigid checklist of conduct types that will be adjudged by the WRC to be unacceptable and warrant dismissal. It is also relevant under this heading that 'off-duty' conduct – where it has implications for the employer – may be adjudged to constitute grounds for fair dismissal.

Capability/Competence/Qualifications

Dismissal pertaining to the capability, competence or qualifications of the employee, relating to work of the kind which he/she was employed to do, may be justified. Of course, these dismissals often require the employer to advise the employee in advance of the relevant failure, thus enabling him/her to improve. Competence-related dismissals tend to arise where the employee is alleged to demonstrate substandard work. Capability-related dismissals normally surface under the guise of attendance at work. Employees who are persistently late, or fail to attend work regularly, are commonly adjudged to be incapable of performing the work they were employed to do. Indeed, even in those cases of persistent or extensive absence due to illness, the furnishing of medical certification may not protect an employee from a dismissal, where the employer has satisfied him/herself that a return to work is not imminent. Medical certification can even provide conclusive proof that an employee is not capable of undertaking their work. Related to this, it is also notable that the Employment Equality Acts 1998–2015 have implications for employers considering dismissal on the grounds of incapability due to long-term absence. That is, treating a person with a particular disability the same as everyone else is not enough to comply with the law. When faced with such scenarios, prior to taking any precipitative action, employers need to: (1) establish whether the long-term absentee has a disability, (2) establish whether the disability is causing the absence, (3) establish the prognosis that the employee will/will not return to work and (4) consider providing reasonable accommodation to facilitate the employee to undertake the work.

Redundancy

Dismissals on the grounds of redundancy usually constitute fair dismissals. Accordingly, dismissal attributed to the employer ceasing business, reducing workforce size or no longer requiring the employee's kind of work is not unfair. The onus of proving that a genuine redundancy situation exists resides with the employer and the claimant can question the validity of the redundancy. The employer is precluded from using arbitrary criteria when selecting staff for redundancy, although he/she may successfully plead special reasons for departing from an agreed or traditional procedure. Employers also need to be careful that fair procedures are followed in carrying out the selection for redundancy (McMahon 2011). Workers with at least 104 weeks' continuous service, and who have not reached retirement age, are entitled to redundancy pay under the Redundancy Payments Acts 1967–2014. They are entitled to two weeks' pay per year of service plus one week's lump sum, and the calculation of a week's pay is subject to a statutory ceiling of €600.

Any Other Substantial Reason

This has been a 'catch all' category and can include issues such as damage to the employer's business or failure to conform to certain behavioural norms during one's private life, as in *Flynn* v. *Sister Mary Anne Power and The Sisters of the Holy Faith* (1985).

Constructive Dismissal

The term 'constructive dismissal' relates to those cases where the employee terminates their contract on account of the employer's conduct. For example, an employee would be entitled to terminate the contract where the employer's conduct constitutes a significant breach of the contract or in the event of the employer indicating that he/she no longer intends to be bound by one or more of its essential terms, such as refusing to pay wages. Another commonly cited reason in cases for constructive dismissal is an employee claiming that an employer had not adequately dealt with, or protected them from, bullying and harassment. Unlike most other unfair dismissal claims, the onus of proof rests with the employee to show that the employer breached the contract of employment and that the employee acted reasonably. There is:

a high burden of proof on an employee to demonstrate that he or she acted reasonably and had exhausted all internal procedures formal or otherwise in an attempt to resolve her grievance with his/her employers. The employee would need to demonstrate that the employer's conduct was so unreasonable as to make the continuation of employment with the particular employer intolerable. (*Employment Appeals Tribunal in An Employee* v. *An Employer* UD1421/2008)

The Process of Dismissal

A common determinant of a WRC adjudicator's decision is whether the employer followed fair and proper procedures prior to the dismissal. This requirement of procedural fairness is rooted in the common law concept of 'natural justice' and in the provisions of the 1937 Constitution. In addition, the Code of Practice on Grievance and Disciplinary Procedures (Statutory Instrument 146/2000) issued by the WRC provides a clear rationale for the adoption of such procedures and is admissible in proceedings. Related to this, the four basic obligations in regard to disciplinary procedural arrangements identified from case law by Fennell and Lynch (1993: 230–1) are:

- **Investigation:** An inadequate investigation of the situation on the part of the employer may give rise to a dismissal being deemed unfair.
- **Hearing:** The employer must put the relevant case to the employee, thus allowing him/her to respond. A refusal to allow representation at such meetings is likely to render the dismissal unfair.
- **Warning:** Prior to dismissal for misconduct or poor performance the employee should generally be given a series of warnings, thus providing him/her with an opportunity to improve.
- **Proportionate penalties:** A dismissal will be adjudged to be unfair where the employer is seen to overreact, that is, if a lesser penalty would have been more appropriate in the circumstances.

The normal reaction of the WRC and its predecessors to a failure to follow fair procedures (especially those laid down in a collective agreement or written disciplinary procedure) is to adjudge the dismissal to be unfair. However, the extent of the contribution on the employee's part to the circumstances resulting in the dismissal will be taken into account in deciding the appropriate remedy. Consequently, even if the WRC concludes that a dismissal was unfair, it might consider it appropriate to deduct compensation to which the employee would otherwise be entitled. It is also notable that the Circuit Court has concluded that an otherwise 'fair dismissal' does not automatically become unfair due to its procedural defects (Madden and Kerr 1996). Nevertheless, a direct result of this 'procedural fairness' factor is that there have been widespread changes in companies' procedures (see Chapter 7).

Unfair Dismissal Remedies

The Act provides for three remedial options in the event of a dismissal being deemed to have been unfair: reinstatement, re-engagement and compensation.

Reinstatement:
- The employee resumes the same position on the same contractual terms as those applying prior to the dismissal event, i.e. the dismissal is effectively deemed never to have occurred.
- The employee will be paid back-pay, their seniority will be maintained and their pension rights restored.
- Reinstatement is only awarded where the employee is adjudged not to have contributed to the dismissal in any way.

Re-engagement:
- The employee resumes the same or a reasonably suitable different position, on contractual terms which are deemed reasonable.
- The employee's continuity of service is not affected but the period between the dismissal and the re-engagement effectively constitutes suspension without pay.
- Reinstatement is only awarded where the employee is adjudged not to have contributed to the dismissal in any way.

Financial compensation:
- The most common remedial option. A maximum of 104 weeks' net remuneration (including bonus payments). An employee incurring no loss can be awarded compensation up to a maximum of 4 weeks' remuneration.
- Payment takes into account the estimated future loss, pension loss and the present loss of remuneration (from the date of dismissal to the date of hearing) incurred by the employee.
- Earnings since dismissal, where applicable, are deducted and there is an onus on an applicant to seek to mitigate their loss, but social welfare payments are not deducted.

While the redress of reinstatement or re-engagement awards appears to assume that the relationship between the parties is not beyond repair, past research found that re-employment was also ordered where the employer acted extremely badly or where the claimant was in great hardship (Fennell and Lynch 1993).

MINIMUM NOTICE WHEN ENDING EMPLOYMENT

The Minimum Notice and Terms of Employment Acts 1973–2005 entitle employees to a minimum period of notice (or pay in lieu of notice) prior to dismissal. Employees with at least thirteen weeks' continuous service are entitled to minimum notice of one week, and the longer the employee is with an employer, the longer the length of notice they are required to receive. The maximum notice is eight weeks for someone working for an employer for fifteen years or more. Employees with at least thirteen weeks' service are also obliged to give their employer one week's notice of terminating their contract and this amount of notice applies no matter how long an employee is with an organisation. Typically though, employment contracts tend to include notice provisions that are greater than those provided in legislation and, if so, employers and employees are obliged to abide by these.

WHEN A BUSINESS IS SOLD TO ANOTHER BUSINESS

The European Communities (Protection of Employees on Transfer of Undertakings) Regulations (2003), known as TUPE, are designed to protect employees' jobs in the event of a change in their employer's identity, where the business resumes its activities after it has been sold as a going concern. Subject to the employer's right to effect redundancies for economic, technical or organisational reasons involving changes in the workforce, employees are entitled to continue working under the same terms of employment with service and contractual rights maintained. Employee pension rights – aside from those provided for by social welfare legislation – do not transfer to the new employment. However, where there is a pension scheme in operation in the original employer's business at the time of the transfer, the legislation provides that:

- if the scheme is an occupational pension scheme covered by the Pension Acts (1990), then the protections given by that legislation apply; and
- in the case of other pension schemes, the new employer must ensure that rights are protected.

Both the outgoing and incoming employers are also obliged to keep employees informed of developments. An employee whose rights are infringed under the legislation, resulting in dismissal, may bring an unfair dismissal claim to the WRC.

RESTRICTIVE CLAUSES, RETIREMENT AND PENSIONS

Some employment contracts or agreements between an employee and employer can contain clauses which regulate or restrict someone's behaviour after their job has ended, such as in relation to trade secrets or where the employee gets their next job. Employees therefore must check their employment documentation carefully as employers can choose to take legal action against ex-employees for alleged breaches of these clauses (Table 6.7).

If someone's job ends due to retirement, key issues for them are their entitlement to a state pension and the age at which they might be required by their employer to retire. The issue of pensions has become very topical, particularly as the proportion of the population over sixty-five is set to increase significantly in the future and this puts pressure on state resources such as pensions. The state pension is a very important state benefit because of gaps in pension coverage. In 2018 a total of 44 per cent of workers aged between twenty and sixty-nine had no occupational or personal pension (CSO 2019a), and coverage is lower again amongst people not working. While public sector workers are covered by an occupational pension, coverage is much lower in some private sectors. Ireland is one of the few countries in the OECD (Organisation for Economic Co-operation and Development) where it is not mandatory for people to pay into a pension though the government plans to introduce an automatic enrolment retirement savings system for people with no pension coverage in the future.

The age at which people have access to the state pension has increased from sixty-five to sixty-six, and it is planned to rise further to sixty-seven from 2021 and sixty-eight from 2028. These changes created difficulties for people who are required to retire from their employments at sixty-five and experience a gap between employment and access to the state pension. However, political parties campaigning in the general election in 2020 promised to review or reduce the state pension age so the planned increases in pension age may change. In the public sector anyone employed before April 2004 and since January 2013 has a compulsory retirement age of seventy (people employed between April 2004 and December 2012 have no compulsory retirement age), but there is no law on a compulsory retirement age in the private sector. Retirement ages are usually set in employment contracts and have normally been set at sixty-five in the private sector. When setting mandatory retirement ages, employers are required under the Employment Equality Acts 1998–2015 to (i) fix an age which is objectively and reasonably justified by a legitimate aim, and (ii) ensure the means of achieving its aim are appropriate and necessary. So an employer must give serious consideration to the retirement ages they set, and the WRC has established a Code of Practice on Longer Working to give guidance to employers on dealing with retiring employees.

Occupational pension schemes can be the subject of disputes between employers and employees. There are two types of pension schemes. A defined benefit (DB) scheme is one in which the employee will receive a set level of benefits that usually depends on their length of service and their earnings upon retirement. The public sector pension scheme is a DB scheme, and until recently employees' pensions were calculated using their final salary before retirement. However, during the economic recession, the government changed the way in which the pension is calculated for new entrants. For anyone who started employment in the public sector from January 2013, their pension will be based on their average earnings over the lifetime of their employment (known as the 'single scheme') and this is much less beneficial to workers than the previous calculation. In 2019 the Association of Secondary Teachers, Ireland, the Irish National Teachers' Organisation and the Teachers' Union of Ireland called on the government to revert to the final salary pension. A defined contribution (DC) pension scheme is one in which both the employer and employee make contributions but the value of the employee's pension upon retirement depends on a variety of factors such as the amount of contributions paid and the performance of pension investments. DB schemes are considered more favourable to workers than DC schemes, while DB schemes are more expensive for employers. As a result, many private sector organisations have changed from a DB to a DC scheme, leading to disputes with workers such as in Pfizer, Irish Life, Lufthansa Technik Airmotive and AIB.

Table 6.7
Case Study
Getting Another Job and Non-Compete Clauses

Some organisations include post-termination restrictive covenants in employment contracts to protect their business. An example of a restrictive covenant is a non-compete clause, which forbids an employee who leaves the organisation from working for a competitor organisation for a certain period of time and sometimes within a certain geographical area. There is no legislation governing this issue and there are a number of examples of disputes over such clauses in the civil courts. In 2019 Ryanair initiated legal action against its former chief operations officer in the High Court after he left the company for easyJet before the time limit on his non-compete clause ended. The High Court found against Ryanair in its application to prevent him taking up employment in easyJet. In 2013 an ex-employee of Vodafone took legal action against the company in the High Court, seeking a declaration that the non-compete clause in his contract was void and therefore that he should not be stopped from starting a new job with O2 (*Octavio Hernandez* v. *Vodafone Ireland Limited* [2013 IEHC 70]). It is unknown how extensive such clauses are in Ireland but it is estimated that 18 per cent of all workers in the US are covered by them, and there has been increasing concern in the US that such clauses are being used in low-paid workers' contracts and in regard to independent contractors (Belitz 2016).

CONCLUDING COMMENTS

This chapter has provided a brief synopsis of key employment legislation. The law regulates many aspects of the employment relationship but often sets minimum standards which can be exceeded in someone's employment contract. Some aspects are not regulated at all through legislation; for example, there is no employment law which provides employees with a right to overtime pay generally or to sick pay by their employer or to bonuses, so regulations on these and other issues might be regulated in an employment contract or through custom and practice. Many organisations try to ensure that they adhere to their legal obligations, and try to deal with conflict over terms and conditions, by having workplace procedures. These are discussed in detail in the next chapter.

Table 6.8
Summary of Key Employment Legislation

Access to Employment	
Employment Permits Acts 2003–2014	Rules on permission to work for non-EEA nationals

Information to Workers About Employment/Business	
Data Protection Acts 1988–2003; General Data Protection Regulation (EU) 2016/679 (GDPR)	Access to and accuracy of (personal) automated/computer and manual/paper files Rights on the processing of personal data by companies processing the personal data of data subjects residing in the EU
Employees (Provision of Information and Consultation) Act 2006	Right to information and consultation for employees from their employer on matters which directly affect them in undertakings with at least fifty employees
Minimum Notice Act and Terms of Employment Acts 1973–2005	Minimum notice periods on dismissal and terms and conditions of employment
Employment (Miscellaneous Provisions) Act 2018	Employees entitled to a written statement with core terms of employment
Terms of Employment (Information) Acts 1994–2001	Employees entitled to a written statement with extended list of terms and conditions of employment

Treatment of Employees	
Employment Equality Acts 1998–2015	Right of employees to non-discriminatory treatment, protection from harassment

Non-Standard Employment Relationships	
Protection of Employees (Part-Time Work) Act 2001; Protection of Employees (Fixed-term Work) Act 2003	Extends protection of employment legislation to all part-time workers and ensures equal treatment on a pro rata basis with full-time colleagues (2001 Act); and protects fixed-term employees by ensuring that they cannot be treated less favourably than comparable permanent workers and that employers cannot continually renew fixed-term contracts (2003 Act)
Protection of Employees (Agency Work) Act 2012	Equal treatment of agency workers vis-à-vis regular workers in regard to basic working conditions

Working Hours	
Organisation of Working Time Act 1997	Maximum working hours, rest breaks, rest periods, annual leave, public holidays, Sunday working

Table 6.8 (contd.)
Summary of Key Employment Legislation

Protection of Young Persons (Employment) Act 1996	Working hours and age limits for young persons at work
Employment (Miscellaneous Provisions) Act 2018	Regulates zero-hours contracts and banded hours

Pay and Pensions

National Minimum Wage Act 2000 and Employment (Miscellaneous Provisions) Act 2018	Minimum hourly wage depending upon age of workers
Payment of Wages Act 1991	Regulates methods of payment and deductions from wages
Pensions Acts 1990–2009	Administration of pension schemes

Employee Leave

Maternity Protection Acts 1994 and 2004	Right to maternity leave and other protections before, during and after a pregnancy
Adoptive Leave Acts 1995–2005	Right to leave from work in the event of adoption
Carer's Leave Act 2001	Right to leave from work to care for a person in need of full-time care and attention
Parental Leave Acts 1998–2019	Right to leave from work for both parents from the birth or adoption of a child up to the child reaching twelve years of age
Parent's Leave and Benefit Act 2019	Right to two weeks' parent's leave for a child up to one year
Paternity Leave and Benefit Act 2016	Right to paternity leave within the first six months of birth or adoption

Ending/Transferring the Employment Relationship

European Communities (Protection of Employees on Transfer of Undertakings) Regulations 2003	Protects employees' rights in cases of change of ownership of a business
Minimum Notice Act and Terms of Employment Acts 1973–2005	Employees' and employers' right to minimum notice when either party terminates the employment relationship
Protection of Employees (Employers' Insolvency) Acts 1984–2012	Protects certain outstanding entitlements relating to employees' pay in the event of their employers becoming insolvent
Protection of Employment Acts 1977–2014	Employer obligations to consult employees prior to collective (multiple) redundancies and to inform the minister
Redundancy Payments Acts 1967–2014	Right of employees with minimum two years' service to redundancy pay
Unfair Dismissals Acts 1977–2015	Right of employees to challenge a dismissal in a legal forum after the dismissal has taken place

Chapter 7

Collective and Individual Workplace Procedures

INTRODUCTION

This chapter examines the regulation of industrial relations in the workplace. Such regulation is extensively governed by procedures either jointly agreed between union and management or unilaterally determined, normally by management. The procedural regulation of workplace relations has its genesis in collective bargaining, which originated in the second half of the nineteenth century to regulate relations between unions, their members and employers (Pelling 1976). It aimed to introduce norms to limit disputes. As Webb and Webb (1897) pointed out, it was part of union efforts to provide a 'common rule' promoting the equitable treatment of workers. These early collective procedures subsequently influenced procedural regulation in non-union companies, notably in the areas of discipline and grievance, and have also informed the principles incorporated in codes of practice published by state agencies. Apart from their collective origins, there are two other influences on the development of workplace procedures. These are the perspectives offered by organisational psychologists/organisational behaviourists and, most importantly, the growth in legal regulation from the 1970s onwards. This chapter explores the nature of collective agreements, the arrangements for procedural regulation at the workplace, practical prescriptions for dealing with individual workplace disputes and the skills identified as desirable to effectively deal with such issues.

THE NATURE OF COLLECTIVE AGREEMENTS

Collective agreements are commonly used to regulate relations in unionised companies and they are the obvious and standard outcome of a collective bargaining process. Indeed, the International Labour Organisation deems collective bargaining 'to be the activity or process leading up to the conclusion of a collective agreement' (Gernigon *et al.* 2000). As Dunlop (1958) has pointed out, the contents of collective agreements can be divided into *substantive* and *procedural* terms. Substantive terms are concerned with the terms and conditions of employment. Examples of substantive terms include wage rates, overtime and shift work rates, hours of work, holiday entitlements and pension arrangements. Substantive rules are also found in contracts of employment, company rules and handbooks. In contrast, procedural terms lay down the rules for regulating the relationship between the parties and for how substantive terms are to be agreed and changed. These are normally associated with regulation via collective agreements. Examples of procedural terms are union recognition and negotiating rights, management's right to manage, and the ways in which employees can contest management decisions. Procedural terms are normally contained in an overarching agreement – a procedure agreement (or procedural agreement).

Procedure agreements differ in their contents across organisations. Some procedure agreements are short and concise, while others are long and detailed. Agreements may be quite general, or technical and specific (even quasi-legalistic), in terms of how they are drafted and worded. The contents of procedure agreements also vary widely, although they tend to have common elements. They usually contain initial clauses dealing with union recognition and negotiating rights, the competence of both parties and provisions for dealing with disputes when they arise. In the area of individual disputes, procedure agreements will normally contain specific sections dealing with disciplinary and grievance issues. Nowadays, they may also cover individual issues such as gender equality, health and safety, dignity and respect, bullying and harassment, and sexual harassment. However, even in unionised companies such issues are now likely to be specified in a staff handbook. This is because of legal obligations to which organisations are subject, with equality legislation being a notable example.

Disputes procedures are a central part of any procedure agreement. They are most important in collective disputes, but they also cover individual issues. Disputes procedures will invariably contain a peace clause that will normally specify a requirement for local negotiations and referral to third parties, up to and including the Labour Court (or another specified body), in advance of industrial action by either union or management. They may also include arrangements for continued emergency cover in the event of a strike. Individual disputes often require employees to use internal disciplinary and grievance procedures before any referral to a third party.

In some instances a disputes procedure may extend to a no-strike clause. Some no-strike clauses have been inserted in agreements in return for a pay increase and these are only designed to apply for the duration of the agreement. In rarer cases no-strike clauses are designed to be a permanent part of the arrangements between the parties. In such cases some alternative mechanism for the resolution of disputes needs to be specified, e.g. binding arbitration. In some areas of the public sector there is legislative provision for arbitration under the public sector conciliation and arbitration (C&A) schemes, and the government can only refuse to pay an arbitrator's award if it places a motion before the Dáil and that motion is passed. However, that legislation fell into disuse with the development of social partnership agreements in the 1990s, and this has remained the case following the emergence of public sector agreements, with the legislation now considered to be largely redundant (see Table 2.3, Garda Case Study, in Chapter 2).

A key issue in the operation of dispute procedures has been the maintenance or non-maintenance of the status quo while the dispute is in progress. Pluralist writers generally consider that the onus is on the side seeking change to maintain the status quo until procedures are exhausted but this principle was narrowed by the development of functional flexibility in the 1980s. Functional flexibility requires employees to be flexible between tasks, thereby limiting the range of issues over which a status quo requirement applies. Despite this, observation of the status quo can apply as part of the normal requirement on management in unionised companies to negotiate on change. Obviously, a requirement to maintain the status quo has implications for companies in fast-changing technology sectors and this may be one of the reasons that non-unionised companies dominate in that sector. Procedure agreements commonly specify that individual employees are required to accept change and work under protest while appealing a management instruction. However, there are limits to changes that can be required. Arbitrary alterations to an individual's contract can fall foul of unfair dismissals legislation and, depending on the nature of the change, amount to constructive dismissal.

COLLECTIVE AGREEMENTS AND THE LAW

Collective agreements are generally not considered to be legally enforceable. The Commission of Inquiry on Industrial Relations (1981: 214) noted that this reflects the view that collective bargaining – not the law – should be the primary source of regulation in the employment relationship. While the commission's view is generally accepted in industrial relations circles, it is not settled from a legal point of view. To industrial relations observers and practitioners, the legal position can seem quite unclear. In *Holland* v. *Athlone Institute of Technology* (2012), Justice Hogan suggested that collective agreements 'are, in my judgment, not contracts and not enforceable in the legal sense' (Kerr 2017: 898). However, in the same case, Justice Hogan said there was 'no *a priori* rule on the matter', adding 'at most there is a loose presumption that … they are designed to operate *in the sphere of industrial relations only*' (Kerr 2017: 898). A quite opposite opinion was offered by Justice Charleton in the 2016 Supreme Court in *Reid and Turner* v. *Health Service Executive* (HSE). He considered that 'in general, collective agreements bind the union and bind the employer in the ordinary way. They are a contract between two bodies and enforceable as such.' There are strong reasons why collective agreements should not be considered legally enforceable. The main one is that parties in industrial relations generally consider that 'there is no intention to create legal relations'. However, in *Reid and Turner* v. *HSE*, Justice Charleton seemed to strike at this presumption, indicating that it is difficult to argue that no legal effect is intended, and that the onus of proof on those who assert that no legal effect was intended is a 'heavy one' (Kerr 2017: 899).

The impact of the uncertainty over the enforceability of collective agreements was evident in a 2019 Ryanair case where the company successfully applied for a High Court injunction to prevent a strike by the Irish Airlines Pilot Association (IALPA). Among other reasons, Ryanair argued that the proposed strike over terms and conditions was in breach of a collective agreement that required a mediation process to be exhausted before industrial action. Justice McDonald in the High Court found there was a 'fair question' to be tried on the issue of the legal enforceability of that agreement (Goodbody 2019a). In 1985 Kerr and Whyte had considered this a possibility and, despite the Industrial Relations Act 1990 carefully refraining from specifying any requirement that procedures had to be observed in collective disputes, nothing seems to have changed in the intervening years. Justice McDonald's decision indicates that the wording of the agreement between Ryanair and IALPA might lead to a conclusion that the agreement was legally binding. This suggests that the wording of collective agreements can be interrogated by the courts to establish the intent of the parties and not the existence of some a priori principle. In the Ryanair case, as the strike did not go ahead, the dispute itself was not the subject of a full High Court hearing, leaving a continuing uncertainty.

There are other reasons why collective agreements might lack legal enforceability and these are more generally accepted. Neither a trade union nor a union official is normally considered to have a right of 'agency' (Wallace 1989). Agency is where a person or organisation can conclude legally binding agreements on behalf of an individual or organisation. Agency can exist in limited circumstances, most notably when the number of employees is 'small and definite and the matters dealt with are confined solely to that group' (Kerr and Whyte 1985: 161). The aspirational nature of terms of agreements also poses a problem for legal enforceability, a point accepted by Justice Charleton in his *Reid and Turner* v. *HSE* judgment, and this can mean a collective agreement is not capable of legal adjudication.

Some collective agreements are legally binding, most notably where the parties to an agreement have registered them with the Labour Court. Collective agreements can also have legal effect if the parties intended to create legal relations. For instance, the substantive terms of a collective agreement can become legally enforceable through the principle of 'incorporation'. Incorporation describes a process whereby an act of either party permanently alters the contract of employment. Thus, when an employer pays a wage increase provided for in a collective agreement, this normally becomes a contractual entitlement that can only be altered with the employee's agreement. Similarly, a wage reduction specified in a collective agreement can permanently alter the contract of employment not through the terms of the agreement but by its incorporation into the employee's contract of employment (Kerr and Whyte 1985). Some provisions of a collective agreement, however, are not suitable for incorporation.

The legal principle of 'incorporation' does not generally apply in the same way to the procedural elements of an agreement. Nonetheless, procedures covering individual issues such as grievances, discipline, bullying and harassment can also have legal effect. Third parties with legal competence (such as the Workplace Relations Commission (WRC) and the Labour Court, as well as the civil courts) may look at workplace procedures in much the same way that the rules of the road would be regarded in the event of a car accident. It is common to see dismissals declared unfair because the rules of fair procedures and rules of natural justice (which are often specified in disciplinary procedures) have not been observed. Examples include where an employee was not allowed representation during the disciplinary process, if they were not adequately informed of the charge against them, or if they were not allowed an opportunity to respond to any charge.

The absence of legal enforceability does not mean that collective agreements are unimportant. They are 'binding in honour' and the parties to industrial relations set much store on them. Furthermore, third parties such as the WRC or Labour Court are likely to pay careful attention to claims that the terms of an agreement, which were freely entered into, have been breached. Perhaps the most instructive illustration of the need to honour agreements occurred in 2012 when the Croke Park Agreement (CPA) came under pressure during the life of the Fine Gael/Labour coalition government. Tánaiste Eamon Gilmore said: 'If you make an agreement, you keep the agreement, and there's a good reason for that. Because if you break an agreement, the people you make it with are unlikely to reach agreement with you again' (RTÉ 2012a). However, faced with budgetary constraints, and pressure from the troika and public commentators critical of the CPA, this did not preclude government subsequently demanding a renegotiation of the CPA (see Chapter 13).

Renegotiation of agreements is not uncommon and both governments and unions have sought changes to agreements midterm. In 1992 the government achieved reductions in agreed public sector wage increases under the Programme for Economic and Social Progress, while in 2001 trade unions achieved increases above those provided for in the Programme for Prosperity and Fairness. More recently, in 2017 trade unions sought, and achieved, improvements to the pay awards under the Haddington Road Agreement in response to increases to pay and allowances of Gardaí following a Labour Court recommendation in November 2016. At one level these developments demonstrate a lack of certainty attaching to collective agreements and may be regarded as a weakness. However, at another level they indicate their considerable flexibility and capacity (relative to legally binding contracts) to be adapted to changing economic circumstances.

DISCIPLINARY AND GRIEVANCE PROCEDURES

The nature of industrial organisation creates the need for disciplinary measures and gives rise to grievances. Industrial organisations need employees to attend on time, conform to certain behaviour and meet standards of performance, and discipline is one way of seeking to ensure these are delivered. Likewise, employees will typically have expectations of equitable and fair treatment in employment and of an entitlement to bring grievances to management's attention and have them addressed. Both discipline and grievances are then an integral aspect of the employment relationship and, in part, represent an expression of the potential for conflict in that relationship.

Torrington and Hall (1998: 538) describe discipline as the 'regulation of human activity to produce a controlled performance'. This definition draws attention to the essence of discipline as an exercise in control. That exercise of control involves the use of power by one party to the employment relationship (the employer) over the other (the employee), a feature of industrial relations emphasised by radical writers (Fox 1974). A grievance procedure, on the other hand, is 'an operational mechanism which defines, and may limit, the exercise of managerial authority and power through establishing a formal regulatory framework for handling specified issues' (Salamon 1998: 533). In effect, it is explicitly designed to limit managerial control and give the employee a voice to raise concerns over matters that affect them.

Despite the existence of grievance procedures, employees can be reluctant to raise issues, and this is known as employee 'silence' (Donaghey *et al.* 2011). Employee silence has long been acknowledged in the organisational behaviour literature and is seen as arising from ineffective management. In this view, silence is seen as dysfunctional and limits employee input (voice) which might lead to greater efficiency and improved organisational performance. Alternatively, silence can be seen as a rational response to the potential adverse outcomes of exercising a voice option. Examples of adverse outcomes include higher turnover rates, reputational damage, sanctions and management retaliation (Dundon *et al.* 2004). The potential for these outcomes to occur can make employees afraid to utilise a voice mechanism, such as raising a grievance, or can lead them to believe doing so would be futile and not improve their situation. However, writers in the labour process school of employment relations go further. They see the procurement of silence as part of the struggle for control (Beale and Hoel 2011; Holgate *et al.* 2011). Rather than viewing employee silence as something management want to correct, the labour process perspective views employee silence as potentially useful to management, furthering organisational objectives and increasing management control (Donaghey *et al.* 2011; MacMahon *et al.* 2018).

Contextualising Individual Procedures

Historically, conflict over discipline was dealt with at the sole discretion of management. Common law (judge-made law) interpretations did not regard disputes arising out of the contract of employment as being subject to legal adjudication. That approach embodied the principle of 'employment at will' and this is a principle which still applies in the US today, although it is modified by legislation such as the Civil Rights Act 1964. Under the employment at will principle, an employer was entitled to dismiss for any reason or none. As a result, trade unions came to fill the vacuum created by the absence of the law. With collective solidarity, they sought to counterbalance the right of employers to impose discipline unilaterally (Cole 1913). By the 1920s, disciplinary procedures had been developed in some employments (notably public ones), which laid down rules and procedures for disciplinary action (Flanders 1956). Such disciplinary procedures were not entirely detached from the law but borrowed procedural aspects from common law notions of due process and natural justice. Thus, in general, trade unions did not seek to contest management's right to impose discipline but sought to impose requirements on how discipline was to be carried out.

Since it developed over time, the procedural regulation of discipline and grievance was haphazard and sporadic. Flanders (1956: 320) noted 'in many industries the employers' power "to hire and fire" was limited, if at all, only by the restraint imposed by the fear of "trouble"'. This absence of formal regulation at the level of the workplace was highlighted by the UK Donovan Commission, which argued there was a need to put in place workplace procedures for the regulation of industrial relations (Donovan 1968). The commission's approach was based on the pluralist notion of management 'regaining power by sharing it'. Although largely ignored by the political establishment in the UK, the Donovan Commission recommendations had a major impact on the emerging personnel management profession. In Ireland procedural regulation grew substantially (especially in manufacturing industry) from the late 1960s – a development led by personnel management professionals (Wallace 1989). Although emerging in unionised companies, these procedures also came to influence rules for handling discipline and grievance in non-union companies with the introduction of 'parallel procedures' that reflected provisions in unionised companies (Wallace 1989).

Growing legal regulation has promoted greater formality in common law systems that previously eschewed legal intervention in individual disputes (Saundry et al. 2011). Roche and Teague (2011: 439) argue that 'the growth of legislation on individual employment rights may impact on workplace conflict management procedures, as organisations seek to stay on the right side of the law'. The necessity for disciplinary procedures became paramount as a result of the Unfair Dismissals Act 1977. This was despite that Act not laying down procedural requirements for a dismissal to be adjudged fair. In practice, the Employment Appeals Tribunal, which heard cases under the Act, paid great attention to procedural regularity (as arising under the rules of natural justice) when deciding if an employer had acted reasonably in dismissing an employee. The Equality Acts of the 1970s also promoted procedural formalisation, a trend that has been accentuated by the growth in employment legislation since the 1990s (Roche and Teague 2011).

The WRC (previously the Labour Relations Commission) has published codes covering a wide range of issues. Extending beyond discipline and grievance, the codes can have legal implications. While not legally required to be in place, the absence of company procedures in areas such as discipline, bullying and harassment, or equality can make it difficult for an employer to defend a case to a third party. This requirement is highlighted by the *McGuinness* v. *Marco Moreo* (2017) case in which the Labour Court determined that in order 'to avoid liability it is essential for the respondent to establish that it had in place, at the time at which the harassment occurred, arrangements intended to prevent and deal with the occurrence of such content' (Prendergast 2017). Equally, a failure on an employee's part to utilise internal company grievance procedures can lead to a case being lost by the employee irrespective of its substantive merits.

The WRC Codes of Practice on Discipline and Grievance do not prescribe actual procedures but leave it up to organisations to draft their own procedures, taking account of the code of practice. As a result, discipline and grievance procedures can vary quite widely. Table 7.1 contains an example of the contents that disciplinary procedures typically contain.

Table 7.1
Typical Contents of a Disciplinary Procedure

- Indication of conduct and other issues that may lead to disciplinary action
- Provision for a formal pre-disciplinary counselling phase in the case of lesser issues
- Employee is entitled to know the complaint
- Requirement for a full investigation
- Entitlement of employee to representation by shop steward, union official or fellow employee
- Manager hearing the case should not have a personal conflict of interest
- Employee is entitled to challenge any evidence/allegations
- Provision of graded penalties for lesser issues (e.g. conduct, performance); usually an oral warning, written warning(s) and final written warning
- Provision for support action by management to assist improved performance/conduct, e.g. training, use of employee assistance programme
- A step-back provision where, after a defined time period, a warning reverts to the stage below it (i.e. a final written warning becomes a written warning, a written warning becomes an oral warning)
- Removal of warnings from the employee's record following a specified time period
- In cases of alleged gross misconduct, provision for suspension with pay to allow for an investigation
- Provision for suspension/reassignment of duties/dismissal for a first offence for major issues of gross misconduct or persistent failure to address lesser issues
- An appeal to senior management
- Provision for referral to third party in the event that disciplinary action is challenged; this may be absent from a disciplinary procedure in a non-union company but in the event of dismissal is, of course, an option for a former employee

---

The Right to Representation

An entitlement to representation is a central requirement of fair procedures, especially where a discipline interview may have consequences for an employee, and there is an obligation on an employer to inform an employee of this entitlement. The question arises as to how far this right extends, particularly if it includes a right to legal representation, an issue considered by the Supreme Court in *McKelvey* v. *Irish Rail* (2019). That case involved alleged theft through the claimed misuse of a fuel card. McKelvey challenged the internal Irish Rail disciplinary process used because he was not allowed legal representation (Carolan 2019). The Supreme Court determined that the courts should be reluctant to interfere in the 'employers' ability to run fair disciplinary procedures in a timely manner' (Prendergast 2019b). It acknowledged that, in an 'exceptional' case, a right to legal representation might be required, but nothing in the case 'would be beyond the competence of an experienced trade union official' (Carolan 2019). This judgment seems to leave open the question of whether, and under what circumstances, a right to be accompanied by a fellow employee (as often specified in non-union discipline procedures) would meet the requirement of fair procedure in the case of a dismissal.

In the UK Saundry *et al.* (2011: 204) report that in cases of discipline in non-union companies the use of 'non-union companions … did not necessarily help their colleague's case' and could get them 'into more trouble'. This negative assessment arose because fellow employees lacked the requisite skills and knowledge. In contrast, union involvement in the disciplinary process was (surprisingly) positively perceived by managers but only where their role was significant (Saundry *et al.* 2011). Where respondents saw union representation as effective, it tended to be because they were able to persuade employees to own up and make a plea for mitigation, with that being often the most effective strategy (Saundry *et al.* 2011). In weaker unionised or non-unionised companies where they only had a representational role, union involvement tended to be more adversarial and was perceived less favourably by managers (Saundry *et al.* 2011).

There appear to be two main reasons for managers perceiving the role of unions positively in the research by Saundry *et al.* First, having a union test a case will make it less likely that the company will lose it at a subsequent tribunal hearing. Second, the union can 'reality check' the employee – that involves bringing home to them the gravity of their situation and emphasising the need for compliance with management's requirements in the future. As a result, the warning system can work more effectively, and management have reported a benefit from being able to hold on to otherwise good employees in such cases. Saundry *et al.* (2011) suggest that, as was the case historically, unions still seldom challenge management's right to determine and impose discipline.

Management Approaches to Discipline and Grievance

In addition to the influence of collective procedures in non-union companies, there is a distinctly managerial influence on such arrangements and these influences have extended back to discipline in unionised companies. These managerial influences owe much to the work of organisational psychologists and organisational behaviourists, particularly in the US. These approaches are described under the heading of 'corrective' or 'positive' approaches to discipline. The most significant development in management approaches to discipline in Ireland is the *corrective approach*, which appears in the textbooks from at least the 1970s and is now widely espoused. The corrective approach is contrasted with

Table 7.2
Corrective and Positive Approaches to Discipline

Standard Corrective Approach Variant A	Corrective/Positive Approach Variant B	Counselling Positive Approach Variant C
Basic Corrective Approach • A series of warnings provided for, typically oral warning, written warning, final written warning, suspension and/or dismissal • Employee is given an opportunity to improve, except in the case of gross misconduct, where dismissal is specified for a first offence • Normally specifies that a corrective approach should not be punitive but sanctions/penalties are invariably provided for	**Enhanced Corrective Approach** • In addition to all features of Variant A, there is an emphasis on using (i) a diagnostic and (ii) a joint problem-solving approach • A diagnostic approach involves a review of *why* a problem has arisen, e.g. has the employee been properly trained, are the targets reasonable, is there another reason that may entail responsibility on the part of management? • Joint problem-solving between supervisor/manager and employee on *how* the problem is to be resolved and how the employee will meet management's requirements. Emphasis on using counselling rather than penalties, but warnings are also provided for	**Counselling Positive Discipline Variant** • This approach uses problem-solving, as in Variant B. Employees are given a number of staged opportunities to improve. There is no provision for penalties. If they do not meet the employer's expectation and cannot commit to doing so, they are expected to voluntarily resign

the *punitive, coercive* or *negative* approaches in traditional procedures (Hawkins 1982). This can be seen as an attempt to deal with or, alternately, mask the power and control aspects of imposing discipline (Fenley 1998; Osigweh and Hutchison 1989, 1990; Wheeler 1976;).

The terms 'corrective' or 'positive' are used quite loosely in differing texts. In some, the corrective approach is presented as an employee-centred approach to discipline; in others, it merely involves a stepped procedure as developed in standard pluralist 'natural justice' approaches. What various texts identify as a corrective approach can fall anywhere along a spectrum and these are outlined in Table 7.2. A corrective approach may mean little more than the issuing of a series of oral, written and final written warnings. The employee is given an opportunity to improve but there may be little engagement with the underlying issues that have led to the poor performance or behavioural issue. The aim may be to achieve improvement but the punitive element of the warnings is to the fore. It can also be viewed as a bureaucratic exercise designed to comply with legal requirements of due process (see Variant A in Table 7.2). Moving along a spectrum, a 'corrective' or 'positive' approach can involve a more employee-centred, mutual problem-solving approach (see Variant B in Table 7.2). However, Variant B still makes provision for penalties and thus retains the punitive elements of Variant A.

There is a separate positive approach identified in the literature, referred to as a *counselling approach*. This approach is highly critical of the traditional corrective approach precisely because of punitive elements it contains (Osigweh and Hutchinson 1989, 1990; Riccucci 1988; Sherman and Lucia 1992). In this positive approach, there is an absence of any provision for warnings (either oral or written) or dismissal, with counselling to the fore and the employee given several opportunities to improve (see Variant C, Table 7.2). However, at the final stage, if they cannot meet the employer's expectation, they are expected to leave their employment voluntarily. In the US this approach is said to produce higher levels of satisfaction by those experiencing discipline (even in unionised companies). However, the research is extremely limited and the approach does not appear to be widely used. It is not clear if it exists in a formal sense in any Irish employments. Indeed, there must be a risk that the requirement on an employee to resign could constitute a form of constructive dismissal. Finally, it is also worth noting that not all writers see punitive methods as dysfunctional. For instance, Arvey and Ivancevich (1980: 131) argue that 'punishment may be a very effective procedure in accomplishing behavioural change'.

By the early 1980s, some texts had begun to advocate *preventive* discipline, whereby the culture of an organisation is designed to mitigate the need for discipline. This involves *autonomous discipline*, whereby teams regulate discipline or *self-discipline* and individuals are encouraged to take responsibility for their own performance (Strauss and Sayles 1980). Edwards (2005: 376–7) notes that self-discipline still involves control, being 'one aspect of the way in which control has to be negotiated'. There are some impressive examples of reductions in the use of discipline (and grievances) associated with responsible autonomy promoted by teamworking, most notably in Rusal Aughinish – although there the introduction of annual hours arrangements seemed to be the main causal variable (Ryan and Wallace 2016). This suggests that the nature of work organisation greatly influences employee performance and behaviour and can be more important than personal issues, which are the focus of disciplinary procedures, whether of the traditional, corrective/positive or counselling variety.

In the employment relations literature there is a degree of scepticism as to how management approaches to discipline affect workers and the extent to which their prescriptions are operated in practice. Saundry *et al.* (2011: 197) suggest that 'without the countervailing power offered by effective union representation, workplace discipline may be reduced to a stark exercise of managerial discretion'. They note that repeated surveys in the UK have found the imposition of discipline to be two and a half times lower in strongly unionised establishments. Also, Saundry *et al.* (2011: 201) found that non-union organisations had 'less scope for resolving disciplinary disputes informally' and consequently had a greater reliance on procedures. Should a similar effect prevail in

Ireland, this would modify somewhat the pessimistic conclusions arising from Browne's (1994) findings that Irish unions coped poorly with the law in dismissals cases. If unions influence the disciplinary process in advance of dismissal, this would arguably be of much greater benefit to workers were it to lead to them keeping their job rather than having to challenge a dismissal – a far more difficult process given the costs of legal representation, if needed. However, there is clear evidence of a decline in collective approaches to discipline. Kevin Duffy, former Labour Court chairperson, notes that, in the 1970s, employment rights were determined through collective bargaining, but 'that has changed, and changed utterly' (Prendergast 2016). Professor Andrew Neal, himself a barrister, suggests that in the UK:

> the space for in-house resolution has narrowed, I would suggest, by a new generation of much more aggressive, procedurally driven and normative HR officers. … The whole shift has been away from sorting out the issue at the workplace … you end up transferring the issue into a legal issue. (Prendergast 2016)

Professor Neal's observations cast a quite different light on management approaches to discipline than indicated by prescriptive corrective and positive approaches, and strongly suggest a dominance of legal procedural considerations.

Extent of Disciplinary and Grievance Procedures

Given the influences promoting the development of procedural regulation, it might be expected that such procedures would by now be almost universal. However, as of 2011, this was not the case. A study of 500 companies in Ireland found that only 60 per cent of organisations had formally written disciplinary and grievance procedures (Roche and Teague 2011). Written procedures for discipline and grievance were more likely to be found in the following organisations: unionised, medium/large size, manufacturing and foreign-owned (Roche and Teague 2011). While a 60 per cent coverage rate is reasonably widespread, it is far from universal and, given the legal and other pressures for procedural regulation discussed above, it requires some explanation. Research indicates a resistance by some managers to the formalisation involved in the procedural regulation of discipline and grievance. Jones and Saundry (2011) suggest that operational managers (as distinct from human resource managers) in the UK would prefer to avoid procedures, and favour a pragmatic and informal approach to disciplinary issues. Although such preferences may have some effect on the way procedures operate within organisations, it is doubtful it determines the presence or absence of procedures.

Labour market pressures are a more likely cause of the non-universal diffusion of disciplinary and grievance procedures. These pressures seem to be pulling workplace conflict management systems in different directions. Roche and Teague (2011: 438) point to the growth in knowledge-based workers – a development which may promote the adoption of 'innovative ADR-style conflict management practices', 'ADR' referring to alternative dispute resolution. Roche and Teague also note an opposite influence, due to the expansion in relatively low-wage and low-skilled jobs. They suggest that this may have led to 'a significant number of employees … working in organisations where even traditional workplace conflict management practices are absent' (Roche and Teague 2011: 438). Also, a hybrid between the traditional and innovative can exist, with a four-way typology borne out by the results of Roche and Teague's (2011) survey of 500 organisations (Table 7.3). Most notable is the finding that a majority (54 per cent) of the minimal conflict management group appeared to favour a largely improvised approach to managing workplace conflict, although, even in this group, 37 per cent still had formal, written, stepwise procedures.

Table 7.3
A Typology of Workplace Conflict Management Systems

Workplace Conflict Management System	Percentage (%)
Minimal conflict management system	41
Traditional industrial relations conflict management system	30
A high level of usage of ADR practices, combined with formal, written, stepwise conflict management practices	25
Hybrid ADR conflict management system	5

Alternative Conflict Management Systems

ADR practices grew up in the US in the 1980s as an alternative to processing disputes in civil courts. They aim to resolve disputes and improve future relationships, with examples of practices and comparisons to traditional methods provided in Table 7.4. A variety of factors can affect the extent to which ADR is used, e.g. firm size, firm type, whether the firm is unionised or non-unionised, if the company is an MNC, and the demographics of the workforce (Teague *et al.* 2012). The most common ADR mechanism is that of traditional open-door policies, which have been around since at least the 1960s, with Teague *et al.* (2012) finding them present in 53 per cent of companies. Of the firms surveyed, 40 per cent had formal written procedures for dealing with disputes involving groups of employees, 30 per cent used intensive formal communications regarding impending change, 20 per cent used external experts to assist in negotiations, and 31 per cent used brainstorming and problem-solving techniques (Teague *et al.* 2012: 14). Overall, the evidence suggests that ADR is not diffusing on any widespread basis in Ireland (Teague *et al.* 2012). Although not widely used, they can be deployed in some cases by non-union companies – the case study of Hirem

Table 7.4
Conflict Management Practices

Type of Conflict	Conventional Approach	ADR Approach
Conflict involving individuals	• Formal written grievance and disciplinary procedures	• Open-door policies • 'Speak-up' systems • Ombudsmen • External and internal mediators • Review panels of managers and peers • Employee advocates • Arbitration
Conflict involving groups	• Formal written procedures • Resort at final stage (when deadlocked) to state agencies, e.g. LRC	• Assisted bargaining/mediation • Brainstorming • Interest-based bargaining • Private arbitration • Intensive communications surrounding change management

Source: Teague *et al.* (2012).

Recruitment (in Table 7.5) illustrates an assisted bargaining ADR case in a non-union setting.

BULLYING AND HARASSMENT

There has been major growth in attention to the bullying and harassment aspects of interpersonal conflicts in recent years. They are some of the most complex issues for managers to deal with and the most unpleasant for employees affected. Health and safety legislation requires employers to provide a safe place to work, and equality legislation states that they must take all reasonably practicable steps to prevent and address harassment. In addition to the WRC, the Health and Safety Authority and the Equality Authority have published codes in these areas. These codes of practice advocate that an employer should develop a bullying and harassment policy and it should be communicated to all staff as well as customers/clients. The codes provide that an individual complainant could be encouraged to use an informal process whereby they alert the perpetrator to their inappropriate behaviour. If the complainant rejects the suggestion, or it does not resolve the issue, provision needs to be made for a formal written complaints procedure and an employer investigation into the issue.

The issue of what meets the legal requirement for bullying arises. It is considered to be repeated inappropriate behaviour that can reasonably be regarded as undermining

Table 7.5
Case Study
ADR: Assisted Bargaining in Hirem Recruitment PLC

Mary has worked for a recruitment agency called Hirem for four years. She has become very experienced and has direct contact with a wide range of clients. The company has had a high labour turnover and Mary is, in fact, the longest-serving employee. Realising her value, Mary negotiates a substantial salary increase, hinting that she would leave if not satisfied by the company's offer. She is offered a 15 per cent increase, which she accepts. She is also given an assistant to help because the manager has noted she has been working extremely long hours. Some weeks afterwards, Mary comes across a note. It is addressed to Mary's direct manager and it is in the handwriting of the general manager. This note indicates that the general manager considers that Mary has become too independent in her work, has too many direct contacts with clients and that there is a risk she will leave and take clients with her. The note also says that her recent salary increase (she now earns €57,000 per annum) has made it too expensive to continue to employ her. The note indicates that it is not possible to replace her at present, but that the new assistant will take over her job in six months and preparations can then be made for her dismissal.

Mary is shocked at this note and decides to photocopy it. She continues to work and, after four months, her immediate manager begins to raise complaints at her work. At the end of two months, her manager sends for her and indicates that her work is not satisfactory and she is to be made redundant. Mary informs the manager that she knows that the real reason for her dismissal is not redundancy. She hands her manager a copy of the general manager's note. Mary informs the manager that she feels she has been 'bullied and harassed' and that this has caused her substantial stress. She says that she cannot continue to work with the company, but she expects a 'handsome package' to leave. The manager informs Mary that the note she copied was confidential and that copying any confidential material is a matter for disciplinary action.

Following further discussion, the manager indicates that she will accept Mary's resignation and will make a goodwill payment of €2,000 to 'dispose of the matter'. Mary rejects this as 'totally inadequate' and indicates that she 'will sue' and 'take a case for constructive dismissal'. The manager indicates a willingness to 'negotiate' further. Mary asks to have her solicitor negotiate on her behalf but the company say they want 'to keep the law out of it'. Mary proposes instead using an expert negotiator from Alternative Dispute Resolution PLC to negotiate on her behalf. After consideration, the general manager agrees to this and a negotiating meeting is set up. Due to prior commitments of both parties, they agree that the meeting will last no longer than an hour and that, if an agreement is not reached, the parties 'will go their separate ways'.

This case study is designed for use in analysis, discussion or role-play negotiation.

the individual's right to dignity at work – a once-off incident will not suffice (LRC 2006). The requirement to establish bullying was considered further by the Supreme Court in 2017. The court found in *Ruffley* v. *The Board of Management of Saint Anne's School* that disciplinary action was not bullying and that 'the test for bullying is of necessity to be set very high'. The court determined that, to constitute bullying, (i) an action had to be repeated over a period of time, (ii) it had to be inappropriate and (iii) it had to undermine the dignity of the employee at work. Furthermore, to undermine the employee's dignity, the action would have to be 'outrageous, unacceptable, and exceeding all bounds tolerated by decent society'. The case study in Table 7.6 outlines some of the difficulties that can present themselves to management when dealing with an alleged bullying case among workers.

Table 7.6
Case Study
The Allegation

Lisa worked as a cleaner in a large factory for five years. In February she was notified that management and the union had agreed to introduce a new morning shift of 6am–2pm. The cleaners were not consulted about the change and were unhappy with it but did not do anything about the issue. A few weeks into the new shift, Lisa approached her manager and told him that the new shift was unsuitable for her as she had to get her children ready for school. The manager agreed to reduce her number of weekday shifts and to put her on Sunday shifts, which Lisa was happy about as Sunday hours were paid at double time. Following this, she experienced changes in her colleagues' behaviour towards her. She felt excluded from conversations and she felt that her colleagues were whispering and laughing at her. On one occasion, a colleague spilt a drink on a floor Lisa had just cleaned – Lisa felt this was deliberate. Lisa's supervisor told her that Lisa's work was getting sloppy and that she was stupid. Following this, Lisa met the HR manager and told her about what was happening. She also met with the company occupational health nurse, who believed that Lisa was severely anxious and stressed. Lisa took a month off work. However, when she returned, she felt that the bullying continued, and she submitted a formal bullying complaint.

Discussion Points
1. What difficulties does this case cause (a) for an employee who feels bullied and (b) for an organisation faced with an allegation of bullying?
2. If you were the HR manager, what steps would you take regarding the bullying complaint?

In contrast to the requirement that behaviour must be repeated to constitute bullying, harassment and sexual harassment can include a one-off incidence. Harassment is defined as behaviour which is unwelcome to the employee and could reasonably be regarded as offensive, humiliating or intimidating (Equality Authority 2002). An individual's colleagues, customers or clients can engage in bullying but often it is alleged to be perpetrated by an individual's supervisor or manager (Hodgins *et al.* 2014).

Early research on bullying focused on the personalities of the victim and the bully to explain why bullying occurred. However, many authors have cautioned against this approach and have focused instead on the culture, power and hierarchy of the organisation and external factors (MacMahon *et al.* 2009). Organisations with 'destructive' leadership can trigger or sustain bullying behaviour, and can lead to management not intervening when bullying behaviours occur (Einarsen and Skogstad 1996; Salin 2008; Skogstad *et al.* 2007). Also, bullying can become institutionalised where it is ignored or accepted (MacMahon *et al.* 2009). That is not to suggest that employers can ignore the issue since bullying/harassment can have serious consequences for an individual's health and well-being as well as for the organisation (Kelly 2006; McMahon 2009; O'Connell *et al.* 2007).

The imbalance of power between the possible victim and perpetrator can 'provide fertile soil for bullying' (Salin 2003: 1218). Further considerations are that victims rarely report bullying and that there is a reluctance to use procedures – the silence effect discussed earlier. Recent research has explored the twin phenomena of the silence effect and the consistent empirical findings that it is those in superior power positions who are consistently most reported to engage in bullying behaviour (MacMahon *et al.* 2018). Using the labour process lens of power and control, some writers have suggested that bullying may be in management's interests if it becomes so normalised that it extends management control and prerogative (D'Cruz and Noronha 2014).

MacMahon *et al.* (2018) set out to test some of these propositions in a large-scale study of over 2,000 nurses in both the public and private sectors. Their most significant finding was that bullying was endemic in nursing in Ireland and employee silence widespread, with a marked reluctance among respondents (55 per cent) to use bullying procedures. Qualitative answers by respondents indicated a strong belief that it could negatively affect them if they did speak up, with some of those who had made formal complaints reporting they had been labelled 'troublemakers' and regarded as 'deviants' (MacMahon *et al.* 2018: 483–6). They found that, in the 'context of a recessionary environment and increased budgetary pressures', some respondents perceived that management used bullying to ensure that certain duties or performance expectations were delivered (MacMahon *et al.* 2018: 483). Overall, they concluded that 'rather than just viewing bullying as an individual act, there should be a focus on bullying as rooted in the organisational/institutional context' of nursing (MacMahon *et al.* 2018: 485). This finding casts a quite different light on bullying than the individualised perspective that informs codes of practice and the legal system.

HANDLING GRIEVANCES AND DISCIPLINE

Prescriptive texts often present the handling of discipline, grievance and other individual employment relations issues in non-problematic terms but, as outlined above, many considerations may come into play in dealing with them. Despite the elaborate procedural norms that characterise disciplinary and grievance administration, many of the underlying concepts are quite subjective. Of particular note are concepts such as 'reasonableness', 'fairness' and 'consistency'. As far back as the 1950s, the sociologist Gouldner (1954) noted that workers had an indulgency expectation, believing that procedures would be implemented in 'an indulgent' way, i.e. that the full force of formal rules and procedures would not be used against them where they had not previously been applied. There is a long-standing recognition that custom and practice can modify the operation of formal rules. Edwards (2005: 384) points out that 'any manager sticking to the letter of the rule book might well be surprised not merely by the workers' reactions but also by line managers, who have negotiated a form of workplace equilibrium that turns on rules in practice'. It would also be wrong to imagine that managers have a gung-ho attitude to discipline, with Jones and Saundry (2011: 263) reporting findings of a Chartered Institute for Personnel and Development UK survey that managers are 'often reluctant to deal with emerging disciplinary issues'.

The above *caveats* should be borne in mind when considering the remainder of this chapter, which deals with prescriptive norms and practices for handling such issues in the workplace. The case studies presented in Table 7.9 reflect the real-world complexities that handling grievance and discipline regularly bring to the fore. These are based on actual cases and provide material for debate and role play.

Handling Grievances

Prescriptive management texts claim grievance procedures have several benefits. Grievance procedures provide an opportunity for an employee to: 'voice' concerns, provide feedback to management, limit misunderstandings and disputes over what is appropriate, provide an avenue of communication, and increase fairness and consistency (Hawkins 1979; Thomason 1984). In effect, they can be considered as a mechanism to match the expectations of an employer and employee. However, as in the case of discipline, the act of initiating a grievance can be influenced by the underlying power dynamic. It is not clear that employees will be comfortable initiating a grievance and this can result in silence. Also, those who decide to raise a grievance may be filled with apprehension and find difficulties with interviews and meetings connected to the grievance process.

It would be wrong to think that raising a formal grievance is the only way of dealing with an employee's grievance. Most employee concerns will be resolved informally through the normal 'give and take' that characterise workplaces and we have seen earlier that some organisations and managers prefer an informal or improvised approach (Jones and Saundry 2011; Roche and Teague 2011). However, those issues that are unresolved may need to be processed through formal written procedures. Line management/team leaders and employees/employee representatives handle most workplace grievances, so they need to be familiar with grievance procedures and have the skills to handle them. Table 7.7 contains summary guidelines for managers involved in grievance handling.

Table 7.7
Management Checklist for Grievance Handling

- Management should make every effort to understand the nature of, and the reasons for, grievances
- All levels of management should be aware of the potentially significant influence that grievance handling has on industrial relations and company performance generally
- Companies should have a written policy that sets out an orderly and effective framework for handling employee grievances
- Line management, particularly first-level supervision, should be aware of their key role in effective grievance handling
- Managers need to be aware of the need for consistency and consider if a proposed resolution to a grievance sets an undesirable precedent

A written grievance procedure will normally set out the requirements on employees and the employer in the event of a formal grievance and will outline the stages and approaches to be followed by managers and employees. In order to prevent grievance procedures being seen as a delaying tactic, it is recommended that they are handled promptly, with an employee receiving a response quickly. Grievance procedures will normally specify short time limits for each phase of the process. The standard elements of a grievance procedure are outlined in Table 7.8.

Table 7.8
Elements of a Typical Grievance Procedure

- Clear steps specifying the level at which a grievance should be raised
- A requirement that the issue should be first discussed between employees and their immediate manager or supervisor
- Provision for referral to higher levels of management if not resolved
- Provision for a speedy response
- Time limits to be specified for each stage of the procedure (if the issue is not dealt with in the specified time, the next stage of the procedure may be invoked)
- A right of employees to be represented by their trade union or an employee of their choice at the various stages of the procedure
- Provision for referral to a third party if agreement cannot be reached 'in house' (this may be absent in non-union procedures but may still be an option for an employee)
- A 'peace clause', with both parties forgoing the use of industrial action prior to all stages of the agreed procedures being exhausted (this will not be present in non-union companies)

Discipline

Salamon (1998: 545) defines discipline as 'formal action taken by management against an individual who fails to conform to the rules established by management within the organisation'. Management will normally determine what is seen as acceptable rules and standards in areas such as employee performance, attendance and conduct at work. Inevitably, situations will arise where employees are considered to have failed to have met expectations or, less commonly, where employees will wish to contest management rules and standards. Disciplinary procedures provide a formal mechanism for processing issues. They can serve to (i) bring alleged offences to the notice of employees, (ii) indicate how employees can respond to such charges, (iii) find there is no case to answer, (iv) identify any disciplinary action that may be taken if a complaint is upheld, and (v) make clear the right of appeal. Legally, it is almost always essential that a full investigation precedes any disciplinary hearing and that the hearing complies with the rules of natural justice.

If disciplinary action is considered justified, it can range from counselling to more serious forms, e.g. formal warnings, suspension or dismissal. In issuing warnings, clarity is very important and a warning should specify the ways in which the employee's behaviour or performance was unsatisfactory, how that behaviour or performance can be improved, the standard that is expected and the consequences of not improving. Management are obliged to take any reasonable measures that might facilitate improvement, e.g. extra training. Of course, improvement may not ensue, and suspension, dismissal or demotion may result, even for relatively minor repeat issues where these remain unresolved.

It is a common misconception that disciplinary action requires a series of progressively escalating warnings. Discipline procedures will normally specify that, in the case of gross misconduct, options such as suspension, dismissal or relocation to other duties may be applied for a first offence. However, because of the requirement of fair procedures, instant dismissal is rarely capable of being justified before a third party.

There are certain offences, if proven, where dismissal will invariably be justified. Theft is the most obvious of these, although an employer must be able to establish that the theft took place and that the employee was involved. In terms of unfair dismissals legislation, an employer must be able to meet the reasonableness test and is only required to establish facts on the balance of probability – not beyond a reasonable doubt. Nonetheless, this is not always unproblematic, especially where white-collar managerial employees are involved. The parties involved may perceive the same events quite differently, even in the case of alleged theft, as illustrated in the White Goods case study in Table 7.9.

It is important to appreciate that offences that warrant dismissal for a first offence in one organisational setting may not merit dismissal in another. This is especially the case in the 'grey area' of fighting and substance abuse. Being intoxicated on the job might, depending on the circumstances, merit dismissal but in another context an employee might be referred to a company employee assistance programme. The latter would especially apply where this was the first time an employee had exhibited this behaviour.

Table 7.9
Case Study
White Goods: White-Collar Theft?

Your name is Joanna Mooney and six months ago you were appointed general manager of White Goods Distributor PLC. You were hired 'to shake up' the company and make it more competitive. You made it clear from the start that you intend to be 'tough but fair'. You have just discovered that Tom Mallon, a sales manager, has been taking traded-in fridges, washing machines, dishwashers and ovens (the property of the company). He refurbishes them and sells them on privately and keeps the money. You confront Tom and give him a chance to admit the offence but he denies any impropriety. He also admits he did not have permission for this activity. You have direct evidence from two people who have bought refurbished fridges. You feel that, given Tom's position, his activity will inevitably reflect on the company, and you are determined to put an end to this theft. You feel the company has been taken advantage of and you wonder what you should do. You are seriously considering Tom's dismissal.

***

Your name is Tom Mallon and you have been working as sales manager for White Goods Distributor PLC for twelve years. In an informal arrangement over the years, you have taken goods in good condition that were traded in to the company and you have refurbished them and sold them on privately. The company previously had to pay to dispose of them. Today you were confronted by the new general manager, Joanna Mooney – who makes no secret of being tough – and you were accused of stealing company property. You were totally shocked and did not know how to respond except to deny any impropriety. She asked you if you had permission to do this and you answered honestly that you did not. However, you do not see that as relevant, since it was well known that you did this and previous general managers never had a problem with it. Presumably, they knew about the practice, even though you never had formal permission to do it. You are not in a union. You feel very vulnerable and wonder what you can do.

Discussion Points
1. How should Joanna Mooney proceed if she wishes to discipline Tom Mallon?
2. What options does Tom have should he face disciplinary action?
3. What factors in the above account might justify or not justify disciplinary action?
4. In your opinion, is dismissal justified? If yes, why? If no, why not?
5. What additional factors might an investigation uncover which might justify or not justify dismissal?

This case study can be used for analysis, discussion or role-play negotiation.

In relation to fighting at work, while traditionally seen as falling in a grey area, the requirements of modern health and safety legislation may require a stricter view to be taken.

The Interview Process

Any discipline or grievance situation, and many bullying and harassment situations, will require interviews to be conducted and records retained. If handled well, interviews can contribute to a successful resolution of the dispute; and if the dispute is unresolved, a good interview can strengthen management's case in front of a third party. Equally, for an employee, a structured and considered response to an issue is likely to be most effective. Because grievance or discipline issues can be stressful and emotional, it is desirable to avail of a right of representation if an appropriate one is available. If handled badly, issues can easily escalate and lead to difficulties when third parties become involved. It is important to understand that any interview is, in effect, a negotiation and that the principles of negotiations apply. In that regard, this section should be read in conjunction with Chapter 11. In particular, the approach used in an interview will inevitably fall into one or more styles, which are outlined and briefly explained in Table 7.10. A style or choice of style may often happen unconsciously with several of these being suboptimal or negative.

Table 7.10
Possible Approaches to Grievance and Disciplinary Interviewing

- **Frank and friendly:** Inform the person about the problem in an open and friendly way
- **Tell and listen:** Inform the person of the problem and then listen sympathetically
- **Tell and sell:** Inform the person of the problem and tell them of the consequences if they do not take a particular course of action
- **Sweet and sour:** Issue dealt with by two people from the one side; one adopts a hard approach and the other a 'softer' approach – the aim is to manipulate the other party into agreeing to the 'softer' settlement
- **Intimidation:** Use of threats
- **Joint problem-solving:** Both sides explore the problem from their differing perspectives, search for possible solutions, evaluate identified solutions, and agree on a solution and action plan for implementation

---

A 'frank and friendly' manner may work in straightforward situations but is unlikely to be effective where there is a fundamental difference between the parties. In negotiation terms, it is an accommodation approach and means the supervisor/manager is placing a low priority on the organisation's concerns and a higher priority on the employee's concerns. If the employee is also accommodating in their attitude, it may work, but not otherwise. The 'tell and listen' approach places no obligations on the other party to come up with solutions and, as a result, an employee or manager may deploy an avoidance strategy and not really address the issues subsequently. The 'tell and sell' is a power-based approach and it is, in fact, implicit in the notion of progressive warnings – i.e. 'If improvement does not happen, then your job is at risk!' The approach does not require the employee to be part of generating solutions and this may result in them having little commitment to any 'selling' in which the supervisor/manager has engaged. It may also create resentment in the employee and promote an adversarial approach, leading to a legal response. The 'sweet and sour' approach (a variant on the 'good cop/bad cop' approach to negotiations) is generally considered unethical. Since it is based on contradictory management approaches, it has the potential to lead a company into legal difficulties. Intimidation involves the use of threats, which is unethical and can lead to accusations of bullying. Such accusations may not have legal merit if they are one-off events, but they are hardly likely to promote good relations and may seriously undermine the wider reputation of a manager who engages in such intimidatory action.

The recommended best-practice approach to conducting grievance and disciplinary interviews/meetings is the 'joint problem-solving' approach (Table 7.11). The conceptual basis for joint problem-solving is that it attempts to remove, or at least limit, the 'power' dimension in the interview process. Joint problem-solving requires a high level of skill. It requires assertiveness on the part of the interviewer but also active involvement on the part of the employee, who should be encouraged to outline the issue from their perspective and suggest solutions. Solutions advanced by either the supervisor/manager or employee should then be evaluated on their merits, as in Fisher and Ury's (1986) approach to negotiation.

The implementation of a problem-solving approach to either grievance or disciplinary administration may be difficult for a variety of reasons. First, it requires special skills and is likely to require training to be implemented successfully. Second, it may be unpopular with supervisors/managers who may see it as limiting their traditional role and making unreasonable demands on them. Third, in a disciplinary case, there is a requirement to inform employees of the seriousness of the issue and that future offence could result in dismissal. Complying with this requirement can result in the prioritisation of legal technical compliance with procedures over the identification of mutually agreed solutions. Fourth, an employee may feel threatened because of the inherent punitive nature of disciplinary action and may refuse to engage for this or a variety of other reasons. Finally, employees can be very emotional where they have a grievance, or are faced with disciplinary action, and may, as a result, find it difficult to address an issue in a problem-solving way, even where supervisors or managers try to use such an approach.

Despite these reservations, problem-solving approaches represent the prescribed ideal in handling individual issues and appear to have substantial benefits for supervisors and managers who are adept at it, with Saundry (2016) reporting that managers who adopt a problem-solving approach are more likely to resolve conflict. Wichert (2002: 169) notes that 'the better a person is as a listener, the more likely he or she is to rise rapidly up the organisation hierarchy'. She goes on to note that managers overestimate their listening skills and are unaware of how employees view them. Training has been found to increase employees' ratings of the effectiveness of management's listening skills, suggesting 'it might be a good investment in managers' (Wichert 2002: 169).

Table 7.11

Joint Problem-Solving Approach

Elements

- **Non-directive, open-minded interviewing:** Questioning and active listening are required.
- **Establishing the issue from the employee perspective:** Employee's interests must be addressed.
- **Stating the issue from the employer perspective:** Supervisor/manager must show assertiveness.
- **Problem-solving aspect:** Employee is invited to suggest solutions. The solutions are evaluated with reference to objective, mutually agreed standards.
- **Implementing:** Employee must meet company's needs; employer must meet employee's needs.

Dangers

- **Employer may not engage with the process:** Supervisor/manager may be unconvinced at the effectiveness of this method and may believe that it concedes too much power. They may also lack the skills and understanding necessary to execute the method effectively.
- **Employee may not engage with the process:** Employee may be reluctant to be open about issues. They may regard this method as mere manipulation on the manager's part.

Record-Keeping and Administrative Considerations

As with the outcome of all negotiations, the keeping of accurate records on grievance and disciplinary meetings is essential. Since equality and unfair dismissals legislation primarily places the burden of proof on the employer, they must be able to back up reasons for discipline with adequate documentary evidence. The keeping of records is equally important for an employee where an issue proceeds to a third party. Contemporaneous records of events will be adjudged more reliable and will have greater credence than memory; they will be especially important where events are contested. In addition to their usefulness at third party hearings, records also provide data on the extent and nature of discipline and grievances in the organisation and can highlight issues beyond the personal ones that need to be addressed.

While record-keeping is an important dimension of grievance handling, it should not be allowed to distract from its primary purpose. An overemphasis on recording all details may create excessive red tape and cause frustration among employees. The details that need to be retained will vary according to the level that an issue has reached. Grievances that go beyond an informal stage need to be in writing, and details of reasons for any decisions taken must be recorded and retained. At the counselling stage in a disciplinary process, a brief note of the issue, the individual concerned, the date and the nature of the discussion is enough. At verbal and written warning and all subsequent stages, records need to be more elaborate. Written records are especially important at, and after, the final warning stage in disciplinary cases and grievance cases if unresolved internally. A copy should be signed by the employee (as evidence that they received and understood the letter) and placed on their personnel file. A copy should also be given to the employee's trade union (if they are a member and have requested representation) and to the manager(s) involved.

Concluding Comments

Workplace procedures are now widespread and represent an established way of handling both collective and individual conflict. They are important whether employees are in unionised or non-unionised employment. Surprisingly, research has indicated that procedures are not universal. While informality may work in many instances, the absence of procedures in an organisation can cause problems should a dispute proceed to a third party. The requirements of procedural and natural justice will apply whether formal procedures are in place or not. In implementing procedures, managers and supervisors should have an appropriate skill set. Employees must remember that, as well as giving them rights, procedures place obligations on them.

Chapter 8

The Management of Industrial Relations

Introduction

This chapter considers management approaches to industrial relations, placing considerable focus on the impact of contextual considerations on management strategy and behaviour. This is done despite the fact that many organisations do not make deliberate strategic choices in the area of industrial relations. That is, their approach may be variously described as reactive, opportunist or 'fire-fighting' (Boxall and Purcell 2016). In contrast, some organisations do adopt a strategic approach on industrial relations matters (Guest 1987). Thus, management approaches to industrial relations can vary along a continuum from more ad hoc styles, characterised by little or no strategic decision-making, to more deliberate and considered strategic approaches.

Across such a span, this chapter addresses:

- the relevant and changing economic, market and organisational contexts within which entities devise and adapt their human resource management (HRM) and industrial relations styles, policies and practices; and
- the range of possible management styles in industrial relations and the variety and nature of influences thereon.

Contextual Influences: External and Internal

In order to identify and explain management approaches in industrial relations it is necessary to examine a range of external and internal factors that impact management decisions on business strategy and, ultimately, industrial relations (for greater detail see Gunnigle *et al.* 2017). We begin by considering factors in the external environment.

The External Context

The *external environment* exerts a major influence on organisational decision-making. It is widely acknowledged that the economic environment, political systems and regimes, increased product market competition, advances in technology, and changes in the composition and operation of labour markets significantly affect the context of enterprise-level industrial relations (Poole 1986; Roche 2011). For example, the severe recession experienced after the demise of the Celtic Tiger era in Ireland significantly altered industrial relations and HRM priorities and practices (Gunnigle *et al.* 2019; Roche *et al.* 2011). In this respect, it is acknowledged that such downswings generally:

affect the conduct of employment relations. They do this by inclining employers towards more market-responsive postures that may involve downsizing and more flexible employment arrangements, less investment in training and development and general restructuring activities that may weaken internal labour markets and assured career progression. (Roche *et al.* 2011: 221)

A key feature of the changing economic context is the *globalisation of competition,* which has acted as a significant driver of change (at various levels) for many years. Globalisation has been facilitated and encouraged through greater trade liberalisation emanating from developments under the General Agreement on Tariffs and Trade. Globalisation has significant industrial relations implications, since organisations 'benchmark' their activities and costs against international 'best practice'. This has prompted accusations of an 'international race to the bottom' (in respect of both pay and terms and conditions of employment) and so-called 'social dumping' as firms relocate their activities/ production to jurisdictions with lower wages and weaker labour regulation (Blyton and Turnbull 2004; Dundon *et al.* 2017). The effects of globalisation are particularly evident in the Irish context given its success in attracting multinational companies (MNCs) from the US and many other countries which service diverse international markets. On the positive side, trade liberalisation provides greater opportunities to develop and access new markets. However, in order to capitalise on such opportunities, employers often have to improve their performance in areas such as unit production costs, delivery times and customer support. This in turn may force regular reviews of industrial relations, with potential, and sometimes negative, implications for pay levels, labour flexibility and job security.

Associated with increased globalisation is the impact of a greater *intensification of competition.* In addition to traditional sources of competition from jurisdictions such as the US and Japan, the competitive threat from later industrialising countries such as Singapore, South Korea, China, India, Mexico and Vietnam is increasingly evident. Many of these jurisdictions may combine a low cost base with strong performance on dimensions such as productivity and labour skills. Nearer home, a number of Eastern and Central European countries have undergone restructuring in the post-communist era and now offer stiff competition through their low cost base, strong industrial tradition and an educational system with a strong technical and scientific foundation. A case in point was the decision of Dell Computers to relocate manufacturing activity from Ireland to Poland in 2009, with the loss of approximately 2,000 jobs.

In responding to such challenges, organisations have followed two broad strategies:
• rationalisation, wage restraint, lay-offs, outsourcing and 'de-layering' (Gunnigle *et al.* 2017; Roche *et al.* 2011);
• Increased merger, acquisition and strategic alliance activities (Sparrow and Hiltrop 1994).

A common element to these responses is an increased focus on securing greater efficiencies at workplace level, e.g. seeking productivity improvements and reduced labour costs. Related strategies can include the increased use of atypical employment patterns, task flexibility initiatives and improved performance management systems. These revisions bring into focus the role of management in securing changes to industrial relations in a manner that serves to enhance enterprise-level performance and improve the bottom line.

Organisational performance in its *product/service market(s)* can significantly influence strategic decision-making and management approaches or styles in industrial relations. Clearly, firms operating from a strong market position (e.g. high market share/high levels of demand for their products or services) possess greater scope to deploy more benign and worker-friendly industrial relations and HRM policies, e.g. high pay, attractive benefits, and good training and development opportunities that, in turn, may contribute to a more cooperative industrial relations climate. In contrast, firms operating under high levels of market pressure (contracting market share, high levels of price competition, etc.) have generally less choice and may be forced to adopt a more traditional 'cost and labour control' approach to industrial relations. In turn, this may contribute to a more adversarial industrial relations climate. Consequently, the nature of a firm's product/service market is a key contextual factor influencing competitive strategy, with important implications for the management of industrial relations.

Kochan *et al.* (1986) provide a broad model of the impact of product/market change on strategic decision-making and industrial relations. This model illustrates how changes in product/service markets influence strategic decisions at different levels of the organisation, namely:

- long-term strategy formulation at management level;
- HRM/industrial relations policy at middle-management level;
- workplace and individual organisation relationships at workplace level.

It also explains how a product and service market change can lead to a variety of senior management decisions with important implications for industrial relations. One such decision might be to relocate organisational activities across different jurisdictions and/or from unionised to non-union sites. In this regard, Roche (2007b) explains that the preference – or even the insistence – of many US MNCs to avoid trade unions in their foreign subsidiaries is largely attributable to the perception that product and process dynamism in fast-changing and turbulent product and service markets may be seriously compromised by engagement in time-consuming collective bargaining. Evaluating the impact of increased product and service market competition, Kochan *et al.* (1986: 65) further explain that:

> When competition increases, the initial decision a firm must make is whether it wants to remain active in that line of business and compete in the new environment or withdraw and reallocate its capital resources to other opportunities. If the firm

decides to remain in the market, the next decision it must make is whether to compete on the basis of low prices (costs) and high volume or to seek out more specialised market niches that will support a price premium. The central IR effect of this increased sensitivity to prices and costs is that firms shift their priorities away from maintaining labour peace to controlling labour costs, streamlining work rules (so as to increase manufacturing efficiency) and promoting productivity. The pressure to control or lower costs is especially intense if a firm attempts to compete across all segments of its product market on the basis of low prices and high volume.

Public policy (the government's influence) is another important external factor affecting industrial relations. It is particularly important in explaining variations in national industrial relations systems and in the nature and extent of local- or enterprise-level industrial relations practices. For example, the revised approach of Ireland's industrial development agencies towards trade union recognition for MNC newcomers from the early 1980s heralded a significant rise in the incidence and extent of non-union establishments (Gunnigle 1995; McGovern 1989; Lamare *et al.* 2013). Likewise, the anti-union policies of successive Conservative governments in the UK during the 1980s gave legitimacy and support to 'macho' management practices that often undermined trade unions. At another consequential policy level, the influence of the EU via a series of directives on almost all day-to-day workforce management interactions have served to promote worker–management engagement and cooperation and to enhance worker rights and protections in the workplace. In a similar vein, Poole (1986) identified centralised regulation of industrial relations by the state as a potentially constraining influence on managerial prerogative/discretion (cf. Ackers 2010). That is, the greater the level of centralised control, the more limited the scope for employers to develop industrial relations approaches or styles that might undermine pluralist principles (see later in this chapter). Conversely, low levels of central regulation afford management greater discretion, rendering more likely the emergence of management approaches to industrial relations that diverge from the traditional pluralist–adversarial model.

As noted in Chapter 1, *technology and technological change* represent another key external environmental factor affecting managerial approaches to industrial relations (Beer *et al.* 1984; Taras and Bennett 2002). It impinges on a range of issues related to industrial relations, e.g. cost structure, job security, upskilling, deskilling, demarcation lines and reward systems. Marchington (1982) suggests that in labour-intensive sectors, where labour costs are high and market competition intense, organisations may adopt 'harder' approaches to industrial relations, characterised by high levels of work intensity and worker surveillance. However, in capital-intensive sectors, where labour costs constitute a small proportion of total costs, organisations may have greater scope to adopt 'softer' or more benign management approaches. The 'soft' approach places an emphasis on more cooperative relations between management and employees, via initiatives designed to increase employee involvement and satisfaction (see Chapter 12). From an industrial relations perspective, advances in technology can impact on relative bargaining power positions, whether it be to strengthen the employer's position (e.g. information technologies that facilitate access to global markets and investment relocation opportunities) or the employee's position (e.g. jobs that require substantial human capital in the form of high levels of education, training and skills).

The *labour market* represents an especially important contextual influence on industrial relations, specifically with regard to recruitment, training and reward systems. For example, high unemployment affects the power balance in industrial relations and can often lead to more authoritarian employer approaches. Such conditions also facilitate increased 'atypical' work patterns, job insecurity, lower pay, displacement, 'race to the bottom' initiatives, and reduced trade union power and density, and they force workers and trade unions to accept less favourable levels of pay and working conditions. A notable development in the Irish labour market in this regard is the exponential growth in the services sector. This has exerted a drag effect on trade union membership and recognition since union density is generally lower in this sector, particularly in the information and communications technology sector and other private services such as domestic services, contract cleaning and hospitality. In contrast, low unemployment puts the focus on the attraction and retention of labour. This was especially evident during the Celtic Tiger years, where tight labour market conditions exerted upward pressure on wages and employment conditions, with the balance of power tipping back towards workers and trade unions.

The Internal Context

While an organisation's external context influences and helps inform management approaches to industrial relations, it is generally the factors in an organisation's *internal environment* that determine unique organisational managerial responses and behaviour at the level of the firm. Such factors include, inter alia, managerial ideology, business strategy, and organisation size and structure (see Gunnigle *et al.* (2017) for detail).

Management ideology and values incorporate the deeply held beliefs of senior management that serve to guide decisions on various aspects of workforce management, including industrial relations (Dundon *et al.* 2017; Gunnigle 1995; Purcell 1987). In relation to managerial values, Kochan *et al.* (1986: 14) highlight their significant impact upon management approaches and strategies in industrial relations, acting as a 'lens' through which 'managerial decision makers weigh their options for responding to cues from the external environment'. The impact of management ideologies and values is addressed later in this chapter in the context of managerial frames of reference and management styles in industrial relations.

Organisation structure and size are key internal factors affecting management approaches to industrial relations (Salamon 2000). With regard to *organisation structure*,

Purcell (1992) argues that senior (corporate) management in highly diversified organisations are primarily concerned with financial issues. Consequently, industrial relations and related considerations are not a major concern of corporate decision-makers but rather an operational concern for management at the business unit/subsidiary level. A corollary of this argument is that organisations with a highly diversified product or service portfolios are more likely to adopt differing industrial relations approaches and practices suited to the needs of constituent divisions, subsidiaries and establishments. By comparison, 'core business' organisations with a narrow product range are arguably more likely to integrate industrial relations and other HRM issues into strategic planning. Daniels (2006: 18) presents three basic categories of organisational structure that have important implications for industrial relations, namely functional, divisional and matrix structures, as described below.

- **Functional:** This applies to a structure whereby employees are grouped according to the type of work they do, i.e. by function; for example, marketing, research and development, operations, finance. Argued limitations of this commonly used structure are that employees may only have a partial view of the organisation's activities and goals, are arguably less likely to be innovative, and operate in a business environment characterised by poor coordination across functions (Daft *et al.* 2010; Duncan 1979).
- **Divisional:** This applies to a structure where employees are grouped via product/service markets. For example, the Virgin Group has a number of different product and service offerings, including an airline, a mobile phone company, and media and financial products. It thereby organises and groups employees according to the division in which they work. Likewise, Coca-Cola has a presence in over 200 countries and opts to structure its sales and marketing on a divisional basis by country. This enables the company to market the product differently across various jurisdictions. Bank of America deploys a similar service line structure via their retail, commercial, investment and asset management arms. While it is argued that this structure may be more efficient for the management of industrial relations, it may also experience poor coordination across product/service lines (Duncan 1979).
- **Matrix:** This structure endeavours to overcome weaknesses in 'functional' and 'divisional' structures by locating employees to functional groups and divisions that reflect their area of expertise. For example, engineers may be located in a single engineering department and report to an engineering manager. However, particular individuals may be assigned to different projects and report to different engineering or project managers while working on specific projects. Thus, to effectively execute their job roles, individual engineers may have to work under several managers. An emphasis on specific projects may enable empowerment and team working to the advantage of customer service and delivery. Under such arrangements, working

relationships are constantly changing. However, a potential downside identified by Daniels (2006) is that assignees to different products or services for varying durations may result in fragmented and poorly developed working relationships. Furthermore, requiring employees to report to two or more managers (e.g. a divisional and functional manager) can lead to divided loyalties and role ambiguity.

Turning to the industrial relations implications of an *organisation's size*, numerous studies have noted that trade union recognition and the presence of a specialised HR function are positively correlated with size. In the Irish context Gunnigle and Brady (1984) found that management in smaller organisations tend to veer towards a unitarist frame of reference (see later in this chapter) and adopt less formality in industrial relations than their counterparts in larger organisations.

A firm's *competitive strategy* is concerned with achieving sustainable competitive advantage in a particular industry or segment. This might entail a low-price strategy (e.g. Lidl or Aldi in the retail sector). Alternatively, firms may seek to differentiate their product or service offerings on some dimension that might command a higher price from consumers, such as high quality or branding (e.g. Marks & Spencer in the retail sector). Either way, employers and management will generally seek to align their industrial relations (and HRM) policies and practices to facilitate implementation of their chosen competitive strategy. This is often characterised as a desire to secure adequate 'fit' between competitive strategy and industrial relations (and HRM) strategies and behaviours. Here the suggestion is that if an organisation seeks to pursue a specific competitive strategy, it should adopt and implement a complementary set of industrial relations and HRM approaches. It is further argued that organisations will experience severe problems in strategy implementation if it is not effectively linked with appropriate industrial relations and HRM policy choices (Fombrun 1986).

Towards Strategic Industrial Relations?

From the foregoing contextual review, we can see how business strategy, product/service market circumstance and choice of competitive strategy can have important knock-on effects on industrial relations and HRM practices. This premise is particularly pertinent given the growing evidence that effective deployment and utilisation of an organisation's workforce can positively affect competitive advantage (Boxall and Purcell 2016; Guest 1987). A useful analysis of this topic is provided by Wood and Peccei (1990), who differentiate between 'strategic HRM' (i.e. where HR and industrial relations issues are fully integrated into the strategic planning process) and 'business-led HRM' (i.e. where such issues are linked to the commercial imperatives of the organisation). Differences in these approaches lie in the level of strategic consideration of HRM and industrial relations issues. In relation to 'strategic HRM', industrial relations issues are integral to strategic planning and form part of the organisation's long-term business strategy. From the 'business-led' perspective, policies and practices are very much lower-order strategic activities, linked to higher-order strategic decisions in areas such as product development or market penetration. As noted earlier, the traditional perception advanced by Purcell (1992) is that strategic decision-making in organisations largely focuses on 'primary' business issues such as finance, while any attention devoted to industrial relations issues is secondary and somewhat incidental. At the other extreme, some organisations incorporate industrial relations and HRM considerations into their strategic decision-making processes, taking well thought-out strategic decisions relating thereto.

Collings *et al.* (2018) emphasise the centrality of industrial relations to organisational competitiveness, while Dibben *et al.* (2011: 308) posit that in the face of increasing investor and customer mobility, technological change and economic and political uncertainty, it is 'all the more important' that industrial relations be 'managed in a strategic way' to 'impact on the broader organisational context'. As further delineated by Gennard and Judge (2010: 235), the bottom line on this theme is as follows:

> The key is to develop an employment relations strategy that is responsive to the needs of the organisation, that can provide an overall sense of purpose to the employment relations professional and assist employees to understand where they are going, how they are going to get there, why certain things are happening and, most importantly, the contribution they are expected to make towards achieving the organisational goals.

Implications for the Management of Industrial Relations

In evaluating the implications of these various contemporary developments for industrial relations, we point to specific challenges for collective bargaining and trade unions (see Chapter 3; also see Bacon and Storey 2002; Guest 1987). In essence, these challenges entail a reduced emphasis on collective bargaining and management/trade union interactions, enabled through increased union avoidance.

Management may deploy particular combinations of HRM policies to exclude/avoid trade unions using either *trade union suppression* or *trade union substitution* tactics (Kochan *et al.* 1986; Roche and Turner 1998). Union suppression entails aggressive resistance to trade union organising and trade union recognition, e.g. by dismissing or threatening to dismiss workers associated with union organising. In contrast, trade union substitution seeks to secure union avoidance by creating a benign workplace environment where triggers or causes of union activity are eliminated or minimised. This approach has achieved widespread resonance, often resulting from its association with non-union greenfield sites in the US (Gunnigle *et al.* 2009; Lavelle *et al.* 2010). Roche and Turner (1998) argue that a union substitution strategy is most likely to emerge in larger firms that operate in the more profitable sectors of the economy. In such instances, firms have the financial wherewithal to provide pay levels, employment conditions and the overall working environment necessary to underpin such a strategy (Roche 2001; Roche *et al.*

2011). Ireland has experienced extensive union avoidance since the late 1970s, particularly among US-owned firms (Gunnigle *et al.* 2001, 2019). Undoubtedly, many of these firms (e.g. IBM and Intel) have done so via 'union substitution', involving the adoption of comprehensive HRM policies, including competitive pay and working conditions, designed to eliminate employees' need for collective representation (Dundon *et al.* 2017).

From the employer's perspective, there are advantages and disadvantages to union recognition. In this regard, there has been considerable focus on the impact of unionisation on organisational performance, and specifically on issues such as profits, productivity and return on investment (Huselid 1995). In evaluating this literature, Roche and Turner (1998) find the evidence regarding the impact of unionisation on productivity inconclusive. However, they argue that the evidence from the manufacturing sector (particularly in the US) indicates that unionisation may lead to reduced profitability. Flood and Toner (1997) identified a number of disadvantages associated with both union substitution and union recognition strategies, as summarised in Table 8.1.

Table 8.1
Disadvantages of Union Substitution and Union Recognition

Disadvantages of Union Substitution	Disadvantages of Union Recognition
• Firms need to provide pay and employment conditions at least on a par with those in similar unionised companies	• Unions make changes in work organisation more difficult
• Management may be reluctant to enforce discipline	• Unions give rise to demarcation problems and impose restrictions on production
• Absence of adequate structure to deal with grievances (particularly collective issues)	• Unions impose higher manning levels
	• Unions protect unsatisfactory workers
• Fear of unionisation a constant concern	• Unions inhibit individual reward systems
• Supervisors are monitored too closely	• Unions promote an adversarial industrial relations climate and can cause industrial action
• Management in non-union firms must work harder at communications	• Unions encourage the pursuit of trivial grievances
• Need for expensive, well-resourced personnel/HR function	• Unions make communication with employees more difficult

Source: Flood and Toner (1997).

As evident from this table, the disadvantages associated with union substitution are categorised as a 'catch-22' situation, whereby firms pursuing union substitution cannot take advantage of their non-union status (Flood and Toner 1997). For example, by reducing pay and diluting employment conditions or disciplining/dismissing unsatisfactory workers, there is the fear that such action will lead to union recognition. This leads the authors to conclude that the major advantages of union substitution lie not in clear economic 'cost–benefit' criteria but rather in allowing the firm greater scope to develop a unitary company culture and to foster 'warm personal relations' between management and employees (see next section).

MANAGEMENT VALUES, FRAMES OF REFERENCE AND MANAGEMENT STYLES IN INDUSTRIAL RELATIONS

All organisations are characterised by particular values and philosophies with respect to industrial relations. In some organisations these values are explicit, as might be demonstrated via mission statements and HR policies regarding how workers (and possibly their representative organisations) are treated. In others, managerial values are more implicit and must be inferred from management practice in areas such as supervisory style, pay levels or the nature and extent of management–worker communications (see Chapter 12). Of particular significance is the suggestion that managerial opposition to pluralism (see Chapter 1) and trade union recognition is especially characteristic of the value system of managers from the US. On the other hand, certain HRM approaches, which emphasise individual freedom and initiative, direct communications and merit-based rewards, are very much in line with this value system (Jacoby 1997; Kochan *et al.* 1986; Lamare *et al.* 2013). This interpretation is significant for Ireland, where the economy is heavily dependent on foreign direct investment, much of which comes from the US (Lamare *et al.* 2013; Lavelle *et al.* 2009).

In his seminal work on the management of industrial relations, Fox (1966, 1968) posits that management approaches are primarily determined by the frame of reference adopted by line managers at the level of the firm. A frame of reference, as originally defined by Thelen and Withall (1949: 159), incorporates 'the main selective influences at work as the perceiver supplements, omits and structures what [s]he notices'.

In turn, a manager's frame of reference affects how they approach industrial relations since it:
- defines how management expect people to behave at work and how it thinks they should behave (viz. values and beliefs towards industrial relations);
- determines management reactions to actual behaviour (viz. management practice);
- shapes the methods management chooses to employ when it wishes to change the behaviour of people at work (viz. strategies, policies and practices).

Fox (1968, 1974) identified two alternative frames of reference to help evaluate management approaches to industrial relations, namely employment relations. These were termed (i) the unitarist and (ii) the pluralist frame of reference, as outlined in Chapter 1 and summarised in Table 8.2.

Table 8.2
Unitarist and Pluralist Frames of Reference

Unitarist Frame of Reference	Pluralist Frame of Reference
Emphasises the dominance of common interests. Everyone – management and employees – should strive to achieve the organisation's primary business goals since everyone will benefit	Organisations comprise different interest groups with diverse objectives, but linked instrumentally by their common association with the firm/corporate entity
There is only one source of authority (management) and it must command full loyalty	Management's role is to achieve some equilibrium, satisfying the various interest groups and thereby helping to achieve the organisation's goals
Anyone who does not share these common interests and does not accept managerial authority is viewed as a dissenter/agitator	A certain amount of conflict is inevitable since the objectives of the parties will clash on occasion
Since dissenters endanger organisational success, they must fall into line, either appreciate the overriding importance of corporate goals and accept managerial authority, or risk elimination from the organisation	Management must expect and plan for conflict so that it can be handled successfully and not endanger the achievement of the organisation's primary objectives
	Management should not seek to suppress conflicting interests but rather aim to reconcile them in the organisation's interests

Source: Fox (1968).

In illustrating the workplace application of these differing frames of reference, Marchington (1982), as well as Marchington and Parker (1990) and Gunnigle *et al.* (2017), considered how managerial behaviour in three different facets of workplace industrial relations – namely dealings with trade unions, management prerogative and industrial conflict – might differ depending on the particular frame of reference adopted.

Regarding *approaches to trade unions*, Marchington (1982) argues that managers adopting a unitarist frame of reference perspective see no role for trade unions. Rather they generally view unions as a malign force, encroaching on management's territory and on their 'right' to manage, making unreasonable demands, inhibiting change and flexibility, and negatively affecting competitiveness and performance. They would also view unions as an externally imposed institution that introduces conflict into the organisation and prohibits the development of 'good' industrial relations/HRM. Consequently, workers associated with union organisation are viewed as 'disloyal', 'agitators' or 'troublemakers'. In contrast, managers adopting a pluralist frame of reference accept the legitimacy of union organisation in representing the voice of workers and articulating their views on matters of workplace management. They would also accept that employees might have loyalties to groupings other than management, notably trade unions.

The second area of difference depending on the frame of reference adopted was with regard to *management prerogative*. Management prerogative refers to areas of decision-making where management see themselves as having sole decision-making authority, i.e. management's right to manage and make decisions (Salamon 2001). Managers adopting a unitarist frame of reference would be unwilling to accept any diminution of management prerogative because of trade union organisation. Rather they would view management as the sole legitimate decision-making authority. On the other hand, managers adopting a pluralist frame of reference would acknowledge the legitimacy of other interest groups in the organisation, such as trade unions. They would also acknowledge the right of trade unions to participate in decision-making in areas of germane interest and, consequently, accept some reduction in managerial prerogative.

The final area where managers' approaches to industrial relations may differ depending on their frame of reference is in relation to *industrial conflict*. Salamon (2001) notes that the underlying assumption of the unitarist frame of reference is that 'organisational systems exist in basic harmony and conflict is unnecessary and exceptional'. Consequently, managers adopting a unitarist frame of reference would view the enterprise very much along 'team'/'family' lines, with everyone (management and workers) working together to achieve the same business/organisational objectives. These managers would therefore see conflict as an aberration, only occurring because of a breakdown in management–worker communications or from the work of troublemakers. However, managers adopting a pluralist frame of reference accept that some degree of industrial conflict is inevitable since the interests of management and labour will inevitably clash on occasion. Since the pluralist perspective accepts the legitimacy of conflict, managers adopting this frame of reference will tend to plan for it by, for example, following agreed grievance, disputes and disciplinary procedures.

These contrasting frames of reference represent dominant orientations that may be adopted by management. In practice, one finds that management do not strictly adhere to any one of these approaches but may adopt different approaches in different situations and/or change their approaches over time. Nevertheless, these frames of reference provide a useful foundation for evaluating management approaches to, or styles in, industrial relations at the level of the enterprise/firm.

Rollinson (1993: 92) describes management styles in industrial relations as 'management's overall approach to handling the relationship between the organisation and its employees'. While employer organisations can play an important role in helping organisations manage industrial relations, as outlined in Chapter 4, individual employers are primarily responsible for the development and implementation of their own style, and associated policies and practices. The link between ownership and the legitimacy of managerial authority is a critical characteristic of organisational life. Despite the fact that management are responsible to other interest groups – such as workers and trade unions – they exercise considerable power by virtue of their capacity to take strategic decisions on behalf of their owners' interests.

On the theme of management styles in industrial relations, Purcell (1987) notes that employers' policies and practices cannot be fully explained by structural variables such as size, product markets and technology. Accordingly, he identifies strategic choice, exercised by senior management, as a key factor in explaining differences in management

---

Table 8.3
Indicative Managerial Decisions Impacting on Industrial Relations

Decisions	Impact on Industrial Relations
Location	Influences labour supply, nature of labour force, labour costs, labour/employment law application and prospect of unionisation
Size	Influences span of managerial control, communications, leadership/managerial style
Recruitment and selection	By deciding on the nature of the workforce (e.g. propensity of workers to join trade unions)
Training and development	Nature and extent of training and development can influence management and employee approaches and attitudes to industrial relations
Union recognition	In a greenfield situation, management may be able to decide whether to deal with trade unions, which will have a significant impact on the subsequent nature of enterprise-level industrial relations
Employer association membership	Deciding whether to join an employer association may influence subsequent industrial relations decisions (e.g. pay negotiations)
Procedural formalisation	The extent and nature of formalisation of industrial relations procedures will impact on enterprise-level industrial relations (e.g. grievance and dispute handling)
Use of HRM policies and practices	By introducing techniques such as performance appraisal or performance-related pay, management can limit the scope of trade unions

styles. Management can therefore use their power to make strategic choices in respect of industrial relations matters, albeit within the all-important constraint of environmental context. Furthermore, management can take strategic decisions that either directly or indirectly influence industrial relations matters. For example, the impact is direct where senior management decide not to recognise trade unions in a new greenfield start-up. In contrast, the industrial relations implications are more indirect where, for example, a product line is terminated (due to poor sales) and consequential redundancies may detrimentally affect industrial relations. However, the precise effects may be difficult to discern. Table 8.3 provides a sample list of managerial decisions potentially impacting upon industrial relations.

Several commentators have attempted to develop categorisations of management styles in industrial relations in order to better illustrate and explain the differences in organisational approaches. However, Purcell and Sisson's (1983) five-fold categorisation of 'ideal-typical' management styles in industrial relations, which is based on differing management approaches to trade unions, collective bargaining, consultation and communications, is arguably seminal (see Table 8.4).

Table 8.4
Management Styles in Industrial Relations

Management Style	Characteristics
Traditionalist	'Orthodox unitarism': opposes role for unions; little attention to employee needs
Sophisticated paternalist	Emphasises employee needs (training, pay, conditions, etc.), discourages unionisation, demands employee loyalty and commitment
Sophisticated modern	Accepts trade unions' role in specific areas, emphasises role of industrial relations procedures and consultative mechanisms Variations: (a) **Constitutionalists:** emphasise codification of management–union relations through detailed collective agreement (b) **Consulters:** collective bargaining established but management emphasises personal direct contact and problem-solving, playing down a formal union role at workplace level
Standard modern	Pragmatic approach, unions' role accepted but no overall philosophy or strategy developed, 'fire-fighting' approach

Source: Adapted from Purcell and Sisson (1983).

However, despite the appeal of such categorisations, in reality it is hard to categorise management styles in industrial relations into clearly discernible 'ideal-typical' groupings. Using data from over 1,400 organisations, Deaton (1985) empirically investigated the utility and relevance of Purcell and Sisson's (1983) typology. He concluded that attempts to classify firms into a small number of 'ideal' styles were problematic and, while the distinction between organisations that recognise trade unions and those that do not is crucial, it is more problematic to further subdivide styles in organisations where unions are recognised. Using more anecdotal evidence to examine variations in management styles in industrial relations, Poole (1986) also found an assortment of hybrid styles as opposed to convergence towards any predominant pattern. As Daniels (2006) observes, one model with five categories cannot hope to capture all the various complexities of the employment relationship. However, Purcell and Sisson's (1983) work does provide indicative examples of management styles in industrial relations within each category, and is therefore particularly useful for purposes of illustration.

THE MANAGEMENT OF INDUSTRIAL RELATIONS IN IRELAND

Based on our preceding review of environmental influences on management styles in industrial relations and the key dimensions thereof, we propose a broad categorisation of such styles, drawing on the available Irish evidence. This categorisation is set out in Table 8.5 and represents an attempt to apply the typology pioneered by Purcell and

Table 8.5
Categorisation of Management Styles in Industrial Relations in Ireland

Anti-Union Style
Organisations in this category are characterised by a commodity view of labour. Manifestations of this approach might include a preoccupation with retaining managerial prerogative, rejection of any role for trade unions or other modes of collective representation, little or no attention to HR/industrial relations except where deemed necessary, a low-level HR function, absence of procedures for communicating or consulting with employees, and an authoritarian management approach. The available research evidence suggests that 'anti-union' styles are predominantly confined to smaller indigenous entities managed in the classic 'small firm/entrepreneurial' mode and to some foreign-owned firms.

Paternalist Style
With this style, top management prioritise the need to 'look after' employees, and be benevolent and welfare-oriented. However, the management approach is essentially unitarist. There is little focus on deploying systems or procedures for employee representation or involvement. Opinions adjudged divergent from those of management are considered disloyal and potentially damaging. Indeed, the paternalist style may incorporate high levels of management complacency regarding the convergence of management and employee interests. HRM policy manifestations include a caring supervisory style but also a work system that limits employee involvement and participation, limited communication mechanisms and a low-level HR function whose role is of an administrative support nature.

Traditional Industrial Relations Style

The 'traditional industrial relations' style is characterised by adversarial industrial relations and primary reliance on collective bargaining. Management–union relations may be formalised through procedural agreements dealing with, inter alia, union recognition, and disciplinary, grievance and disputes procedures. Other manifestations of this style may include a bureaucratic organisation structure, job demarcation, limited communications mechanisms and a 'contracts manager'-type HRM function whose primary role is to handle industrial relations (see Gunnigle *et al.* 2017; Tyson and Fell 1986). In Ireland this style is most common in the public sector and semi-state sector, and in larger, long established, indigenous organisations and some MNCs (i.e. primarily those established prior to the 1980s).

'Soft' HRM Style

The 'soft' HRM style is characterised by a managerial desire to create an organisational climate where employee needs are addressed through positive employee-oriented policies designed, in part, to render collective representation unnecessary. It is grounded in a unitarist perspective and a 'union substitution' approach. Manifestations of this style include competitive pay and employment conditions, extensive management–employee communications, direct employee involvement, and procedures to address grievance and disciplinary issues, together with a highly developed and influential HRM function. This approach appears most common in US-owned firms operating in high-technology sectors.

'Hard' HRM Style

This style is strongly focused on 'transaction costs'. The objective is to source and manage labour in as cheap and cost-effective a fashion as possible to ensure achievement of the organisation's 'bottom line' objectives. This style equates to what has been termed 'union suppression', incorporating low employment standards. It represents a direct contrast to the 'soft HRM' approach, and may be found among some foreign-owned assembly and service firms, often operating in a subcontracting mode. Manifestations of this style might include use of 'atypical' employment forms to improve cost-effectiveness and the application of performance management techniques in order to achieve high productivity.

Dualist Style

The 'dualist' style is characterised by the acceptance of trade union recognition and collective bargaining to deal with overarching industrial relations issues, e.g. pay negotiations. However, workplace industrial relations is characterised by a strong individualist orientation. Organisations adopting this style differ from 'soft HRM' with regard to trade union recognition and collective bargaining but otherwise they pursue broadly similar policies. At workplace level, management seek to keep formality to a minimum, with the management focus on minimising the extent of collective bargaining, preferring direct dealings with employees. This style might be termed 'neo-pluralism' and it involves the use of selected HRM techniques, including sophisticated recruitment and selection, extensive direct communication with employees, performance-related pay systems and established collective bargaining procedures. Further characteristics can include extensive employee development, encouragement that employees deal directly with management on issues of concern, line management training in industrial relations, and a well-developed, influential HR function.

Sisson (1983) and Fox (1974) in the Irish context. It identifies six 'ideal-typical' management styles, with differences derived from variations via, *inter alia*, the strategic significance that management attributes to industrial relations and management approaches to collective employee representation, as manifested through management practices in areas such as communications, reward systems and the role of the specialist HRM function.

While this typology is indicative of the predominant styles adopted by Irish-based organisations, in practice one often finds overlap in these styles within organisations. Given the caveats outlined above (i.e. the limitations of 'ideal-typical' categorisations) and reflecting on the Irish scenario, a most notable feature of the typology relates to the 'soft HRM', 'hard HRM' and 'dualist' styles. These styles are significant because they indicate a planned and coordinated approach to the management of industrial relations, in contrast to other styles that are indicative of a more arbitrary approach.

The 'traditional industrial relations' style equates to the pluralist-adversarial model, which was historically the most pervasive in medium and large organisations in Ireland. In contrast, the 'anti-union' and 'paternalist' styles reflect opposition to the pluralist model, as manifested through forthright attempts to curb or eliminate moves towards collective employee representation. It is sometimes argued that these latter styles were most commonly found in smaller organisations and that – in the event of growth – they would succumb in time to the 'traditional pluralist' model. However, the available evidence indicates considerable change in enterprise-level industrial relations in Ireland. In terms of management styles, these developments are characterised by the increased adoption of HRM-based styles ('hard' or 'soft' variants). As outlined earlier we have witnessed a strengthening of unitarist managerial ideology, greater opposition to union recognition, the emergence of a strong non-union sector and a continuing decline in union density. These various developments may often contribute to 'union marginalisation' (viz. reducing or eliminating the role of trade unions in enterprise-level industrial relations), and seemed to gain favour among employers during the most recent economic downturn. In the case of Ireland Roche *et al.* (2011: 228) observed:

> a pattern where employers and HR managers sought to bypass unions and implement change unilaterally. They also sought to rescind or ignore collective agreements and to change the established rules of collective bargaining and industrial relations. Unions officials were of the view that their role was often only to rubber stamp decisions already made.

A quick review of the literature on the historical development of the specialist personnel/HR function in Ireland also helps advance our understanding on the evolution of management styles in industrial relations. This literature identifies industrial relations as traditionally the most significant area of activity (Gunnigle *et al.* 2017; O'Mahony 1958). This is largely due to the growth in influence of trade unions up to the early

1980s, with many larger employers engaging specialist 'personnel' managers to deal with industrial relations matters (particularly collective bargaining and grievance/discipline administration) at enterprise level. As Gunnigle (1998a: 4) notes:

> For the personnel function, industrial relations became the priority, with personnel practitioners vested with the responsibility to negotiate and police agreements. Industrial harmony was the objective and personnel specialists through their negotiating, interpersonal and procedural skills had responsibility for its achievement. This industrial relations emphasis helped position the personnel function in a more central management role, albeit a largely reactive one.

From these rather humble origins, the specialist HR function developed to a stage where it has become widely accepted as an integral part of the management structure of larger organisations, charged with the establishment and maintenance of stable industrial relations. Often more reactive than strategic, this industrial relations orientation was significant: it served to define what HR work involved and it helped to position the function as an important component of the managerial infrastructure.

However, this role orientation had peaked by the end of 1970s. By the early 1980s 'industrial relations orthodoxy' as the accepted model for the personnel/HR function had begun to unravel. The change may be traced to numerous sources, most particularly increased competitive pressures on organisations. As Roche and Gunnigle (1997: 445–56) observe, contingency approaches became the order of the day, with the role of the HR function influenced by a variety of factors such as sector, managerial values and market context:

> Never before has the analysis of industrial relations practices and policies been so closely tied to an appreciation of commercial and national and international political pressures. In the past, the worlds of industrial relations practitioners and academics alike tended to be much more introverted and preoccupied with the internal dynamics of industrial relations systems, agreements and procedures. The professional preoccupations and vocabularies of industrial relations experts tended to revolve around distinctly industrial relations themes: disputes and grievance procedures, anomalies in pay structures, productivity bargaining … Currently, these concerns, though not altogether displaced, often take second place to such issues as company performance, the union's role in contributing to business success, mission statements and quality standards, business units, employment flexibility and so on.

The most widely accepted explanation of these changes is the aforementioned increasingly competitive nature of product and service markets. These pressures appear to create a 'flexibility imperative' whereby organisations seek to be increasingly responsive to consumer demand on dimensions such as price, customer service and product quality.

It is also significant that these competitive trends are increasingly penetrating the state sector, due in large measure to the erosion of monopoly status because of EU-imposed pressures (see Hastings 2003). One example of a hitherto state-owned company grappling with a changing and more competitive environment is Aer Lingus. Deregulation in the airline industry left the company facing increased competition, particularly from low-cost airlines (notably Ryanair and easyJet). Resultant restructuring has led to significant changes in employee numbers, employment patterns and reward systems.

Although industrial relations remains an important component of the specialist HR function's organisational role, we have witnessed a considerable reorientation in this role in many organisations. As noted above, this involves a broadening of the HR remit to embrace core areas of HR activity beyond industrial relations, such as training and development, performance management and an increased role in more generic management initiatives, e.g. organisation change initiatives (Carbery and Cross 2019). In some organisations, this change has led to a greater strategic role for the HR function, involving the development of closer linkages between business strategy and HR/industrial relations practice.

CONCLUDING COMMENTS

This chapter has considered management approaches to industrial relations and the various contextual influences impacting thereon. This review suggests that many organisations do not make any deliberate strategic choices with regard to industrial relations, but rather adopt somewhat more reactive and ad hoc approaches. However, we also present evidence that some organisations employ more strategic approaches, and the characteristics of such approaches or 'styles' in the management of industrial relations have been outlined. We have placed considerable focus on management approaches to collective employee representation (and particularly on trade union recognition and avoidance) and how this has changed over time, with particular emphasis on developments in Ireland.

Chapter 9

The Nature of Industrial Conflict

INTRODUCTION

Industrial conflict is one of the most emotive aspects of industrial relations and it often makes headlines in the media. Inevitably, media commentary seldom discusses underlying causes of conflict, with the narrative often dominated by the immediate concerns of those involved. The causes of disputes are rehearsed from differing perspectives, be they management, workers, government or citizens. The media frequently pronounce implicitly on the 'rights' and 'wrongs' of disputes. They sometimes seem to become actors in disputes and can influence its direction and even its outcome. For example, the Association of Secondary Teachers, Ireland received cold treatment in the media in their attempts to have the two-tier system of employment abolished through industrial action (see Chapter 10). In contrast, Vita Cortex workers, who occupied their former place of employment from December 2011 to May 2012, enjoyed widespread sympathetic media treatment even though such occupations are illegal. Sometimes media treatment varies from understanding and sympathy to condemnation, as with the coverage of the threatened withdrawal of labour by Gardaí in November 2016. In this chapter we explore the dimensions of industrial conflict, both collective and individual, to provide a more nuanced and deeper understanding of its nature. It is not possible to cover all approaches in this chapter and the major focus will be on micro-level conflict; however, macro factors are touched on, before receiving more extensive treatment in Chapters 10 and 13.

NATURE AND FORMS OF INDUSTRIAL ACTION

The most obvious form of industrial conflict is that which occurs between employers and workers. However, industrial conflict is not confined to such disputes but is arguably inherent in the nature of industrial competition (Dahrendorf 1959). Some of the most bruising examples of conflict take place between businesses (e.g. disputes over patents involving Samsung and Apple), between companies and governments (e.g. Microsoft and the US government), and between companies and international organisations (e.g. Apple and the EU over the €13 billion tax the EU claims is owed from the alleged unfair application of Irish tax law). The dispute between the Quinn Family and the Irish Bank Resolution Corporation (formerly Anglo Irish Bank) is a graphic example of such conflict. The courts normally deal with such commercial disputes, while industrial action has wider societal dimensions and is not always appropriate to legal adjudication. The

Irish system of immunities for industrial action reflects this consideration; however, even in industrial relations systems based on rights, disputes of interest are normally not subject to resolution by the courts.

Classifying Conflict

Given the difficulties in defining industrial conflict, industrial relations scholars have drawn attention to the diverse forms that it can take (Gall 2017). It is pointed out that conflict can be collective or individual, organised or unorganised (spontaneous); and it may occur between workers and management, between workers themselves, or between managers themselves (Jackson 1991). Conflict can also be inherent in the employment relationship but may remain latent and unexpressed, or only be 'expressed in informal or often in covert ways' (Saundry 2016: 15). In this way, covert conflict can be distinguished from disputes which are, of their nature, visible (Dix *et al.* 2009). The possibility that conflict can be latent implies that an absence of conflict cannot be assumed to be a 'good thing'. Conflict may not be expressed because management 'buy it out' to the long-run detriment of the organisation, something Irish industrial relations practitioners refer to as 'cheque book' industrial relations. Workers may be unable to express conflict because they have insufficient power resources at their disposal or it may be illegal and suppressed in some societies. Conflict can shift between forms, a phenomenon associated with the 'balloon theory'. Godard (2014: 37) expresses this as follows: 'if the prevalence of one form of conflict reduces … the volume of conflict does not change, only its shape does, as happens when one squeezes a balloon'. While the implicit preservation of the volume of conflict seems a somewhat heroic assertion, there are many examples of conflict being displaced and expressed in different forms, not least the consequences on the Irish political system of austerity policies from 2008, as discussed in Chapter 1.

As an example of unexpressed conflict, women did not engage in widespread strike action against historical gender discrimination in pay and the 'marriage bar'. The marriage bar involved forced retirement on marriage and was only abolished in the civil service in 1973, and made illegal in the private sector in 1977 with the passage of the Employment Equality Act 1977 (Bambrick 2019). It is not credible to argue that potential grievances did not exist. The question arises as to how these grievances were limited so that they did not end up in widespread conflict. The reality was that society sanctioned such arrangements and women did not have sufficient power to challenge these social norms. Up to the late 1960s the collective bargaining system institutionalised gender pay discrimination, with women generally receiving pay rises that were only 60 per cent of those of their male counterparts. In the early national agreements of the 1970s, anticipating equal pay legislation, increases were raised to 85 per cent of the male rates. It was only with social mobilisation via the women's movement in the 1970s that women were able to press their case, but equal pay legislation only took effect because of the obligations arising from our membership of the European Economic Community.

While legislation has now narrowed the pay gap to some 14 per cent, it has not been eliminated and the reasons for its continuation are a matter of continuing public policy concern.

While it is difficult to define industrial conflict, collective industrial action is considered to be 'any temporary suspension of normal working arrangements which is initiated unilaterally by either employees (whether through their union or not), or management, with the aim of exerting pressure within the collective bargaining process' (Salamon 2000: 411). However, this definition only applies to collective industrial action, and industrial action can exist outside of collectively organised action. Thus, two broad categories of industrial conflict can be recognised as follows:
- explicit and organised collective industrial action; or
- unorganised and implicit individual industrial action.

The conceptual difference between the two forms of action is that individual unorganised action represents a 'withdrawal from the source of discontent' by individuals, while organised collective action is more likely to be a conscious strategy to change the situation that is the source of the discontent (Hyman 1989: 56).

Table 9.1 contains examples of the main forms of both individual and collective industrial action. Individual conflict such as absenteeism, labour turnover and dismissals are less visible forms of conflict. Even actions such as sabotage, theft, industrial espionage, silence and passive non-cooperation can be expressions of individual conflict. Such unorganised or individual action by workers represents a largely spontaneous, reactive and random response to the employment relationship and generally does not involve any conscious strategy. The growth of individual disputes referred to the Employment Appeals Tribunal (EAT) from 2000 to 2015, and their continuation since responsibility transferred to the Labour Court in 2015, is an indication of quite a dramatic increase in individually based conflict in Ireland in recent times.

Table 9.1
Forms of Industrial Action

- **Strike:** Collective in nature, involving temporary withdrawal of labour.

- **Lockout:** The most conspicuous form of organised industrial action instigated by employers, which involves preventing the workforce, or a proportion thereof, from attending work.

- **Withdrawal of cooperation:** Collective in nature, involving the withdrawal of representatives from joint institutions, strict interpretation of and rigorous adherence to procedures, absence of flexibility.

- **Work to rule:** Collective in nature, involving working only in accordance with the strict interpretation of written terms and conditions of employment, job description or other rules, such as those concerning safety or hygiene.

- **Overtime ban:** Collective in nature, involving refusal to work outside normal contractual hours of work.

- **Go slow:** Collective in nature, involving working at a lower-than-normal level of performance.

- **Work-in/sit-in:** Occupation of the workplace or section thereof, denial of access to management. This approach is often used to prevent movement of plant and equipment and is associated with plant closures. An example was its use in Vita Cortex in Cork.

- **Blacking of goods/services:** Refusing to handle goods or cooperate with services from a particular employer(s).

- **Unilateral management changes:** Changes to the agreed speed of work, work intensification, job insecurity, unilateral changes to terms of contract of employment by employer – if considered unreasonable by the Labour Court, may constitute grounds for constructive dismissal.

- **Other management action:** Blacklisting of workers, harassment and intimidation, industrial accidents due to improper safety, speed-ups, etc.

- **Sabotage and industrial espionage:** Individual or collective in nature, involving conscious action to damage goods or equipment, illegitimate leaking of commercial information to competitors, distributing false, damaging information about an organisation.

- **Whistleblowing:** Unauthorised release of internal company information to the media, government or other source on commercial, health and safety, or other matters. Generally individual but may be collective.

- **Pilfering and theft:** Individual in nature, involving stealing by employees, either from the organisation or customers; also unauthorised deductions of wages by management.

- **Absenteeism:** Generically defined as all absences from work other than authorised leave. It is estimated that only a small proportion of absenteeism may represent a form of industrial action. Where it does, it can represent an individualised response to perceived problems in the workplace.

- **Labour turnover:** High turnover can be an expression of underlying employee dissatisfaction. Only a proportion of labour turnover in organisations may represent a form of industrial action.

- **Motivational withdrawal:** Lack of trust, passive non-cooperation, low productivity.

- **Suicide:** Suicides in Renault and France Telecom have been individual responses to work stress. In Taiwan and China there have been both individual incidences and threats of mass suicide in response to grievances over working conditions.

- **Bossnapping:** Kidnapping of managers.

The most common examples of organised industrial action arising from workers are strikes, go-slows, overtime bans, work to rules and non-cooperation. Lockouts are a well-recognised form of collective management conflict, but there are other less obvious forms arising from industrial restructuring, e.g. plant closures and relocation. Hebdon and Stern (1998: 204) suggest that third-party measures such as 'arbitration' are also correctly viewed as expressions of conflict, with arbitration and strikes acting as direct substitutes. This is a variant on the notion that diplomacy is war by other means!

Individual Unorganised Conflict

Edwards and Whitson (1989) identified control of attendance and discipline as having a social as well as a personal dimension. While absenteeism can be an indicator of individual conflict, an inability to attend work due to illness or other factors is, of course, not necessarily an indication of conflict. Absenteeism can be due to a range of factors, including such things as the ability to attend work, the motivation to attend, family circumstances, gender, the level of social welfare provision, and sick pay. This reservation aside, absenteeism and turnover rates can be affected by the nature of the job: a job that has low discretion, is unrewarding, has high levels of stress, or where bullying is tolerated can lead to higher absenteeism or/and high levels of turnover and are rightly regarded as expressions of conflict. Royle and Towers (2002) claim high levels of absenteeism in McDonald's is an expression of unorganised individual conflict against its work system. Looking at the issue of turnover, it is well established that the nature of industrial relations affects turnover. Wood and Allen (2019: 176) note that 'voluntary labour turnover has been found to be higher in countries with low levels of collective bargaining, employee representation and unionisation'.

Other forms of individual unorganised conflict can be subtle and virtually impossible to detect or measure. Employees may engage in passive non-cooperation, underperform or exhibit low-trust behaviour (Fox 1974). Such individual action may not even be conscious but it can have long-term effects on productivity and the employment relationship (see case study in Table 9.2). Indeed, underperformance has been a common concern of management theorists since Taylor's development of scientific management in the early twentieth century (Rose 1977).

Management can also engage in unorganised individual conflict. Examples include overly strict supervision, arbitrary discipline, bullying, victimisation, speed-ups, industrial accidents and unauthorised deductions of wages. Beynon's (1973) celebrated study of the Ford motor plant in Halewood in the UK (*Working for Ford*) paints a vivid picture of the reality of speed-ups as management-initiated conflict. He notes that 'production managers out to make a name for themselves' engaged in speed-ups, resulting in 'unofficial walkouts' (Beynon 1973: 138). Management eventually conceded to shop stewards the right to hold the key that locked the assembly line, thereby ensuring the agreed production line speed could not be exceeded – in this way an individual-initiated conflict was resolved through collective regulation.

Table 9.2
Case Study
Unorganised Individual Conflict – Withdrawal

Following the completion of her PhD, Dr Monica Murphy was recruited by a start-up technology company employing fifteen people. In her first six months she found the work rewarding and the CEO praised her for helping to deliver on a key aspect of an EU contract. She enjoyed being involved in all discussions and decisions at weekly company meetings. At these meetings she noted that suggestions made were often not followed up and suggested a tracking system. As a result, the project manager took responsibility for monitoring and compliance. He put in place a requirement to report mid-week and at the end of a week on all issues via email. Gradually, Monica realised that issues, even inconsequential ones, never disappeared from a list which got ever longer. When she raised this, nothing changed. Monica was especially annoyed at the nitpicking nature of the production manager's monitoring of her work and they ended up 'having words' on several occasions. She thought he was a 'jerk' and grossly incompetent but kept her opinion to herself, although the CEO seemed to have the same view as they fought regularly. She did discuss her annoyance with the five other technical and engineering staff, who were also frustrated and, like Monica, had stopped making suggestions at the weekly meetings. As her motivation ebbed, Monica sent her CV to several more established companies where she expected to find better management systems in place.

Discussion Point
What examples of individual conflict are evident in the above case study?

The issue of job insecurity and work intensification associated with flexibility and performance management systems can impact on employees in terms of 'stress, psychological health and family tension' (Burchell *et al.* 2002: 2). MacMahon *et al.* (2018) point to the negative effects of budgetary cutbacks and recessionary pressures affecting Irish nurses. Nolan (2002: 131) points to the limitations of family-friendly policies when commercial pressures arise as 'the inclination of managers to develop family friendly policies diminishes'. Burchell *et al.* (2002) argue that pro-employee policies are not independent of the neo-liberal imperatives of economic competition.

Collective Conflict

The 'fact' that the employment relationship may be characterised by conflict only rarely gives rise to any public concern or comment, yet collective industrial action is commonly regarded as extremely negative and damaging. Rollinson (1993) identifies three principal reasons why this is the case:

1. When initiated by workers, it is normally vertical in nature and therefore challenges the legitimacy of management authority/prerogative in decision-making.
2. It tends to be highly visible, both within and outside the organisation, and it can involve large numbers of workers.

3.   Its objective tends to be misunderstood: such action is commonly seen as irrational
     or dysfunctional, with most conflict situations viewed as being capable of
     resolution by discussions and negotiation, i.e. they should not result in industrial
     action.

Collective conflict is generally associated solely with the existence of trade unions – a
view that, while largely correct, is not fully accurate. The resistance of the 'Luddites' to
the new lace machines and factory production in the period 1811–1813 was notable for
the fact that the resistance came from groups of workers who were not organised in the
early trade unions, or 'combinations' as they were then called (Darvall 1964). While
collective conflict is not necessarily confined to trade unions, it is uncommon to find
unorganised workers engaging in formal collective action. In effect, trade unions provide
an ordered mechanism for expression and potential resolution of conflict. The main
mechanism for achieving this is the process of collective bargaining; but strikes, go-slows,
ban on overtimes or a work-to-rule may be deployed. However, trade unions are
moderating influences on industrial conflict, as emphasised by US sociologist C. Wright
Mills, who famously described trade union leaders as the 'managers of discontent'
(Wright Mills 1948).
     A major defect in much theorising about the causes of industrial action has been the
insufficient attention to the role of employers and managers (Edwards 1992). The
lockout is a commonly recognised but nowadays quite rare form of management-
initiated organised conflict. Some employer conflict is masked because it is normal
commercial activity. Plant closures, relocations and unilateral changes to terms and
conditions of employment can constitute employer conflict. Salamon (2000: 421) notes
that, because of its permanency, plant closure or a threat of closure 'may be considered
a more powerful sanction than the employees' temporary stoppage of work through
strike action'. Conceptually, these options can serve the same function as strikes because
both are a party's BATNA (best alternative to a negotiated agreement – see Chapter 11).
In contemporary industrial relations, multinational companies often have a ready
capacity to switch production (either temporarily or permanently), to limit the capacity
of workers to take industrial action or to limit the effectiveness of industrial action if it
occurs.
     Even where unions are the clear initiators of collective conflict, this is almost invariably
a reaction to management action or inaction. Salamon (2000: 424) notes that by
passively resisting union demands or by unilaterally initiating change, management
can 'place the onus on the employees or union to take direct industrial action'.
Conceptually then, all collective industrial action should be viewed as joint industrial
action in that both union and management will have decided to allow the action to
proceed by making too few concessions to meet the demands of the other side or by
demanding too much.

Crossover Between Individual and Collective Action

Not all conflict can be neatly divided into individual unorganised and collective organised forms. Gall (2017) draws attention to the dramatic employee responses to employer-initiated conflict of 'bossnapping' and employee suicide or threats of suicide. In China up to 200 workers threatened to jump from the top of the Foxconn dormitory in Wuhan in 2012, with at least 10 suicides in the plant in the previous two years (Coonan 2012). Their dispute was in pursuit of severance payments which they claimed had been promised following a decision to close the Xbox 360 assembly line. In France three Renault executives committed suicide after they were dismissed following company accusations of industrial espionage (later proven to be false). The most dramatic case involved industrial restructuring in Orange, formerly France Telecom. In 2019 three senior Orange corporate executives (including the CEO) received jail sentences and fines following at least eighteen suicides and thirteen suicide attempts, with one employee reported as stabbing herself in the stomach during a company meeting (RTÉ 2019). A French court found the managers bore responsibility for 'collective moral harassment' and 'institutional harassment' designed to create a conscious climate of fear to force people from their jobs. These examples illustrate the limits of legal protection in the face of employer-initiated conflict (France has strong laws protecting employees) and individual employee responses borne of desperation.

Bossnapping, which involves the kidnapping of managers and holding them overnight or for some hours to demand concessions, occurred in several French plants in 2009 and included companies such as Sony, Caterpillar and 3M. The actions were carried out by groups of workers and, similar to the Foxconn case, were used to enforce demands over redundancy. Unusually, it involved unorganised groups of workers kidnapping managers. Vahabi (2011) argues that bossnapping was used as an effective substitute for large strikes, and that it worked because essentially the action had an implicit political intent, which saw the state recoil from taking legal action against what were clearly illegal acts. He argues:

> The recent state intervention to rescue and bail out banks was not accompanied by sanctions against employers who massively lay off workers … But if the state that had previously given carrots to bankers had used sticks against the bossnappers, then it would have run a high risk of provoking another wave of strikes, as seen in November 2005.

EXPLAINING CONFLICT: CONCEPTUAL FRAMEWORKS

As noted in Chapter 1, there are two broad conflicting assumptions as to the nature of industrial conflict. The first is the unitarist approach, which proceeds on the implicit assumption that conflict is frictional and is not a fundamental aspect of the employment relationship. The second is the range of pluralist approaches, which see industrial conflict as being inherent in the employment relationship and the nature of society. This unitarist–pluralist dichotomy is a standard starting point for the analysis of conflict. It was introduced into the study of industrial relations by Alan Fox in a seminal working paper for the UK Donovan Commission 1965–1968 (Fox 1966). He presented unitarism and pluralism under two distinct but related headings, as:

- competing conceptual frameworks for viewing the industrial enterprise; and
- alternate employer approaches to the management of industrial relations.

Fox (1966) categorised unitarism as a view of the industrial enterprise in which there is one source of authority and one focus of loyalty. Organisations are viewed as essentially cohesive and harmonious units in which all members of the organisation (management and employees) have common interests and share common goals – a team view (Fox 1966; Marchington 1982). This means that there is no place for factions and that people 'accept their place'. Unitarism allows that differences of interest may arise at an individual or group level, but 'class' as a unit of analysis is not deployed and the possibility of class conflict is not recognised (Dahrendorf 1959). Conflict, when it does occur, is viewed as dysfunctional and the result of misunderstandings, the action of troublemakers, a breakdown in communications, a lack of management leadership, or other non-fundamental reasons, i.e. frictional factors.

Because industrial conflict is not seen as inevitable, a need for institutional arrangements to deal with conflict, even at a societal level, hardly arises in unitarist perspectives. Appropriate management initiatives (e.g. effective communication, proper recruitment and selection, voice mechanisms, employee involvement and effective leadership) should be capable of either preventing conflict or resolving it when it arises. Trade unions are contradictorily viewed as either too powerful or no longer necessary. Marchington (1982: 38) points out that they are viewed as either achieving 'too much for their members in that they block change and inhibit efficiency or, conversely, as being irrelevant in that management is much more able than trade unions to identify and satisfy employees' needs'.

Fox (1966) contrasted unitarism with a pluralist conceptual framework that he considered offered a more realistic view of the industrial enterprise. This claimed realism is based on the assertion that different interests characterise the employment relationship and, as a result, there is an inherent potential for conflict. Insofar as there are shared goals within an organisation, these are instrumental: workers need to earn a living and the employers need workers to produce output or provide services – they are a factor of production. Factions and different groups are likely to emerge in organisations and these cannot be eliminated or integrated fully into the organisation. In resisting unionisation, long-term damage may be caused to industrial relations, since union recognition may only be achieved after a trial of strength, involving attempted dismissal of union activists (troublemakers), strikes or other industrial action. This is a picture which has contemporary resonance with the Ryanair experience, which saw difficult industrial relations after the company surprisingly recognised unions in 2018 after many years of resistance.

Politicians and public policymakers in the UK largely disregarded the recommendations of the Donovan Commission and looked instead to legal reform based on the ill-fated Industrial Relations Act 1971 (Goldthorpe 1974). In contrast, the pluralist analysis had a major impact on industrial relations practitioners and a seminal persisting influence on academic analysis. Practitioners in the emerging personnel management profession embraced the recommendation for procedural regulation, which has been explored in Chapter 7; in this chapter, we concentrate on academic influence.

Table 9.3 contains an outline of the unitarist–pluralist conceptual frameworks, together with the Marxist and radical approaches. Indeed, Marxist and radical approaches are properly considered to be pluralist explanations, since, at a fundamental level, pluralism means the recognition of differing interests in the employment relationship. It is also important to note that Marxist and radical approaches are systems theories. They differ from Dunlop's systems theory in that they focus on issues of power and control in the employment relationship, whereas Dunlop (1958) gives greater attention to rules and institutions and is, therefore, more conservative. All systems-based theories envisage industrial relations actors as being constrained by factors such as historical influences, economic factors and societal structures. They have only limited room for manoeuvre, although the extent of that room is a matter for debate (Hyman 1975).

Unitarism Developed

The various unitarist approaches all have an underlying assumption that industrial conflict is frictional, not fundamental, and its elimination is within management control. Implicit examples of unitarist ideology are found in the various human relations approaches, which originated with the work of Mayo in the 1920s (Mayo 1949; Rose 1977). Although it did not consider class conflict, human relations was paradoxically a reaction to the class conflicts associated with the growth of mass production. It also developed in opposition to the growth of Taylorist scientific management in the US in the early decades of the twentieth century. It presented a more employee-friendly approach to workplace regulation and promoting maximum employee productivity than the anomie (a form of alienation) it saw Taylorism promoting. However, as Coser (1956: 24) points out, Mayo 'never considers the possibility that an industrial relations system might contain conflicting interests, as distinct from different attitudes or "logics"'.

To Mayo, management embodied the central purposes of society and all his research was conducted to help management solve its problems (Coser 1956). In the human relations school and its modern managerial derivations, conflict is variously seen as a failure to meet the social needs of workers, incompatible personalities, overly strict supervision, the action of troublemakers or deviants, inadequate management, or a breakdown in communications (Mayo 1949; Rose 1977; Scott and Homans 1947; Whyte 1951). According to Mayo (1949: 128), the elimination of conflict and different interests is merely a matter of 'intelligent organisation that takes careful account of all the group interests involved'. He envisaged management achieving this desired end by deploying certain 'social skills' to ensure good communication and mutual understanding (Mayo 1949: 23, 191). Dahrendorf (1959: 111) points to the influence of this school on popular writers on management – e.g. Drucker – who echo and adopt this implicit unitarist view that the individual must understand the goals and functions of the industrial enterprise as their goals and functions (Drucker 1950: 156–65).

Arguably, the most significant omission in the human relations treatment of conflict arises not from a priori theoretical considerations but from the systematic suppression of the evidence of both individual and collective conflict observed during the Hawthorne studies. Bramel and Friend (1981: 874), writing in *American Psychologist*, point out that 'worker resistance to management was commonplace at Hawthorne (despite the absence of a union), yet tended to be covered up in the popular writings of Mayo and Roethlisberger'. They noted that management employed dismissals, threats, removal of breaks and increased hours of work, restrictions of output among workers and a concern for the job security of fellow workers but they wrote them off as irrational (Bramel and Friend 1981). Thus, Bramel and Friend (1981) argue that the very evidence uncovered in the Hawthorne studies contradicted the conflict-free view of the capitalist firm which Mayo and the human relations school promoted.

The Depression of the 1930s was not a fertile ground for the 'soft' policies advocated by the human relations school and, in truth, it was not popular among supervisors. Rose (1977: 170) notes 'the rapid decay of the approach with the spread, and relative failure, of human relations training for supervisors'. The growing unionisation in the US following the introduction of Roosevelt's New Deal and the 1935 Wagner Act, promoting collective bargaining and union representation, saw a move away from human relations (Rose 1977). Finally, the approach was subject to devastating critical assaults, the exposure of fatal methodological flaws in the Hawthorne studies and, perhaps most tellingly, criticism of its neglect of 'economic factors' (Rose 1977: 172). Despite these defects, the human relations approach was to survive and evolve.

Neo-human Relations

The development of the neo-human relations school post World War II was a reaction to the limitations of the earlier Mayo approach, particularly the neglect of financial rewards (Rose 1977). Maslow (1945) provided an explanation for conflict arising at an individual level. He identified a hierarchy of needs, with the implication that failure to meet the need at any level could lead to conflict (Maslow 1954). Thus, when basic needs were met, employees were identified as possessing a need for personal growth or self-actualisation. Meeting these needs could avoid conflict and lead to more productive and happier workers (Huczynski and Buchanan 1991). Herzberg (1968) introduced the distinction between satisfiers and dissatisfiers: poor pay may create dissatisfaction (and conflict) but good pay will not necessarily create satisfaction (absence of conflict). This led to a policy prescription that managers needed to attend to what motivates employees, as well as hygiene factors, i.e. pay and working conditions. While the neo-human relations approach was influential in management circles in the 1960s and 1970s, it had little impact on the practice of industrial relations, not least because (like the earlier human relations approach) it sought to deal with conflict in an exclusively managerial framework excluding collective actors (Rose 1977). Its greatest relevance was in personnel policies involving the management of white-collar staff, professionals and managers themselves.

Human Resource Management and Conflict

The human resource management (HRM) approach to conflict is conceptually like its human relations predecessors, i.e. an implicitly unitarist framework. However, it is much more sophisticated than simple unitarism. While it does not imply an absence of conflict, it does retain the key feature of the earlier human relations approaches that conflict is not fundamental and can be handled through appropriate management measures. There is greater sophistication inherent in the panoply of policies and measures that HRM can deploy. Teamworking, team briefings, merit pay, performance management and appraisal, and a host of other techniques are indicative of an awareness of a highly developed need for planning in order to promote motivation and avoid conflict.

Thus, unitarism has a degree of permanence as management's default or preferred approach to employment relations. Hence, Doherty and Teague's (2011) survey found that non-union organisations assume that management–employee interactions are based largely on 'trust and unity of interest', while workplace conflict is regarded as 'deviant'. This tallies with the unitarist perspective, as outlined by Fox (1966), that conflict is 'frictional' (due to incompatible personalities or 'things going wrong') and that it results from poor 'communications', stupidity (in failing to appreciate common interests) or the work of agitators inciting the (otherwise content) majority.

It may be argued that HRM has had a greater impact in tackling conflict than its conceptual predecessors. There is indeed evidence to support a substantial decrease in conflict (as measured by strikes and changes in workplace relations) since the early 1980s. However, the contribution of HRM to such a decrease is uncertain. Globalisation, the failure of state socialism as an alternative to capitalism, social partnership, neoliberal economic policies and, most notably, the decreased power of labour vis-à-vis capital in a globalised world are just some alternative causal variables to be considered. Even if HRM has worked to reduce overt conflict, Edwards (1992: 363) argues it 'has not dissolved the bases of conflict' and it is crucial to understand where lines of tension remain.

Pluralism Developed

As with unitarism, there is a range of approaches to understanding conflict that can be classified under the banner of pluralism. In its broadest sense, pluralism means a recognition that the employment relationship is based on a 'plurality of interests'. All pluralist approaches share the proposition that, to a greater or lesser degree, the potential for conflict is inherent in the employment relationship. It is not hard to sketch out a priori reasons why this might be so. Employers' needs for productivity, cost-effectiveness and change can be at odds with workers' needs for job security and 'good pay' (Allen 1971; Huczynski and Buchanan 1991; Hyman 1989; Jackson 1987). The 'financial exchange' dimension is only one potential conflict of interest as others are also inherent in other aspects of the employment relationship. The management of organisations requires the exercise of employer/managerial authority over employees on dimensions such as working time, workflow and task allocation (Morley *et al.* 2004; Reed 1989). Any of these factors hold the potential for conflict and they are emphasised to a greater or lesser degree by differing pluralist approaches. Here we focus on three pluralist approaches: (1) institutional pluralism, (2) the Marxist and (3) the radical approaches. As with the unitarist approaches, they do not provide definitive answers as to the cause of conflict, since there are fundamental differences between the various pluralist approaches. Their merit is to offer insights into the nature of industrial conflict and provide a degree of sophistication to the research and analysis of conflict.

Institutional Pluralism

Fox's original 1966 contribution is classified under the heading of institutional pluralism and is just one of a number of approaches that emphasise the role of institutions. In general, this approach focuses on the organisations into which the differing interest groupings form, and on the rules that regulate their relations (Dunlop 1958). Among early writers in the institutional tradition are Allan Flanders, W. E. J. McCarthy and Hugh Clegg in the UK, and John T. Dunlop, Clark Kerr, Arthur M. Ross and Paul T. Hartman in the US. Institutional approaches are considered functionalist in nature since although they see conflict as normal and inherent in the employment relationship, they regard it as capable of being accommodated and controlled by institutional mechanisms (Goldthorpe 1974). Temporary compromises (or collective agreements) are seen as helping to align the opposing aspirations of business to earn profits and increase productivity and efficiency with workers' demands for improved pay and working conditions. These regulations or procedures manage an ongoing dynamic tension, which is sourced in conflicts of interest and loyalty.

As Dubin *et al.* (1954) explained, collective bargaining was the great social invention that served to institutionalise industrial conflict. Just as the electoral process democratically institutionalised political conflict, collective bargaining created a dependable means for the resolution of industrial conflict.

The focus on rules is very evident in the work of the UK Donovan Commission and its recommendations for institutional reform, which had an inherent institutional-pluralist perspective. This approach was also based on the tradition of voluntarism and aimed at developing workplace systems for channelling and resolving conflict. Fox (1966) noted that a pluralist view allowed for the development of appropriate procedures (notably disputes, grievance and disciplinary procedures) and included relevant social actors (e.g. shop stewards) in the processes of conflict resolution. In effect, management, by adopting a pluralist approach, was urged to 'regain power by sharing it', with management's role being to balance competing interests. The case study in Table 9.3 provides an example of how the conceptual frameworks approach can be used to shed light on differing perspectives of conflict, allowing for analysis without resort to the distortions thrown up by interpersonal and emotional factors.

Table 9.3
Case Study
Perspectives on Conflict in a Small–Medium Enterprise

Clancy Motors has a small main dealer franchise in a medium-sized town in Co Kerry. The company is owned and managed by Tom Clancy, who served his time as a mechanic many years ago. Tom has recently heard that a few disgruntled employees are unhappy with their pay and overtime payments. He is very surprised at this because he feels he has always treated his employees very well – like family, really. He operates an 'open-door policy' and sees no need for rules and procedures, since each person has to be handled differently. Over the years, he has had a number of approaches from a local union official saying that employees want to be represented by a union. The official refused to supply names and Tom shrugged off the approaches, telling her that he refused to entertain 'any involvement in his business by any outside body'. Tom talks to a few senior employees whom he can trust. He asks them what is behind the current unrest and he hears that there are only a small number of employees involved. He concludes that they are just causing trouble and are showing no regard for the difficult financial pressures that all small businesses are under at this time. As a result, he decides to 'ignore the gripes'. However, while investigating, he finds that some employees (not the same ones behind the gripes) are putting petrol in their own cars from the company fuel tank without signing for it. He allows employees to do this in lieu of overtime if they have a call-out. He has always felt that this is a win-win, since they are not taxed on it. He discovers that three employees are filling up weekly. Tom is appalled at their action and feels betrayed. He calls in the three employees separately, telling them that he has clear proof of the theft and they have 'gone to town on a good thing'. He dismisses them without notice.

***

Mick Murphy has worked for Clancy Motors for six years. He thinks things are badly regulated, with pay below the norm compared to other main dealerships. Employees can be called in without notice at weekends to deal with breakdowns and towing people. There is no overtime or call-out pay for this, although employees do get a few gallons of petrol in lieu. Mick has bought a new house and is planning on getting married, and he feels he should be paid the going rate for his work. There are rumours that some mechanics are getting paid more than others but no one knows for sure. Mick feels he cannot do anything about this. While Tom Clancy says he operates an open-door policy, everyone knows you have to be careful what you say to him. Employees often say that it is 'Clancy's way or the highway' but no one dares say anything like that directly to Tom! Mick hears that three fellow employees are being sacked because Clancy said they were 'going to town on the petrol'. He thinks this is very unfair, since he knows these three employees are paid less than him, even though they are fully qualified.

Mick and a number of employees get together and join the Services Industrial Professional Technical Union (SIPTU). They tell the union official that they are going to strike. She insists that they do not strike. She explains that she will seek a meeting first thing on Monday with Tom Clancy in order to try to resolve issues and have the employees reinstated. Over the weekend, a number of employees get together and decide that there is 'no use in waiting' and that 'you need to strike when the iron is hot'. They decide they will picket Tom Clancy's home and the dealership. As a result, when Tom Clancy arrives to open on Monday at 9am, he finds himself confronted by seven disgruntled employees picketing the premises and they stay there all day. At the same time, two employees arrive to picket Mr Clancy's home – but they do this without telling any of the other striking employees. Mrs Clancy is surprised and upset to see them there when she returns from taking her children to school.

Discussion Points
1. Through what implicit conceptual frameworks do Mr Clancy, Mr Murphy and the union official view the employment relationship? Give reasons for your answers.
2. If Mr Clancy asked you on Monday evening for advice on how he should handle the situation, what suggestions could you make? Give developed reasons for your recommendation and for your rejection of the other options.

This case study can be used for analysis, discussion or role-play negotiation.

Marxism

Marx regarded capitalism as a major advance on the pre-existing feudalist system. It brought with it enhanced productive capacity, economic growth and a greater capacity to create wealth. Despite this approval, Marx considered capitalism as inherently flawed because the system would lead to great inequality in income and wealth distribution, and thus it held the potential for societal and workplace conflict. He saw this potential for conflict as rooted in two factors – the nature of capitalist societies and the nature of work under capitalism. Capitalist society is divided into two main classes – the propertied capitalist and working class (proletariat) – with the former expropriating the latter. Capitalist accumulation and profit come from the worker being paid less than the value of their labour. This leads to 'surplus value' accruing to the owners of capital – this is known as the labour theory of value. Marx predicted that the extraction of surplus value would lead to the 'immiseration' (or impoverishment) of workers. Expropriation would lead to the development of class consciousness among workers, with industrial conflict taking place along class lines between the proletariat and capitalists. Marx also predicted that capitalism would be gripped by recurring crises, making it unstable.

Marx's analysis is rooted in class and is concerned with exploring the effects of common economic conditions leading to organised action with the possibility for revolution (Dahrendorf 1959). Classical Marxism sees conflict as not just being inherent in the employment relationship but also irreconcilable. It predicted that as capitalism matured, a growing and ever-impoverished working class would create the conditions for a working-class revolution. Industrial conflict is therefore part of a broader class-based conflict, with the potential to lead to revolution and overthrow capitalism.

Contemporary Marxists have grappled with the failure of several of Marx's predictions to materialise. Revolution was supposed to occur in highly developed capitalist economies but Marxist revolutions have actually been associated with dislocation (war) in underdeveloped countries. Marx's prediction of periodic capitalist crises has been borne out by the 1930s 'Great Depression' and the 'Great Recession' from 2008; however, they have not led to revolution. Marxism not only spawned revolutionary parties but also led to reformist social democratic parties. The stability of capitalist (democratic) states has been explained as being due to an awareness of Marx's writings and the reforms in capitalist societies after the Great Depression of the 1930s, Keynesian demand management policies and the welfare state reforms being key developments.

Globalisation is seen as easing the potential for conflict in western societies (Arrighi 1990). It is argued that the extensive strikes in Korea in the 1980s and 1990s represented the displacement of traditional capital–labour conflicts to newer developing economies (Cho 1985; Edwards 1992). The modern consumer electronics industry is seen as depending on exploitative working conditions – for example, Foxconn, where extreme forms of labour conflicts (including, as previously noted, threats of mass suicide) have arisen. The death of nearly 300 workers in a factory fire in Karachi in September 2012 echoes historical experiences such as the infamous 1911 Triangle Shirtwaist Factory fire in New York City, which led to the death of 146 garment workers. In both cases, the workers were locked in with windows barred; as a result, they could not escape.

Radicals and Neo-Marxists

There is a substantial crossover between Marxist and modern radical industrial relations academics, with the terms being used interchangeably by some writers (Salamon 2000). However, there are significant differences. The radical perspective is focused on the basic premise of a fundamental inequality in the employment relationship – capital is considered more powerful than labour (Fox 1974; Goldthorpe 1974). As with Marxism, there is a focus on the hierarchical nature of society, the unequal rewards and unrewarding work. The key difference is that the radical view does not approach the comprehensiveness or extremities of classical Marxist explanations. In fact, the term 'radical' is an elastic one, stretching from social democrats such as Colin Crouch to the radical pluralism of Alan Fox and neo-Marxists such as John Kelly, Paul Edwards, Richard Hyman and many others who analyse contemporary society using Marxist concepts in a non-doctrinaire way. This diverse group is united by an effort to understand the fundamental *root causes* of industrial conflict in a societal as well as an organisational context. Just as the human relations school tends to reflect managerial concerns, the radical school concentrates on workers' experiences and conditions in the context of modern capitalism.

The development of a radical critique dates from the 1970s. It was a response to the growth in industrial conflict post Donovan and the failure of the pluralist prescriptions to stem the tide of strikes, especially unofficial ones. It owes much to further work by Alan Fox, who revised his earlier pluralist analysis in a series of publications from 1973 onwards. In doing so, he focused on the issues of power and control – not rules and institutions – in the workplace 'blending Marxian and liberal pluralist elements' (Ackers 2019: 41). While continuing to assert the superiority of pluralism over unitarism, he pointed to limitations in the pluralist approach and advocated a radical alternative interpretation for conflict. He wrote, 'like the pluralist approach, it [the radical approach] emphasises the gross disparity of power between the employer and the individual employee' (Fox 1977: 141). He continued, 'unlike the pluralist, however, the radical does not see the collective organisation of employees as restoring the balance of power (or anything as yet approaching it) between the propertied and propertyless' (Fox 1977: 141). Fox now sees pluralism's need to bind workers ever closer with procedures as evidence of a low-trust relationship between those who manage and those who are managed. In essence, radicals (such as Fox) point to the limits of institutional and procedural provisions where these are not underpinned by a degree of value consensus (Goldthorpe 1974).

Unlike classical Marxists, Fox (1974) does not anticipate any radical or revolutionary change. He argues that the approach of many rank-and-file employees probably consists of low-key acceptance of the organisation's essential characteristics, accepting it without 'enthusiasm and commitment' (Fox 1977: 143). In essence, the industrial enterprise is divided by a 'them and us' mentality and involves control rather than commitment (D'Art and Turner 2002; Whelan 1982). In this scenario, conflict is institutionalised through collective bargaining, but agreements may only be observed on the basis of expediency. Accordingly, radical writers have been more concerned to explain the limited extent of industrial conflict. Fox (1977: 142) argues that if workers go too far in challenging management power, privilege, values and objectives, they face the combined power of employer and government, which 'would soon reveal where ultimate power lay'. This point anticipated developments in the UK in the 1980s where the Thatcherite 'revolution' was a response to trade unions challenging both managerial and state power in the 1970s. The lessons of the Thatcherite revolution influenced Irish industrial relations, with trade unions moving from an adversarial approach to a more consensus or partnership approach from 1987 onwards (see Chapter 13).

The prediction of the immiseration of workers arose directly from the labour theory of value. That theory is widely regarded as wrong, if not absurd, by most economists, and rising real wages and declines in inequality after World War II seemed to disprove the prediction. However, from the early 1980s, inequality in wealth and income distribution started to grow and is now an issue of major concern again (Piketty 2014). Inequality matters because, as Wilkinson and Pickett (2009) in their influential work *The Spirit Level* have shown, inequality leads to inferior outcomes for societies on a large series of indices such as health, life expectancy and incarceration rates. In contrast, individuals at all levels of the social hierarchy do better in societies that are more equal, although people at the lower end benefit most (Wilkinson and Pickett 2019).

Extreme inequality in income and wealth has appeared to give a degree of vindication to Marxist predictions. However, Piketty (2015) has made clear that the reason for the growth in inequality he identified is based on returns to capital outpacing economic growth rates, and that he has not explored the growth in labour inequality. Wilkinson and Pickett's (2009) approach also differs from that of Marxists, who see inequality as being based on materialism. They see the negative effects of inequality as being grounded in 'our evolved psychology to do with dominance and subordination, superiority and inferiority … Inequality increases status competition and status insecurity [leads] to anxieties about self-worth, and intensifies worries about how we are seen and judged' (Wilkinson and Pickett 2019). In this they reject as naive the 'view that inequality only matters if it creates poverty or if income differences seem unfair'. While the labour theory of value is therefore not in any way vindicated by either Piketty or Wilkinson and Pickett's work, the issue of labour market inequality is very much a live issue, with the decline in union power and the growth in non-standard forms of work directly bearing on inequality.

While several classical Marxist predictions have not been realised, the notion that industrial conflict arises from an inherent antagonism between capital and labour remains a powerful hypothesis to explain the permanence of such conflict, its underlying causes and periodic resurgence despite pluralist or managerial efforts at containment. Many industrial relations writers, neo-Marxists included, now regard the organisation of work in a capitalist society as a complex mix of conflict and cooperation. The interdependence of employers and workers mediates the simple zero-sum game inherent in classical Marxist analysis. Controlling workers is only one way of achieving effective work organisation (Grint 1991). Edwards (1992: 390) notes that 'there are aspects of new employment systems which benefit workers, and critical analysis does not imply that workers' and managers' interests are totally opposed'. The possibility of worker resistance to the introduction of new information technology, which was of much concern to the European Commission in the 1980s, now seems misplaced, since workers willingly embraced such technology.

Indeed, workers have an interest in effective management, and management have an interest in tapping their workforce's initiative and creativity. While differences of interest may underlie the employment relationship, there are also strong imperatives that limit conflict and promote cooperation. Globalisation and international competition can heighten the need for collaborative engagement to protect employment. Indicative of this interdependence are findings that workers and their representatives (shop stewards) prefer competent managers (Edwards 1992; Sturdy *et al.* 1992). Studies have also shown that management in unionised organisations have generally positive perceptions of the role played by shop stewards, findings which are at odds with the militant image in which shop stewards are sometimes portrayed (Ackers and Black 1992; Donovan 1968; Wallace 1982).

Labour Process Theory

In addition to the hierarchical nature of society and unequal rewards, the tendency for capitalism to promote the unrewarding and alienating nature of work is regarded as a fundamental cause of conflict at the level of the workplace (Hyman 1975). Writing from a Marxist perspective, Braverman's (1974) seminal work has led to the development of contemporary labour process theory (LPT), which today spans neo-Marxists to radical pluralists and other researchers in the area of critical management studies. Braverman was concerned with understanding the nature of the labour process under capitalism. The starting point is the indeterminacy of the employment relationship. An employer hires the capacity to work (labour power) but has no guarantee that capacity will be delivered (Chillas and Baluch 2019). Workers are likely to seek intrinsically rewarding and stress-free work while employers, faced with the imperatives of competition, are likely to prioritise productivity and effort. Taylor had sought to solve this problem with his system of scientific management. He had hoped to eliminate underperformance (what he referred to as soldering) by breaking tasks down to their essential element, measuring these and then rewarding workers for achieving a certain standard above the norm. It was a win-win idea but contained the hidden potential for conflict as it created repetitive, deskilled work (Braverman 1974). It also led to disputes over the distribution of the win-win, which Taylor had arbitrarily set at 25 per cent for workers. This provided negotiating opportunities for trade unions and promoted their growth – the opposite of what Taylor had hoped, as he had suggested scientific management would make unions redundant.

Surprisingly, there are some similarities between LPT and management approaches to understanding conflict. Both LPT and human relations approaches identify unrewarding work, anomie/alienation and over-close supervision as leading to conflict. Thompson (2016) notes that LPT also shares many of the concerns of HRM but considers these factors are inherently bound up with the nature of capitalist production. In the human relations tradition conflict is only incidental, requiring a technical fix by enlightened management. HRM has many such technical fixes but Chillas and Baluch

(2019) question the extent to which the claims of HRM, and associated high-performance work systems, actually produce a win-win for companies and employees in practice. Labour process researchers have delivered a rich vein of case study research that shows such systems 'are often accompanied by stress, work intensification and job strain' (Thompson 2016: 73). While LPT theory has been influential in analysing the underlying reasons for conflict, it has little practical impact on the practice of industrial relations. Work organisation tends to be a management function and largely outside the influence of unions. Conflict, when it occurs, tends to be over the appropriate remuneration for the job and non-agreed changes to established work organisation.

Although based on an analysis of conflict between capital and labour, LPT sees private sector management approaches as extending into the state and non-profit sector. Chillas and Baluch (2019: 74) write that 'increasing pro-market practices and intensified competition amongst non-profits undermine efforts to sustain and encourage staff commitment, demanding instead a "hard" HR agenda that increases the disposability and insecurity of workers'. Arguably, this is not straightforward as workers are also tax payers and pro-market practices can be seen as being driven by government desires to reduce or limit taxation, including taxation on workers.

Conceptual Frameworks and Conflict: The State of Play

Table 9.4 provides a summary of the conceptual frameworks' perspectives on conflict. While the various schools are at odds with one another on explanations of workplace conflict, the debates surrounding the approaches and modern empirical research have led to a more nuanced understanding of conflict. Whatever its limitations, Fox's (1966) contribution remains one of the most insightful and influential works in industrial relations theorising (Ackers 2019). However, it projected a conservative, steady-state view of the regulation of employment relations, at odds with the dynamic and changing nature of industry and society. However, employment relations practice since the 1980s has moved in the opposite ideological direction towards unitarism. It is now clear that unitarism has many more strings to its bow in informing managerial policies than the 'straw man' model advanced by Fox in 1966.

Fox's pluralism was developed at a time of high union density and was rooted in that perspective. Union growth has now reversed and the high union density levels up to the 1980s appear to be the product of economic and social circumstances of that time – notably Keynesianism aggregate demand management, full employment and factory-based production. The re-emergence of widespread unemployment from the 1970s, combined with globalisation, the growth of multinational enterprises, an expansion in service sector employment and gig employment, has changed the dynamic of employment relationships.

Table 9.4
Summary of Perspectives on Industrial Conflict

Unitarist Perspective

The basic unitarist position is a non-conscious and reactive one. Conflict is seen as an aberration that occurs because 'something has gone wrong'. Harmony and unity are seen as the natural state, with conflict being an abnormal phenomenon that occurs as a result of some failure in the normal functioning of the organisation (e.g. poor communications, bad management, a lack of management leadership or the work of 'troublemakers'). While viewing conflict as abnormal, the unitarist perspective also sees conflict as essentially negative and damaging to the normal harmonious, productive state of the organisation. Thus, conflict is viewed as something that can and should be avoided. Where it does occur, management should take appropriate steps to eradicate it, probably by addressing the alleged source (e.g. improve communications or organisational design, train managers or get rid of troublemakers). The role of collective representation hardly arises at an analytical level in unitarist perspectives, with trenchant opposition to union recognition being common at a practical management level.

Pluralist Perspective

The pluralist perspective views conflict as a naturally occurring phenomenon in organisations. It arises from the differing perspectives and interests of all the groups and individuals who make up the organisation. At an organisational level, the emphasis is on management to plan for and manage conflict. This can be done by using procedures and negotiating with representative bodies (e.g. trade unions). At a societal level the role of the state is to provide institutional support for those engaged in trade unions in the form of provisions for conciliation, adjudication and arbitration on disputes. It may also provide for organs of worker participation (e.g. works councils). The pluralist perspective is also consistent with the view that conflict is not necessarily negative but can have beneficial effects. Efforts should therefore be concentrated on channelling conflict to limit damage and realise such organisational benefits.

Classical Marxist Perspective

Conflict in capitalist societies is seen as a symptom of the structural enmity that exists between capital and labour, employer and employee. Such enmity arises from the organisation of work in capitalist societies and the unequal distribution of power between the dominant establishment group that owns the means of production (employers, shareholders) and those whose labour is required to produce goods and services (workers). Therefore, conflict in organisations is simply a manifestation of broader class conflict in relation to the distribution of power in society, and organisations themselves are simply a microcosm of a broader class conflict between the bourgeoisie (who control economic resources and political power) and the proletariat, with managers representing the interests of capital. In the Marxist perspective, conflict is seen as instigating revolutionary change designed to dismantle the capitalist system, redistribute power in favour of workers and the working class, and ultimately achieve a classless society.

Radical Perspective

The radical perspective overlaps with Marxist analysis – it sees conflict as endemic in industrial societies, with a major cause being the unequal power distribution both in society and in organisations. Efforts by employers to organise work lead to a need for control, which tends to lead to compliance rather than commitment. Revolution or radical social change is not to be expected, since workers generally accept the system and their place in it. However, there are limitations to any efforts to contain conflict through institutions or procedural regulation. Workers may observe agreements on the basis of expedience. More recently, the complex interaction between conflict and cooperation and the mutual interdependence of managers and workers are emphasised. HRM is seen as another form of control, leading to work intensification, stress and long working hours – the new forms of social conflict.

In employment relations practice, unitarism has become more attractive for many employers. Ackers (2019) notes that American HRM and organisational behaviour have been exported globally and they are now the dominant frame of reference for many employers. Non-unionisation is now the private sector norm, and unitarist models for ordering employment relations are common. These models range from the 'soft' HRM approaches of Google or Intel to the 'hard' versions of Dell and Amazon. Such companies have successfully used unitarist approaches to managing people. However, there are situations where such approaches cannot be maintained, as can be seen from Ryanair's decision to recognise trade unions in 2018. Structural conditions, notably a shortage of pilots and the difficulty of coordinating a non-union approach across many different employment relations systems, saw the company abandon its previous non-union approach and enter collective agreements with unions.

Functions of Conflict

Rollinson (1993: 252) suggests that the argument that industrial action is irrational or dysfunctional is a fundamentally flawed perspective, and that industrial action is 'simply a rational extension of the negotiation process'. Indeed, collective bargaining requires the possibility of industrial action since, without it, there would be a much-reduced incentive for either party to reach an agreement during negotiations (Clegg 1975). In effect, the costs that industrial action may impose on both parties bring a reality to the negotiation process. Conflict exposes the actors to the shifting power balances, altered norms in employment relationships and the changes in the wider society and economy, and forces adaptation to them.

Within the Irish industrial relations system, many aspects of current Irish employment practice and regulation are derived from the resolution of former conflicts. The general provision for a forty-hour working week was established in the early to mid 1960s in a series of groundbreaking industrial disputes. Irish equality legislation of the 1970s arose in large part from European Community requirements but its introduction was also a result of campaigning by the women's movement and the trade unions, which brought them into conflict with government and employers. The current statutory redundancy entitlement to two weeks' pay per year of service first arose from union demands in a sit-in at Peerless Rugs in Athy, Co Kildare, and a strike in the Irish Glass Bottle Company in Dublin during 2002, and only later was it incorporated in legislation. More recently, the garda representative associations were granted ad hoc access to the Workplace Relations Commission and Labour Court as part of efforts to resolve threatened industrial action by individual Gardaí – this access was then made permanent in legislation, as noted in Chapter 2.

It is not just on the workers' side that conflict can be regarded as functional, as it has benefited both employers and government. In the 1980s a series of disputes in which unions were relatively unsuccessful led to greater labour market flexibility, the reduction of traditional effort bargaining, and union givebacks or concession bargaining (Wallace and Clifford 1998). Equally, the willingness of union members to accept the modest terms of the Programme for National Recovery in 1987 cannot be separated from these developments and the Irish trade unions' concerns at the negative strike outcomes for UK trade unions under Thatcherism.

The Dual Face of Conflict

In many situations conflict can have a *dual nature*, having both positive and negative aspects to it. When company closures occur, there are frequently harrowing TV interviews with employees who are traumatised by the immediate impact and express great anxiety for their future – the proposed closure of Molex in Shannon in October 2019 with the loss of 500 jobs being just one case in point (Goodbody 2019b). The negative personal aspects of such conflict are manifest, yet the alternative for an economy as a whole is the stagnation of state socialism. Faced with competition from low-cost countries, employers advocate 'moving up the value chain'. This is a functional strategic choice for an economy. While industrial restructuring can see a heavy price paid by workers, this has been mitigated by the provision of statutory redundancy payments – sometimes enhanced through collective bargaining – and the common use of voluntary selection for redundancy within companies that continue to trade. This Irish approach to redundancies, of course, imposes costs on employers, and it is at odds with the 'flexicurity' approach used in Denmark, where union density rates are around 67 per cent and employment rates high and unemployment rates low (3.7 per cent as of 2019). Flexicurity provides for easy dismissal, and litigation around dismissals is limited. In return, employees who are laid off have extensive access to social security provisions and retraining opportunities (Wilthagen and Tros 2004). Flexicurity is in effect a claimed mutual gains approach to the apparently competing issues of organisational adaptability and worker security. It has been an aspiration of the EU to promote flexicurity as part of a European Employment Strategy. However, this has had minimal success because, as Pedaci (2016: 150) notes, the concept has been used in different ways and is not specific as to 'what level of security and flexibility are appropriate'.

In contrast to the practice in their home country, many US non-union multinationals pay redundancy terms well above the statutory minimum. In this way, employees in non-union companies enjoy benefits first negotiated by unionised employees. While enhanced redundancy terms sometimes apply in non-union companies, this is far from always being the case and, where it does occur, there is evidence of the terms now being more modest. The redundancy terms when Dell Limerick laid off around 1,900 workers in 2009 were much lower than those paid in non-union companies like Digital and Wang in the 1980s. This trend has also been evident in the unionised sector, with the government insisting that Bank of Ireland reduce the redundancy payouts for bank employees from six weeks per year of service (plus statutory) to three weeks per year of service (plus statutory) when redundancies were being negotiated with the Irish Bank Officials Association in 2012. In addition, even where there is an advance agreement on enhanced redundancy pay, its delivery cannot be guaranteed, as evidenced by the Vita Cortex dispute in 2011–2012 (see case study in Table 9.5).

A Macro Perspective on Conflict

Industrial conflict has wider societal considerations beyond the immediate workplace. How societies choose to allow, disallow or regulate industrial conflict has major implications for the nature of society and there is a strong tradition in social science which argues that conflict is functional at a societal level. Coser (1956) thought it important to contain conflict within communal bounds (trade unions and employer organisations being classic examples). However, conflicts can and do take their own course and are not necessarily capable of being contained within 'the social structures which give rise to them' (Hyman 1989: 108). The demonstrations against globalisation in the early 1990s and early 2000s, the demonstrations against austerity during the global financial crisis in Greece (and other countries), the *gilets jaune* movement's resistance to the carbon tax in France and the climate action movement are all conflicts not fully contained within communal or pre-existing institutional boundaries. In contrast, discontent in Ireland against austerity after 2008 was largely confined within the Irish political and industrial relations systems (see Chapter 13), although the political system struggled to contain the dispute over water charges, which were dropped.

Those who see conflict as functional oppose its suppression and warn of the dangers inherent in such a utopian venture. For example, Dahrendorf (1959: 224), a noted critic of Marxism, declared that 'effective suppression of conflict is in the long run impossible'. At a societal level, it is not hard to think of examples of failed attempts to contain, suppress or eliminate conflict. In the Soviet Union, free trade unions were not allowed, with the primary function of unions being to serve the needs of the state – or, as it was known, to be the 'transmission belts of the party'. This suppression of industrial conflict

Table 9.5
Case Study
Longer than the Dublin Lockout – The Vita Cortex Dispute

Thirty-two Vita Cortex workers in Cork were made redundant on 15 December 2011. The company did not pay statutory redundancy pay, claiming inability to pay. As such, the payment fell to be paid by the state social insurance fund. Workers were unhappy with the statutory payment and occupied the company's plant in a sit-in to enforce a claim for an enhanced payment of 2.9 weeks of service, the cost of which was estimated at around €372,000. They claimed they were entitled to this as part of an agreement which had seen this amount paid to workers previously made redundant. The workers occupied the plant over Christmas 2011 and drew support from the local community and a number of local businesses, who supplied them with provisions. Many high-profile public figures, nationally and internationally, sent messages of support: Alex Ferguson, Mary Robinson, Katie Taylor, Christy Moore and Noam Chomsky. The company pointed out that there was no legal entitlement to the enhanced payment, that SIPTU had ignored the company's inability to pay and that the sit-in by the workers was 'unlawful' and 'unofficial'. Despite these points, the long-service of the employees – some over forty years – and the dignified nature of the protest continued to garner widespread support. In January the employees were offered €1,500 per person to leave the plant – an offer which was seen as derisory – and subsequently the owner (not the company) Jack Ronan offered €180,000, which was also rejected. The dispute was the subject of unsuccessful Labour Relations Commission intervention and a recommendation made by a group of three mediators, led by Labour Court chairman Kevin Duffy, was rejected by the company. However, within days, and following direct negotiations between the parties, a confidential settlement was agreed. Following the settlement SIPTU Manufacturing Division Organiser Gerry McCormack issued a statement: 'The workers are satisfied that these proposals, which were agreed following direct talks between SIPTU representatives and the owners of Vita Cortex earlier today in Cork, provide the basis for the full and final settlement of this dispute' (*Industrial Relations News* 2012: 1). Taoiseach Enda Kenny welcomed the settlement and praised the workers for their enormous 'dignity and fortitude' and said they 'deserved respect for their long years of committed and diligent service' (RTÉ 2012b). The occupation ended on 24 May 2012 – 161 days after it began – after payment of the agreed enhanced redundancy terms had been made.

Discussion Points
1. What lessons does the above case have for managing redundancy situations?
2. Why might the employer not have used the law even if the dispute was illegal?
3. Why might the offers above have been made by the owners and not the company?

Source: Various *Industrial Relations News* articles, including 2012; RTÉ, various news programmes from 2012; http://vitacortexworkers.wordpress.com/

only led to greater upheavals and the eventual collapse of state socialism in Eastern Europe. Right-wing dictatorships have experienced similar developments, as exemplified by the collapse of apartheid in South Africa, the fall of the Pinochet regime in Chile and the overthrow of Fascism in Franco's Spain and Salazar's Portugal.

Neither Fox's pluralism, the various schools of unitarism or classical Marxism has any explanatory power when it comes to establishing the differences in strikes (collective conflict) between countries. However, Godard's impressive review, written from a neo-Marxist perspective, identifies institutional variations as playing 'a critical role in addressing the sources of conflict and managing it' (Godard 2014: 37). Scandinavian countries have generally combined high levels of unionisation together with generally low levels of strikes and economic prosperity. In Germany and Holland systems of co-determination involving workers at board level and works councils produced a less adversarial system of industrial relations in the 1960s and 1970s than that in the UK and Ireland. In France extremely low levels of unionisation combine with frequent dislocation from a comparatively high level of strikes. Such differences have motivated a search for overarching theoretical explanations focused on differences in capitalist systems.

Hall and Soskice (2001) coined the term varieties of capitalism (VoC) to encapsulate the differences in western democracies with market economies. They distinguished between liberal market economies (LME) and coordinated market economies (CME). In the VoC taxonomy LMEs are 'characterised by deregulated, decentralised and adversarial employment relations ... and are dominated by considerations regarding shareholder value' (You 2016: 473). In contrast, CMEs are 'characterised by a more regulated industrial relations landscape that fosters a cooperative approach to employee relations', with stakeholder value (not shareholder value) driving corporate governance (You 2016: 473). The role of labour is central in the VoC approach. In CMEs labour is treated as a key asset in strategy formulation and business planning, with trade unions and works councils involved in planning processes and day-to-day development of products, and processes and performance are located at the firm, rather than, individual level (Morgan and Doering 2019). In contrast, in LMEs labour is treated as a variable cost, with little incentive to invest in employees, individual-level performance applies, and lower-level employees are given little autonomy or discretion beyond that provided by teamworking (Morgan and Doering 2019).

A major strength of the VoC approach is the simplicity of the model and it provides a significant contribution to understanding the different paths taken by countries like the UK, Germany and Sweden since the 1980s. The latter has seen its industrial base eroded and replaced by a move to services and finance, while in contrast Germany has maintained a thriving industrial base. Godard (2014: 45) claims that it is these underpinning features that have a determining influence on the level and long-run expression of organised industrial conflict, not the 'micro conflict management system popularised in recent decades' (Godard 2016: 45). The VOC analysis has resonance with the longer established neo-corporatist explanations of conflict and has led to coordinating national industrial relations systems. Given the importance of social partnership in Ireland from 1987 to 2008 and its links to neo-corporatist thinking, we develop these areas more fully in Chapter 13.

Concluding Comments

Industrial conflict takes many differing forms, both individual and collective, which can impose personal, commercial and societal costs. It can be initiated by workers or management and it can be seen as being inherent in the nature of industry and business. Different approaches provide a range of perspectives on the causes of conflict, with none providing the last word. Collective organised conflict has been in decline generally but there is evidence of greater pressure on workers from individual forms of employer-initiated conflict. However, conflict can also be functional, and the ways in which societies allow and disallow conflict can have significant implications for the stability of those societies. Past conflicts have shaped major areas of work organisation in ways often unrealised. Trade unions and employer organisations have been instrumental in reaching accommodations on areas of differences between employers and workers, and this has contributed to societal stability. However, such arrangements are now giving way to unilateral employer regulation only constrained by any legal arrangements which do not always adequately cover, if at all, new forms of employment – notably in the gig economy.

Chapter 10

Strikes and Lockouts as Forms of Organised Conflict

INTRODUCTION

Strikes are the most visible manifestation of industrial conflict. A strike can be defined as 'a temporary stoppage of work by a group of employees in order to express a grievance or enforce a demand' (Griffin 1939: 20). For the purposes of the collection of statistics, the International Labour Organisation (ILO 1990) has based its slightly broader definition on Griffin's as follows:

> a temporary work stoppage wilfully effected by a group of workers with a view to enforcing or resisting a demand or expressing a grievance, or supporting other workers in their demands or grievances.

A lockout is similarly defined as a wilful act involving one or more employers. Griffin's long-standing definition emphasises that strikes are a temporary interruption in normal working. It also implies that strikes are rational actions since they are undertaken to remedy a grievance or achieve a demand. Strike action is the most visible type of industrial action but, as already noted, they are far from the only form of conflict. Salamon (1998: 402) notes:

> the strike is often depicted as the ultimate and most favoured form of collective action in that, by stopping work and leaving the workplace, the employees clearly demonstrate both the importance of the issue in dispute and their solidarity.

Strike action, however, can involve considerable hardship for strikers through lost income and the risk of job loss. Thus, strikes can be a double-edged sword. If successful, a strike can strengthen a union's position, but a defeat can fundamentally damage it, as in the outcome to the British miners' strike in 1984–1985. In contrast, a recent study by Hodder *et al.* (2017) found that strikes were positively associated with an increase in members joining the UK civil service union. Sometimes, the resort to strike action can be an expression of weakness in workers' bargaining power rather than strength, something which Wallace and O'Shea (1987) found to be particularly the case in unofficial strikes.

Not all strikes are aimed against an employer. They can also take place because of disputes between unions (inter-union disputes) or because of disputes internal to the union (intra-union disputes). In Ireland there were a small number of damaging intra-union and inter-union strikes in the 1960s and 1970s but these have been absent in recent years. Indeed, such strikes are no longer accorded legal protection as a result of the changes to trade disputes law in the 1990 Industrial Relations Act.

A lockout is the employer equivalent of a strike; however, no distinction is made between strikes and lockouts in published strike statistics. In some countries the lockout is illegal (e.g. France), while in others (e.g. Germany) it is legal. In Ireland lockouts are legal but also extremely rare, and this may, in part, be due to the historical reverberations of the 1913 Dublin Lockout making them socially unacceptable. However, as Stokke and Thörnqvist (2001) note, 'pure' lockouts are uncommon internationally: most lockouts are a response to strike action or the threat of strike action. Even in Germany, where the lockout is socially acceptable, it is seldom used by employers (Fuerstenberg 1987). Of course, the opposite can also be the case. A strike can be provoked by an employer to engineer a shutdown – in other words, a disguised lockout.

HISTORICAL IMPORTANCE OF STRIKES

Historically, some strikes have been very influential and their outcome has set the tone for the industrial relations of an era. In many countries the establishment of trade union representation and recognition, especially among unskilled workers, was only achieved after successful strike action. The 1888 strike in Bryant & May by the London matchgirls presaged a rash of strike action over the following three years, resulting in the first widespread permanent unionisation of unskilled workers (Pelling 1976). As noted in Chapter 1, after the 1913 Dublin Lockout, union membership declined initially but resentment at the militant actions of the employers during the lockout, combined with the events of the 1916 Easter Rising and the subsequent War of Independence, saw the membership of the union involved in the lockout – the Irish Transport and General Workers' Union – recover dramatically (Roche and Larragy 1986). These historical experiences contrast directly with the outcome of key conflicts since the 1980s. Failed strikes in the UK and the US in the early 1980s saw trade union influence and power recede. The most notable were the year-long National Union of Mineworkers strike in the UK in the period 1984–1985 and the Professional Air Traffic Controllers Organization strike in 1981 in the US (Kelly 2015). Unions also experienced unsuccessful outcomes to strikes in the mid 1980s in Ireland, which was influential in trade unions embracing social partnership in 1987.

In addition to achieving industrial aims, strikes can mobilise collective interests in the broader social and political sphere. In France strikes in 1936 and 1968 led to major social and industrial changes. While strikes may express a popular desire for change, it is unusual for strikes to lead to revolutionary social change. A notable exception is the case of Poland dating from 1980 when martial law was used in an attempt to suppress the Polish Solidarity trade union (*Solidarność*). This attempted suppression was unsuccessful and led to major changes in Poland, which were to be influential in the eventual fall of state socialism throughout Eastern Europe in the early 1990s. The overthrow of these regimes and their replacement with capitalist systems contrasts starkly with the role Marx envisaged for industrial conflict, where communism was predicted to replace capitalism. In recent times strikes against government policy have become comparatively more common internationally (Hamann *et al.* 2013). In coordinated market economies, Kelly and Hamann (2010: 11) see this as being linked to 'radical government intervention on an issue salient to union members; and union exclusion from policymaking in countries with strong corporatist traditions'. However, despite the abandonment of social partnership and a period of austerity, Ireland has had only one rather muted national public sector strike in recent years (in March 2009) (Roche and Gormley 2017b).

Political strikes have also occurred in Ireland, although they do not constitute a legally recognised trade dispute and therefore they are not protected by the immunities in the Industrial Relations Act 1990 (or its predecessor, the Trade Disputes Act 1906). In the early 1980s there were a series of large-scale nationwide strikes against the disproportionate burden of taxation on PAYE workers. These were unsuccessful, with eventual tax reform concentrating on reducing the tax burden rather than redistributing it through a broadening of the tax base. A further notable example of a strike with political dimensions was the 1984–1987 strike by twelve Dunnes Stores workers, led by Mary Manning. This strike lasted for two and a half years and attained widespread international recognition. The workers refused to handle South African fruit in protest against apartheid in that country, and they were dismissed as a result (RTÉ 1985). Such altruistic strikes are unusual, however, with most strikes being concerned with terms and conditions of employment.

STRIKE CAUSES

Recording the cause for a strike involves a degree of subjectivity, since this may be disputed by the parties. Although a strike cause may be unclear in any single instance, the overall distribution indicates clear differences between the potential areas of dispute that contribute to strike activity. Table 10.1 contains details of the causes of strikes over the period 2012–2018. The top three contributors to the number of strikes are (1) wages; (2) reorganisation, demarcation and transfers; and (3) hours of labour. Wages made by far the largest contribution to working days lost (WDL), followed by reorganisation and hours of work. The 'Other matters' category included strike causes cited as being over a Labour Court recommendation, health and safety, and union recognitions. In the 'Reorganisation, demarcation, transfer' category, all except one of the strike causes (over transfer of workers) related to reorganisation, and this presumably indicates the impact of reorganisation as a consequence of competitive pressures resulting from the 'Great Recession'. No strike in that category related to demarcation, indicating the extent to which such once-common disputes now appear to have become virtually extinct.

Table 10.1
Causes of Strikes, 2012–2018

	Number of Strikes	% Strikes	WDL	% WDL
Wages	23	34.3	135,460	58.3
Hours of labour	7	10.4	13,508	5.8
Engagement or dismissal of workers, redundancy, etc.	5	7.5	766	0.3
Holidays with pay	0	0.0	0	0.0
Reorganisation, demarcation, transfers, etc.	19	28.4	73,657	31.7
Other matters	13	19.4	8,903	3.8
Not stated	0	0.0	0	0.0
	67	100.0	232,294	100.0

Source: CSO (data derived from industrial disputes).
Note: Because strikes have multiple causes, the number of strike causes exceeds the total number of strikes in the period (63) and the WDL causes exceed the total WDL (226,313).

EXPLANATIONS FOR STRIKES

While the above data indicate that strikes generally occur over terms and conditions of employment, they do not provide any explanation for the trends over time. Strikes do not occur in a homogeneous fashion. There are wide variations across countries, over differing time periods and between industries. As with theories of conflict, there is no one theory of strikes which can fully account for their incidence (Kelly 2015). However, theories do offer insights into the variables influencing strike activity, and they point to the role of factors that can influence the level and nature of strike activity. It is beyond the scope of this text to review all such approaches; instead, we focus on four particularly influential ones. These are: (1) the role of industrialisation and the effect of institutions and collective bargaining, (2) economic factors as expressed by both the short-run business cycle and long waves, (3) industrial sector effects and (4) the impact of political economy, including the role of centralised collective bargaining. The aim is to give an insight into the leading theoretical and empirical approaches explaining strike incidence, as a prelude to examining the Irish strike record.

It is a truism that the movement of workers into large-scale factory production was the cause of the emergence of strike action. As discussed in Chapter 1, early craft unions used strikes as a method to defend their craft, while unskilled workers used the strike weapon to gain union recognition and improve pay and conditions of employment. Battles for recognition were often bruising contests, with employers making frequent use of the lockout, especially where unskilled workers were involved. Ross and Hartman

(1960) and Kerr *et al.* (1962) drew on these historical factors to construct an institutionalist explanation for strikes and their variation over time and between countries. They suggested that conflicts were especially intense between labour and capital in the early twentieth century, under the influence of syndicalist union policies and trenchant employer opposition to unionisation. As societies matured, these conflicts decreased; employers and unions came to accept each other, collective bargaining became established and more sophisticated, and the state provided dispute resolution policies and procedures (Ross and Hartman 1960).

Ross and Hartman (1960) saw the development of industrial relations institutions, especially the growth of multi-employer bargaining and state intervention to assist dispute resolution, as having moderated 'primitive attitudes' to industrial action. Among the primitive aspects of industrial relations they identified was the nature of union movements, with communist-dominated and fragmented trade unions leading to higher levels of strikes. On the other hand, they saw the rise of labour/social democratic parties in power as leading to a decrease in strike activity. Controversially, they predicted the strike would, in time, wither away in certain societies, notably Northern Europe (Ross and Hartman 1960). This prediction was confounded by the dramatic events in Europe in the 1960s and 1970s, which saw a widespread growth in strikes. The broadening of strikes to groups that had traditionally not been involved in strikes (e.g. white-collar workers) also undermined the prediction (Crouch and Pizzorno 1978).

Despite the confounding of Ross and Hartman's prediction in the short term, it remains a persistent question as to whether industrial conflict is cyclical in nature or whether it will decline with the modernisation of economies and societies. It is salutary to note that, even in the UK, 'working days lost due to strikes remained at historically low levels from 1927 through to 1970' (Smith 2003: 206). Furthermore, the intensity of conflicts experienced prior to 1922 (as measured by violence on the part of the state, workers or employers) was generally not exceeded even in the strike-prone 1970s and 1980s in the UK (Kelly 1998). However, strikes and demonstrations against austerity in Greece and other European countries indicate the capacity for continuing violence to erupt. Despite this, it remains the case that in northern European states, such events are not the norm. Indeed, a generally unacknowledged aspect of Irish strikes is that they are moderate and carried out according to generally understood rules of industrial relations, consistent with the Ross and Hartman picture of a maturing industrial relations system. In developing countries quite a different picture can still exist – as exemplified by police shooting dead thirty-four miners during a goldmine strike in South Africa in August 2012.

Cyclical Explanations

In contrast to the institutional thesis of the withering away of the strike are explanations that suggest that strike action is cyclical. There are two variants of the cyclical approach: one based on the link between strikes and the *short-run* or Keynesian business cycle; and the other based on variation in strikes over *long-run cycles* or Kondratieff waves (also spelt Kondratiev). Analysis of the link between the short-run business cycle and strikes dating back to the early 1920s has heavily influenced economists' approach to the analysis of strikes (Jackson 1991). The key idea underlying the existence of such a link is that in good times the prospects for successful strikes are greater than when economic conditions are bad. Brannick *et al.* (1997: 299) write, 'obviously, unions are most likely to maximise their gains when business conditions are favourable'. In this regard, 'revolt' is most likely not when conditions of extreme misery exist but when conditions are improving (Hoffer 2002). In seeking to test the link between strikes and the short-run business cycle, economists have linked strike action to the key macroeconomic variables: the rate of unemployment, changes in real or nominal wages, the rate of inflation, and change in the profit ratio of organisations (Brannick *et al.* 1997; Edwards 1992). Thus, strikes should decrease as unemployment rises and increase in line with inflation or profits. We will see later that historically the Irish strike record displays just such an effect.

While the economic analysis of strikes has a degree of utility in explaining strikes, there are limitations. While a link between low unemployment and higher strikes is the most common economic variable to be tested, Brannick *et al.* (1997: 301) note that 'there is little consistent agreement as to the economic variables that influence strikes across countries'. Market forces are only one of several determinants of strike action, and other factors such as the nature and extent of unionisation (Shalev 1992) and the nature of collective bargaining (Clegg 1976) can counteract them. A further consideration is that certain sectors of the economy may be in a growth phase, even though the overall economy can be in decline; thus, there is a need to supplement any macroeconomic analysis with sectoral studies. Most critical for the economic approach is Paldam and Pederson's (1982) finding that the relationship between unemployment and strikes held in only one-third of seventeen countries examined for the period 1948–1975. Rigby and Aledo (2001) also note a lack of fit between unemployment and strikes and the rate of economic growth in Spain across the two decades of the 1980s and 1990s.

Kondratieff cycles, or long-wave theory, imply the periodic resurgence of strikes over historical time – not their withering away (Kelly 1998). The idea of Kondratieff waves is based on the claimed existence in capitalist economies of long-run business cycles of boom and depression. These waves are claimed to be driven by the creative/destructive waves of capitalist innovation and new technologies. Long waves are posited to occur across approximately fifty- to sixty-year cycles with '25–30 years of upswing, 25–30 years of downswing' (Kaufman 2018). Strike incidence and intensity increase at the upswing of long waves as the economy prospers and as the prospects for success of strikes improve. Strike incidence reaches its highest point before or at the peak of the waves. Strikes continue at a lower level during the downswings as workers seek to protect and retain any gains achieved during the upswings (Edwards 1992; Kelly 1998). At the bottom of the cycle, during extended recessions or depressions, strikes continue to occur but at a much lower level. The reduction is due largely to the poor prospects for their success and is similar to the short-run business cycle effect but stretched over a much longer time.

Kelly (1998) claims to identify a number of strike waves coinciding with the peaks and downswings of Kondratieff cycles. Reviewing a range of international empirical studies, he writes, 'overall it can be argued that there are major strike waves towards the end of Kondratieff upswings (1860–1875, 1910–1920, 1968–1974) and minor strike waves towards Kondratieff downswings (1889–1893, 1935–1948)' (Kelly 1998: 89). Thus, there is a degree of evidence to support the Kondratieff hypothesis. There are, however, difficulties with empirical testing. First, the fifty- to sixty-year cycle means that there has been only a limited time frame in which to test for long-run cycles. Second, empirical testing also throws up anomalies (Edwards 1992). For example, within long-run cycles, there will be variations caused by short-run business cycles, which can, and do, vary across countries. Finally, if a new wave is to occur, Kaufman (2018) notes that it would be due to peak between the years 2018 to 2034. However, he is deeply sceptical of this happening, claiming that union decline and other developments make it unlikely.

Account needs to be taken of the displacement effect, with evidence of the migration of social conflict beyond the workplace, as seen by the French *gilets jaunes* protests in France in 2018 and 2019. Notably, this movement had a right-wing character and concerned opposition to increases in taxes designed to help tackle climate change. In Ireland the campaign to resist water charges, led by the Right2Water movement, in 2014–2017 was a further recent social conflict extending beyond the industrial arena.

Sectoral Factors

Historically, strike levels vary across different industries. Some industries, such as mining and docking, have been noted to have high strike activity. In the case of Ireland Brannick *et al.* (1997: 315) note that from 1922 to 1992 'the mining and turf sector has produced more strikes and work-days lost per employee than any other sector [and] the agriculture forestry and fishing sector … rarely experiences strike activity'. The question arises as to what accounts for this phenomenon. Kerr and Siegel (1954) attempted to explain the inter-industry propensity to strike based on the characteristics of the job and the nature of the workers. They examined the relative strike rankings of industries in eleven countries and posited a two-factor explanation to account for the common rankings they found. Industries characterised by hard jobs – which attract tough, combative workers, living in isolated mass communities – have high strike proneness (e.g. mining and docking). Industries characterised by easy or skilled work performed in pleasant surroundings – whose workers are integrated into the wider community – will attract more submissive men or women and will have low strike proneness (e.g. railroad and agriculture).

While giving an insight into extremes of strike occurrence in some industries, the theory has been criticised on a number of grounds, e.g. there are contradictory experiences in the same industries in different countries. In addition to this, the methodology used in the research was flawed: they excluded results that did not fit (e.g. steel industry) and the empirical results did not justify the conclusions (Edwards 1977). The low strike proneness of certain industries (e.g. agriculture) can ignore counter-examples. In Ireland agriculture experienced widespread strikes and agitation in the period 1917–1923, which has been documented by the labour historian Emmet O'Connor (1988). The portrayal of agricultural work by Kerr and Siegel (1954) also seems oddly romantic, since not everyone shares the view that farm work is 'easy', as they suggested.

Kerr and Siegel's analysis leads us to ask if the 'men' were made hard and combative by their jobs or if they were this way to begin with. Thus, Edwards (1977: 564) notes that Kerr and Siegel ignored alternative explanations, notably the uncertainty caused by 'perpetual problems over the planning and organisation of work, and over earnings when these are related to output' – a feature that mining shared with casual dock work at the time. Most pointedly, the theory pays inadequate attention to economic and political factors and management action. In Germany, after World War II, the system of codetermination enabled the rationalisation of coal mining without the levels of conflict that accompanied that industry's rationalisation in the UK.

Political Factors and Collective Bargaining

Political economy explanations of strikes came to the fore in the 1970s with the development of neo-corporatist theories. Edwards (1992: 366) notes that this approach seeks to address the question: 'Why in particular have strike rates been low in Scandinavia and Germany and high in the US, Australia and France, for example, as well as in Britain?' Ross and Hartman's (1960) institutional explanation had drawn attention to the mitigating effect of Labour and Social Democratic parties on strike levels; however, there is an important difference between their explanation and the later political economy explanations. The latter focuses not only on the institutional aspects of Social Democratic parties in power but on the political exchange dimension between capital and labour.

The reasoning behind the political economy approaches is that strikes impose high costs on workers and trade unions, and they can better achieve their aims through Labour or Social Democratic parties, which they control and which are sympathetic to them. It is suggested that such countries tend towards neo-corporatism where collective bargaining is carried on centrally. The centralised organisation of collective bargaining accords trade unions and employer organisations a monopoly position in representing the interests of workers and employers, and limits workplace conflict. Trade unions exchange industrial action for political action and pursue a higher social wage (through redistributive social policies) instead of using their industrial muscle to achieve higher money wages. Employer-initiated conflict is reduced by the capacity of employer organisations to bind members in collective agreements or by general applicability of such agreements through their extension, making them legally binding on all employers (Kelly 2003). In particular, industry-wide wage agreements take wages out of competition and limit employer conflict over wages, which is generally the main cause of strike action.

The political economy approach has been particularly useful in drawing attention to the different strike experiences in strikes across countries and the need to be aware of the wider political and social context; however, it has a number of limitations (Edwards 1992). Franzosi (1989) notes that political economy theories are 'labour movement theories' and that they focus on the role of labour, paying insufficient attention to the role of employers or the state. Thus, there are limits to which even Labour governments can meet the expectations of labour, as exemplified by the socialist government of François Mitterrand in France in the 1980s. Furthermore, the accession of Labour or Social Democratic parties to power does not necessarily lead to lower strikes, since there are several counterfactual examples, e.g. Australia (late 1940s and early 1970s) and the UK (1978–1979, the 'winter of discontent'). More pointedly, since the mid 1980s, neoliberal policies have been associated with dramatic reductions in strike levels in the UK and also in the US. Such reductions have involved government exclusion of unions rather than any involvement in political trade-offs.

Not all political approaches are amenable to analysis in terms of an economic trade-off between capital and labour or workplace factors. Hamann *et al.* (2013: 1035–6) point out that 'general strikes differ fundamentally from economic strikes' as they have a strong political character. In the years from 1998 to 2006 (when economic strikes were in decline) general strikes grew in Western Europe. These strikes were frequently aimed against government policy and the exclusion of trade unions from policy influence through governments' legislative action. Minority governments were less likely to face general strikes than majority governments because they were 'more likely to include unions in policy formation' as part of blame sharing for unpopular policies (Hamann *et al.* 2013). In this regard, it is worth noting that the Irish Labour Party was in power between 2011 and 2016 and at a time when discontent was contained although that party suffered as a result of the austerity policies pursued by that government.

The approaches reviewed above are most useful in drawing attention to structural, economic, temporal and political underpinnings of strikes, for which unitarist-type explanations cannot account. Thus, diagnoses based on unitarist notions such as bad communications, troublemakers or bad management (the conceptual equivalent of troublemakers) cannot explain why strikes should vary across countries, industries and time. It is not credible to argue that strike-prone industries or countries are related to poorer communications and attract more troublemakers or bad managers. Undoubtedly, such factors may be present in strikes but they are more properly regarded as symptoms rather than causes of industrial conflict.

MEASUREMENT OF STRIKES

Information on strikes is the only source of data collected internationally on industrial conflict. Before looking at strike statistics, it is necessary to discuss two general problems that arise in their compilation. These are the issues of *completeness* and *reliability* of strike data.

Completeness relates to the extent to which statistics include all strikes. Countries have adopted different definitions of strike for inclusion in their statistics. An absence of completeness in data is something which particularly affects the statistic on the number of strikes but also distorts WDL and numbers of workers involved. In Ireland there is a low threshold for recording strikes – with strikes being counted once they last at least one day or involve a minimum of ten WDL. Irish strike data also include workers indirectly affected (those not working in the establishment affected but not on strike), unlike some countries, e.g. Germany, Spain and Sweden.

In contrast, some countries have much higher thresholds for their figures, most notably the US, which only counts strikes involving more than 1,000 workers. Furthermore, some countries do not count strikes in the public sector, e.g. Belgium, France, Greece and Portugal (Gall 1999). Other countries exclude political strikes from their official figures, with Spain excluding general strikes from their statistics since 2009. These inconsistencies make the inter-country comparisons of strikes suspect, but if the data are regularly collected within a country using a consistent methodology, trends within those countries can be more reliably examined. However, it is common for information on strikes in many developing countries, and even some developed countries, to be inconsistently collected. Data are frequently missing for countries for some years and this makes comparisons across time difficult, if not impossible (Wallace and O'Sullivan 2006).

The second problem with strike statistics is one of *reliability*. Reliability is determined by the extent to which the strikes (within the defined criteria) are actually recorded. This raises the issue of either under-reporting (most frequently) or over-reporting (rare) (Brannick and Kelly 1982). Under-reporting most affects the strike frequency statistic, making it smaller than what it should be, with short strikes more likely to be missed than larger and longer ones (Kelly and Brannick 1989). The number of workers involved can also be less than reliable since this statistic can be affected by variations in numbers involved throughout a strike. The WDL statistic tends to be least affected by problems of reliability. However, even this statistic can be wide of the mark, with German official figures for 2004 to 2014 under-reporting WDL by nearly three-quarters of the total picked up by an alternative source in the period (Dribbusch and Vandaele 2016).

The general unreliability of strike statistics poses particular difficulties for making comparisons between countries (Lyddon 2007). In this regard, the Irish statistics are likely to be more reliable and complete than those in many countries. The small size of the country and the media reporting of strikes mean that few strikes are likely to be missed. In addition, Dribbusch and Vandaele (2016) note that other countries exclude sectors of their economy and, unlike in Ireland, do not count workers indirectly involved – workers not directly striking but out of work.

Strike Indices

It is standard practice to collect information on the number of strikes (*frequency*), the number of workers involved (*breadth*), the duration of the strike, WDL and the causes of strikes. We have already dealt with the causes of strikes and will now examine the other four indices.

Strike frequency is simply the number of stoppages in a defined time period. Strike frequency has been used in many econometric studies and is advocated as indicating the general impact of strikes on management and the economy (Kelly and Brannick 1989). However, it is subject to the limitation that it gives equal weight to large and small strikes (Turner 1969). It is also the index with the greatest reliability problems due to two factors: the different criteria used by different countries for the inclusion of strikes, and the likelihood that many smaller strikes that meet the definition for inclusion may not be counted.

Strike breadth is measured by the number of workers involved in strikes. It gives an indication of the size of strikes but it can be open to error if the numbers involved vary during a strike.

The third index is *strike duration*, which refers to the length of strikes in days and can reflect differing strike 'cultures' across countries. For instance, French strikes have traditionally been short due to French trade unions not making provision for strike pay and the fact that strikes can be demonstration strikes with a political purpose. Traditionally, Irish strikes were quite long and this was taken as an indication of employer and union intransigence. However, that has changed since the 1990s and Irish strikes now are now much shorter, with a tendency for one-day periodic strikes having emerged since the 1980s.

WDL is the final measure of strikes. As this statistic is a measure of the impact of strikes, if not actual costs, it is widely considered the most informative indicator of the pattern of strike activity. It is calculated by multiplying the number of workers involved by the strike duration. In making comparisons across countries or sectors, WDL should be standardised for the level of employment. This is done by dividing the number of WDL by the numbers in employment. It is necessary to be aware that the WDL index is affected by a small number of large strikes. Kelly and Brannick (1983: 69) note that the Irish strike pattern is extremely sensitive to the 'comparatively small number of large strikes'. This historical feature of Irish strikes has continued in the 2000s, with only two strikes (2.5 per cent of the total) accounting for 75 per cent of all WDL in the period 2003–2018.

TRENDS IN IRISH STRIKE STATISTICS UP TO THE 1990s

Only a small proportion of all Irish employments experience strike action in any one year. The number of recorded strikes in Ireland has exceeded 200 in only one year, 1974, with 219 strikes. The number of strikes has only exceeded 100 in 30 of the years since 1922. There have been 38 years in which the level of strikes has been between 50 and 100 (Figure 10.1). The number of strikes has been under 50 in only 30 years, 28 of which have occurred since the commencement of social partnership agreements in 1987. The trend of declining strike incidence has become particularly marked since 2000, with the annual strike incidence exceeding 20 in only 5 years up to 2018.

In looking at the variation over time, the evidence from the three strike indices in Figures 10.1, 10.2 and 10.3 indicate certain periods of higher and lower strike activity, combined with a large degree of fluctuation from year to year. Much of this movement, at least up to the 1990s, can be linked to economic factors. Two main economic influences can be identified: both the short-run and long-run cyclical explanations discussed earlier, and industrial restructuring linked to the role of industrial policy.

Brannick *et al.* (1997: 310) emphasise that all three indices of strike activity over the period 1922–1995 are 'broadly pro cyclical with respect to economic changes'. This means that strike activity (most notably as represented by the frequency and WDL indices) rose and fell roughly in line with the short-run business cycle. There was a decline

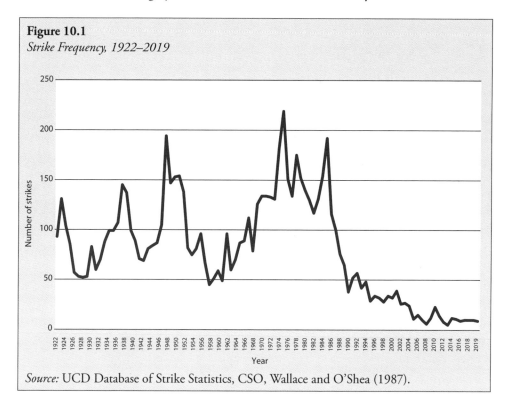

Figure 10.1
Strike Frequency, 1922–2019

Source: UCD Database of Strike Statistics, CSO, Wallace and O'Shea (1987).

Figure 10.2
Workers Involved in Strike Activity, 1922–2019

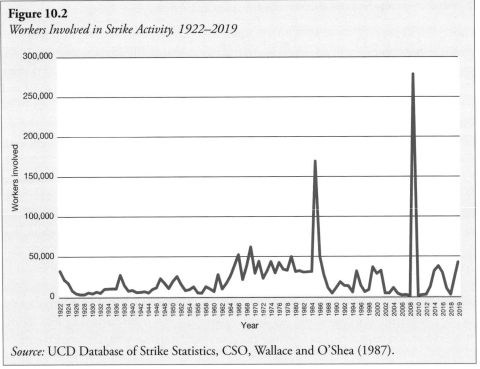

Source: UCD Database of Strike Statistics, CSO, Wallace and O'Shea (1987).

Figure 10.3
Working Days Lost Through Strike Activity, 1922–2019

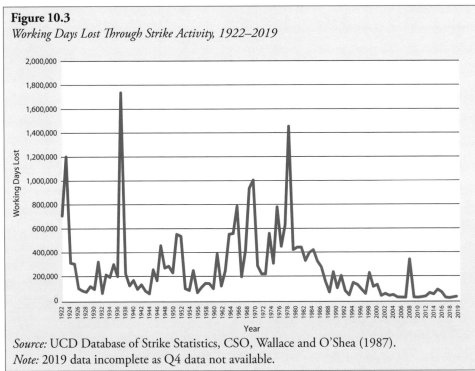

Source: UCD Database of Strike Statistics, CSO, Wallace and O'Shea (1987).
Note: 2019 data incomplete as Q4 data not available.

in strikes in the 1920s, which coincided with a period of recession and stagnation (Brannick *et al.* 1997). Strike levels increased during the 1930s, corresponding to a period of increased industrialisation and economic protectionism (with 1937 being the year with the largest number of WDL up to now). After that, there was a decline in strike activity, coinciding with World War II and the Wages Standstill Order, which placed restrictions on wage increases and made strikes over wages largely impractical.

The general increase in the strike frequency and WDL indices from 1945 to 1952 follow on from the austerity of the war years and the removal of the Wages Standstill Order. This represented an effort by workers to restore pay levels, which had declined dramatically since 1939. From 1952 the economic depression of the 1950s (when the Irish economy was out of sync with the rest of northern Europe) saw both large-scale emigration and increased unemployment, which led to a decline in strike activity. The growth in economic activity associated with an opening up of the economy in the 1960s was accompanied by a return to a higher level of strike activity, which reached a peak in the late 1970s. Although there was a decline thereafter, up to the mid 1980s the indices remained at relatively high levels by historical norms.

Domestic and International Influences on Strike Trends

In addition to the short-run pro-cyclical economic factors outlined above, Irish strikes were influenced by international developments and industrial development policy. The years 1922–1924 coincided with the end of an earlier international strike wave. The rise in strikes in Ireland in the 1960s coincided with the Kondratieff wave, which Kelly (1998) identifies as lasting from 1968 to 1974 but others suggest it ended in 1985 (Kaufman 2018). While it was part of an international trend, the Irish strike wave starts well before 1968 and lasts well beyond Kelly's 1974 end date. The international influences on the Irish strike experience can be summarised in the following simplified narrative.

After the 1950s Irish recession, wages were low and the 1960s economic growth led to increases in strike activity as workers sought to gain improvements in their terms and conditions of employment. The buoyant economy of the 1960s led to low levels of unemployment and increased the prospects of a successful outcome to a strike. This combined with rising inflation, and the decentralised nature of collective bargaining based on wage comparability with other workers and with open-ended agreements (see Chapter 13), led to increased strike activity as measured by the three indices. These strikes led to significant improvements for workers, notably in terms of the introduction of the forty-hour week in 1964 and increased pay.

The successes emboldened workers and led to union growth, and this coincided with the international strike wave, starting around 1968. Efforts at reforming collective bargaining with the introduction of national wage agreements led to some fall-off in the strike indices in the early 1970s but this reduction was limited in size and only temporary. The second half of the 1970s saw strike activity increase, coinciding with historically high levels of inflation but still relatively low (although increasing) levels of unemployment. The early to mid 1980s saw a severe downturn in the Irish economy associated with the second oil crisis and, as a result, employers sought concessions or 'givebacks' from workers and unions. The demands for givebacks led to a series of defensive strikes, as predicted by long-wave theory. These were generally unsuccessful and, following this lack of success, strike activity declined.

The decreased strike activity was sustained in the period of social partnership, 1987–2008, with a marked break in the previous pro-cyclical strike experience. From 2008 onwards, during the financial crisis, or 'Great Recession' as it has been called, Ireland continued with a low strike experience. There were a large number of WDL in 2009 due to a general public sector strike against government policies, formally against pension and other cuts, but, as Teague and Donaghey (2012) note, this was muted. It was more a demonstration of discontent than any serious challenge to those policies. There was some strike resurgence in 2015–2017, as indicated by increases in the workers involved and WDL figures but not the number of strikes (Figures 10.1, 10.2 and 10.3). This increase can be seen as marking a return of a short-run business-cycle effect and does not represent a long-wave strike trend. This return of a procyclical effect was limited, and appears short-lived, as the level of strikes, workers involved and WDL returned to historically low levels in 2017 and 2018. This consolidation of the change in the nature of the Irish strike experience beyond the social partnership years makes it difficult to imagine any re-emergence of a long-run Kondratieff strike wave. What seems to have happened since the late 1980s is a long-run *attenuation* of strikes but not their *withering* away.

Industrial Policy Influences on Strikes

Cyclical factors at a macro level mask the influence of the role of industrial development and industrial restructuring in the 1960s to 1980s. A seminal paper by Kelly and Brannick (1988) disentangles the strike record of British, Irish and US companies in three separate time periods: 1960–1969, 1970–1979 and 1980–1984. In the period 1961–1969, British companies in Ireland had the lowest strike record of the three groups, with US companies having the highest strike record. This low strike record changed dramatically in the period 1970–1977, with British companies becoming the most strike-prone and strike activity declining in US companies in the 1970s and reaching a low level in the 1980s. Kelly and Brannick (1988: 45) locate the reason for this change in the 'disjunctive impact' of industrial policy, which opened up the country's economy. They point especially to the effect of the Anglo–Irish Free Trade Area Agreement of 1965, which required a progressive reduction in protective tariffs of 10 per cent *per annum* up to 1975.

The protectionism of the 1930s saw British companies set up behind high tariff barriers to supply the Irish market, with little of their production exported. These companies were exposed to competition by the progressive removal of the trade barriers in the 1970s. This led to 'a sharp disjuncture in the traditional relationship between the companies and their employees', resulting in a change from low to higher levels of strike activity (Kelly and Brannick 1988: 52). These new competitive policies led to 'slimming down policies' and 'new tougher stances by managements' (Kelly and Brannick 1988: 52). The picture that emerges from Kelly and Brannick's research is one of the workers and managers bearing the price of industrial adaptation. It is clear from these findings that the increased strike activity in British companies in the 1970s was a symptom of industrial change and the dislocation this caused. This finding is destructive of the notion that the industrial conflict was caused by 'troublemakers' or indeed its intellectual equivalent – 'bad managers'. Even more so, it exposes the limitations of the frequently invoked 'lack of communications' as a cause of strikes.

A CONSIDERATION OF CURRENT STRIKE LEVELS

Public and Private Sectors

Figures for strike activity in the public and private sectors over the period 1960–2018 are contained in Table 10.2. The figures in that table indicate that the private sector was the source of most strike activity, as measured by all three indices, during the decades of the 1960s and 1970s. However, this might be expected – since employment was greater in the private sector. The private sector continues to have the largest number of strikes, although there has been a decline in the proportion of strikes accounted for by the private sector, from 80 per cent in the 1970s to 62 per cent in the period 2012–2018. The decline in the numbers of workers involved in the private sector is much greater – down from 67 per cent in the 1970s to only 18 per cent over the years 2012–2018, although this is an increase on the period 2003–2011, when it was only 6 per cent. The main reason for this increase is the distorting effect of the 2009 large one-day public sector strike (involving 265,000 workers and resulting in 237,000 WDL) in protest at the government pension levy. When the average length of strikes (strike duration) is examined, a different pattern emerges. Strike duration has been longer in the private sector since 2003: it was six days on average in that sector in the period 2003–2011 compared to slightly over one day in the public sector. The gap closed significantly since then as over the period 2012–2018 the average duration was 2.7 days in the private sector as against 2.3 days in the public sector. Both of these are dramatic reductions over the period 1990–1995, when the average length of public and private sector strikes was six and a half days and twenty-one days, respectively (Brannick *et al.* 1997). This reduced strike duration makes a major contributor to the overall reduction in WDL and reflects a change in the historical nature of strike action in Ireland. Workers now often opt for rolling one-day strikes and not the much longer strikes that characterised Irish strike action in the past.

Table 10.2
Proportion of Strike Activity in the Public Sector and Private Sector, 1960–2018

Year	Strike Frequency (%)		Workers Involved (%)		Working Days Lost (%)	
	Public Sector	Private Sector	Public Sector	Private Sector	Public Sector	Private Sector
1960–1969	17.9	82.1	36.3	63.7	23.3	76.7
1970–1979	18.3	81.7	32.5	67.5	37.8	60.2
1980–1989	29.1	70.9	68.9	31.1	37.7	62.3
1990–1995	47.0	53.0	61.0	39.0	27.0	73.0
1996–2002	45.1	54.9	75.0	25.0	58.7	41.3
2003–2011	34.0	66.0	94.0	6.0	74.0	26.0
2012–2018	38.1	61.9	82.1	17.9	79.5	20.5

Source: 1960–1995 data from Brannick *et al.* (1997); 1996–2018 data supplied directly by the CSO.

Official and Unofficial Strikes

In Ireland unofficial strikes tend to be subject to considerable opprobrium and state institutions have had a general policy of not involving themselves in meetings to resolve unofficial strikes until work is resumed. Unofficial strikes are strikes that do not have the sanction of the relevant union authority (Wallace and O'Shea 1987: 2). Unofficial strikes can be distinguished from unconstitutional strikes, which are strikes in breach of procedures – not strikes in breach of the Constitution! The utility of the official and unofficial distinction has long been questioned. Kelly and Brannick (1983: 10) found that among union officials there was substantial variation in what was considered an unofficial strike. In some instances, a strike may not be official because the union did not know of the strike; making a strike official would involve payment of strike pay, which a union could not afford; or it may be official at one level of the union but not at another level (Jackson 1982). In addition, strikes that start as unofficial may subsequently be made official to allow for retrospective strike pay to be paid. Even within unofficial strikes there are different categories. Wallace and O'Shea (1987) found that longer unofficial strikes tended to be more like official strikes because they had perceived collective validity by the workers. In contrast, unofficial strikes without such perceived validity (so-called cowboy strikes) tended to be of very short duration – only one or two days and sometimes even only hours' long. Despite the general militant image of unofficial strikes, the evidence is that, even in the early 1980s, they were generally a weak weapon for workers (Wallace and O'Shea 1987).

The figures in Table 10.3 indicate that unofficial strike action is now rare. There were only three unofficial strikes in the period 2012–2018 and the number of WDL, at only 787, was insignificant. It was not always thus. During the years 1976–1979, unofficial strikes averaged 67 per cent of the total number of strikes and almost 16 per cent of total WDL. Table 10.4 charts the decline in unofficial strikes and shows they have fallen to an all-time low. In the period 2012–2018 they accounted for just under 5 per cent of the total number of strikes and 0.3 per cent of total WDL. Looking at the distribution of WDL, there is a similar dramatic decrease in the period 2012–2018. A number of factors may account for the decline in unofficial strikes. For example, their weakness during the 1980s and the greater role of employment law, which provides an alternative to strikes (particularly the Unfair Dismissals Acts dating from 1977), are likely to be contributory factors. Unofficial strikes were already in decline before the Industrial

Table 10.3
Summary of Official and Unofficial Strike Activity, 2012–2018

Number of Strikes, 2012–2018			WDL in Unofficial Strikes
Official	60	Number of days lost	226,313
Unofficial	3	Unofficial days lost	787
Total	**63**		227,100
			% of total WDL
% Official	95.2		99.7
% Unofficial	4.8		0.3
	100.0		100

Source: CSO data on industrial disputes.

Table 10.4
Trends in Official and Unofficial Strike Activity, 1976–2018

Year	Unofficial Strikes (as a Percentage of All Strikes)	WDL in Unofficial Strikes (as a Percentage of All Strikes)
1976–1979	66.8	15.5
1980–1989	42.1	19.3
1990–1999	27.4	6.8
2000–2011	18.7	7.4
2012–2018	4.8	0.3

Source: Wallace and O'Shea (1987); Department of Enterprise, Trade and Employment; 2012–2018 data supplied directly by the CSO.

Relations Act 1990 but the greater regulation of balloting in that Act, and the requirement for seven days' notice of strike action, may have contributed to driving down the incidence further and keeping them at a low level. Whatever the specific factors contributing to their decline, it is evident that there has been a major change in strike culture in Ireland.

National and International Influences on Recent Irish Strike Activity

Up to about 1993, the narrative in Ireland is largely consistent with a pro-cyclical hypothesis; however, there is no upswing in strike activity with the economic boom of the Celtic Tiger years as the former pro-cyclical relationship breaks down. The reasons for this disjuncture are a matter of debate, with the two main reasons being identified as (i) social partnership and (ii) other national and international factors. A disjuncture in Irish strike levels is already evident from the mid to late 1980s, with fewer than sixty strikes in each year since 1988 and the other strike indices generally, if not consistently, declining. The decline provides prima facie evidence for what Thomas *et al.* (2003: 36) identify as 'a peace dividend' attaching to Irish centralised agreements dating from 1987. Thomas *et al.* (2003: 36) see this dividend as being driven by union leaders who have sought to move away from 'an overtly adversarial style of industrial relations'. However, this suggestion is a labour movement theory à la Franzosi (1989) and can only offer a partial explanation for decreased strike activity.

The weakness of the strike weapon in the 1980s, the shift in the economy to services (where unionisation has traditionally been lower), the decline in unionisation and the openness of the Irish economy (promoting a need for competitiveness to ensure firm survival) are all factors that would have tended to depress strike action, irrespective of partnership. Also, many employees now have mortgages and other fixed financial commitments, which previous generations of workers did not have, and these may explain the movement to short strikes and act as a brake on strike action. The decline in Irish strikes reflects a common international trend, with a dramatic decline in strikes occurring across most countries since the 1980s (Kelly 2015; Kelly and Hamann 2010; Wallace and O'Sullivan 2006). The UK has experienced an equivalent drop in strike activity with an entirely different market control approach – the opposite of social partnership.

Focusing on the EU, Thomas *et al.* (2003: 42) claim that 'while there has been an overall fall in strike activity within the EU, the decline in industrial action within Ireland has been one of the sharpest'. However, international evidence is somewhat mixed for WDL – the most useful strike statistic. In respect to the rank order of WDL per 1,000 employees across nineteen developed countries, the Irish position only changed marginally for much of the social partnership period (Table 10.5). It was fifth highest in 1981–1985, it fell to seventh highest in the period 1991–1995, but then it returned to being fifth highest in the period 1996–2000. The period 2000–2005 does, however, show a substantial drop in the Irish position down to only eleventh highest out of the nineteen countries – a fall of six places over the Irish position in the period 1981–1985. While this does indicate a sharp reduction, the period of 2001–2005 was also when social partnership drew the most criticism. Thus, the low WDL levels of that period may only have been sustained by 'give-away' deals such as benchmarking, which critics at the time argued were not in the interest of the economy.

Table 10.5
International Comparison of Annual Average WDL per 1,000 Employees, 1981–2005

Country	1981–1985	1986–1990	1991–1995	1996–2000	2001–2005
Australia	386	224	130	85	42
Austria	2	2	6	1	83
Belgium	n/a	(48)	32	21	71*
Canada	532	429	159	215	215
Denmark	306	41	45	296	35
Finland	326	410	218	56	78
France	78	111	94	68	72
Germany	52	5	17	2	3
Greece	516	6,316	1,148	29 (1996–1998)	87
Ireland	474 (fifth highest)	242 (sixth highest)	109 (seventh highest)	91 (fifth highest)	30 (eleventh highest)
Italy	774	315	183	76	71
Japan	10	5	(3)	1	0
Netherlands	24	13	33	4	12
Norway	58	142	62	134	29
Portugal	176	82	34	20	19
UK	440	137	24	21	27
Spain	584	602	469	182	171
Sweden	40	134	50	9	34
Switzerland	n/s	n/s	1	2	5

Source: 1981–1995 data from Brown *et al.* (1997); 1996–2000 data from the Office for National Statistics (January 2003); 2000–2001 and 2003–2005 data from EIRO; 2002 data from ILO; there are some inconsistencies in the data sources.
Note: Brackets indicate averages based on incomplete data; n/a = not available; n/s = less than five days lost per 1,000. Some figures are estimated.

The strongest argument in favour of a significant social partnership effect is the break in the previous procyclical strike trend and it may be improbable that this would have happened without a domestic initiative, such as the partnership agreements. The growth of the Celtic Tiger years would have placed workers in a position to achieve favourable outcomes to strike action. Thomas *et al.* (2003: 36) point out the relatively low level of conflict secured and sustained by the continual striving of the social partners 'through a series of dense personalised networks and an array of informal, formal and ad hoc institutions'. These personalised networks and the strength of the third party institutions were influential in the sustained low strike levels during the period 2010–2019.

However, the underlying national and international dynamics were also working to reduce strikes. Most notable in that regard is the greater openness of the Irish economy, with Piazza (2005) demonstrating that there is a strong inverse relationship between WDL in strikes and the openness of an economy. Within the unionised private sector, companies are now open to international competitive pressures, are more mobile internationally and can switch production between different plants within groups. Thus, while favouring a partnership effect, Thomas *et al.* (2003: 45) recognise that 'the shared understanding of the interdependent mechanism within Ireland's small open economy allied to the "cold wind" of reality generated by the intensification of international competition' made a wave of industrial militancy (reminiscent of the period 1965–1985) unlikely.

Of interest also is the non-return to anything like high strike levels after the collapse of social partnership in 2009. Roche and Gormley (2107a) acknowledge the enduring influence of partnership but also draw attention to the openness of the Irish economy. They see the low levels of strikes as, in part, a response to competitive pressures and the limited potential for success that strikes would have enjoyed, a point that accords with Piazza's (2005) finding. Within the public sector, substantial pay cuts and changes to conditions of employment were introduced from 2010 to 2019 without major strike activity and, as in the private sector, there were constraints on industrial relations actors in initiating strikes. The dispute over two-tier pay in the teaching profession is illustrative of these constraints and the limited prospects for success for those who operated outside the Public Sector Stability Agreements (see Table 10.6).

CONCLUDING COMMENTS

The occurrence of strikes and their impact are affected by underlying structural, economic and political factors, as well as the nature of collective bargaining arrangements. Neo-corporatist systems tend to have low strike rates because of a political exchange between capital and labour. In Ireland in the 1960s the decentralised pay rounds were seen as being behind increased strike activity. However, this also coincided with a booming economy and international strike wave. Thus, both the short-run and long-run economic waves are linked to the increased strike levels in the 1960s to mid 1980s. An economic influence is also evident in an increased strike proneness in British companies as a result of industrial restructuring consequent on the opening of the Irish economy following the Anglo–Irish Free Trade Area Agreement and entry to the European Economic Community. Internationally, strike incidence and impact have

Table 10.6

Principle and Pragmatism: Two-Tier Pay and Croke Park Hours

The Croke Park Agreement (CPA) (2010–2014) committed members of secondary teaching unions to work an extra one non-teaching hour per working week (thirty-three hours per year). Subsequently, the Association of Secondary Teachers, Ireland (ASTI) rejected the Lansdowne Road Agreement (LRA) (2016–2018) and balloted to take limited industrial action in that its members would not work the thirty-three additional CPA hours, as it considered the CPA commitment had then lapsed. The government, however, judged the ASTI to have 'repudiated' the LRA and so it imposed an increment freeze and other penalties on ASTI members for doing so. In addition, ASTI members no longer qualified for the restoration of payments for supervision and substitution (S&S), which had been removed temporarily in 2013 but were due to be restored from September 2016 under the Haddington Road Agreement. In autumn of 2016 the ASTI announced its withdrawal from S&S duties 'since they were not being paid for them'. Separately, it also announced a series of seven one-day strikes against the two-tier pay system for new entrant teachers who had been recruited after January 2011. The Teachers Union of Ireland (TUI) and the Irish National Teachers' Organisation, while opposed to two-tier pay, had accepted the LRA and decided to address the issue under the LRA pay restoration process. Involvement in the LRA meant these unions continued to work the CPA hours. Government strenuously resisted the ASTI's demands, as it feared concessions would have undermined the LRA. The ASTI actually only took strike action on two days, together with one day of withdrawal from S&S duties – which resulted in schools being closed – before the industrial action was suspended and the dispute referred to the Teachers' Conciliation Council. ASTI members narrowly rejected the report from that council hearing in February 2017. The ASTI did not resume any industrial action that would have closed schools but maintained its ban on the CPA hours, keeping it outside the LRA. As ASTI members continued to be subject to penalties, discontent grew within the union and a Special Convention of the ASTI was held on 10 June 2017. At that convention, ASTI delegates decided to resume working the CPA hours, thereby giving their members access to payments under the LRA from 10 June 2017. By the time of opting into the LRA, 1,069 ASTI members had left that union and transferred to the TUI, thereby making them eligible for payments under the LRA. An inter-union dispute resulted, with ASTI making a complaint against the TUI to the Irish Congress of Trade Unions (ICTU) under rule 46(c) of congress, which debars a trade union from accepting members from another union in a dispute situation. The complaint resulted in an ICTU recommendation that the TUI pay compensation of €279,799 to the ASTI. On 4 February 2020 (after the period covered by the LRA), the TUI engaged in a one-day strike over two-tier pay and made its abolition a precondition for the union's involvement in any new public sector agreement. The ASTI also indicated an intention to return to strike action but this time only in conjunction with one or both of the other teacher unions.

Discussion Points
1. What lessons can be drawn from the differing stances adopted by the teachers' unions to addressing their grievances?
2. What differences exist in the government's approach to the two-tier dispute in teaching and the treatment of the Garda and nurses' disputes?

Source: Various editions of *Industrial Relations News*, *The Irish Times*, TheJournal.ie, ASTI (2019), O'Kelly (2020). Special thanks to Colman Higgins of IRN for commenting on a draft of this case study.

declined greatly in a majority of countries since the 1980s. In the Irish case social partnership and other domestic factors, along with competitive pressures from the openness of the economy and common international developments, are likely to have contributed to a disjuncture in Irish strike experience, which continues at a historically low level in the absence of social partnership. In post-partnership the low level of strike activity has been maintained by active industrial relations policies in both the public and private sectors.

Chapter 11

Negotiations

INTRODUCTION

This chapter aims to provide an introduction to negotiation theory and practice for use in third-level modules on negotiation and for negotiation training generally. Naturally, exposure to one chapter in a single text is insufficient to make someone a skilled negotiator – but even a basic understanding can significantly improve performance. One of the difficulties of modern negotiations textbooks is that it can be a challenge to assimilate and apply the detailed analysis and exhaustive prescriptions therein. A short introductory review has its own merits as it can simplify and highlight key points.

Previous chapters have sketched out the dynamics of employment relations and the underlying tensions, with the potential for damaging conflict and the need for cooperation. Many employment disputes will involve informal negotiations, although individuals may not even realise they are involved in a negotiation process. Where disputes arise in unionised employments, negotiations at workplace, sectoral or national level are the normal way to seek to resolve disputes and these may be more or less formal. In non-union companies, even where issues are subject to unilateral management determination, some engagement involving informal negotiations with employees is inevitable. Also, many potential legal disputes will involve negotiations in an effort at resolution before a need for third-party adjudication.

The question 'Can negotiations be learned?' is often asked. Natural ability will influence negotiation performance but even natural ability will benefit from critical study and practice. Formal negotiations tend to have norms and procedural conventions attached to them, and an understanding of these and their application in a specific context requires experience. Skilled negotiators also need an understanding of negotiation theory and research findings to inform performance. Practitioners who do not have an understanding of negotiation theory and research are likely to be at a substantial disadvantage, irrespective of their experience. Therefore, no more than becoming skilled in any other activity, negotiation requires study and practice.

NEGOTIATION: CONCEPTS AND THEORY

Kennedy (1998: 11) defines negotiation as 'the process by which we search for the terms to obtain what we want from somebody who wants something from us'. The advantage of this definition is that it emphasises that negotiation is fundamentally an act of 'exchange', which is reached by a 'searching' process. Emphasising the exchange aspect of negotiation also draws attention to the idea that it requires movement: a negotiator can only attain some, or all, of *their* needs by being prepared to take account of, and concede, some or all of the *other* party's needs. If this were not the case (i.e. if a negotiator could achieve their needs without taking account of the other party), there would be no need to negotiate. Searching is necessary because parties do not have perfect information and often disguise, and even misrepresent, their true intentions. Since negotiation is a searching process, an ability to uncover the other party's needs is an essential part of the skilled negotiator's repertoire. Unskilled negotiators tend to focus excessively (and sometimes even exclusively) on their *own* needs and are less skilled at discovering the needs of the other party.

STRATEGIC CHOICE

Parties can pursue a number of strategic options in any negotiation. These options are often discussed under the heading of negotiation styles – but can be understood as strategic choices that have to be made (Figure 11.1). Parties can choose among the following approaches: (i) *avoiding*, (ii) *accommodating*, (iii) *competing*, (iv) *compromising* and (v) *collaborating*. These represent extremes and the choice for a negotiator is which of these options they deploy and to what extent they use them (i.e. a greater or lesser use of avoidance, accommodation, competition, collaboration or compromise). Avoiding involves a decision to have limited or no engagement with the conflict at hand. Accommodating implies giving priority to the other party's needs and having less concern for one's own. Competing (or controlling) is where each side seeks to maximise their outcome. Collaborating involves working together to find solutions to simultaneously meet both parties' needs, i.e. a search for mutual gains.

It is not uncommon for parties to adopt a negotiation approach by default and without conscious thought, and even to move between 'styles' without any consistency. Adopting a negotiating strategy without conscious consideration has the potential to be a serious mistake. Using a compromise strategy in a potential win-win (mutual gains) situation will 'leave value on the table'. A party that uses an accommodation approach when the outcomes are important to them are likely to end up dissatisfied if faced by a power-centred negotiator. For instance, a company that is in financial difficulty and uses an accommodation approach in response to a too-high wage demand may damage the company and cause the loss of employment, so that both sides lose.

Avoidance

From a rational point of view, it is not always correct to negotiate. Entering into a negotiation process is justified when:
- we need something from someone or need someone's consent;
- the time and effort of negotiating are justified by the potential outcome; and
- the outcome is uncertain.

Figure 11.1
Negotiation Choices

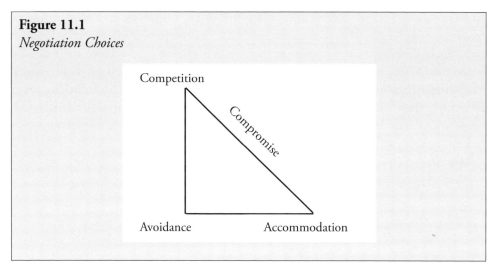

In certain (maybe many) industrial relations situations, the rational option may be unilateral action (this does not imply any moral approval or disapproval of the action). Where there is an extreme power imbalance, it can mean there is no need to negotiate. Ryanair avoided negotiating with trade unions for many years because of its superior power position vis-à-vis unions seeking recognition. It was only the change in the power balance that made its approach no longer tenable in 2018.

Accommodation

Accommodation is a potentially good choice when parties are more concerned about the other party's outcomes than their own. An accommodation approach was widely used by employers during Ireland's appearance in the World Cup in 2002. Production stopped in many companies and widespread arrangements were made for employees to watch games. The employers placed the 'relationship' aspect ahead of their legal entitlements to insist on 'performance' during the games. All negotiations involve the balancing of a range of factors, with relationships being particularly important in those interactions that are not 'one-off', e.g. employment relations situations. Sebenius (2001) calls attention to the error of focusing solely on price in negotiations to the exclusion of intangibles such as relationships. He suggests that 'most deals are 50 per cent emotion and 50 per cent economics' (Sebenius 2001: 89). This does not mean that negotiators can neglect the *hard* elements of negotiation such as price; rather, focusing solely on price is seldom sufficient in complex negotiation typical of industrial relations situations (see case study in Table 11.1).

Competition

Competitive bargaining is a 'controlling' or 'power-centred' approach to negotiations (Hiltrop and Udall 1995). A competing strategy arises when two parties have high concerns about their own outcomes and lower or even minimal concerns about the other's (Lewicki *et al.* 2010). Use of this approach involves parties relying on their power position in an attempt to control the negotiation process and achieve their desired outcomes. Competition is typically characteristic of distributive and adversarial bargaining. It also leads to *compromise* solutions where neither party has sufficient power to enforce their will on the other party and is typically used in industrial relations negotiations over the *substantive* aspects (pay, hours of work, etc.).

Table 11.1
Case Study
The 'Logic' of Accommodation

One party is given €100 to divide with another party as he/she likes; the second party can agree or disagree to any proposed arrangement. If the second party agrees, the €100 is divided in line with the first party's proposal; if not accepted, neither party gets anything. Price logic would suggest that the first party should propose something like '€99 for me and €1 for you'. Although this is an extreme allocation, it still represents a position in which the second party gets something rather than nothing. Pure price negotiators confidently predict the other side will agree to the split. In laboratory experiments, however, most players turn down proposals that do not let them share in at least 35–40 per cent of the €100. This also holds true in laboratory-based experiments even when much larger stakes are involved and the amount forfeited is significant. While these rejections are 'irrational' on a pure price basis, studies show that when people feel a split is too unequal, they reject the offer as unfair, are offended by the process and perhaps try to teach the 'greedy' person a lesson. If the first party is to get anything, they have to 'accommodate' to the second party with an offer well above that suggested by pure price-based logic.

Source: Adapted from Sebenius (2001).

Compromise

Compromise involves the division of a resource and a way of resolving negotiations when both parties deploy a power-centred strategy. It is distributive as it involves 'cutting up the pie'. It is common to hear practitioners comment after a negotiation that it was a 'win-win outcome: we both compromised'. While it is possible to understand why the context would lead to such a comment, at a conceptual level it is a contradiction. A negotiation in which there is a compromise on an issue involves a win-lose outcome: what one party gains, the other loses. Where mutual gains are to be discovered, a compromise is a suboptimal outcome.

Collaboration

A collaboration strategy promotes problem-solving and is the optimum approach where the potential for mutual gains exists. In this approach, both sides try to assist each other in gaining the other's desired outcomes. The problem-solving approach is essential since mutual gains are not always obvious; it may require considerable ingenuity to generate or discover them. A mutual gains process is often called 'enlarging the pie'; however, once enlarged, the pie still has to be divided and this, of necessity, involves distributive bargaining. Thus, negotiation is a two-way process of creating value and claiming value (Allred 2000). A negotiator who concentrates on creating value (enlarging the pie) but fails in claiming value cannot be considered an effective negotiator.

The Merits of Different Approaches

It is important to stress that the adoption of an avoidance, accommodative, collaborative, compromise or competitive approach is normally an issue of degree. Any or all approaches may be used during a negotiation. A negotiator may refuse to engage and say 'That is not up for negotiation', a more accommodative approach may prevail as in 'We are open to movement on Z', a collaborative approach might proceed as in 'We would require movement on Y in order to make any concession on X', or there may be a compromise as in 'We can only pay a percentage of what is demanded'. The central issue is which approach dominates.

In principle, a collaborative approach is superior and parties who fail to collaborate, where the potential for mutual gains exist, will likely depart the negotiating process leaving 'value on the table', i.e. with suboptimal outcomes. However, where resources are fixed or decreasing, collaboration may involve a long and costly search for a non-existent solution. As discussed in Chapter 1, in the face of an existential financial crisis in 2009, the Fianna Fáil/Green Party government abandoned the collaborative approach of social partnership in favour of a power-centred one and introduced legislation. However, it followed that up with a social dialogue process in the Croke Park Agreement and subsequent public sector agreements. This example illustrates that a power-centred approach and a collaborative approach are not mutually exclusive. Avoidance may be a preferred approach if an item is unimportant or if one's power position is such that the involvement of the other party is unnecessary to reach one's desired outcome. As seen in previous chapters, employees can favour avoidance where they may opt not to utilise 'voice' mechanisms, preferring 'silence,' because of their inferior power position.

Negotiation Outcomes

In addition to outlining the possible options that parties may pursue in a negotiation, Figures 11.1 and 11.2 also indicate possible negotiating outcomes. These are expanded in Figure 11.3 to include all possible outcomes, notably the outcome of absolute loss. An efficient compromise option is indicated along the compromise line. Who gains most in a compromise is indicated by the movement along the compromise line – with a position higher up, A gains more, while a position lower down means more is gained

Figure 11.2
Negotiation Choices Expanded

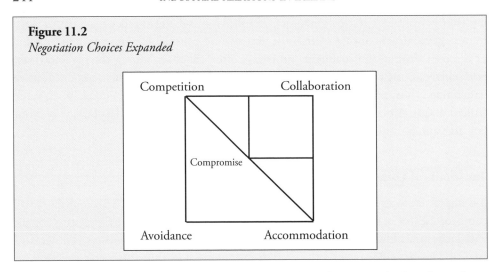

by B. The space below the compromise line within the top-right-hand quadrant represents an inefficient outcome, or what industrial relations practitioners refer to as 'value being left on the table', although the same can be said of the failure to realise potential mutual gains. Mutual gains are represented by the space above the compromise line within that top-right-hand quadrant. The bottom-right-hand quadrant represents an absolute loss for A but a gain for B, while the top-left-hand quadrant indicates gains for A with B losing in absolute terms. The lower left quadrant represents mutual absolute losses arising from injury and self-damage from badly conducted negotiations. These are the kinds of outcomes represented by wars and extreme social conflicts. Losses caused by strikes and lockouts can also inhabit that quadrant, depending on the extent of the losses.

Figure 11.3
Negotiating Outcomes

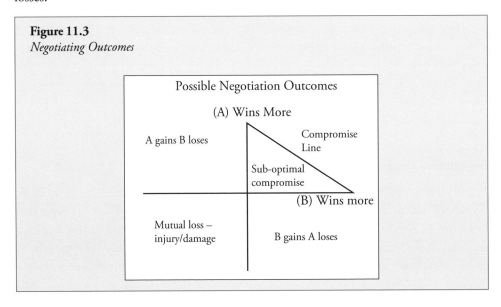

Negotiations and Trust

Commentators frequently ascribe difficulties in negotiations to a breakdown of trust. However, the issue of trust is not clear-cut. It is simply incorrect to suggest that it is not possible to negotiate with a party one does not trust. People often have to negotiate with others they do not trust. Fisher *et al.* (1997) suggest that it is a mistake to either trust or not trust another party in a negotiation. They offer negotiators a way out of the trust dilemma by suggesting that negotiators should 'proceed independent of trust'. Thus, a party can take account of the revealed behaviour of the other party, or objective protection can be built into any proposed agreement. Such measures are common – e.g. a warranty on a second-hand car is a practical example of objective protection, the revocation of bail if a criminal does not abide by specified conditions, etc. In industrial relations specifying in agreement that both parties will refer any dispute over its interpretation to the Labour Court for binding adjudication is an option frequently used (see case study in Table 11.2).

Table 11.2
Case Study
To Trust or Not to Trust?

TEX Engineering employs 500 employees but, due to competition, it is forced to lay off 250 employees. A negotiating meeting is arranged at which the HR director announces to the union representing the workers that she wants to handle this in a constructive way and get away from the adversarial high-ball/low-ball approach. She says the company wishes to deal with its employees in a fair way but there is a limit to what they will pay. Instead of starting low, then haggling and eventually going to the Labour Court, she is prepared to tell the union what is on offer. Pointing to her briefcase she says there is one-and-a-half weeks' pay per year of service 'in the bag' in addition to statutory redundancy entitlements. She says that the union can take this or drag negotiations out and go to the Labour Court, but 'that is all there is'. The HR director has a reputation for being a tough but honest negotiator.

Discussion Point
What kinds of issues should the union consider in evaluating the offer on the table?

This case study can be used for analysis, discussion or role-play negotiation.

TYPES OF BARGAINING

The strategies outlined above map on to the types of bargaining that are identified in negotiation theory as follows.

Distributive Bargaining

Distributive bargaining involves dividing up resources and tends to involve a power-centred approach. The difference between the opening positions of both parties sets the bargaining range. It is conventional for parties to have identified (for themselves) their opening position and intermediate position(s) – or realistic positions – to which they are prepared to move during a negotiation. If these positions prove insufficient to gain agreement, then they should have a fallback. A fallback is the least favourable offer they will accept from the other side to avoid breakdown and referral to a third party or other such action (Figure 11.4). Skilled negotiation should result in a settlement if, *at a minimum*, the fallback positions of the parties overlap. If they do not overlap, then non-agreement will be the outcome – even with skilled negotiation – unless one party adjusts their fallback. Of course, parties may be unrealistic in setting a fallback position. It may be set too high (on the worker side) or too low (on the management side) and, as a result, a fallback or walk-away point needs to be kept under review during the negotiations as new information comes to light.

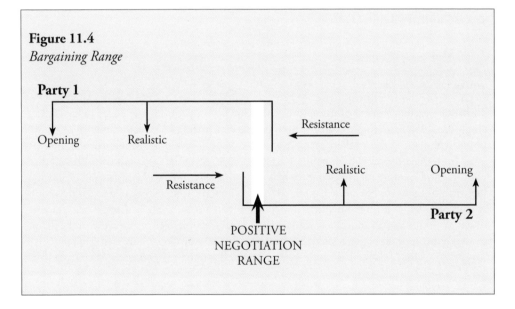

Figure 11.4
Bargaining Range

The main task of a negotiator in a distributive situation is to maximise the 'negotiator's surplus', i.e. the portion of the overlap between the two parties. The negotiator's surplus is the difference between the fallback position (sometimes called the resistance point) of parties 1 and 2 in Figure 11.4. The incentive to maximise the negotiator's surplus contains within it the potential to derail a negotiation. Distributive negotiations, by definition, involve compromise rather than collaboration (see case study in Table 11.3). In attempting to maximise the negotiator's surplus, there is a strong temptation for negotiators to deploy hardball tactics. However, such tactics can make settlement more difficult, if the other party responds in kind and relationships are damaged. Breakdown can then occur for personal and emotional reasons even though the respective fallback positions overlap.

Table 11.3
Case Study
The Negotiator's Surplus in Action

During the 'Great Recession' an employer organisation seeks a reduction in the pay of electricians. They are seeking 17 per cent but they will settle for 8 per cent. During its preparations for negotiation, the industry union that represents electricians decides it is willing to agree a 12 per cent reduction, but no more. Neither side is aware of the other's fallback. The eventual settlement is for an 11 per cent reduction. In this distributive example, the employer organisation has gained 75 per cent of the negotiator's surplus and the union 25 per cent.

In workplace negotiations, there can also be incentives for parties not to reach an agreement even where fallback positions overlap. Management and unions may keep offers in reserve for hearings at the Workplace Relations Commission (WRC) and the Labour Court. There is long-standing and repeated evidence of such an effect in practice, with a criticism of the parties' failure to engage in meaningful negotiations long attracting comment from various Labour Court chairmen (Horgan 1989; Sheehan 2019c). The provision of assisted bargaining by the WRC is an effort at promoting engagement prior to a Labour Court hearing. It allows for facilitation and longer engagement on issues of a complex nature (Roche 2016).

Integrative Bargaining

Integrative bargaining involves an effort to address interests rather than positions in negotiations. Lewicki *et al.* (2001: 94) define interests as 'the underlying concerns, needs, desires or fears that motivate a negotiator to take a particular position'. The notion of interests can sometimes be difficult to grasp and it may be easier to think in terms of addressing 'needs'. The central proposition in interest-based bargaining is that focusing on interests allows parties to achieve superior outcomes than those achieved using positional bargaining. Focusing on positions (bargaining demands) leads to distributive negotiations and can make it more difficult to gain agreement.

The notion that a focus on interests will aid the negotiation process is something of a paradox since industrial relations theorists have identified differing interests as being at the root of employment conflict. However, the following example demonstrates how a focus on interests can work in a common Irish industrial relations situation. In a negotiation over restructuring, a company may wish to reduce costs by lowering the headcount and gaining higher productivity. The position of workers might be no redundancies and no worsening of terms and conditions of employment. Their interests, on the other hand, might be a need for job security for the majority of workers, with older workers open to early retirement if adequately compensated. It may only be possible to achieve job security (the union need) by lowering costs and improving competitiveness (meeting the employer's need). Improved competitiveness may necessitate new work methods and a reduction in employee numbers. The worker *position* (of no worsening of terms and conditions of employment, and no redundancies) must then give way in order to meet the underlying primary *need* of job security for the largest numbers. Of course, there is still distributive negotiation to be done over (i) the level of redundancy payment to be offered, (ii) the numbers to be made redundant and (ii) the specific new work arrangements.

A key feature of pure integrative negotiations is the free sharing of relevant information and the open exchange of ideas. A free flow of information is essential, along with concerted efforts by both sides to understand the needs of the other party and have concern for meeting those needs. One method for developing ideas is 'brainstorming', where ideas are generated and then evaluated with reference to pre-established and mutually agreed criteria. Such criteria are usually of a broad nature, e.g. acceptability to the parties, workability and fairness. In the brainstorming process, all ideas are noted down but only those ideas that meet the agreed criteria are retained for further discussion and negotiation.

Integrative bargaining does not involve the parties setting ideal, realistic or fallback positions. However, it is accepted that a party needs to identify their walk-away point, which is very similar to a fallback. Nor does integrative bargaining involve concealing of material information. Some negotiators may claim to be negotiating on a win-win basis, but may really be attempting to manipulate the other party. A test of a party's true intentions is to see if the party making the claim of engaging in a win-win negotiation is sharing all relevant information and if an adequate concern is being shown for the other party's needs. A negative answer to either of these questions indicates that a distributive approach is, at least, partly being adopted. However, there are limits to an information-sharing obligation; it does not extend to disclosing one's walk-away point. A party that does this is unlikely to achieve any more than their fallback as a result, thereby foregoing any *negotiator's surplus* that is available. The case study in Table 11.4 indicates the transformative changes to working relationships of an integrative approach but also the limitations when faced with the cross-national decision-making process of a multinational company.

APPROACHES TO INTEGRATIVE BARGAINING

A particular approach to integrative bargaining known as 'principled bargaining' or 'interest-based bargaining' has been popularised by Fisher and Ury (1986) in their influential book entitled *Getting to Yes*. The approach focuses on the following principles and is similar to other integrative approaches:

- separate the people from the problem;
- focus on interests, not positions;
- invent options for mutual gain; and
- insist on using objective criteria.

Table 11.4

Case Study
Partnership and Relationship Change – WILO Pumps

WILO Pumps Ltd (WPL) is a Limerick-based Irish subsidiary of the German-based WILOSALMSON Group, which specialises in the manufacture and marketing of central heating pumps primarily for the European market. Since 1996 WPL endured intense competition from sister plants to produce and supply its motors at very competitive prices, thereby forcing it to adopt a highly focused approach of cost reduction within an environment demanding high-quality standards. WPL's management expended much effort in focusing on many improvement initiatives over a five-year period. While definite progress was made, management perceived that the results did not give the return for the effort expended. Consequently, it was agreed that relationships between the maintenance team and management, which were extremely adversarial, would need to be drastically developed to ensure the long-term future of the plant. Discussions took place with the assistant general secretary of the Technical Electrical Engineering Union in Limerick. Critical outcomes of these discussions were the acceptance of each other's bona fides and the mutual acceptance of the principle of achieving a win-win outcome for all parties. With the assistance of an independent facilitator, it was agreed that the extended management team and the entire maintenance department would meet off-site to explore the possibility of a way forward. This joint session became the major turning point for the plant, since both parties realised they had far more common interests than the differences that divided them.

The group agreed to meet on a monthly basis over an eight-month period in order to develop their relationships, improve communication channels and work on partnership initiatives. As a result, management became much more attuned to the underlying needs of its employees in bringing about change. These needs included respect, involvement and trust – the real drivers of sustainable change. On the union side, a keen appreciation of the business needs of the company developed. This ultimately led to negotiated reductions in labour headcount (reductions of approximately 25 per cent), increased employee efficiencies of 60 per cent and 110 per cent in its two key departments, and a dramatically changed working environment where much greater levels of mutual respect and trust prevailed. The key to achieving these solutions was the systematic use of problem-solving and mutual gains bargaining, with employees being an integral part of defining and producing mutually agreed solutions.

Within twelve months of these successful changes, the core motor manufacturing business of WPL was closed, resulting in a reduction of 85 per cent of the workforce. This was done for group strategic reasons that were outside the Limerick facility's control. Despite the trauma of the closure, the development of relationships within the plant had dramatically changed attitudes on both sides; these relationships survived the closure decision and created a supportive environment for everyone in dealing with the closure. Subsequently, members of management, union officials and shop stewards have made joint presentations to the partnership network on their experiences in effecting a change in relationships.

Source: Contributed by Brendan Lyons, former managing director, WILO Pumps.

Depersonalising issues, as in separating people from the problem, is essential in a negotiation. However, understanding the motivations and personal characteristics of individuals one is negotiating with is also essential. Integrative approaches, including those of Lewicki *et al.* (1999), identify a number of key steps in the integrative negotiation process:

- identify and define the problem in a mutually acceptable way;
- keep the statement of the problem to be addressed simple;
- state the problem as a goal and identify the obstacles to reaching that goal;
- be solution, not problem, focused;
- depersonalise the problem; and
- identify the needs of the other party.

Fisher *et al.* (1997) insist that adopting a principled approach is not an easy option and requires 'real toughness'. Paradoxically, while espousing their attachment to collaboration, new negotiators find collaboration very difficult to *implement* in practice. That is because they lack the requisite skills to implement their desire in the context of a specific conflict. Even for experienced negotiators, mutual gains bargaining can be challenging, especially if only one party is committed to the process. A party attempting to operate in an integrative way can end up merely accommodating the party using a distributive approach. Nonetheless, Fisher *et al.* (1997) claim that a principled approach can even be adopted with distributive or 'difficult' negotiators. A negotiator should not abandon their critical faculties just because they are engaged in principled win-win negotiation. They are entitled to, and should, test rigorously the propositions advanced by the other party and insist on them justifying their demands on objective grounds. They suggest that the aim should be to bring difficult negotiators to their senses – not to their knees!

Mixed-Motive Negotiations

In the 1980s it became common for writers to categorise distributive bargaining in somewhat garish terms and compare it unfavourably with integrative bargaining. For instance, Fisher and Ury (1986) claimed that it is the process of distributive bargaining that impedes effective conflict resolution – and that a principle bargaining approach is superior. If this were the case, it would be expected that principled negotiations would have displaced distributive approaches over time. There is, however, no evidence that this has happened: distributive bargaining remains a commonly used approach to negotiations. There has been a counter reaction to the somewhat evangelical promotion of integrative approaches. Thompson (2009: 41) points out that 'even in win-win negotiations the pie of resources created by negotiators eventually has to be sliced' and this involves distributive bargaining. Lewicki *et al.* (2010: 103) concurs and suggests that 'purely integrative or purely distributive negotiation situations are rare'. More recently, efforts have turned to identifying those situations where traditionally pluralist distribute-type negotiations are best suited, where high-trust mutual gains bargaining will work best and where unitarist options may be the rational option (Bray *et al.* forthcoming; Budd *et al.* forthcoming).

Lewicki *et al.* (2010) refer to a negotiation that has both integrative and distributive characteristics as '*mixed-motive*' bargaining and this is common in industrial relations situations. The capacity to manage the complexities involved in mixed-motive bargaining is a key negotiation skill. Negotiators need to be able to handle both distributive and integrative elements of the bargaining process. A useful way to approach mixed-motive negotiations is to separate the two phases. The integrative element can be dealt with first by using problem-solving techniques and sharing information, and the distributive element (agreeing on dividing the gains) dealt with afterwards. Even within the distributive phase, the use of creative and integrative techniques can ensure a greater prospect of success and solidify the relationship between the parties. Fisher *et al.* (1997) suggest using objective criteria to reach agreement on the compromises necessary in distributive negotiations. An example in industrial relations is the frequent reference to precedents and norms in comparable employments. These often form the basis for pay rates and other terms and conditions of employment. Other integrative techniques that can be applied in mixed-motive negotiations are discussed below.

THE NEGOTIATION PROCESS

Industrial relations negotiations tend to be highly ritualistic processes in which both parties engage in an elaborate game. Normally, the formal initiation of industrial relations negotiations begins with one party presenting a claim or demand to the other. It is a convention of normal industrial relations that a claim, once served, will be the subject of negotiation. The negotiating process can be divided into stages. These may be categorised as (1) preparation for negotiations, (2) bargaining and (3) post-negotiation follow-up action. It is useful to further distinguish the second stage as being divided into three phases as follows: (i) beginning, (ii) middle and (ii) end. Table 11.6 contains a simplified checklist of items needing attention in the negotiation process.

Stage 1: Preparation for Negotiations

Administrative Arrangements
Advance attention to the 'boring' administrative details is essential. While many of these will be agreed as a matter of course, it may be necessary to negotiate them – a process known as 'negotiating the negotiations'. Effective engagement on these issues can set a positive tone in advance of negotiations commencing, while the opposite is likely to be the case where parties are unwilling to address each other's concerns. Typical issues that require attention in advance are an agenda, appropriate physical facilities and a spacious

venue free from interruptions, with appropriate seating and breakout rooms available. Setting protocols for the length that negotiations are to last on any day can avoid tired negotiators making mistakes late into the night. This is essential in problem-solving technical negotiations since cognitive abilities decline at night due to circadian rhythm effects.

However, in the pressure of mixed-motive negotiations, late nights can be difficult to avoid and there may be no option other than 'to suck it up' if that happens. Often, crucial concessions and trades only become possible under the intense pressure of late sessions. This pressure can bring home to parties the realities of the situation that 'each side ultimately must choose between two options: accepting a deal or taking its best no-deal option' (Sebenius 2001: 88). A graphical illustration of late-night negotiations was the negotiation session leading to the Good Friday Agreement (the Belfast Agreement) in 1998. Neither unionists nor nationalists were fully happy with the proposals but the alternative of breakdown, with the risk of a return to the violent conflict, was much less attractive.

Preparation

Many authors have stressed the importance of preparation for negotiations (Hawkins 1979; Hiltrop and Udall 1995; Lewicki *et al.* 2010; Thompson 2009). Adequate research is the key to good preparation: it helps to focus negotiations on facts rather than opinions or value judgments. Preparatory research on substantive terms of employment issues (pay and conditions) is likely to require establishing the terms and conditions in comparable employment and precedents. An evaluation of the knock-on effects of the potential outcomes is also something for advance consideration. All negotiators will at some time be faced with situations where they have not been able to prepare. Hiltrop and Udall (1995) strongly advise that when faced with this, negotiators should listen, ask questions for information and adjourn at an early opportunity. Finally, while preparation is important, Rackham (1993) found that effective negotiators *do not* spend more time in preparation than average negotiators. Equally, they do not spend more time accumulating information but devote more time to considering how to use the information they have (Rackham 1993).

Establishing Negotiating Objectives

The most important decision in preparing for negotiation is for each party to identify *what* it wants to achieve; this can often be quite difficult. What one wants can depend on a multiplicity of factors like future demand for a product, maintaining relationships and other intangibles. Not all elements within an organisation will have the same objectives and this can be particularly true of a trade union, where the aggregation of interests can be a difficult process. Any disagreements or differences should be aired and resolved in advance. Not infrequently this can be the most difficult part of a negotiation. The same principles apply here as apply to general negotiation theory, with an even stronger emphasis on the benefits of an open, integrative approach.

Establishing bargaining objectives relative to one's interests is preferable to deciding on emotional or other grounds. That requires a critical examination of a case's strengths and weaknesses. There is now a growing body of psychological and behavioural economics research that has identified cognitive biases as part of the human thinking process and challenged the traditional economic assumption that people are rational and make rational calculations (Malhotra and Bazerman 2008). Such biases mean that negotiators tend to underestimate the strengths of the other party's case and overvalue the strengths of their own. Ignoring the other party's interests and thinking (cognition) is a serious mistake (Lewicki *et al.* 2010).

A technique to attempt to address cognitive biases is 'perspective taking' (Thompson 2009). Perspective taking involves looking at things through the eyes of the other party. It is an essential skill: 'since the other side will say yes for its reasons, not yours, agreement requires understanding and addressing your counterpart's problem as a means to solving your own' (Sebenius 2001: 88). It can be difficult to do honestly; role reversal exercises (where some members of one's negotiating team take on the role of the other party) are helpful in achieving a realistic perspective of the other side's concerns and options. Remember that the objective of gaining this understanding is to use it to achieve your objectives by making exchanges that enable the other party to meet its interests. An illustration of this principle worth consulting is given by Sebenius (2001: 92) in 'Solving Teddy Roosevelt's Negotiating Problem', an example which also provides a useful entrée into discussing ethics in negotiation.

The Bargaining Mix and Prioritising

The bargaining mix refers to the items for negotiation. Advance prioritising of items within the bargaining mix allows identification of those items that can be traded. Negotiation conventions require that parties be prepared to move during negotiations. Trading is an integrative approach that is a superior form of movement to pure compromise. There are two conventional ways of prioritising. Parties can attach labels to items to classify them in decreasing order of importance as follows:

- items they must get;
- items they intend to get;
- items they would like to get.

Alternatively, items can be labelled 1, 2, 3 and so on in decreasing order of priority. If the first method is used, there is a great temptation to place a large number of items in the 'must get' category. Kennedy (1998) points out that the more items one has to achieve from a bargaining mix, the lower one's power position is in a negotiation. That arises because one has fewer items to trade in return for concessions one wants from the other party. However, many negotiators think the opposite is the case: that the more issues in the bargaining mix they define as 'must get', the higher their power position. This is a serious mistake that can impede the reaching of agreement.

A bargaining mix will contain both tangible (improved productivity, more pay) and intangible items. The intangibles can be vitally important. For managers, they might include issues such as ensuring good relations with workers and their representatives. Ensuring one's opponent does not lose face is a common intangible, encapsulated in the phrase 'Leave your opponent the bus fare home.' Bargaining objectives will vary according to the issue at hand. While parties should be clear on their walk-away position, flexible objectives are generally preferable to rigid ones because information uncovered during negotiations can alter the perception of one's interests and what is achievable. Thus, setting bargaining objectives as a range is better than setting point goals.

Mandate

A clear mandate is one of the crucial issues to be tied down in advance. That means articulating objectives and having them approved by constituents – top management on the employer's side and trade union members/representatives on the union side. Clarity on objectives enables more effective engagement with the other side – illustrated in the maxim 'It's hard to negotiate with someone who doesn't know what they want'. It also maximises the chances of ratification of any proposed agreement with which a negotiating team returns. Outright rejection is a more frequent occurrence where a large constituency is involved, such as in a trade union, but management-side non-implementation can arise where operational managers at workplace level may not operate an agreement as intended, even if the deal is ratified at senior level. In such cases, a negotiator can suffer reputational damage. Rackham (1993) identified skilled negotiators as having fewer implementation failures than those of average negotiators.

Bargaining Power

Bargaining power can be understood as the degree to which one party can achieve its negotiating goals despite the opposition of the other side or, as Boulding (1993: 341) writes, 'power is the ability to get what one wants'. Relative bargaining power significantly influences the outcome of negotiations, with outcomes likely to favour the party with the greatest bargaining power. Bargaining power depends on a range of factors that are both external and internal to the negotiations process. The relative strengths and weaknesses of the case in question are the starting point and, as noted previously, the perception of these can be subject to cognitive biases. Much power will be determined outside the bargaining process: by economic factors, the level of demand for a product, the skill possessed by workers and levels of unemployment. Thompson (2009) points out that one way to increase bargaining power is to form alliances and, of course, the formation of alliances is the underlying rationale for the existence of trade unions and also employer organisations.

The relative perceived strength of each party's BATNA (best alternative to a negotiated agreement) is a crucial component of power (Fisher and Ury 1986). A major mistake, made by even experienced negotiators, is a failure to pay attention to assessing BATNAs (Sebenius 2001). A strong BATNA represents the best defence against concluding an unfavourable agreement and thereby confers negotiating power and leverage. Thus, it is essential in preparing for a negotiation to attempt to assess the relative strengths of differing parties' BATNAs. There are two important points to bear in mind: (i) a BATNA is not necessarily fixed, and (ii) a BATNA is a perception and therefore subjective. The first point indicates that it may be possible to improve a BATNA. It may be possible to discover an alternative and stronger BATNA through the discovery of new information or the formation of alliances. The second point indicates that it is the perception of relative BATNAs that is important. A credible BATNA, delivered by a negotiator with a reputation for credibility, is likely to be seen as strong. This leads us to a consideration of the temptation of bluffing. While individuals may engage in bluffing, and it may work, it is a risky venture as it can come at a high cost to long-term personal credibility if discovered.

A BATNA should not be confused with a fallback (bottom line) or walk-away point. A fallback can prevent a negotiator from making concessions beyond their mandate but offers no real power advantage. Disclosing one's fallback position (or bottom line) is rarely a good idea. Statements such as 'That is our bottom line' may simply be disbelieved and result in pressure for further concessions. If these are then made, one's credibility can be damaged. An alternative is to indicate that 'No further concessions are possible in the current circumstances'. This qualified statement is an integrative approach that invites an exploration of changes in circumstances that might close the gap between the parties. A negotiator should think carefully before disclosing their BATNA but, disclosing information on which it is based may be helpful. Information needs to be credible to lead to the perception of a strong BATNA. However, even a very strong BATNA will have no effect if the other party has reached their reservation price and that is not moveable. A case study from outside the industrial relations arena is provided in Table 11.5 to illustrate the utility of a BATNA and to distinguish it from a fallback.

Team Organisation

Careful advance consideration should be given to the selection of a negotiating team. The size and composition of the negotiating team may depend on the issues up for negotiation. In industrial relations, it is inadvisable to enter negotiations with fewer than two people. Having at least two people provides a witness to what is said and can allow for greater objectivity. With more than two people, the question arises as to the optimum size. Increased numbers can give solidarity, ensure greater technical knowledge and aid planning. A greater number also allows the allocation of responsibilities in presenting the case, analysis of verbal and non-verbal responses, record-keeping and consideration of the consequences of various settlement options and management responses (Nierenberg 1968). However, greater numbers increase the possibility of internal disagreement and the likely inclusion of unskilled negotiators prone to making errors and

Table 11.5
Case Study
Fallback and BATNA: Jean's Car Purchase

Jean is interested in purchasing a family car and has found a year-old model of the car she wants. The local main dealer has advertised it for €31,950. There are two models with similar mileage and same spec on the web for €31,495 but the dealers are a distance away and she does not see any point in contacting them. She phones the local dealer and he tells her the car was acquired from the distributor's head office and has only 9,000km on the clock. She says she has no trade-in and is told, in that case, there is a €1,000 discount but the salesman indicates that if she comes in, he may be able to do a 'little better'. She considers herself a tough negotiator and decides not to pay more than €30,000 (her fallback) but hopes to do better than that. Before going to the dealer, she searches the Internet one more time and is very surprised to find the same model (and spec) with similar mileage advertised for €28,000 at a dealer 250km away. She immediately rings that dealer and makes an offer but is told 'I sold it within two hours of it going up this morning'. She asks the dealer if they will be getting any others in and is told that it is uncertain but the dealer expects one in about six weeks. She asks could she have the first refusal (at the same price) and she is told certainly – but again is warned there is no guarantee she will get one. Being curious, she asks how they are able to sell them 'so reasonably' as other dealers are asking a lot more. The dealer says 'I get them from the distributor at a good price and I'm happy to leave them go reasonably as I still have a good cut.' After hanging up, Jean realises she has new information that needs to be assessed. She must decide if she should wait or go into the local dealer and negotiate with an adjusted fallback. And, if she does go in, what should she say to the local salesperson to reach an agreement and how much should she be prepared to pay?

Discussion Points
1. How strong is Jean's potential BATNA?
2. How might her new knowledge be best used if Jean decides to visit her local dealer?
3. What considerations might the local salesperson have if Jean made an offer of €28,000?

being 'picked off' by the other party. The size and composition of a team may be outside the control of the parties. For trade unions, large numbers of shop stewards may attend negotiations to ensure that the lead negotiation (union official) represents various constituencies fairly. In such situations, strict internal rules for making contributions can be laid out in advance to ensure coherence and discipline. However, irrespective of its size, a team needs to provide for three functions. These are:
- **Lead spokesperson:** The role of the chief representative is to present arguments, control strategy and tactics, and make major on-the-spot decisions.
- **Observer/analyst:** Their role is to evaluate progress relative to objectives, spot key reactions, identify changes in approach and advise the chief negotiator.
- **Recorder:** This involves recording key points in negotiations and documenting the final agreement.

More vital than any allocation of roles is how a team gel. During the negotiation process, team members should support the lead spokesperson without supplanting her/him. Team members should display empathy and be mutually supportive. A clarification or digression can be of enormous benefit to a team member who is under pressure or who has made an error. Negotiations have an inevitable ebb and flow and there are few mistakes that cannot be retrieved with an appropriate and *prompt* 'clarification' or 'amplification'. In conclusion, we provide a simple checklist for preparing for a negotiation in Table 11.6.

Table 11.6
Checklist for Industrial Relations Negotiations

1 **Preparation**
   • Make appropriate administrative arrangements
   • Conduct relevant research
   • Agree negotiating objectives
   • Prioritise
   • Check mandate
   • Assess relative bargaining power
   • Organise team

2 **Bargaining**
   • Opening phase
      • Parties outline their case (expectation structuring)
      • Explore the other side's case
   • Middle phase
      • Movement and solution building
      • Exchange
   • Closing phase
      • Final movements
      • Ensure clarity on agreement
      • Recording agreement
   or
      • Noting areas of disagreement
      • Noting subsequent action
      • Referral to appropriate third party
      • Option for industrial action

3 **Post-negotiation**
   • Document agreement/disagreement
   • Agree action plans
   • Communicate
   • Implement action plans
   • Review

Stage 2: Bargaining

First Phase

The phase involves each side setting out its case and seeking clarification from the other side. It is vitally important to set out all the demands in the bargaining mix clearly. The subsequent introduction of new demands is considered to be outside accepted negotiation conventions. That does not exclude integrative exploration of previously unidentified options and creative solutions. A key skill in the opening phase is the use of open questions that focus on what, how and why, with the most effective questions exploring the other side's interests (Thompson 2009). Interests are the reasons for pursuing a negotiating objective and explicitly exploring them is crucial. Following an initial outline of the issues, parties are likely to wish to adjourn to consider any new information, to consult with their principals and to check on their mandate. In particular, unions need to keep in touch with their members. In complex negotiations, the opening phase of a negotiation can be spread over many meetings.

A key activity identified by Walton and McKiersie (1965) in the opening phase is that of *attitudinal structuring*. This involves attempts by either party to frame the negotiation and concentrate discussions on issues of most concern to them. To do this, parties deploy generalised arguments – these are different from bargaining objectives, which are concrete and can be traded. In a situation where management wants to introduce a pay pause, the bargaining objective is the pay pause and management's underlying arguments might be to contain costs and remain competitive. Where a union is seeking a 5 per cent pay increase, that is their bargaining objective and its underpinning arguments could be to compensate for inflation, to keep pace with pay increases in other companies or to reward employees for increased productivity already delivered. Different types of framing arguments will promote a greater integrative or a more distributive approach. Arguments based on interests allow for a more integrative approach.

Research by Rackham (1993) for the Huthwaite group has found that skilled negotiators deploy fewer arguments than average negotiators (www.huthwaite.co.uk). The use of more and more arguments leads to the problem of *argument dilution* and negatively affects a negotiator's credibility. This is a mistake because later arguments tend to be weaker and are easier to counter. However, average negotiators tend to be drawn into advancing multiple arguments when they find their initial arguments do not seem to gain acceptance. In the opening phase of mixed-motive negotiations, it is vital for negotiators not to be fazed by an apparent non-acceptance of one's underlying arguments.

Middle Phase

The middle phase involves further testing of the arguments advanced and exploration of the possible solutions. Identifying areas for movement and solution building is a critical aspect of this process. We now discuss some key processes involved in movement and solution building.

Movement and Solution Building

Movement is a vital point in a negotiation. Remember: once an offer is put on the table, negotiation conventions dictate that it must not be removed unless the other party rejects it. Movement is best approached as a trading process. Less skilled negotiators tend to blurt out offers without adequate preparation and without linking them to any requirement for concessions by the other party. Making a concession, in the expectation that it will create an obligation on the other to respond in kind, can frequently lead to disappointment. The other party may immediately indicate that the offer is inadequate and demand further concessions. They may have concluded that the other party is an accommodator and will move again without a need to make any concession to them.

Indicating Movement

When making movement, skilled negotiators tend to talk in terms of 'proposals', not offers. They talk about their proposal and show how it is designed to respond to the needs of the other party. For example: 'The reason we are making this proposal is that we have listened carefully to the points you've made. We feel a number of them have merit and we want to try to meet them within the limits of our mandate. To do this, we are proposing the following...' Rackham (1993) found skilled negotiators tend not to describe their own proposals as 'fair', 'good', 'generous', etc., since such descriptions have been found to act as irritants to the other side. As previously advised, using objective standards is a good basis for justifying proposals, with examples being the going rate in the industry and the terms of national agreements.

Size of Offers

It is common for the initial movements to be large and for later movements to decrease in size. Such an approach is contrary to a hardball tactic of making small concessions initially. The benefit of a larger initial movement followed by subsequent smaller ones is that each subsequent move signals decreasing room for movement to the other party. More importantly, one can ask for greater concessions on items of importance in return for a larger movement: a small concession may very well be reciprocated in kind, making progress difficult.

Trading

The essence of negotiation is trading. When making a concession, it is desirable to link it to something you want in return. A standard technique used by skilled negotiators is to make a concession *tentative* in the first instance and *conditional* on the other party agreeing to their demands. Making conditional proposals has the dual advantage of identifying what a party wants in exchange and allowing a withdrawal of an offer if that exchange is not agreed (see example in Table 11.7). In this way, it is possible to establish if the other side values the likely linkages you have identified. If they do not, then they need not be pursued further and other options can be explored. If they are valued, then they can be 'firmed up' to see if progress is possible.

> **Table 11.7**
> *Exploring Trades – A Practical Example*
>
> '*If* the union can agree to a 10 per cent increase in productivity and to work reserve hours as required, then that *would* be sufficient for us to consider a significant move on the pension scheme and to make improvements to the sick pay scheme.'
>
> Note that management have put their requirement *first* and their proposal is less specific than the demand from the other party. If the union is interested, they can ask: 'By how much do you propose to increase the pension and the sick pay scheme?' If the union does not agree to increased productivity, there is no obligation on management to leave the *conditional* offer on the sick pay scheme or pension on the table.

Responding to Proposals/Offers

In responding to offers, it is generally not a good idea to talk down or make little of an offer, even if that offer is considered inadequate. A better response is to welcome the fact that an offer has been made and then to indicate the improvement necessary to enable further progress to be made. Put simply, effective negotiation involves opening doors rather than closing them. Care should be taken in making counterproposals – research shows that skilled negotiators use much fewer counterproposals than average negotiators (Rackham 1993). Immediate counterproposals are often weak because they tend to arrive at a time when the other party is concerned with *its* proposals and they can be perceived as designed to block the other party's proposals. They can also signal anxiety to concede, i.e. that one's negotiating style is one of accommodation. This does not exclude the possibility of an immediate counter demand near the end of a negotiation where the final shape of a deal is clear and it appears a small concession from the other side might close the deal.

Adjournments

Adjournments are useful for considering new information and reviewing progress. A good idea before adjourning is to ask the other party to reflect on key issues you have raised. Then after the adjournment, the other party can be asked if they have come up with any proposals to respond to the issues you raised. Using adjournments in this way can prevent negotiations from getting 'stuck in a rut' or going around in circles. It is best not to use adjournments to release pressure and 'blow off steam'. Proper preparation can ensure that this is not necessary. Remember the other party will be alert for non-verbal behaviour. Inappropriate adjournments can inadvertently reveal a lot about one's negotiation position and a team's lack of internal coherence.

Closing Phase

Three tasks normally have to be undertaken in the closing phase: (i) finalising the agreement (if one is reached), (ii) noting issues for further negotiation and (iii) recording details of any area of failure to agree. This phase carries many traps for the unwary as offers and counter-offers may come very quickly after little has happened in the earlier phase, which can especially be the case where parties have *unwisely* used a 'chicken tactic' – waiting until the last stage to make any significant movement. In this situation it is all too easy to lose sight of the cost or value of proposals – careful costing in advance will limit the prospect of errors and a 'winner's curse' effect. The winner's curse arises where someone concludes an agreement, and is happy with it, but subsequently discovers new information that leads them to feel they could have got a better deal. A further danger is that both parties can have different beliefs as to what *has* been agreed. Not infrequently, this leads to subsequent accusations of bad faith on the part of one or both parties and to implementation difficulties.

Slowing down and proceeding in a deliberate, considered manner can limit misunderstandings. At this stage active listening (using paraphrasing) and asking direct and leading questions can aid in ensuring there is a mutual and agreed understanding of what is proposed. Here is an example: 'So are we agreed on twenty-five voluntary redundancies? If insufficient employees opt for redundancy to make up these numbers, compulsory redundancies will take place on a last in, first out basis – are we agreed on that?' Any provision for reviewing an agreement should be specified and agreed before the parties leave the negotiating table. If an agreement is not reached, it is normal in Irish industrial relations for the dispute to be referred to an appropriate third party – the WRC, Labour Court, etc. As seen in Chapter 7, disputes procedures normally specify that neither party can use industrial action until these procedures have been exhausted.

Stage 3: Post-Negotiation

Once negotiation has concluded, the parties will normally 'report back' on the outcome. The way in which any agreement is communicated to employees should be agreed upon, as should decisions on any administrative obligations. Problems can arise in the implementation of an agreement, especially on the management side, particularly with giving effect to concessions, such as productivity ones, made by the other party. Thus, details of implementation should be worked out and responsibilities clearly allocated within organisations. Implementation of an agreement is the key post-negotiation consideration. Non-implementation can arise from bad-faith negotiation but also from the winner's curse effect. Non-implementation, or implementation in a way other than mutually understood, potentially sours relations and can permanently damage a negotiator's credibility. While it is desirable to review and assess the lessons learned from the negotiation experience, this has been found to be done infrequently (Rackham 1993).

INTEGRATIVE TECHNIQUES

Enlarge the Pie

The most obvious integrative technique is to enlarge the 'pie'. While this can be difficult, especially in recessionary times, ingenuity can lead to an identification of ways in which this can be achieved. A standard way to enlarge the pie is the use of reciprocal concessions – pay for productivity being the most common. As with all integrative techniques, enlarging the pie needs to be evaluated against rigorous criteria. For example, by the early 1980s, some management had become disenchanted with aspects of productivity bargaining, some of which failed to deliver any real productivity gains.

Negotiate on a Package Basis

Lewicki *et al.* (2010) refer to this technique under the US term of 'log-rolling'. It increases the possibility of exchanges (trading) and reduces the need for suboptimal compromise. Less effective negotiators negotiate on an item-by-item basis, especially when they are making 'offers'. They treat each item in a bargaining mix separately, moving through an agenda one item at a time. This reduces negotiation on each item to a win-lose situation. While it may be somewhat more difficult to deal with several issues at a time, the prospects of a superior outcome are increased by negotiating on a package basis. As discussed earlier, making proposals conditional facilitates trading. Also, a practical way to circumvent the difficulty of negotiating on a package basis is to agree in advance that 'nothing is agreed until everything is agreed'.

Prioritise and Then Trade

If a team has prioritised in advance, appropriate trade-offs are easier to identify and agree. Identifying trade-offs is typically an iterative process of trial and error and may require the parties to redefine problems by separating or unbundling issues – referred to as 'fractionating' – in order to come up with a mutually acceptable package. The best possible outcome is where each party can concede on their low-priority items in return for gaining their high-priority items. Thompson (2009) points out that trade-offs work not because they build common ground but because they exploit differences. It is somewhat counterintuitive to think that differences can promote agreement but this *is* the case. Sebenius (2001) emphasises that negotiators often search too hard for common ground, neglecting the exchange options that differences offer.

Non-specific Compensation

Non-specific compensation can be used where a mandate is excessively restrictive. An example is where management is attempting to attract a job applicant but cannot meet their salary demand due to a wage cap. Examples are an offer to pay for educational courses or provide an enhanced job title or a company car.

Cutting the Cost of Compliance

This involves reducing the cost to the other party of agreeing to your proposals. Cutting the costs for one party is a staple of employee relations. For example, paying relocation expenses is standard when recruiting employees from abroad where the move would impose a cost on the individual.

'Finding a Bridge' Solution

When using this technique, both sides attempt to invent novel options that satisfy their interests. A classic example of this occurred during negotiations on the Partnership 2000 agreement. The employers' maximum offer was a 7 per cent basic pay increase (excluding the local bargaining clause) while the Irish Congress of Trade Unions said it would not accept less than 8 per cent – an apparent impasse. An agreement was reached on an overall 8 per cent increase through the novel use of phasing. The increase was paid in phases so that the employees achieved an 8 per cent pay increase by the end of the agreement but the cost to employers over the duration of the agreement was 7 per cent – the circle was squared!

HARDBALL TACTICS

Research indicates that some negotiation hardball tactics are outside the accepted norm while others are regarded as 'part of the game'. Hardball tactics which are generally regarded as unacceptable include deliberate lying, refusing to accept reality and failure to implement agreements. These are examples of bad-faith tactics and are viewed as unethical (Lewicki *et al.* 1999). Between the acceptable and unacceptable, some hardball tactics can be viewed as ethically 'questionable'. Numerous writers have noted that the acceptability of hardball tactics is blurred and negotiators have to be prepared to deal with them (Lewicki *et al.* 1999; Ury 1992). Lewicki *et al.* (2010: 62) note that hardball tactics 'can do more harm than good in negotiations'. They point out that 'each tactic involves risk for the person using it, including harm to reputation, lost deals, negative publicity and consequences of the other party's revenge' (Lewicki *et al.* 2010: 62). Risky hardball tactics include the common one of 'chicken', intimidation, good cop/bad cop, fait accompli (introducing unilateral change) and dead leg (asserting there is no room for movement), and the kiss (a concession of no substance designed to place an obligation on the other party). Anyone who negotiates is likely to encounter such tactics.

The most common acceptable hardball tactic is probably the highball/lowball tactic and it has some advantages. A high/low opening position provides room for movement and concessions. In addition, research indicates that, where an exaggerated opening position is taken seriously by the other party, it exercises a strong influence on the outcome to the advantage of the side using it. Thompson (2009: 49) notes that the common perception that an extremely high or low opening offer may insult the other party 'is more apparent than real'. She goes on to note that opening offers have a strong anchoring effect and they have an 'at least 0.85 correlation with final outcomes' – that is an 85 per cent correlation! This indicates that dealing with a highball/lowball opening position is very difficult. One option is to respond in kind but probably the best response is to refuse to table a counter highball/lowball offer, explain why and indicate it will be necessary for the other party to substantially revise their initial offer/demand for the negotiations to make progress. There are also disadvantages to a highball/lowball tactic since it can backfire on those who use it. The main disadvantage is that the other party may decide there is no point in negotiating and may move directly to their BATNA – this is the lost deal outcome!

Concluding Comments

Since the 1960s, the process of negotiation has been the subject of considerable theoretical development, which has provided valuable insights. These insights have promoted a more sophisticated and informed understanding of the negotiation process, the main thrust of which has been the advantages of focusing on an interest-based approach. This approach promotes integrative strategies and techniques. However, there is no evidence of integrative bargaining replacing distributive bargaining, and most negotiations involve both integrative and distributive approaches – so-called mixed-motive bargaining. As a result, those involved in industrial relations negotiations, whether of a collective or individual type, need to understand both integrative and distributive techniques and be able to handle both.

Chapter 12

Employee Participation, Employee Involvement and Workplace Partnership

INTRODUCTION

The terms 'employee participation' and 'employee involvement' encompass any means of increasing employee input into managerial decision-making. While these terms are often used interchangeably, some important distinctions can be made, as we will see later. The concept of employee participation springs from the premise that people who work in an organisation should have the opportunity to influence decisions affecting them. This is sometimes seen as the political democratisation of the workplace, since it facilitates the redistribution of decision-making power away from management and towards employees (Chamberlain 1948; Lavelle *et al.* 2010; Thomason 1984; Wilkinson *et al.* 2004).

The structure of industrial organisations, with the support of the legal and business systems, has traditionally placed decision-making power in the hands of employers. Notwithstanding the primacy accorded to the employers' position, employee participation in organisational decision-making has a long history and various initiatives have been taken to promote this end. These range from a basic level of information sharing, through consultation with employees on certain issues, to joint decision-making and even worker control. These initiatives may result in a variety of institutional arrangements to facilitate employee participation and involvement, e.g. suggestion schemes, quality circles, empowerment, joint consultative committees, works councils or board-level participation.

EMPLOYEE PARTICIPATION AND INVOLVEMENT

In analysing the subject of employee participation and employee involvement, it is customary to make two important distinctions. The first is between direct and indirect participation and the second is between task-centred and power-centred participation (Dundon *et al.* 2008).

Direct employee participation encompasses any initiatives that provide for employee involvement in, and influence on, decisions affecting their work and immediate work environment. Employees are directly involved themselves. Direct participation and involvement are generally introduced at management's behest, and can take a variety of forms, such as briefing groups, quality circles, consultative fora and teamworking. Since the 1980s, direct employee participation was frequently introduced as part of change initiatives in which management reassigned responsibility for a limited range of job-related decisions to employees, e.g. decisions on working methods, recruitment of team members and task allocation.

In contrast, *indirect participation* is more power-centred and often referred to as representative participation. It is an indirect form of employee influence insofar as employee views and input are articulated through the use of some system of collective employee representation, e.g. via works councils or on company boards (Lavelle *et al.* 2010; Salamon 2001). These employee representatives are usually elected or nominated by the workforce and thus carry a mandate to represent the interests and views of the broader body of worker whom they are selected to represent. They do not act in a personal capacity but as a conduit through which the broader mass of workers can influence organisational decision-making. Indirect participation is considered power-centred because it involves the redistribution of decision-making power in the workplace. Axiomatically, it thereby seeks to reduce the extent of management prerogative and bring about greater employee influence in areas that have traditionally been the remit of senior management.

The distinction between task-based direct participation and power-centred indirect participation tends to delineate the respective positions of employer and trade union positions. Employers tend to favour task-centred participation while trade unions have generally sought to extend power-centred participation. However, on occasion some ambiguity has been evident in trade union postures. For example, certain trade unions may oppose the appointment of worker directors (a form of indirect participation), fearing it may undermine the enterprise-level role of trade unions and collective bargaining. They may be especially concerned as to the capacity of unions to take an independent position to oppose company policy if workers were involved in the formulation of that policy, e.g. through board-level participation. Others view the appointment of worker directors as a positive development that introduces joint regulation in the enterprise, particularly in relation to higher-level strategic decisions.

THE DYNAMICS OF EMPLOYEE PARTICIPATION AND INVOLVEMENT

Many descriptions of employee participation tend to be somewhat 'elastic' in character and it is necessary to be more precise in outlining the principal components. Marchington and Wilkinson's (2005) analysis highlights the dynamic nature of employee participation and involvement and deconstructs its various components according to degree, form, level and range of subject matter.

The *degree* of participation and involvement addresses the extent to which employees can influence management decisions, namely whether they are simply informed of changes or, at a higher level, are consulted and have a substantial input in decision-making or, at the highest level, actually make decisions. This is illustrated in Figure 12.1, which outlines the differing levels of progression in the degree of employee participation and involvement (Marchington and Wilkinson 2005: 401).

Figure 12.1
Ladder of Employee Participation and Involvement

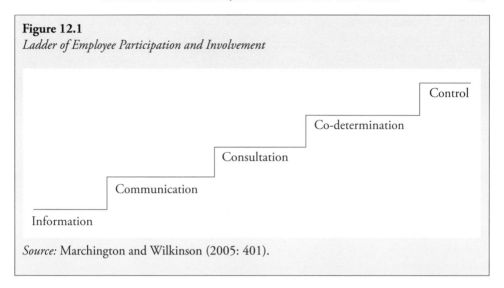

Control

Co-determination

Consultation

Communication

Information

Source: Marchington and Wilkinson (2005: 401).

Second, there is the *level* at which such employee influence is exercised. This may occur at task, departmental, establishment or corporate level. Many of the developments at enterprise level in Ireland focus on increasing direct employee involvement on work/tasks, namely in decisions related to their immediate work role. However, we also find employee influence exercised at higher levels in the organisational hierarchy – for example, at business-unit level (through collective bargaining) or at corporate level (through worker directors/board level participation).

Third, we have the scope or *range* of subject matter. This dimension addresses the type and number of issues over which employees have the opportunity to influence decision-making. The most commonly used categorisation differentiates between influence at the operational level and influence at a strategic level. Influence at the strategic level implies a capacity for employee input on the future nature and role of the organisation, while operational level covers more day-to-day matters (e.g. working arrangements and employee autonomy in carrying out work-related tasks).

Fourth, there may be variations in the *form* of participation and involvement. For example, employees may be involved through structures that provide for 'financial' or 'equity' participation. Financial involvement generally involves profit-sharing or gain-sharing schemes, whereby employees participate directly in the commercial success (or failure) of the organisation. Such schemes may allow workers to secure an equity share in their organisations. In such instances, financial rewards to employees are normally linked to some measure of corporate or establishment performance.

We now summarily outline the main ways in which workers or their representatives become involved in influencing decision-making in organisations, namely through 'industrial democracy', 'participation' and 'employee involvement'. As noted earlier, while these terms are sometimes conflated or used interchangeably, it is possible to distinguish between each in turn.

Industrial Democracy

Industrial democracy is generally understood to involve situations where workers exert primary control over organisational decision-making. Salamon (2000: 370) describes industrial democracy as follows:

> Its central objective is the establishment of employee self-management within an organisation, whose ownership is vested in either the employees or the state and whose managerial function is exercised ultimately through a group, elected by the employees themselves, which has the authority over all decisions of the organisation, including the allocation of 'profits' between extra wages and reinvestment.

This approach is sometimes seen as the ultimate form of employee influence, involving a fundamental restructuring of control and power in industrial organisations in favour of employees.

Employee Participation

Salamon (2000: 371) argues that employee participation denotes a distinct evolutionary development aimed at extending collective employee influence beyond the traditional remit of collective bargaining into 'much wider areas of organisational planning and decision making at both the operational and, more importantly, strategic level'. The collectivist element is a critical distinguishing characteristic of employee participation. This approach involves establishing and extending employee influence through representative structures such as trade unions, works councils or other forms of elected employee representation. Salamon (2000) further notes the importance of power equality between capital and labour in giving effect to what he terms 'real' employee participation. Citing Pateman (1970), Salamon (2000: 371) states that '"real" participation ideally requires both sides to have "equal power to determine the outcome of decisions"'. In the absence of such power equality, employees can only rely on management goodwill, i.e. its acceptance of, and commitment to, a participative philosophy or style of organisational management. As Wilkinson *et al.* (2010) argue, there should be more than merely information provision to employees or their representatives. Rather, there must be genuine opportunity for employees to influence major strategic organisational decisions.

Employee Involvement

Employee involvement embraces any means of increasing the direct involvement of workers in decisions affecting their work situation, e.g. work scheduling or quality monitoring. Salamon (2000) identifies the following most commonly used means of operationalising employee involvement, namely empowerment, teamworking, briefing groups and quality circles. He goes on to argue that employee involvement is generally introduced as a means of advancing management objectives:

> These measures have been introduced by management in order to optimise the utilisation of labour (in particular, to improve organisational quality and flexibility) and at the same time to secure the employee's identification with and commitment to the aims and needs of the organisation. Such measures may allow employees greater influence and control over decision making, but only in relation to their immediate work operations; hence the phrase sometimes used of 'task participation'. (Salamon 2000: 372)

The suggestion that employee involvement tends to be primarily management driven is also evident from Marchington and Wilkinson's (2005: 398) conclusion that 'more recent EI (employee involvement) initiatives have been management sponsored and, not surprisingly, have reflected a management agenda concerned primarily with employee motivation and commitment to organisational objectives'. Similarly, Wilkinson's (2002) analysis of the concept of employee 'empowerment' found that it largely focused on 'task-based involvement and attitudinal change' and did not incorporate any acknowledgement of workers having a right to a say. Rather, it remained an employer (managerial) decision concerning whether and how to empower employees. Wilkinson (2002: 1720) further notes the potential variation in the extent of power that employees may be afforded under such schemes:

> Most [empowerment initiatives] are purposefully designed not to give workers a very significant role in decision making but rather to secure an enhanced employee contribution to the organisation with 'empowerment' taking place within the context of a strict management agenda. Empowerment schemes tend to be direct and based on individuals or small groups (usually the work group), a clear contrast with industrial democracy and participative schemes such as consultative committees which are collectivist and representative in nature.

The above distinctions reiterate the point that various approaches to employee participation and involvement may differ concerning both the degree of employee influence on decision-making and the level of institutional sophistication of the differing forms of employee influence. As we will see below, early initiatives in the area of employee influence revolved around worker participation and industrial democracy. More recently, however, we have witnessed a significant shift in the employee influence debate towards more management-sponsored forms of employee influence (Gunnigle et al. 2017). This has been accompanied by a move away from indirect (representative) forms of participation and towards a greater focus on the direct involvement of individual employees in decisions of immediate work relevance. We now proceed to review these developments.

INDIRECT EMPLOYEE PARTICIPATION AND INVOLVEMENT: DEBATES AND DEVELOPMENTS

The movement for worker influence in organisational decision-making has its roots in early attempts to achieve worker control dating from the Industrial Revolution in the UK (Chamberlain 1948; Coates and Topham 1968). These initiatives entailed a rejection of an economic order rooted in capitalism and wage labour. This movement for workers' control and self-management addresses an important question, namely whether employee participation should aim to fundamentally change the established economic order by redrawing decision-making mechanisms within organisations, or whether it should try to bring about greater employee participation within the current structure of industrial organisations. It is clear that most, if not all, recent developments follow the latter route. Hyman and Mason (1995: 8) observe thus:

> Industrial democracy has little currency in contemporary market-driven economies where any worker or activist concern for industrial control has been fragmented and displaced by defensive struggles to retain individual employment and to protect employment rights.

A further 'big question' is whether promoting employee participation actually contributes to increasing employee influence. Salamon (2000: 398) argues that the appointment of worker directors is 'unlikely to affect significantly the power and decision making of senior management'. In the UK the famous Bullock Committee report favoured worker participation at board level in larger organisations (Bullock 1977). However, Salamon (2000) was less enthusiastic and identified a number of factors that might mitigate the influence that worker directors have on management decision-making, namely:

- infrequency of board meetings;
- exclusion of worker directors from other director and senior management meetings;
- main role of the board of directors is to formally endorse senior management proposals/decisions; and
- board-level decisions rely heavily on senior management for information.

These issues are further considered in the next section, which provides a brief comparative perspective, particularly with regard to the German system of co-determination.

A COMPARATIVE PERSPECTIVE

Developments aimed at increasing employee influence in organisational decision-making have taken varying directions in different countries. With the demise of the early movements for workers' control, employee participation achieved its most concrete form through the extension of collective bargaining. More far-reaching developments took place in the era post World War II, with various institutional arrangements developed to further employee participation, particularly in a number of continental European countries. While these developments fall considerably short of full industrial democracy, they entail institutional arrangements that provide for considerable democratic input. This occurs within what Salamon (2000: 370) terms 'only a limited modification of the capitalist managerial authority system rather than a fundamental restructuring'.

The most widely cited example is the German system of *co-determination*, which provides legal support for the right of workers to participate in management of companies for whom they work. This system comprises two key pillars, namely *board-level participation* (worker directors) and *works councils*, and dates back to the restructuring of the then West German economy after World War II.

Like a number of other European countries, Germany is characterised by a two-tier board structure: a supervisory board to deal with policy issues and a management board to deal with operational affairs. In structural terms, co-determination entails the appointment of worker directors to the main (supervisory) board of companies. In companies employing between 500 and 2,000 workers, a third of seats on supervisory boards are reserved for worker representatives, while in companies employing more than 2,000 workers, half the seats are reserved for worker representatives.

During the 1970s there was extensive debate in Ireland and the UK on the desirability of extending the representative participation of other members of the then European Economic Community (EEC), with a preference for a system along the German lines. In contrast to Germany, neither the UK nor Ireland have any established tradition of co-determination. Company structures in both countries are based around a single (unitary) board of directors, as opposed to the two-tier systems that characterise a number of European countries. Stimulated by moves to extend the German system to other EEC countries, debate on worker participation intensified in the 1970s. In the UK a Committee of Inquiry, known as the Bullock Committee, investigated employee participation, with special reference to worker directors (Bullock 1977). The final Bullock Committee report favoured the retention of the existing unitary (single) board structure but supported the idea of worker directors on the main board of large companies. However, this report encountered widespread employer opposition and was never acted upon. Nonetheless, these historically conflicting positions are broadly representative of historical employer and labour standpoints regarding worker representation at board level in Ireland.

Works Councils form the second pillar of co-determination in Germany. These are shop-floor-level organisations comprising members elected by the organisation's workforce. Operating at workplace level, these organisations are under a legal remit to consider and agree on a wide range of employment and other matters affecting the firm. Works councils have a long-established tradition in many European countries, often enjoying legislative support and exerting considerable influence on the organisations in which they operate. As noted above, they represent a method of providing formal employee representation at workplace level to facilitate consultation and discussion of enterprise-related issues between workers and management.

However, the respective roles of works councils vis-à-vis collective bargaining is normally delineated as follows. Major decisions on pay movements and related matters are decided through general labour agreements decided at sectoral level by national trade unions and national employer associations. At local level, works councils then have scope to become involved in 'non-pay' issues (see below) and also to fine-tune sectoral agreements to local circumstances.

In Ireland many of the activities handled under the remit of works councils, such as those related to terms and conditions of employment, are subject to management prerogative. However, in Germany – and some other continental European countries – these matters are the subject of discussion and joint agreement between managers and the workforce within using the forum of works councils. Works councils thus represent an important means of delivering high levels of legally mandated worker participation in decisions on work and employment matters within organisations. They also provide a forum for formal employee representation to facilitate consultation, discussion and information exchange between workers and management. Regarding the German context, Torrington *et al.* (2011: 440) comment thus on the role of Works Councils:

> German managers cannot impose any decision relating to changing workplace rules, disciplinary procedures, working hours, holidays, bonus payments, overtime arrangements, health and safety matters, training or selection methods, without first securing the agreement of their organisation's Works Council … In addition, the (German) law requires that managers share a great deal of financial and planning information with Works Councils that goes well beyond the employment sphere.

DEVELOPMENTS IN IRELAND

Irish industrial relations came comparatively late to the employee involvement and participation debate. Kelly and Hourihan (1997: 405) note that 'the only opportunity to participate in Ireland was through the collective bargaining process'. By the mid 1960s, with the apparent success of the German model and the prospect of Ireland's entry into the Common Market, interest was aroused in the idea of advancing worker participation and involvement. In 1967 the Irish Congress of Trade Unions adopted a pro-industrial democracy stance. However, a later report by Tom Morrissey concluded that even in Germany there was no evidence to suggest that co-determination had in fact 'made any direct contribution to the sharing of managerial authority' (Morrissey 1986: 32–3). The report advised that the best way for employees to influence managerial decisions was through collective bargaining, supporting a standard employer position on the topic and one similar to the stance of UK employers, as alluded to above.

Board-Level Participation

Meanwhile, developments at European level dealing with both board-level participation and works councils, as discussed above, highlighted the potential of extending European-type participation in Ireland. As it transpired, most activity in this sphere was confined to the state sector from the late 1970s until the turn of the millennium. In 1977 the Worker Participation (State Enterprises) Act was passed and subsequently augmented by the Worker Participation (State Enterprises) Act 1988. This legislation provided for the appointment of worker directors to the boards of seven semi-state companies: Bord na Móna, Córas Iompair Éireann (CIÉ), the Electricity Supply Board (ESB), Aer Lingus, British and Irish Steam Packet Company Limited (B&I), Comhlucht Siúicre Éireann Teoranta (CSE) and Nitrigin Éireann Teoranta (NET). The 1988 Act extended board-level participation to include (among others): Aer Rianta, An Post, Bord Gáis, Bord Telecom Éireann, Irish Steel, the National Rehabilitation Board and the Voluntary Health Insurance Board (VHI).

The spread of privatisation from the early 2000s had obvious and dramatic consequences for Irish worker directors. Among the first four organisations initially privatised (B&I, NET, CSE and Bord Telecom Éireann), one (B&I) immediately abolished their system of worker directors and two (NET and CSE) retained worker directors on a consultative board, but this was arguably ineffectual since 'all commercial, operational and policy decisions are taken by a second board' (O'Kelly and Compton 2003: 7). In the remaining organisation (Bord Telecom Éireann – now eir) the government removed all the worker directors in preparation for privatisation.

European Works Councils

Increasing employee participation over workplace issues represents a 'key tenet' of the Community Charter of Fundamental Social Rights, generally known as the 'Social Charter', which was initially adopted in 1989 and further developed through the ratification of the Treaty of Lisbon in 2009 (Eurofound 2011; also see Blyton and Turnbull 2004).

Because of the Social Charter, the EU published a draft directive in 1991 proposing that companies with over 1,000 workers operating in two or more member states must establish a so-called European Works Council (EWC). The proposed role for EWCs was to supplement national structures in securing information and consultation rights for workers on transnational company matters. In Ireland this was given effect via the enactment of the Transnational Information and Consultation Act 1996. This provides for the establishment of a works council, or employee forum, in companies employing at least 1,000 workers across the EU and at least 150 workers in two EU member states (Dundon *et al.* 2006).

In addressing the establishment of works councils, the Act outlines three ways in which 'transnational information and consultation' arrangements can be established (Kelly and Hourihan 1997):

1   Through pre-directive agreements on information and consultation concluded before the EU directive came into force (September 1996).
2   After the Act came into force, moves to establish works councils may be initiated by employers or by 100 employees or their representatives. This approach requires the establishment of a 'special negotiating body' of employee representatives. This body then negotiates the establishment of a European employees' forum or works council with management.
3   If agreement is not reached, then employers must establish an EWC in line with the requirements of the 1996 Act. These requirements deal with a number of aspects of the EWC:
    •   composition – a minimum of three and a maximum of thirty members with membership proportional to the number of employees in each state;
    •   frequency of EWC meetings (meeting with central management at least once a year); and
    •   issues for consideration at such meetings. Issues specified included: the state of enterprise, business plans, employment and financial trends, organisation structure and organisation change/new working methods, transfers of production, mergers, cutbacks/closures and redundancy.

The legislation also provides for special meetings with management in 'exceptional circumstances' (such as closure, relocation or collective redundancies). The expenses of EWCs or their equivalent are to be borne by management. Employee members of works councils are entitled to reasonable paid time off to perform their works council functions and cannot be dismissed for performing their representative duties. The legislation deals with numerous other aspects relating to EWCs, such as voting and arbitration. An important employer concern in relation to works councils relates to the disclosure of commercially sensitive information. On this issue, the Irish legal context provides for the appointment of an independent arbitrator to deal with disputes over whether information being passed on or requested is commercially sensitive. Employees who disclose commercially sensitive information are subject to criminal sanctions.

Information and Consultation

The EU Information and Consultation Directive (2002/14/EC) was transposed into Irish law in July 2006 via the Employees (Provision of Information and Consultation) Act 2006 (Butler et al. 2018; Cullinane et al. 2014; Dundon et al. 2008). This meant that for the first time in Ireland there was statutory provision for employee information and consultation rights (with the exception of specific regulation relating to European

Works Councils, and consultation over collective redundancies and transfer of undertakings).

In transposing this directive, the Employees (Provision of Information and Consultation) Act 2006 establishes a right to information and consultation in undertakings in Ireland with at least fifty employees. Dobbins (2009: 1) summarises the main features of the legislation as follows:

- The parties can develop customised 'pre-existing agreements'.
- Otherwise, a 10 per cent employee trigger mechanism is required for negotiations setting up an information and consultation structure (applications either directly to employer or to Labour Court in confidence), unless employers volunteer to introduce information and consultation arrangements.
- Trade unions are not the sole channel for employee representation.
- If a negotiated settlement is not possible, standard fallback rules provide for elected representative information and consultation forums (along the lines of employee representative works councils).
- There is potential for employers to avail of direct forms of information and consultation to suit local circumstances, or a mix of direct and representative, so long as employees are agreeable.
- Provision for the Labour Court to issue binding determinations in instances of dispute/disagreement.

Dobbins (2009) argues that a controversial aspect of the legislation is the provision that negotiations on the establishment of an information and consultation structure must be triggered by workers themselves, unless an employer chooses to establish such a structure on a voluntary basis. Such a trigger mechanism must take the form of a written request from at least 10 per cent of employees in an undertaking, subject to a minimum of 15 employees and a maximum of 100. Once such a request is submitted, the employer is required to enter into negotiations to agree an information and consultation procedure with employees, or otherwise introduce the standard rules provided for in the legislation.

Another area of controversy identified by Dobbins (2009; 2011) is the provision for direct forms of information and consultation. For some time prior to its transposition, trade unions had long expressed its preference for independent and indirect trade union representation as the best way to enhance information and consultation with employees. However, the directive never envisaged trade unions as the sole channel for employee representation. A definition of employee representatives is provided in Section 6. This requires that they be employees of the undertaking, elected or appointed for the purposes of the Act, and that the employer make suitable arrangements for the election or appointment of such employee representatives. In unionised firms, where it is normal practice for employers to engage in collective bargaining with a trade union (or excepted body) representing 10 per cent or more of the employees in the undertaking, the legislation provides that employees who are union (or excepted body) members are entitled to elect or appoint one or more employees' representatives from amongst their members.

Dobbins (2009: 2) also observes that the fallback or standard rules in the legislation provide what he terms are 'pretty strong "continental style" [information and consultation] provisions, in the form of an elected representative employee forum composed of not less than three or more than thirty elected/selected employees' representatives only, who shall be employees of the undertaking'. Under these standard rules, employers are obliged to provide information and consultation on a range of issues, including: probable developments regarding the undertaking's activities and economic situation, the structure and probable development of employment within the undertaking and any anticipatory measures envisaged, and any decisions likely to lead to substantial changes in work organisation or contractual relations. Although the frequency with which an employee forum may meet on its own without an employer presence is subject to the employer's agreement, 'the employer may not unreasonably withhold consent to proposals made by employees or their representatives' (Employees (Provision of Information and Consultation) Act 2006). In addition, the employee forum is entitled to meet with the employer at least twice a year, with the employer obliged to pay for the expenses of the forum, including those relating to members' participation.

DIRECT FORMS OF INVOLVEMENT AND PARTICIPATION: DEVELOPMENT AND DIFFUSION

Direct employee influence encompasses any initiatives designed to provide for personal involvement by employees, individually or as part of groups, in decisions affecting their jobs and/or immediate work environment. Such employee involvement may take a variety of forms, e.g. empowerment, briefing groups and teamworking. As noted earlier, direct involvement is often generally instigated by management and driven by managerial needs and objectives. Salamon (2000: 374) emphasises this point as follows:

> This strategy may be referred to as descending involvement, insofar as management invariably initiates the development for its own purposes (involvement is offered) and, as part of the change, may transfer authority and responsibility from itself to the employees for a limited range of work-related decisions (methods of working, allocation of tasks, maintenance of quality, etc.). However, the content of the process is confined largely to the implementation phase of operational decisions already made by management. This approach is intended to motivate the individual employee directly, to increase job satisfaction and to enhance the employee's sense of identification with the aims, objectives and decisions of the organisation (all of which have been determined by management).

Direct involvement tends to be quite an amorphous concept that may be used in organisations to describe a wide range of activities that vary considerably in their scope and impact on industrial relations practice. Direct involvement initiatives are principally confined to efforts at improving upward and downward communications, with limited provision for employee influence on the decision-making process (Dundon *et al.* 2008).

However, some direct involvement initiatives may influence the decision-making process and it is this dimension of direct employee involvement that is of most interest from an industrial relations perspective. The term most widely used to describe this approach is 'task participation', described by Geary (1994: 637) as follows:

> Task participation is defined as opportunities which management provides at workplace level for consultation with and/or delegation of responsibilities and authority for decision making to its subordinates either as individuals or as groups of employees relating to the immediate work task and/or working conditions.

Task participation involves the devolution of greater control over work-related decisions to employees. Employees are encouraged to become more actively involved in influencing decisions, contributing their opinions and solving problems at the workplace level. Workers are required to assume greater responsibility for the general organisation and execution of work, while also being expected to concern themselves with broader enterprise objectives, e.g. improving productivity, controlling costs and general organisational efficiency. As Geary (1998: 3) again observes:

> With [task participation] … employees are granted more control over their immediate work situation and are invited to participate in decisions that relate to the organisation of work at the point of production. Thus, workers may influence the manner in which work is allocated, the scheduling of work and when to take breaks. They are also actively encouraged to seek solutions to problems and to make suggestions that will improve the organisation's efficiency.

Sisson (1994) identifies two key forms of task participation. The first is *consultative participation*, whereby workers are given the opportunity to become involved in decisions and make their views known but are not involved in joint decision-making. The second is *delegative participation*, whereby workers are empowered to make key decisions without the need for management approval, and this operates on the premise that individual workers assume greater autonomy in their work.

Teamworking is often considered an advanced form of delegative task participation, whereby workers make key decisions such as those concerning the selection of team leaders, team members and team roles, and task allocation. The concept of teamworking has its traditional roots in movements designed to improve the quality of working life (Morley *et al.* 2008; Tiernan and Morley 2019). While these early developments were met with some support in countries such as the US and Scandinavia, they had little impact in Ireland (Geary 1996; 1999; Gunnigle *et al.* 2017). In recent years there has been a significant increase in teamworking, largely instigated by employers in pursuit of organisational change. This contrasts with earlier initiatives that were worker/trade union driven and were designed to improve the quality of working life. In this vein, it appears that teamworking initiatives in Ireland have been few in number and largely efficiency driven rather than quality of work life/people driven. Geary (1996, 1999) further notes that Irish developments have largely involved 'tinkering at the margins' of existing work practices. Although teamworking is certainly more developed in European countries, even there the developments seem mostly modest. As noted earlier, the greatest advances have been in Germany, particularly in that country's automotive sector. In evaluating the European experience of teamworking, Geary (1996) identifies five important issues, as follows:

1   **The regulation of teamwork:** The introduction of teamworking in Europe has been achieved more through agreement with employee representatives rather than via unilateral imposition. This is attributed to the strength of collective employee representation (especially works councils and trade union involvement in industry-wide bargaining) in countries such as Germany and Sweden, which have led the way in its introduction.

2   **The objectives of teamwork:** Achieving a balance between managerial goals of improved efficiency and worker goals of improved quality of work life is a critical issue in facilitating the successful introduction of teamworking. In particular, it appears that trade unions are more willing to engage in teamworking when it is not used solely, or primarily, to achieve managerial aims.

3   **Impact on working lives:** Teamworking has favoured skilled workers, and the 'gender divide' has been left relatively untouched, i.e. a major divide remains, with more limited opportunities for women. However, some specialist categories of staff such as engineers and accountants have been transferred to line positions. Employers have not solely relied on persuasion to introduce teamworking but rather 'more traditional forms' of management control have also been utilised such as increased employee surveillance and more intense work schedules. Overall, increased skill and effort levels have been a common outcome of teamworking. A number of positive changes may be associated with teamworking, such as improved working conditions and job security, which can lead to productive efficiencies and encourage worker acceptance of teamworking.

4   **Teamwork and management support:** The European experience indicates that management commitment and support is an absolute prerequisite for the effective introduction of teamworking. If teamworking is introduced as an 'island solution', it has little chance of success, while line management 'indifference and resistance' are a key impediment to the effective introduction of teamworking.

5   **Integrating teamworking with human resource management (HRM):** The European evidence indicates that teamworking is likely to be most successful where it is integrated with complementary changes in other aspects of HR policy. In particular, a number of key policy changes are identified: a shift from individual-based pay to team-based pay, significant investment in training and development, and the maintenance of job security commitments.

Financial Participation

Financial participation is a generic term to describe mechanisms through which employees can gain some form of financial or equity share in their organisations through various profit-sharing, share-ownership or similar schemes. Financial participation is often seen as a means of developing a sense of ownership among workers by giving them a stake in their organisation while also integrating employees more fully into the market economy. Indeed, increasing employee loyalty, commitment and morale through the closer identification of employee interests with those of the organisation is a key objective of many schemes.

However, financial participation of itself will not normally allow for any significant increase in employee influence, since employees will generally represent a minority of the shareholders. Organisations such as the John Lewis Partnership in the UK and Donnelly Mirrors in Ireland have long been known for their policy of sharing profits with employees, and other companies now offer share options or some other form of profit sharing, such as Irish Cement, Dell Computers and Abbott Laboratories.

Salamon (2000) identifies two major reasons for the developing interest in financial participation. The first focuses on fairness and the argument that workers should receive a share of the profits or other positive outcomes which their work has helped create. Second, such schemes arguably encourage employee cooperation with management strategies to improve performance.

We can also identify two forms of financial participation, namely (i) gain sharing/ profit sharing and (ii) employee share ownership. Gain-sharing or profit-sharing arrangements essentially reward employees for improvements in organisation performance. While profit sharing is self-explanatory, gain sharing refers to arrangements where payments to workers are contingent on some measure of improvement in organisation performance other than profits. Commonly used measures are changes in levels of output or value added. However, gain-sharing arrangements may also be based on less obvious measures of performance, such as lower accident rates, scrap/rework levels or product/service quality. Gain-sharing arrangements are commonly linked to management attempts to instigate particular organisational change initiatives, often embracing attempts to increase employee involvement and commitment. We can identify a number of general objectives underlying such schemes (Armstrong and Stephens 2005):

- to encourage all employees to identify themselves more closely with the company by developing a common concern for its progress;
- to stimulate a greater interest among employees in the affairs of the company as a whole;
- to encourage better cooperation between management and employees;
- to recognise that employees of the company have a moral right to share in the profits they helped to produce;
- to demonstrate in practical terms the goodwill of the company to its employees; and
- to reward success in businesses where profitability is cyclical.

Such schemes are popular in the UK and the US and have been linked to corporate success on criteria such as market share, profitability and quality.

The second form of financial participation is an employee share ownership plan (ESOP). ESOPs involve the allocation of a proportion of company shares to employees according to some agreed formula. In Ireland the utilisation of employee share ownership has traditionally been quite low (Gunnigle *et al.* 2002; Poutsma *et al.* 2012). However, initial growth was stimulated by the Finance Acts of 1982–1984, which provided a number of incentives to organisations and employees with respect to ESOPs. Subsequent government measures have tinkered with tax-exemption limits, which impact on the incentive value of such schemes. However, despite some growth in ESOPs in recent years, the overall scale remains quite modest (D'Art and Turner 2006a). Even in organisations with share ownership schemes, these are often confined to higher managerial levels.

Additional data on the incidence and uptake of various forms of direct employee participation and involvement in Ireland are available through the periodic national workplace surveys of employers and employees conducted by the Economic and Social Research Institute (ESRI) (https://www.esri.ie/news/national-employer-and-employee-surveys, accessed 2019). A further useful source on financial participation and other aspects of information and consultation among the multinational sector in Ireland is the work of Lavelle *et al.* (2009, 2010).

HIGH-PERFORMANCE WORK SYSTEMS, DIRECT INVOLVEMENT AND THE QUALITY OF WORK LIFE

The concept of high-performance work systems (HPWS) is closely associated with many of the new 'high-tech' companies that emerged in the US from the 1970s sites (e.g. Apple, Microsoft and Compaq). The essence of HPWS appears to lie in efforts to adopt a culture of continuous improvement and innovation at all levels in the organisation. This is to be achieved by a combination of work organisation and HRM practices to sustain and develop this culture, particularly teamworking, quality consciousness and flexibility

(Tiernan and Morley 2019). It is argued that a specific characteristic of HPWS is a reliance on high levels of direct employee involvement in decision-making (Huselid 1995; Messersmith *et al.* 2011; Tiernan and Morley 2019). In evaluating the impact of HPWS, an issue of significance is their effect on employees' work experience. It is particularly important to address the coupling of initiatives for direct employee involvement with the application of management techniques designed to improve quality and productivity, especially just in time (JIT) and statistical process control (SPC) systems. The introduction of these initiatives is generally rooted in the premise that greater direct employee involvement and autonomy is consistent with the use of JIT, SPC or related techniques. Indeed, the argument that direct employee involvement/autonomy complements the use of JIT and SPC is often a key selling point in encouraging employees (and trade unions where present) to cooperate in the introduction of such approaches. However, such a complementary beneficial dynamic may always exist.

In her seminal review of the implications of techniques such as JIT and SPC for employees, Klein (1989: 60) argued that such changes in production systems do not necessarily make for a more empowered workforce:

> In Japan … where JIT and SPC have been used most comprehensively, employees are routinely organised into teams, but their involvement in workplace reform is typically restricted to suggestions for process improvement through structured quality control circles or kaizen groups. Individual Japanese workers have unprecedented responsibility. Yet it is hard to think of them exercising genuine autonomy, that is, in the sense of independent self-management.

Using examples from both the US and Japan, Klein found that increased pressures and constraints on workers were a common by-product of such manufacturing reforms (also see Cullinane *et al.* 2012). While allowing for greater employee involvement and autonomy than traditional assembly line systems, they are not conducive to the high levels of employee empowerment often thought to accompany a shift towards HPWS. She observed:

> True, under JIT and SPC, employees become more self-managing than in a command and control factory. They investigate process improvements and monitor quality themselves; they consequently enjoy immediate, impartial feedback regarding their own performance … They also gain a better understanding of all elements of the manufacturing process. On the other hand, the reform process that ushers in JIT and SPC is meant to eliminate all variations within production and therefore requires strict adherence to rigid methods and procedures. Within JIT, workers must meet set cycle times; with SPC, they must follow prescribed problem-solving methods. In their pure forms, then, JIT and SPC can turn workers

into extensions of a system no less demanding than a busy assembly line. These systems can be very demanding on employees. (Klein 1989: 61)

However, this analysis does not necessarily mean that HPWS cannot positively affect workers' job experience. Rather, it points to the fact that these techniques and systems may be applied in differing ways. Thus, the issue of management choice is important. Equally important can be the role of workers and trade unions in influencing management choice as to the nature of deployment of these new systems. It is plausible to argue that unfettered management prerogative in introducing so-called HPWS can contribute to a regression in employment conditions and employees' work experience. Thus, it appears that the key to improving employee involvement and autonomy when instigating HPWS is to provide for greater collaboration between teams, and to allow greater opportunity for teams and individuals to propose and evaluate suggestions for changes in the work process and in the conduct of different jobs (Geary 1996, 1999; Gunnigle *et al.* 2017; Tiernan and Morley 2019).

WORKPLACE PARTNERSHIP

Arguably, the most significant development in Irish industrial relations over several decades was the development and subsequent demise of national-level partnership agreements, principally those involving the so-called social partners, viz. trade unions, employers and government. As outlined in detail in the next chapter, between 1970 and 2009 pay determination was predominantly handled through centralised national-level bargaining between trade unions and employers' associations, with the exception of a short period from 1982 to 1986. Then from 1987 until 2009 national bargaining took on a tripartite character, with the state becoming a full partner at the negotiating table. This extended period of centralised national bargaining came to an abrupt end in 2009 with the onset of the 'Great Recession' (Gunnigle *et al.* 2017; Roche 2007b; Roche *et al.* 2011). For the first time in decades, Ireland embarked on a period of enterprise-level pay bargaining in the private sector, while four public sector agreements were concluded between 2010 and 2020 – see Chapter 13 for greater detail.

However, while national-level social partnership was well established, there had been a failure to replicate the national consensus/partnership model at workplace level, despite numerous initiatives to this effect (Gunnigle 1998b; Roche 2007b, 2008). As Roche (1995: 5) observed during the heyday of national-level social partnership, the Irish model of social partnership was somewhat narrow, involving only the top levels of the union and employer bodies, and had not significantly affected industrial relations at enterprise or workplace level. He described the Irish model as 'truncated' social partnership, inferring that employer–union relations at enterprise level continued to be characterised by adversarialism, despite the standing of national-level social partnership.

In traditionally voluntarist industrial relations systems, such as in Ireland, workplace partnership tends to be characterised by a combination of indirect and direct employee participation and involvement initiatives. These broadly include active cooperation between management and employee representatives, including trade unions, team-working and other direct involvement initiatives like suggestion schemes. These are supported by a variety of complementary HRM practices, including the use of a range of communications fora, access to training and development, and possibly commitments to employment tenure (Dobbins and Dundon 2011).

Proponents of partnership often point to deficiencies in the adversarial industrial relations model, in particular the apparent dominance of distributive bargaining on short-term issues and its emphasis on dividing limited resources (Kochan and Osterman 1994; McKersie 1996; O'Donnell and O'Reardon 1996). It is suggested that this approach leads the parties to develop adversarial positions, believing that any gains can only be made by inflicting losses on the other party. Indeed, distributive bargaining reflects the very essence of the traditional pluralist–adversarial model: claims, offers, bluffs, threats, compromise, movement, agreement or conflict (see Chapter 11).

In contrast, advocates of partnership at enterprise level posit that integrative/collaborative approaches represent a more attractive alternative, with their emphasis on exploring common ground and seeking solutions of mutual benefit for both employers and workers. It is further argued that this new model allows both sides to break out of the traditional adversarial relationship through the adoption of a partnership model based on 'mutual gains' principles, as follows:

- employers recognise and facilitate worker and trade union involvement in strategic decision-making;
- workers/trade unions commit themselves actively to productivity improvements;
- the gains of productivity improvements are shared between employers and workers; and
- productivity improvements do not result in redundancies but rather employers actively seek new markets to keep workers gainfully employed.

In essence, the mutual gains argument on which workplace partnership is based posits that workers and trade unions actively pursue with management solutions to business problems and appropriate work reorganisation, in return for greater involvement in business decisions and in the process of work reorganisation. It is characterised by a strong emphasis on consensual decision-making using integrative rather than distributive approaches in management–union interactions and negotiation (Roche 2007a).

The Characteristics of Workplace Partnership

In analysing the 'ideal-typical' characteristics of enterprise-level workplace partnership, we can identify three principal dimensions, namely its strategic impact, the role of trade unions/employee representatives and the degree of institutional sophistication.

Employee and/or trade union involvement in the strategic decision-making process is probably the key element that characterises a highly developed 'strategic' workplace partnership. The focus on high-level strategic decisions is important and serves to differentiate 'strategic partnerships' from lower-level workplace partnerships that focus on operational-level decisions, such as those related to work organisation or quality. That is not to say that operational workplace issues cannot be a focus of strategic partnership arrangements, but rather to indicate that the 'strategic' element refers to partnership in making long-term strategic decisions that impact on the future nature and direction of the enterprise as a whole. As McKersie (2002: 111) notes, a critical feature of strategic partnership is union or employee involvement in key corporate decisions, with trade unions having the 'opportunity to challenge or confront management before a decision is made'.

Given the critical role played by the Irish trade union movement in national social partnership, unions are generally seen as an equally important facet of the development of workplace partnerships. Indeed, trade unions have played an important role in promoting the idea and providing an institutional stimulus for the introduction of workplace partnership arrangements (Dobbins and Gunnigle 2009; Roche 2007a, 2008). However, we also know that foreign-owned firms, many of which are non-union, generate much industrial activity in Ireland. These firms often claim to have well-developed management–employee partnerships and deploy what have been termed non-union 'high commitment systems' (Cutcher-Gershenfeld and Verma 1994). These generally have their roots in the US and place the primary focus on facilitating direct employee involvement in operational decision-making at workplace level. However, it is often difficult to discern the existence and nature of such partnerships, since most accounts are based solely on a managerial perspective.

Another critical dimension of effective workplace partnership concerns the extent to which there are well-developed institutional arrangements to facilitate a partnership approach. The non-union high-commitment system relies primarily on direct employee involvement through teamworking and problem-solving groups – it does not normally involve formal representative structures (Cutcher-Gershenfeld and Verma 1994; Roche 2007a). However, in high-level workplace partnership (which provide for employee involvement in strategic decision-making) one would expect to find more formal structures. In unionised firms these structures normally exist in addition to established collective bargaining arrangements. For strategic partnership, one would expect to see provisions for union or worker representation at board level. An extract from a joint union/employer task force paper between Communications, Energy and Paper Union and Bell (Canada) illustrates this point:

Union–management partnerships need to involve, through the corporate steering committee and other exchanges of information, appropriate union executives in planning, strategy, training, and policy formulation in areas such as quality, human resources planning, new technology, major product development and market changes, and strategic alliances with other telecommunications companies. (McKersie 1996: 1)

Another key distinction is that these partnerships are at the corporate level, where key business decisions are made that affect the viability of the enterprise. To support well-developed partnership arrangements at the operational level, one might also expect to see the development of management–employee/union institutions to facilitate joint decision-making. However, some workplace partnership arrangements, particularly those of an operational nature, may not necessarily be underpinned by complementary institutional arrangements (Dobbins and Gunnigle 2009). For example, there may be ad hoc arrangements for periodic management–employee briefings where the focus is on information sharing and consultation. Management may use such fora to inform employees of organisational developments and garner employee feedback. However, the employer retains managerial prerogative with regard to final decision-making.

It is possible to identify two additional and important components that may form part of workplace partnerships: gain sharing and job security commitments. As mentioned earlier, gain sharing broadly incorporates arrangements that reward workers for improvements in enterprise performance via profit sharing, share ownership or some other reward mechanism. Such schemes are critical in giving effect to an underlying principle of partnership, namely that the gains from improved performance are shared between employers and workers. An important complementary element one might associate with effective workplace partnership is reasonable assurance of employment security. Such assurances would allow workers, and their trade unions, to engage in discussions on matters such as organisational change without being constrained by the spectre of redundancies/job insecurity.

Workplace Partnership: Pressures and Diffusion

In evaluating the pressures for workplace partnership, we can identify a number of generic stimuli (Roche 2007a, 2008; Roche and Geary 2002). First, the decline in trade union membership and recognition has prompted the union movement to seek mechanisms to increase their legitimacy and representativeness. Second, we have noted the increasingly competitive environment facing organisations. This puts pressure on organisations to reconfigure their industrial relations approaches to facilitate improved performance and productivity. Third, multilocation firms often promote competition between subsidiaries in differing locations/countries as a means of leveraging greater efficiencies and improved performance. Finally, there are pressures for industrial restructuring, stimulated largely by technological change and automation, and by 'social dumping', involving the relocation of processes and services to lower/lowest-cost locations.

Provisions in a number of national social partnership agreements, dating from the late 1990s, represented concerted attempts to promote workplace partnership in Ireland. However, none of these agreements entailed any legislative requirement on workplace partnership. This is arguably an important factor differentiating Ireland from countries where employee participation has taken stronger root. Certainly, the quite limited empirical evidence and patchy take-up of workplace partnership arrangements in Ireland suggest that such arrangements are unlikely to take hold without stronger regulatory support.

The University College Dublin/ESRI Workplace Survey (Roche 2007a, 2008; Roche and Geary 2002) remains one of the most comprehensive sources of information on the diffusion of workplace partnership. This study investigated twelve key areas of workplace change and, where change had occurred, examined the predominant approach used by establishments to handle workplace change. This study also investigated four optional approaches to handling change, as follows:

- management prerogative: change decisions made solely by management;
- traditional collective bargaining;
- partnership: engaging with trade unions to introduce change by consensus; and
- direct involvement: decided by management with the direct input from employees.

As evident from Table 12.1, the data on workplace change in unionised establishments indicate that partnership approaches are very much the exception rather than the rule. It also appears that, where partnership is used, it occurs more in relation to operational rather than strategic issues. However, this table indicates high levels of direct employee involvement in handling workplace change, in relation to both operational and strategic issues.

Looking at non-union establishments, we find even greater use of direct employee involvement on both strategic and operational issues (Table 12.2). Nevertheless, management prerogative remains the most widely practised means of introducing workplace change, and particularly so with regard to strategic issues. The study also looked at how employers planned to handle future workplace change. Respondents in unionised establishments indicated a clear preference for partnership approaches or direct employee involvement rather than collective bargaining. This was especially strong with regard to operational matters. Respondents in non-union establishments revealed a strong preference for greater use of direct employee involvement.

As illustrated in Table 12.3, the more recent National Centre for Partnership and Performance (NCPP) national employee survey (2010) found that approximately one-fifth (21 per cent) of employees reported the presence of formal partnership institutions at their workplaces. The NCPP data indicate that partnership committees are most common in the public sector, where over 40 per cent of employees reported their presence as compared to a private sector figure of just 16 per cent. However, the NCPP data indicated that just 4 per cent of employees (on average) are personally involved in

Table 12.1

Handling Workplace Change in Unionised Establishments

	How Change Is Handled (%)			
	Management Prerogative	Collective Bargaining	Partnership	Direct Involvement
Operational Issues				
Pay levels	17	62	11	10
Payment systems	21	40	18	22
New plant and technology	48	13	11	27
Working time	8	38	16	38
Work practices	13	25	20	41
Numbers employed	65	13	14	8
Employee involvement	26	14	14	46
Promotion structures and criteria	77	8	11	5
Strategic Issues				
New products/services	62	2	8	29
Setting business targets	71	3	3	23
Identifying ways of realising targets	47	4	8	41
Plans regarding mergers, acquisitions or divestments	92	1	2	6

Table 12.2

Handling Workplace Change in Non-union Establishments

	How Change Is Handled (%)	
	Management Prerogative	Direct Involvement
Operational Issues		
Pay levels	62	38
Payment systems	51	49
New plant and technology	52	48
Working time	20	80
Work practices	32	68
Numbers employed	33	67
Employee involvement	81	19
Promotion structures and criteria	76	24
Strategic Issues		
New products/services	56	44
Setting business targets	68	32
Identifying ways of realising targets	38	62
Plans regarding mergers, acquisitions or divestments	97	3

such forms of employee representation. This NCPP survey also investigated the incidence of formal partnership committees according to sector and size. The findings outlined in Table 12.3 indicate that employees in large private sector firms or in the public sector were most likely to be involved in formal partnership arrangements. However, those working in the hospitality sector, financial and other business activities, construction, and small firms were least likely to be thus involved.

Table 12.3
Incidence of Partnership Institutions in the Workplace by Organisational Characteristics (Employee Respondents)

	Partnership in Work (%)	Involved in Partnership (%)
Public	40.9	7.8
Private	15.6	2.9
Other production	24.5	4.4
Construction	7.6	2.8
Wholesale and retail	13.9	3.0
Hotels and restaurants	5.0	1.7
Transport, storage, communication	33.9	5.1
Financial and other business activities	13.9	1.4
Public administration and defence	48.8	9.8
Education	26.4	5.0
Health	27.6	5.0
Other services	12.5	3.4
Size of Local Unit		
1–4	5.0	1.1
5–19	9.5	1.9
20–99	20.5	4.6
100 plus	36.6	6.4
Total	21.0	4.0

Source: NCPP (2010).

More in-depth empirical evidence on direct and indirect forms of employee involvement and participation up to and including formal workplace partnership arrangements has been gathered by a team led by researchers at NUI Galway and Queen's University Belfast (Cullinane *et al.* 2012, 2014; Donaghey *et al.* 2011, 2012; Dundon *et al.* 2008, 2017). The specific issue of workplace partnership in Ireland has been explored in work by Tony Dobbins, John Geary and Aurora Trif, among others (cf. Dobbins 2008, 2010; Dobbins and Dundon 2011, 2017; Dobbins and Gunnigle 2009; Geary 2008; Geary and Trif 2011).

CONCLUDING COMMENTS

This chapter has investigated the nature and extent of employee involvement and participation, with particular emphasis on the Irish context. We have identified the range of initiatives used in organisations to facilitate employee involvement and participation, their evolution over time and the regulatory environment underpinning such initiatives. We have also considered the issue of workplace partnership and reviewed research evidence on its diffusion in Ireland. In the next and final chapter we focus on the key area of collective bargaining.

Chapter 13

Collective Bargaining in Ireland

INTRODUCTION

This chapter first explores selected elements of collective bargaining theory before proceeding to examine the evolution of the Irish collective bargaining and contemporary developments. As we have seen, collective bargaining is a mechanism to reconcile divergent interests in the employment relationship. Its principal feature is that terms and conditions of employment are determined collectively, not individually. For a modern state, it has importance outside of the individual contract of employment, since wages and conditions of employment set under collective bargaining can have major impacts on public finances and the competitiveness of an economy. The outcomes from wage determination, whether through collective bargaining or otherwise, also affect income distribution and whether a society is more or less egalitarian.

THEORETICAL OVERVIEW

There are a number of definitions of collective bargaining that stress different aspects of the process. Sidney and Beatrice Webb were the first to analyse the topic in detail. They saw collective bargaining as being the means that unions used to achieve their objective of 'maintaining and improving the conditions of their members' working lives' (Webb and Webb 1897: 1). Flanders (1968) challenged the Webbs' definition, claiming that collective bargaining is primarily concerned with rulemaking. The International Labour Organisation (ILO 1973: 7) defines collective bargaining as involving 'the negotiation of an agreed set of rules to govern the terms of the employment relationship, as well as the relationship between the bargaining parties themselves'. While collective bargaining has more than economic aspects to it, arguably the pursuit of improvement of terms and conditions of employment (as set out by the Webbs) remains its *raison d'être* (Fox 1975).

Pluralists consider that collective bargaining redresses the disparity of power between capital and labour; although there is a vigorous debate in the industrial relations literature as to what extent this is achieved in practice (Clegg 1975, 1976; Fox 1974). Clegg (1975) argues that the great advantage of collective bargaining is that compromise and agreement is the norm despite the absence of any assurance that compromise and agreement will result from every negotiation. He further contends that this uncertainty and an element of pressure is vital to collective bargaining (Clegg 1976).

A key concept in examining collective bargaining is bargaining structure. Bargaining structure has four aspects: bargaining form, bargaining scope, bargaining units and bargaining levels (Parker *et al.* 1971). Bargaining form describes the degree of formality of an agreement and this may vary from informal unwritten understandings to formal and comprehensive written agreements. Custom and practice can vary the application of collective agreements and can even be incorporated in the individual contract of employment (see Chapter 7). In general, the higher the bargaining level within an organisation, industry or country, the greater the degree of formality. Bargaining scope relates to the range of issues to be covered, which may be comprehensive or limited in range. A bargaining unit refers to the group of workers to be covered by a collective agreement. A bargaining unit may be narrow or wide, e.g. covering all fitters in a single company, all manual employees in an industry or all qualifying public sector workers (as in the case of public sector agreements). It may involve a single union, a group of unions or, for that matter, a confederation of unions such as the Irish Congress of Trade Unions (ICTU). The term 'bargaining unit' can also be applied to employers, where bargaining may take place with a single employer or with a number of employers – the latter is referred to as multi-employer bargaining. Multi-employer bargaining is generally associated with an industry, sector or national bargaining.

The most important aspect of bargaining structure is the level at which bargaining takes place. It is useful to view bargaining as taking place at the level of either the workplace/enterprise, industry, sector or nationally. This is, of course, a simplification since bargaining can overlap and take place at multiple levels. It is common for agreements reached at a higher level to be applied through further negotiation at industry, sectoral or workplace level. Such a process can allow for a degree of flexibility in adapting national agreements to sectoral or local circumstances while retaining the integrity of the overall agreement. However, it can also undermine the integrity of national agreements – most notably in the case of wage drift.

CENTRALISED BARGAINING

At a minimum, centralised bargaining involves negotiation between representatives of trade union confederations (ICTU in Ireland) and employer associations (primarily the Irish Business and Employers Confederation (IBEC) in Ireland). It has been typified by attempts to adopt a corporatist approach to collective bargaining. Corporatist arrangements go beyond the mere level at which negotiations take place. They typically attempt to:
- integrate government intervention in collective bargaining so that negotiations become tripartite;
- establish a consensus on economic and social issues in pursuit of a 'national interest';
- promote a debate over broader issues, such as macroeconomic policy, industrial policy and employment promotion; and
- make provision for pay increases, typically taking account of broader issues such as competitiveness, rates of taxation and welfare provision.

Thus, centralised bargaining is inextricably bound up with greater involvement by government in the industrial relations process than a simple voluntarist model of non-intervention implies. We now turn to examine theories on the role of the state in industrial relations.

COLLECTIVE BARGAINING AND THE ROLE OF THE STATE

While collective bargaining may take place at differing levels, a major factor determining which level dominates is the overall approach governments choose to adopt on the part of the state (Crouch 1982; Schmitter and Lehmbruch 1979). There are three broad options open to governments (Table 13.1). One is non-intervention, or what practitioners call 'free collective bargaining'. The term 'voluntarism' is sometimes used for this approach but it can cause confusion since in an Irish context that term has been used to describe minimal intervention by the law and employers' right not to engage with a trade union. A more formal and accurate term used to describe non-intervention in collective bargaining is 'liberal collectivism' (Palmer 1983). This refers to a situation where governments leave the regulation of industrial relations to unions and employer organisations. Roche (1989: 116) refers to this as an 'auxiliary' approach. He highlights the fact that Irish governments prior to the 1970s, while generally adopting a non-interventionist approach, did not abstain from efforts to influence employers and unions. However, these efforts were limited, with the frequent exhortations for the parties (invariably unions) to exercise wage restraint being the most notable.

Liberal collectivism (free collective bargaining) came under pressure in Europe as a result of the success of Keynesian demand management policies employed in the aftermath of World War II. These policies were designed to prevent a recurrence of the economic dislocation of the Great Depression of the 1930s. Keynesian policies in the 1950s and 1960s led to unprecedented levels of 'full employment', which increased the power of organised labour. Employers could no longer rely on what Marx called the 'reserve army of the unemployed' to constrain the growth of wage rates. Initially, governments addressed this by allowing a degree of inflation to maintain economic growth and full employment. However, by the late 1960s, countries were beginning to experience 'stagflation', i.e. limited growth combined with growing inflation. Faced with this problem, governments had two alternatives to liberal collectivism: 'to move in the direction of greater state intervention in collective bargaining or to jettison the commitment to full employment' (Roche 1989: 116).

Individual Liberalism

Jettisoning the commitment to full employment meant imposing 'discipline' on labour markets and curbing the power of organised labour, namely trade unions. It involved the adoption of an approach variously described in the industrial relations literature as 'individual liberalism' (Palmer 1983), 'market liberalism' (Rollinson 1993) or 'market control' (Roche 1989). The use of differing terms can be somewhat confusing, but they all represent the expression of a common neoliberal economic philosophy that emphasises the primacy of markets. This is the principle underlying modern neo-classical economic theories – notably the monetarism of Milton Friedman, which became widely influential in the 1980s. As with the laissez-faire ideology of the nineteenth century, in the neo-classical view, supply and demand is the ultimate arbiter of the competing interests of capital and labour. Put simply, labour is a commodity to be bought or sold. Wage rates and terms and conditions of employment are to be determined by the market. Trade unions and collective bargaining are seen as distorting the market and governments should move to limit their influence.

Table 13.1
Government Approaches to Collective Bargaining and Industrial Relations

	Liberal Collectivism	Individual or Market Liberalism	Neo-corporatism
Role of government in collective bargaining	• Non-intervention, or at the most, auxiliary approach	• No direct intervention in industrial relations • Indirect intervention via market control	• Direct intervention with unions and employer organisations (social partnership)
Key policy measures	• Appeal to parties to behave responsibly • Reduce the cost of labour via devaluation • Establish dispute resolution bodies	• Tighten monetary policy • Implement industrial restructuring • Impose legal restrictions on unions • Weaken the role of dispute resolution bodies	• Coordinate wage determination with economic and social policy • Strengthen the role of policy and research institutes • Strengthen dispute resolution bodies

In keeping with the laissez-faire doctrine, direct involvement by the state in industrial relations issues is to be avoided. Instead, indirect policies are to be applied. These include the restructuring of older uncompetitive industries and the adoption of a tight monetary policy. A tight monetary policy would mean that companies that conceded too-high wage increases in negotiations with unions would become uncompetitive and would fail. Such thinking informed the Thatcherite revolution in British industrial relations from 1979 onwards as the economy there was restructured away from manufacturing towards services, notably financial services (Roche 1989). In the UK the economic restrictions were augmented by legislation rolling back the trade disputes immunities previously conferred on trade unions and placing successively tighter legal obligations on strike action. Initially, these legislative measures were promoted on the basis of enhancing internal union democracy but it quickly became apparent they had the aim of weakening trade unions.

Individual liberalism promises greater flexibility and superior economic performance but, as Crouch (1982) points out, it subordinates employees to the control and authority of the business owner and promotes an employment relationship that is at best paternalistic and at worst exploitative. It is, in effect, unitarism at a state level. Although no Irish government has deployed a strategy of thoroughgoing market liberalism to date, it would be a mistake to suggest that market forces have not affected the nature of Irish industrial relations. The open nature of the Irish economy, globalisation and EU competition policy have been powerful forces in shaping the nature of collective bargaining (McDonough and Dundon 2010).

Corporatism

The origins of corporatism can be traced back to diverse sources, most notably the Social Christian tradition in the papal encyclical *Rerum Novarum* issued in 1893 by Pope Leo XIII. Corporatist ideas were (and are) opposed to notions of atomistic individual competition inherent in laissez-faire economic theories but are also opposed to the class conflict of Marxism. In contrast to classical and neoclassical economic theories, they recognised the legitimacy of collective organisations representing workers and employers. Corporatism was concerned with avoiding or at least limiting class conflict, and it preached social harmony under organised and representative structures of workers and employers, coordinated by the state. These ideas continue to inform modern neo-corporatist thinking.

The mass unemployment of the 1930s threatened the stability of the liberal democracies and led to the emergence of fascism in several European countries, notably Italy, Germany, Spain and Portugal. Fascist countries turned to state-led corporatism to produce 'social harmony'. In this type of corporatism, free trade unions were abolished or severely restricted and the state acted as the controlling influence in regulating labour management relations. In effect, dictatorship was extended to the labour market. Panitch (1979: 120) notes that the fascist states 'gave a rude answer to the question of how the social harmony trumpeted in theory would in fact come to replace the competition and class conflict of capitalist society'. After 1945 there was a strong appreciation of the merits of independent trade unions and free collective bargaining as essential pillars of democracy acting as a brake on the excessive power of capital and the state. The associations with fascist authoritarianism led to the concept of corporatism being viewed in overwhelmingly negative and pejorative terms post World War II (Panitch 1979; Schmitter 1979).

Neo-corporatism

By the 1970s political scientists and industrial relations scholars had begun to resurrect some corporatist ideas under the term of 'neo-corporatism', or new corporatism (Schmitter 1979). The re-examination of corporatist ideas was driven by the examples of a number of northern European states in the 1950s and 1960s, most notably Scandinavia, with Sweden as the main exemplar. Sweden had strong trade unions with very high union density and equally strong employer organisations. Collective bargaining played a major role in the Swedish economic model and there were none of the dire outcomes predicted in neo-classical economic theory. In fact, the Swedish economy had enjoyed remarkable economic success and modernisation. Sweden also seemed to finesse the problems of stagflation that afflicted some other European countries, notably the UK, and for which its industrial relations system was held by some to be responsible.

The contribution of their industrial relations system was identified as being due to 'political exchange', which involved unions exercising wage restraint in return for commitments from governments to pursue full employment and a high level of welfare provision. Management was allowed a largely free hand in the workplace and modernisation, and technical innovation was embraced by trade unions. High taxation levels allowed the state to deliver enhanced standards of education, health, pension, housing and other entitlements, producing a high 'social wage' that compensated for wage restraint. There was also a large element of wage solidarity, with wage differentials being squeezed and overall income differentials being narrow. Consequently, neo-corporatism of the Scandinavian type delivered higher levels of social and economic equality than alternative models based on liberal ideas. Successful neo-corporatist arrangements, as in Sweden, can be seen as being held together by a 'virtuous circle' of full employment and high welfare provisions, which had the effect of legitimating and reinforcing the unions' policies of wage restraint and government intervention (Roche 1989).

Differing Forms of Neo-corporatism

We can distinguish between different forms of corporatism: *social corporatism*, as in Scandinavia, and *liberal corporatism*, as in Austria and the Netherlands (Pekkarinen *et al.* 1992). Social corporatism is based on a political and ideological analysis that perceives conflict as endemic to capital–labour relations and where compromise arises from a position of power on both sides. In this model corporatism acts to institutionalise conflict as part of a democratic class struggle (Korpi 1983). In contrast, liberal corporatism is based on the view that there is essentially a commonality of interests between capital and labour (Pekkarinen *et al.* 1992). In liberal corporatism there is a gradual institutionalisation of a consensus, particularly between leaders rather than members of organisations. The management of economic adjustment and the sharing of burdens and rewards are controlled by the elites at the top of hierarchies of interest organisations. The gains go chiefly to insiders, reflecting the relative power of peak-level federations (unions such as ICTU and national employer organisations such as IBEC) and their member organisations. There is an absence of (or only weak commitment to) egalitarianism, resulting in the preservation of existing disparities in wealth and life chances (Turner and Wallace 2000).

Contemporary Corporatist Developments

The redistributive and solidaristic policies of social corporatism came under threat following the 1970s. In Sweden the employers broke from the system that had previously been lauded and industry-level bargaining replaced national bargaining as the dominant wage-determination mechanism. By the mid 1980s, it appeared that neo-corporatism as a specific political and economic approach to economic management had declined in many European countries (Golden *et al.* 1999). However, by the 1990s, corporatism had 'undergone an astonishingly lively and broad-based revival' with the emergence of what were called national social pacts in a number of countries (Pochet and Fajertag 2000: 9). Social pacts involved centralised agreements between governments, trade union confederations and employer organisations.

These social pacts have been analysed under the term 'competitive corporatism' and are attributed to increasing competition in a global market (Turner 2006; Turner and Wallace 2000). Competitive corporatism is a search for an alternative or 'third way' to the neoliberal prescriptions of deregulated labour markets and reduced welfare (Ferner and Hyman 1998; Goetschy 2000). Teague and Donaghey (2009) note that such pacts were associated with the introduction of the Economic and Monetary Union (EMU) in the EU and, unlike Irish social partnership, most proved unsustainable once the key motivation of EMU had been achieved and, as a result, they collapsed.

Competitive corporatism is equivalent to liberal corporatism, as is evident from policy measures. Competitive or liberal corporatism represents an attempt to meet the demands for economic efficiency while promoting some equity or at least defending existing social protection systems (Rhodes 1998). Both involve greater flexibility in the labour market together with social security systems tailored more closely to the imperatives of competition. Labour market reforms are used to promote employment rather than government management of aggregate demand as in Keynesian economics (Goetschy 2000). Rhodes (1998: 200) observes that competitive corporatism prioritises competitiveness and 'downplays the equity function of more traditional golden age forms of corporatism'. In effect, the 'policies of competitive corporatism, for example, labour market deregulation and a reduction in corporate taxation, promote increased inequality' (Turner and Wallace 2000: 4).

The distinctions made between liberal (or competitive) corporatism and social corporatism reflect ideal types, and real-life examples tend to fall somewhere along a continuum between these two ideal types. For example, it is now recognised that Swedish neo-corporatism paid great attention to competitiveness. Moene and Wallerstein (1999: 234) note that 'the Nordic variety of corporatism was associated not with protectionism and monopolistic pricing, but with free trade and the subsequent need to remain competitive'. In evaluating any real-world corporatist system, the key question is not whether the example matches either of the ideal types, but to which version the particular example most approximates. In this regard, differences in taxation policy and income distribution are crucial. Liberal corporatism is based on low taxation, which limits the redistributive capability of centralised agreements and government policy. This is an especially important consideration in evaluating where the Irish social partnership agreements lay along the corporatist continuum.

THE DEVELOPMENT OF IRISH COLLECTIVE BARGAINING

As noted in Chapter 1, collective bargaining is a relatively new concept and practice, which arose out of the economic, political and social developments of the nineteenth century.

The period between the two world wars saw collective bargaining still in its infancy in this country. O'Brien (1989: 133) writes that 'while collective bargaining was extensive, it covered only a minority of all workers and it was uncoordinated and rather haphazard'. The onset of World War II brought a cessation to much collective bargaining (see Table 13.2). Wage determination was governed by the Wages Standstill Order (No. 83) of 1941, which limited wage increases. Prices rose steadily during the war period and this, combined with the wage restraint, led to a decline in purchasing power and a substantial erosion of living standards. Unsurprisingly, when the Wages Standstill Order was suspended at the end of the war, there were widespread claims for wage increases and this resulted in the initiation of a wage round system. This system, which lasted from 1946 to 1970, established collective bargaining as the dominant method for determining wages and conditions of employment in the Irish economy. It was also associated with major growth in union density and the increased importance of employer organisations, most notably the Federated Union of Employers (FUE), the predecessor of IBEC.

WAGE ROUNDS, 1946–1970

Wage rounds involved a largely unplanned general upward movement of wages and salaries over a period of time, which recurred at intervals (McCarthy *et al*. 1975). Four of the twelve wage rounds were the result of bipartite agreements between the FUE and ICTU at national level. This prefaced the development of national bargaining. The other eight were decentralised examples of free collective bargaining and were negotiated either 'at industry and trade or company level' (O'Brien 1989: 134). Craft workers were to the fore in the initiation of new wage rounds and this reflected their relative strength within

Table 13.2
Outline Profile of Wage Bargaining, 1922–2020

	Level of Bargaining	**Number of Agreements**	**Name**
Pre-1941	Haphazard and sporadic bargaining	No systematic number of agreements	None
1941–1946	National legal regulation	Wage increases restricted by law	Wages Standstill Order
1946–1970	Industry and local (some national element in four of these)	Twelve	Wage rounds
1970–1981	National supplemented by enterprise level	Seven	National wage agreements
		Two	National understandings
1982–1987	Enterprise and general public sector agreements	Varied in organisations: generally five (max. six)	Decentralised wage agreements
1987–2009	Centralised	Seven	Consensus/ partnership agreements
2010–2020	Public sector national	Four Public Sector (Stability)* Agreements	Croke Park
			Haddington Road
		*Term stability used from Haddington Road Agreement	Lansdowne Road
			Lansdowne Road Extensional Agreement
2010–2019	Private sector enterprise-level	Various number of agreements	IBEC–ICTU protocol on private sector (no distinctly named wage round system)
	2010–2011 limited bargaining	Pharmaceuticals and some others in export sector	
	2012–2019 widespread bargaining	Union-initiated pattern bargaining	

the trade union movement of the time. Over a period of time that settlement would be extended through the economy. Workers covered by later settlements tended to gain higher increases to compensate, although this depended on the type of work they did. There was also huge gender discrimination in wage increases, with increases for women workers of the order of 60 per cent of the male rate.

The wage round process became the subject of much criticism over time. As in other northern European countries, it was the relative prosperity of the 1960s that heightened government concern at the impact of collective bargaining (Hardiman 1988). Critics focused on the wage competition between bargaining groups, the sacredness of 'wage differentials' and sectional interest being pushed to the fore at the expense of the national interest (O'Brien 1989). Sectional wage bargaining was particularly prevalent among craft groups, where the protection of relativities and differentials was deeply entrenched. Roche (1989: 116) argues that the wage rounds 'came to be identified by successive Irish governments as a significant contributor to economic problems, especially inflation'.

The main charge against wage rounds that they caused inflation is unproven. Neo-Keynesian economists saw wages as contributing to inflation – called wage push inflation. As such, economists from this school tended to favour government intervention in collective bargaining in order to constrain wage rises through corporatist-type arrangements. While inflation was indeed increasing, workers saw themselves serving wage claims to chase inflation. Among neo-classical economists a consensus had emerged by the late 1970s that unions did not cause inflation but rather increased unemployment (Hardiman 1988). They argued that by increasing wages above their market level, trade unions decreased the competitiveness of labour, leading to a growth in unemployment. However, Irish unemployment in 1969 (at the end of the wage round system) was only 4 per cent – effectively full employment. Therefore, there is little evidence that settlements from wage rounds were out of line with the underlying growth of the economy, at least in terms of employment. Whatever about the economic arguments, criticisms of the wage round system increased with the heightened level of wage demands and the strike activity of the late 1960s.

CENTRALISED WAGE AGREEMENTS, 1970–1981

A six-week-long maintenance craftsmen's dispute in 1969 crystallised government concern at the unregulated wage round system. That strike, and the wage increases resulting from it, represented a watershed in industrial relations, and high wage demands for an emerging thirteenth round in 1970 prompted government action. In October 1970 the Fianna Fáil government published a Prices and Incomes Bill, which proposed to limit wage increases to 6 per cent until the end of 1971 (Dáil Éireann 1970). Not unnaturally, unions were opposed to the Bill but employers were also concerned at the idea of establishing a statutory system of wage determination. Indeed, it is doubtful if the government really wished to take on this role. Allen (1997: 144) claims the Bill 'was mainly a device by the Fianna Fáil Government to pressurise the union leaders into standing up against their own militants'.

The threat of legislation was effective, and employers and unions entered negotiations under the auspices of a body called the Employer Labour Conference (ELC). This led to an agreement being reached that provided for a wage increase of some 14 per cent over eighteen months – well in excess of the 6 per cent mooted in the Prices and Incomes Bill (Breen *et al.* 1990). The increase reflected the rising expectations of workers and the increasing rate of inflation, which was common to many western economies at the time. It was an indication that the process of national bargaining could not be insulated from worker expectations or external influences. The agreement provided a model for six further national wage agreements, spanning the years 1970 to 1978, and two more developed agreements called *national understandings*.

The initial national agreements were bipartite employer–union agreements, with the government involvement confined to its role as a public sector employer. As the decade progressed, governments became more involved in their governmental role – a trend that culminated in the two national understandings in 1979 and 1980. These last two agreements represented an attempt to establish a more developed form of neo-corporatism, taking account of a wide range of issues, including welfare and taxation policy in the wage-negotiation process. The nine agreements set wage increases for unionised workers across the economy but also became a standard for wage increases in non-union companies. This represented an informal process of the 'extension of collective bargaining', which in a range of other western European countries is given effect through legal provision. Fogarty *et al.* (1981: 19) famously drew attention to this aspect of the process, saying national wage agreements were viewed as 'an award from heaven or Dublin'.

The Performance of Centralised Bargaining, 1970–1981

The centralised agreements were a much more structured system than the pay rounds. Pay was set in specific terms, the duration of the agreements was fixed and specific machinery (the ELC) was provided to deal with disputes arising out of the terms of the agreements and any anomalies. In terms of process, 'they had basically stabilised what had become a chaotic picture' (von Prondzynski 1992: 79). During their existence, they were also endorsed by public commentators and media, with free collective bargaining being referred to in pejorative terms as 'a free for all' and often presented as an unrealistic alternative.

While the national agreements enjoyed strong support initially, over time opinions changed, especially among employers. This was because of a failure to deliver on implicit objectives. McCarthy (1977) identified the following objectives for centralised bargaining:

- control inflation;
- promote full employment;
- reduce industrial unrest;
- moderate income increases; and
- deliver relatively higher increases to lower-paid workers.

These objectives were not met to any great degree, although this was far from being due to the process of centralised bargaining. International developments meant that any attempts to control inflation were certain to be stillborn. Fuelled by the oil crises of 1973/1974 and 1979/1980, inflation rose and fell precipitously during the 1970s, reaching around 20 per cent in both 1975 and 1981. Employment grew over the period of the agreements but the labour force expanded at a greater rate, resulting in a rise in unemployment from 4 per cent in 1969 to 10.7 per cent by 1982 (Conniffe and Kennedy 1984; Hardiman 1988). There was some modest initial impact on industrial unrest, with a decline in strike statistics under the early agreements. However, in the second half of the 1970s strikes and working days lost increased (see Chapter 10).

Of most concern from an employer perspective was that the agreements failed to deliver the promised wage restraint. While national wage increase norms were specified in the agreements, free collective bargaining could still operate at enterprise level. This was because clauses in the agreements provided for above the norm (ATN) increases, which could be negotiated for higher productivity. These on occasion led to 'spurious productivity' deals in which wage increases were conceded but the productivity elements were not realised (Wallace 1982). ATN provisions led to substantial wage drift, i.e. increases above the prescribed amount. Roche (2009: 192) argues that 'while employers and governments complained of the bad faith of union leaders, trade union members saw little reason to moderate their pay demands against a background of high inflation and an escalating income tax burden'. Workers pointed out that national agreements only restrained wages, with no constraints on income increases generally. The growth in the tax burden saw many low-paid workers drawn into the tax net for the first time and this eroded the solidaristic element of the higher percentage wage increases for the lower paid.

Not only do the national wage agreements of the 1970s have to be evaluated in the light of external influences on the economy, they must also be viewed against unwise pro-cyclical policies. The most damaging of these arose from the Fianna Fáil government elected in 1977, which sought full employment through a naive Keynesianism involving the expansion of employment in the public sector. Coinciding with this was a simultaneous narrowing of the tax base brought about by abolishing rates (a property tax) and motor tax. The extensive welfare and social provisions associated with the national agreements now had to be paid from a narrower tax base. Arguably, the most telling defect of the Irish experiment with corporatism in the 1970s was that it represented an attempt to transplant an egalitarian model into a country with an inegalitarian taxation system. This is an example of the acknowledged difficulty that can arise in attempting to transplant industrial relations from one country to another (Godard 2014).

Hardiman (1988: 102) notes that 'by the late 1970s almost 90 per cent of income tax came from the PAYE sector'. The inequities in the tax system resulted in large-scale trade union tax marches. These had little effect as the overall tax burden on wage and salary earners actually rose from 30 per cent in 1979 to 45 per cent in 1981. Figure 13.1 illustrates the tax wedge effect of increased taxation, where employers saw 'labour costs rising steeply while the net value of earnings increased but little' (Hardiman 1988: 99). The result was that the pay terms of the agreements worked against the interests of both employers *and* workers. However, it was employers who were the most dissatisfied with national agreements, chiefly because of their failure to deliver the promised wage restraint and industrial peace. Faced with a deepening recession, resulting from the second oil crisis, and unhappy at the levels of government spending and taxation, they only reluctantly agreed under extreme pressure from the Fianna Fáil government to be party to the second national understanding in 1980, and they declined to enter a new one when that agreement terminated in 1982.

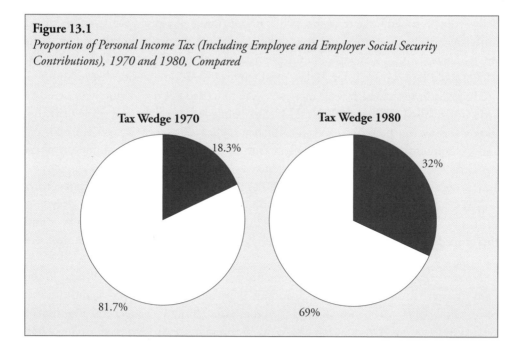

Figure 13.1
Proportion of Personal Income Tax (Including Employee and Employer Social Security Contributions), 1970 and 1980, Compared

Tax Wedge 1970

18.3%

81.7%

Tax Wedge 1980

32%

69%

DECENTRALISED BARGAINING, 1982–1987

The second national understanding was followed by a period of decentralised bargaining which lasted from 1982 to 1987 and coincided with a long and deep recession. Numbers at work fell as redundancies rose to in excess of an average of 20,000 workers per annum and emigration shot up. Unemployment grew from almost 9 per cent in 1981 to 17.1 per cent in quarter two in 1986. Overall, real disposable income was estimated to have fallen by between 8 and 10 per cent between 1980 and 1987 (Turner and D'Art 2000).

Against this backdrop, the focus of private-sector bargaining moved to enterprise level. Viability and economic performance became the key criteria shaping wage increases as a 'new realism' prevailed in employer–employee relationships (Gunnigle *et al.* 1994). The most visible aspect of employer assertiveness in the 1980s involved concession bargaining. Concession bargaining involves 'union givebacks' such as wage cuts, reductions in terms and conditions of employment, and accompanying productivity concessions. These were the reverse of the spurious productive deals of the 1970s. In addition, prominent employers such as the banks introduced two-tier employment systems, with new entrants being paid below the rate of established workers – these were termed 'yellow pack' and 'green pack' employment grades, named after the own-brand products of two large retailers.

There was a major gain in comparative wage competitiveness as private sector unit wage costs rose by only 7 per cent between 1980 and 1985, compared with an average 37 per cent increase in competing countries (Hardiman 1988: 220). As can be seen from Table 13.3, the trend of wage increases decreased greatly in line with a reduction in the rate of inflation. Inflation was driven downward not only by the deflationary effects of the recession but also by the disciplinary effects of the decision in 1979 to link the Irish pound to the European Exchange Rate Mechanism.

Table 13.3
Wage Increases and Inflation Compared, 1982–1987

Round	Average Cumulative Increase (%)	Average Length (Months)	Year	Inflation (%)
22	16.4	14.9	1982	17.1
23	10.9	13.5	1983	10.4
24	9.3	12.75	1984	8.6
25	6.8	12.0	1985	5.4
26	6.0	12.0	1986	3.9
27	4.5–6.5*	15.4*	1987	3.2

* Only a small number of agreements were concluded in the twenty-seventh round, which was overtaken by the Programme for National Recovery.
Source: Department of Finance (2003), McGinley (1989).

The Return to Centralised Agreements, 1987

The 1980s was a period of severe economic difficulties, with a growing crisis in the public finances being especially marked. Three of the principal elements in current government expenditure are foreign debt service, social welfare and the public sector payroll. At the end of 1986, the debt/GNP ratio stood at over 120 per cent of GNP and unemployment had reached some 17 per cent, resulting in expenditure on social services increasing from 28.9 per cent of GNP in 1980 to 35.6 per cent in 1985 (NESC 1986).

Early 1987 brought the election of a Fianna Fáil government with Charles Haughey TD as Taoiseach and Bertie Ahern TD as Minister for Labour. That government's economic strategy was to address public finances with a focus on tackling the public sector payroll. It saw a return to national bargaining as the mechanism to achieve this objective and the government issued invitations to the employers and unions to enter negotiations. The name of the resultant agreement – the Programme for National Recovery (PNR) – reflected the economic circumstances in which the state found itself. Employer support was copper-fastened by the extremely modest wage increases of approximately 2.5 per cent per annum spread over thirty-nine months to January 1991. This was significantly lower than the trend then emerging under the twenty-seventh round, of about 4.5 per cent per annum (see Table 13.3). For trade unions, the agreement delivered a general one-hour reduction in the working week, to thirty-nine hours. It also held out the promise of giving them influence at the national level and avoiding the marginalisation of unions that had happened in the UK.

In addition to the pay terms, a number of broader policy objectives were set out. These included:
- the creation of a fiscal and monetary climate conducive to economic growth, including a commitment that the ratio of debt to GNP should be reduced;
- movement towards greater equity and fairness in the tax system;
- measures to generate employment opportunities; and
- a reduction of social inequalities.

These objectives differed from agreements of the 1970s in that they were expressed as specific targets and not as binding commitments. Over time, these elements expanded greatly in successive agreements – especially from 1997 onwards when the Community and Voluntary Pillar was added to partnership negotiations. The PNR initiated a consensus approach to collective bargaining that in time became known as social partnership. Although called 'partnership', this does not mean that the negotiation process was purely integrative. There were many examples of distributive tactics such as 'sabre rattling' and the use of bottom lines and preconditions. In effect, the process of negotiating agreements conformed to a mixed-motive model of negotiation rather than a purely integrative one.

Wage Terms of the Agreements

The agreements dealt with a wide range of issues and while some of them were devolved to industry or sectoral level, the provisions for wage increases were determined centrally.

The agreements can be divided into two broad groups. Five of the agreements had provision for more modest wage rises while two – the Programme for Economic and Social Progress (PESP) and the Programme for Prosperity and Fairness (PPF) – contained wage increases of a higher order of magnitude. Not all the agreements were implemented as set down. In early 1992 lower than expected growth saw the government delay the agreed increases and pay them a year in arrears with full retrospection – in effect giving government an interest-free loan (von Prondzynski 1992). In 2001 the PPF was renegotiated upwards when inflation exceeded the predicted 2.5 per cent per annum. Employers resisted this renegotiation but they eventually agreed to a 2 per cent additional pay rise plus 1 per cent 'lump sum' payment. Finally, although the Towards 2016 transitional agreement was agreed in September 2008, that agreement quickly unravelled under the pressure of the deteriorating economic situation and it was not implemented as both private sector employers and government abandoned social partnership.

Above the Norm (ATN) and Local Bargaining Provisions

Employers were generally opposed to local-level bargaining, although two of the agreements contained such a clause – PESP (3 per cent) and Partnership 2000 (2 per cent). The latter 2 per cent was based on profit sharing and conditional on 'deepening partnership and securing commitment to competitiveness at the level of the enterprise' (Department of the Taoiseach 1997: 64). This increase was generally paid but did not lead to any deep and sustained workplace partnership (see Chapter 12). These two incidences aside, provisions for ATN were not a feature of the remaining agreements. There is evidence of some wage drift but that appeared to be driven by underlying market conditions and tended to be concentrated on increases for higher-skilled grades. In any event, the wage drift that did exist in the private sector did not lead to major employer complaints as in the 1970s.

Wage Tax Trade-offs

The central feature of the agreements was the trade union movement's exercise of wage restraint in return for reductions in personal income tax (Yeates 2013). This meant that real take-home pay increased at a rate greater than the nominal wage increases in the agreements. Employers also achieved substantial tax reductions on the corporate tax take, which was designed to encourage companies to locate in Ireland and to reward enterprise. Table 13.4 contains outline details of the wage and tax elements of the agreements. However, lower personal taxation was not a creation of social partnership but owed its origin to the political system (notably the influence of the Progressive Democrat party, even before it entered government first in 1989). The lowering of personal tax rates cannot be considered a consensus policy, at least as applied from the election of the Fianna Fáil/Progressive Democrat government in 1997. David Begg, General Secretary of ICTU, argued as follows:

the policy of the Government that came to power in 1997 ... [was that they] were hell bent on cutting taxes for the wealthy and deregulating whole swathes of the economy ... It is a matter of public record that Congress opposed that decision. (Sheehan 2011d: 17)

Like other issues such as union recognition and proportionately higher wage increases for lower-paid workers, the low taxation model was not a deal-breaker for the unions. Indeed, the wage restraint/tax concessions trade-off was the central mechanism underpinning the social partnership agreements. McDonough and Dundon (2010: 548) are highly critical of the after-effects of this policy, pointing out that it left Ireland in a position where 'as a percentage of GDP, Irish taxation remains at a similar level of some of the poorer Eastern European Member States of the EU'. The lower taxation of the social partnership years was accompanied by a widening gap between high- and low-income earners in the years 1987 and 2005 (D'Art and Turner 2011; McDonough *et al.* 2009), and a drop in relative disposable income for the bottom 50 per cent of households, from 25.25 per cent to 23.49 per cent in the years 1987–2007 (D'Art and Turner 2011; Social Justice Ireland 2009). While accepting that employers benefited more from social partnership, Yeates (2013) asserts that workers and the trade union movement benefited immensely from the partnership process.

Employers and their Attitudes to Social Partnership

Private sector employers were generally positive about social partnership. Writing on the Programme for Competitiveness and Work (PCW) agreement, Brian Geoghegan of IBEC argued that the national programme had delivered on jobs, kept inflation and interest rates low, and delivered additional disposable income to an average employee (Geoghegan 1996). IBEC's main concerns were generally with the issues of competitiveness, levels of taxation and public expenditure. The main opposition from an employer side came from the Irish Small and Medium Enterprises Association, which claimed that centralised agreements placed unfair burdens on small firms. Such views were not representative of the broad body of employer opinion. In a survey of employer and union elites, Wallace *et al.* (1998) found that 'not a single employer or union respondent favoured a return to decentralised bargaining'. As late as 2006, social partnership continued to have broad support from business leaders. A survey of chief executive officers reported that 82 per cent of them were of the view that social partnership remained necessary (Fitzgerald 2006).

Trade Unions and their Attitudes to Social Partnership

Trade unions generally supported the agreements. From an early date, ICTU saw a consensus approach as holding out the possibility of the 'development of a modern efficient low inflation economy ... with low levels of unemployment and high levels of

Table 13.4

Wage and Tax Elements of National Wage Agreements (NWAs), 1987–2009

Programme	Years	Duration	Tax Provisions	Wage Increases
Programme for National Recovery (PNR)	1987–1991	39 months (6-month pay pause to apply to the public sector)	• Reduction of IR£225m (IR£750m actually delivered), including increases in the PAYE allowance costing IR£70m • Widening of tax band and cut in tax rates to 30% and 53%	• 3% on the first IR£120 per week • 2% on the remaining weekly pay • Minimum IR£4 increase per week
Programme for Economic and Social Progress (PESP)	1991–1994	36 months	• Reduce bottom rate to 25% (only 27% achieved) plus 1% income levy added • Marginal relief rate of taxation reduced from 48% to 40%	• Year 1: 4% increase • Year 2: 3% increase* *(+ 3% local (exceptional) bargaining clause) • Year 3: 3.75%
Programme for Competitiveness and Work (PCW)	1994–1997	36 months	• IR£900m tax cuts, reduction from 27% to 26% on standard rate • PRSI reduced by 1% • IR£100m cut in business tax and improvements for small firms	• Year 1: 2.5% increase • Year 2: 2.5% increase • Year 3: 2.5% increase
Partnership 2000 for Inclusion, Employment and Competitiveness	1997–2000	39 months	• IR£900m in tax reductions over 3 years • IR£100m cut in business tax, including reductions in corporation tax	• Year 1: 2.5% increase • Year 2: 2.25% increase* * (+ 2% local bargaining clause) • Year 3: 1.5% first 9 months + 1% last 6 months
Programme for Prosperity and Fairness (PPF)	2000–2003	33 months (locally agreed pay pauses on last phase of agreement due to inability to pay)	• IR£1.2 billion in tax breaks: increase personal allowance by IR£800 to IR£5,500 and the PAYE allowance increased by IR£1,100 to IR£2,000 • Widening of the standard tax band: single tax earner from IR£17,000 to IR£20,000; and married from IR£28,000 to IR£29,000 • Reductions in the rates in which tax is levied to 42% and 20%	• Year 1: 5.5% increase • Year 2: 5.5% increase (+ 2% renegotiated) • Year 3: 4.0% increase final 9 months + 1% once-off lump sum
Sustaining Progress	2003–2006	1st phase: 18 months 2nd phase: 18 months 6-month pay pause for public sector	• Progress to be made on removing those on the minimum wage from the tax net • Aim to have 85% of taxpayers on standard rate	• 3% first 9 months • 2% next 6 months • 2% next 3 months • Minimum wage €7 an hour from 1 Feb 2004 • Mid-term review • 1.5% first 6 months • 1.5% second 6 months • 2.5% final 6 months
Towards 2016 Phase 1	2006–2008	27 months	None	• 3% first 6 months • 2% next 6 months • 2.5% next 6 months • 2.5% last 6 months plus extra 0.5% for workers paid less than €10.25 per hour in phase 2
Towards 2016 Extensional Agreement (agreement discontinued in 2009)	2008–2009	36 months in 2 phases 3-month pay pause, private sector; 11 months, public sector	None	• Pay pause 3 months • 3.5% next 6 months • 2.5% next 12 months (extra 0.5% for workers under €11.00 per hour)

Source: National agreements, 1987–2008.

Note: This table simplifies the provisions, and the original agreements should be consulted for the full terms. In particular, the application of public sector pay increases varies from the norms above.

* Indicates the earliest date for payment of local bargaining clauses.

social protection' (*Business and Finance* 1990). This did not mean that the agreements were immune from union criticism – quite the contrary. Among a range of issues that gave rise to complaints was the unfair sharing of the gains arising from economic success, social welfare cuts, the absence of provisions for union recognition, the continued disproportionate tax burden on PAYE workers and a failure to extend partnership to the workplace. None of these issues, however, were to prove deal-breakers.

Teague and Donaghey (2012: 13) suggest that unions remained committed to the process for three main reasons: (i) the 'logic of representation' was preferable to the 'logic of mobilisation'; (ii) real wage increases were higher than those achieved by most other workers in Europe; and (iii) 'the employment boom effectively tied trade unions to social partnership as it would have been widely deemed cavalier to have adopted an alternative strategy'. Perhaps the most serious charge was that the agreements only provided limited pay solidarity for low-paid workers. Unions representing lower-paid workers, notably Mandate and the Civil and Public Services Union, opposed a number of the agreements – a reversal of the position in the 1970s when they supported national wage agreements (NWAs). However, majority union support was not in doubt as all the agreements were approved at special delegate congresses of ICTU. The outcomes of these ballots are contained in Table 13.5.

Table 13.5
Voting Results at ICTU Special Delegate Congresses on National Agreements

Agreement	For	Against
PNR	181	114
PESP	224	109
PCW	256	76
Partnership 2000	217	134
PPF	251	112
Sustaining Progress	195	147
Towards 2016 Phase 1	242	84
Towards 2016 Phase 2	305	36

Source: *Industrial Relations News* (various editions).

Social Provision and Involvement of the Community and Voluntary Sector

The agreements contained a number of social provisions that increased in importance over time. The Community and Voluntary Pillar was involved directly for the first time in the negotiation of the Partnership 2000 agreement in 1997. This was in response to criticisms that they had been excluded from negotiations and that it was insufficient to have the trade unions put forward points for this constituency, as had previously been the case. Groups such as the Irish National Organisation of the Unemployed, the

National Youth Council, the Conference of Religious of Ireland and Protestant Aid were among nineteen separate groups that made presentations as part of the process.

The involvement of the Community and Voluntary Pillar was seen as a move to a new and more inclusive 'deliberative democracy' form of governance (O'Donnell and Thomas 2002). However, unsurprisingly the influence of the voluntary pillar was asymmetrical to that yielded by unions and employer organisations which represented economic interests (Larragy 2010; Stafford 2011). More importantly, few concrete policy initiatives emanated from the many working groups that were established (Hardiman

Table 13.6
Social Provisions of the NWAs, 1987–2008

Agreement	Key Social Provisions
PNR	• Emphasis on government policy on social equity with particular attention to health services, education and housing for the disadvantaged • Maintain value in social welfare benefits and, where resources are available, consider increases for those receiving the lowest payments
PESP	• Seven-year health programme to improve community-based services • Education initiatives at all levels
PCW	• PESP terms for social reform will be carried over • Particular attention to improving social welfare due to 1994 Budget provisions
Partnership 2000	• IR£525 million to be spent on social inclusion • Adoption of National Anti-Poverty Strategy (NAPS) • Particular attention to tackling unemployment
PPF	• Investment of IR£1.5 billion on social inclusion measures • Update and review NAPS and poverty-proofing arrangements • Establishment of Housing Forum to monitor supply and affordability of housing
Sustaining Progress	• Emphasis on dealing with poverty and promoting social inclusion under NAPS, especially pensioner poverty • Structural reform of the health service • Improving employment equality, especially tackling gender inequality and treatment of persons with disabilities
Towards 2016	• Employment law compliance • Commitment to establish the National Employment Rights Authority (NERA)

Source: Various national agreements.

2006; Roche 2012b). Teague and Donaghey (2012: 5) argue that this 'calls into question the view of social partnership as a successful system of new governance'.

In 2004 the government turned to address the perceived social deficit accompanying the Celtic Tiger. This policy shift had little to do with social partnership but was driven by Fianna Fáil's poor electoral performance in the local and European elections of that year, which was blamed on that party's shift to the right. The result was an expansion of welfare provisions in a series of redistributive budgets from 2004 onwards (Roche 2012a: 9). In 2006 the Towards 2016 agreement reflected these concerns in its focus on employment law compliance (Table 13.6). There was a sharp retrenchment in social measures when the economic crises of 2008 struck. Roche (2012a: 31) argues this represented not just a reflection of the economic crisis but also 'long-prevalent political attitudes favouring low taxes over collective consumption or redistribution'.

Economic Developments and Centralised Agreements, 1987–2009

Throughout the centralised agreements, the Irish economy underwent a remark-able transformation, unprecedented economic success followed by a precipitous economic collapse. The economic trends can be broken down into four broad periods: a period of stabilisation and uncertainty from 1987 to 1993, a period of expansion and growth from 1994 to 2000, a somewhat rockier period based on construction and increases in public expenditure from 2001 to 2006, and an emergent crisis from 2007 to 2009.

The *first period* was one of stabilisation and uncertainty. On the positive side, growth was maintained, with an average annual real GNP growth of 4.2 per cent from 1988 to 1993, and the debt/GNP ratio saw a significant decline (Figure 13.2). Growth rates were almost three times higher than the EU average and more than twice the OECD (Organisation for Economic Co-operation and Development) average. Inflation stayed low but at a level higher than the average in the EU. Under the PESP in the early 1990s, uncertainty emerged as the effects of the international downturn associated with the first Gulf War were felt. Interest rates rocketed to around 12–15 per cent before decreasing following the devaluation of the Irish punt in early 1993 – a measure that was initially strongly resisted by the government but that proved irresistible and necessary. The public sector pay bill proved difficult to rein in, growing over 27 per cent between 1990 and 1993. However, the main problem was unemployment, which remained stubbornly high and actually increased from 1990 to 1994 – a trend that masked a slight growth in overall employment (Figure 13.3).

The *second period* commenced around 1994 and saw the economic fundamentals change dramatically in an unanticipated way. Growth rates became extraordinary, budget surpluses became the norm (consistently outstripping Department of Finance predictions) and the debt/GNP ratio was reduced to only 35 per cent by 2002. Real disposable income increased by 27 per cent between 1987 and 1998 – a contrast with the decline between 1980 and 1987 (Turner and D'Art 2000). Led by growth in the services sector, increased female participation rates and inward migration, there was dramatic employment growth accompanied by declining unemployment (Figures 13.3 and 13.4). By 2000, unemployment had reached 4.1 per cent and it was maintained around this level for a number of years, rising to only 4.5 per cent by 2007. Teague and Donaghey (2009: 58) argue strongly that the 'high levels of employment growth can be viewed as the Celtic Tiger's social dimension'.

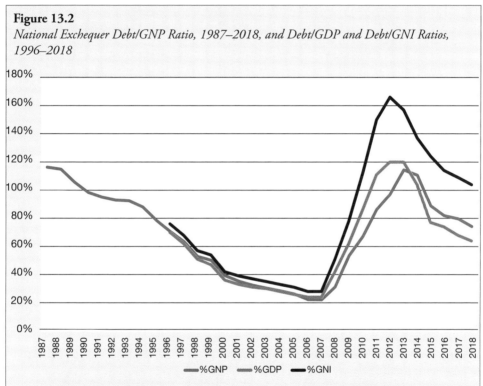

Figure 13.2
National Exchequer Debt/GNP Ratio, 1987–2018, and Debt/GDP and Debt/GNI Ratios, 1996–2018

Source: GNP & GNI ratios, Department of Finance, *Budgetary Statistics 2018.*
Note: GNI = Gross National Income. GNI lessens the effect of the transfer of intellectual property rights to Ireland, notably by Apple in 2015. The ratio based on GNI gives a more realistic picture of national indebtedness than one based on GDP, especially since 2008.
GDP ratio: CSO General Government Debt data using Maastricht Debt and Deficit definitions with revised debt calculation from 1983.
Basis of GNP calculation was revised in 1995; although this led to a decline in the ratio, it is not significant enough to render the growth rates for the two time spans incomparable.

These developments led to the Irish economy being accorded the sobriquet 'the Celtic Tiger'. Hardiman (2000: 292), writing of the period, notes 'real increases in disposable income were delivered, while keeping industrial conflict at low levels'.

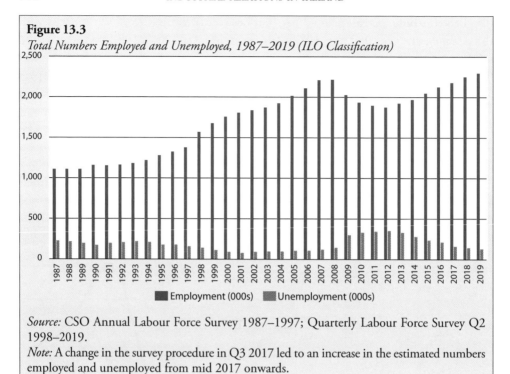

Figure 13.3
Total Numbers Employed and Unemployed, 1987–2019 (ILO Classification)

Source: CSO Annual Labour Force Survey 1987–1997; Quarterly Labour Force Survey Q2 1998–2019.
Note: A change in the survey procedure in Q3 2017 led to an increase in the estimated numbers employed and unemployed from mid 2017 onwards.

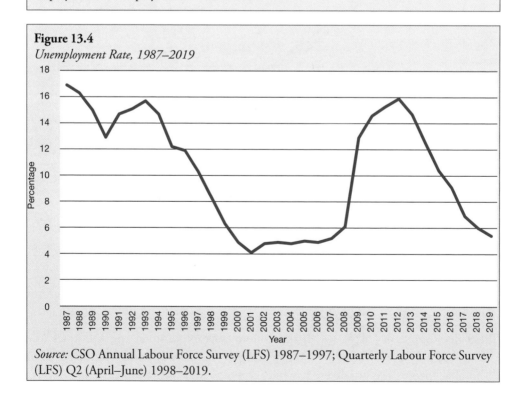

Figure 13.4
Unemployment Rate, 1987–2019

Source: CSO Annual Labour Force Survey (LFS) 1987–1997; Quarterly Labour Force Survey (LFS) Q2 (April–June) 1998–2019.

The general view is that the economic performance during this period marked a genuine productivity and competitiveness boom and was soundly based (Roche 2012b). Employer gains were greatest in relative terms, with a large upward swing in the proportion of national income going to profits accompanied by a corresponding fall in the proportion going to wages. Teague and Donaghey (2009: 68) record that 'in comparative terms, the share of labour in national income was 54.2 per cent in 2001, while the EU average was 67.2 per cent'.

The *third period*, from 2000 to 2006, saw most economic indicators continue to be comparatively healthy. Growth rates tapered off (Figure 13.5) but were still positive, employment continued to expand and unemployment remained low, hovering about 4 per cent. However, internationally, the bursting of the dot-com bubble and the aftermath of the 9/11 attack on the Twin Towers in 2001 meant that the economy

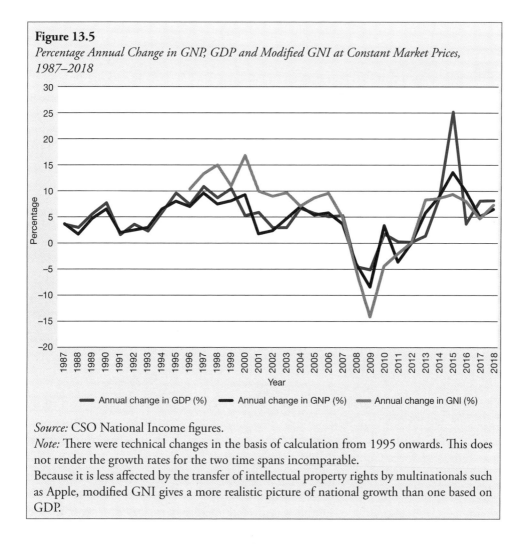

Figure 13.5

Percentage Annual Change in GNP, GDP and Modified GNI at Constant Market Prices, 1987–2018

Source: CSO National Income figures.

Note: There were technical changes in the basis of calculation from 1995 onwards. This does not render the growth rates for the two time spans incomparable.

Because it is less affected by the transfer of intellectual property rights by multinationals such as Apple, modified GNI gives a more realistic picture of national growth than one based on GDP.

was entering a more unsettled period. IBEC had become concerned at 'the loss of competitiveness' and the rise in public sector expenditure (Sheehan 2004: 17). There was substance to these concerns, since 'from the early 2000s pay increases began to diverge from pay trends in Ireland's trading partners, and both pay and unit cost competitiveness declined' (Roche 2012a: 7). As in the 1960s and 1970s, pay pressure was driven by both rising expectations from a buoyant economy and rising inflation, which was also above the EU average from 2000 to 2003. The follow-up agreement to the PPF, Sustaining Progress, represented an attempt to restore stability but actually contributed to problems, with wage increases chasing the high cost of living – a return of the 1970s phenomenon. In addition, the real rise in the cost of living was not captured by the Consumer Price Index as it did not include house price rises. The growth in house prices placed pressure on wages in both the public and private sphere.

Benchmarking

In the public sector, inflationary pressure fed into the first benchmarking process in 2003, with the rather colourful argument that something had to be done about public sector pay because a married guard and nurse together could not afford to buy a house. The average 8.9 per cent increase emanating from benchmarking constituted a form of institutionalised public sector wage drift via social partnership. Benchmarking, which was provided for under the PPF, had the stated aim of matching public and private sector rates for comparable jobs. This can be seen as representing an attempt to use objective criteria as recommended in the principled negotiation model advocated by Fisher and Ury. However, the objectivity of criteria used was not accepted, as the figures on which comparisons were made were not made public. The death knell of bench-marking was marked by the second benchmarking report in 2008. That report provided for overall increases of less than 1 per cent and these were mostly confined to higher-paid workers, with most public sector workers (notably nurses and teachers) receiving no increases (Dobbins 2008). The result was widespread disenchantment with the process and its demise.

The Economy on the Brink

The early part of the *fourth period*, from 2006 to 2007, continued to be marked by confidence, with talk of a soft landing remaining the dominant economic discourse, even from bodies such as the Economic and Social Research Institute and the National Economic and Social Council (NESC). An ambitious ten-year phased agreement called Towards 2016, which was concluded in 2006, seemed to copper-fasten the future of social partnership but this was to prove illusory. By now critical voices were increasingly warning of a property bubble and this was given immediacy by developments in the US sub-prime property market and the consequent collapse of Lehman Brothers Bank in February 2008. The Irish economy was also vulnerable because of the size of the construction sector, which 'accounted for 13 per cent of employment in 2007 compared with an average of about 8 per cent in the EU' (Roche 2012a: 12). The Financial Regulator and the Central Bank made soothing noises about the solidity of the Irish banks. In reality, they were on the brink of a precipice, with the very financial foundations of the state at risk. The main problem for the banks (especially Anglo Irish Bank) was their exposure to property loans. There was also a structural defect in the tax regime, which relied excessively on transactions taxes, a significant proportion of them linked directly or indirectly to property.

Instead of sustainable economic development based on sound financial principles, Ireland was again in a boom–bust cycle, caused by unwise procyclical domestic policies, a sectoral imbalance arising from the concentration on construction, huge levels of public and private debt, and neoliberal light-touch regulation in the bloated property and banking sectors. These were magnified by the international financial crisis, making for the economic version of a 'perfect storm' that broke over the country in 2008 and 2009, and which swept social partnership away in its wake.

THE ECONOMIC CRISIS, 2008–2011, AND COLLECTIVE BARGAINING

The economic dimensions of the crisis that engulfed the country in 2008 are evident in the changes to annual GNP and GDP growth figures, as shown in Figure 13.5. GNP fell most as a result of the deflationary policies pursued to bring the deficit in public finances to a maximum of 3 per cent by 2014. Deflation was accompanied by a startling rise in unemployment from 4.5 per cent in 2007 to nearly 14 per cent by 2009, a level it was to remain at until 2014. Faced with a banking crisis in October 2008, the government decided to act as guarantor for all deposits and liabilities in Irish banks, thereby socialising bank debt and making it sovereign debt (Roche 2012a). The government believed that the banks had a liquidity problem but fatally they were on the brink of insolvency, and this led not to the 'cheapest bailout in history' but to some €70 billion being added to state debt, with no prospect of recovering most of the €34 billion injected into Anglo Irish Bank.

By 2010 the cost of borrowing on international capital markets had risen to unsustainable levels and the government found itself forced to apply for a rescue package to the EU/International Monetary Fund/European Central Bank troika. The consequent loss of financial independence saw Irish budgetary policy and expenditure being directed and overseen by the troika. The loss of financial autonomy rocked the political landscape and led to the decimation of the governing parties – Fianna Fáil and the Green Party – in the general election of February 2011 and their replacement with a Fine Gael/Labour coalition.

Social Partnership and the Crisis

Teague and Donaghey (2012: 20) remark that the 'social partnership process was a bit player in the unfolding Irish economic crisis'. As with the demise of NWAs in the early 1980s, employer commitment 'evaporated with the onset of the recession' (Teague and Donaghey 2012: 20). Conversely, as the crisis loomed, unions became more attached to the process of social partnership (see Table 13.4 above). This reflects the fact that employers need centralised agreements least in recessionary times while unions are most interested in them in such circumstances. Surprisingly, the Towards 2016 transitional agreement was concluded against all the odds in September 2008. It contained a provision for a 6 per cent pay increase (6.5 per cent for the lower-paid) over twenty-one months and a commitment to establish a labour inspectorate body, NERA; however, the agreement was to prove short-lived.

Faced with a looming budget, the government sought to revise the transitional agreement in late 2009. The trade unions were prepared to make concessions but the talks broke down in December 2009 following internal Fianna Fáil disagreement (Roche 2012b). Some in that party favoured retaining the social partnership model but others were opposed, with the latter prevailing. A welter of recriminations from unions accompanied the breakdown. In the private sector, the Construction Industry Federation had declined to be a party to the agreement and it had begun to unravel within months of being concluded, with only a minority of companies honouring the terms. IBEC formally withdrew from the agreement in December 2009, with its director general, Danny McCoy, writing that 'the pay terms are wholly unsuited to our economic circumstances' (Sheehan 2010).

COLLECTIVE BARGAINING: THE CRISIS AND RECOVERY

Following the breakdown of negotiations on revising the Towards 2016 transitional agreement, the main focus of government intervention was in the public sector as it sought to address the deficit between income and expenditure. Some measures applied to both the private and public sector, as seen in Table 13.7. The reductions in the national minimum wage under the Financial Emergency Measures in the Public Interest (FEMPI) legislation were short-lived as the Fine Gael/Labour coalition reversed them after the general election of 2011. A Universal Social Charge (USC), which was introduced in 2011, was retained but with revisions (Table 13.7).

Private Sector (Including Commercial State Companies) Bargaining, 2011–2020

Collective bargaining over wage increases atrophied in much of the private sector in 2009 and 2010, but in March 2010 IBEC and ICTU signed a protocol on private sector industrial relations providing for collective bargaining arrangements in a post-

Table 13.7
Unilateral Changes Applying to all Employees, Public and Private

Finance Act 2011: USC *Note:* USC replaced the 2008 income levy and the health levy	• 2 per cent on the first €10,036 • 4 per cent on the next €5,980 • 7 per cent on earnings above €16,011 Above figures changed over time and by 2015 incomes of €12,012 or less were exempt from USC
FEMPI Act 2010: NMW changes	• NMW reduced from €8.65 to €7.65 for new entrants (reduction later reversed in January 2011)

partnership era (Table 13.8). As early as 2010, pay rises did occur in a small range of companies in the export-led sectors of pharmaceuticals, food and medical devices (*Industrial Relations News* 2010). The focus on the export sector reflected the fact that these companies had been least affected by the recession and were in a better position to afford pay increases. This 'mini round' was not a prelude to the re-emergence of a pay round system as previously understood. Instead, it led to the establishment of a system based on pattern bargaining (Roche and Gormley 2017b).

Pattern bargaining is a strategic form of coordinated collective bargaining in which unions seek to establish a going rate in a firm or sector and then extend this to 'achieve the same or related outcomes in separate negotiations' with other firms or sectors (Roche and Gormley 2017b: 7). From 2011 to 2012 a 2 per cent pay increase target was set by the Services Industrial Professional Technical Union's (SIPTU) manufacturing division and subsequently became a benchmark that unions generally aimed to achieve in other companies. Roche and Gormley (2017b: 8) write 'the two per cent norm was regarded by unions as providing for both earnings and employ-ment security while also preserving competitiveness'. It was clear that the extent of the economic crisis and growth in unemployment strongly conditioned the approach of many unions to private sector pay bargaining. Crucial was the very low rate of inflation, which meant that a 2 per cent per annum increase represented a growth in real income.

The focus on employment security and competitiveness meshed with employers' concerns such that by 2014 the 2 per cent had been established as an informal norm for pay agreements and for pay rises in non-union firms. That norm drifted up over time, with Roche and Gormley (2017a) noting that the mean increase was 2.4 per in 2016. By 2019, even under the pressure of a buoyant economy with near full employment, the general range of increases was in the 2–3 per cent range, with few settlements exceeding 3 per cent or being less than 2 per cent (Higgins 2020).

Table 13.8
Outline of Private and Commercial State Sector Collective Bargaining Arrangements, 2009–2020

Date/Arrangement	Main Terms
2009 Private sector: IBEC withdraws from transitional agreement 2008	Pay terms of Phase 2 effectively lapse. Results in: • Pay freeze in about 80 per cent of companies • Pay reductions in about 10–20 per cent of companies • Wide-scale redundancies and closures
March 2010 IBEC–ICTU protocol on private sector industrial relations	• Adhere to established collective agreements • Use state industrial relations institutions to resolve disputes • Cooperation with ongoing change • Sustain employment • Local engagement
2011–2012 Private sector: mini pay round 2011	Limited local bargaining: • Low pay rises (around 2 per cent) in export-led sector: pharmaceuticals, food and medical devices
2013–2020 Pattern bargaining	Precedent of average 2 per cent rise extended • Length of agreements varied, 1–5 years • No discernible pay round system • Increases had to account for company survival and competitiveness • Amount of pay increases rose over time to between 2–3 per cent per annum by 2019

Source: Industrial Relations News, various editions.

Most agreements were concluded without the threat or use of strike action except for the transport sector, notably the Luas strike. In that case, a series of days of strike action and a Labour Court recommendation failed to resolve the dispute. A second Labour Court recommendation was accepted after further strike action. As that involved a reduced pay award over the first recommendation, albeit with an adjustment to unpopular rostering arrangements, this seemed to indicate the limit to which industrial action could be effective.

Public Sector Stability Bargaining, 2010–2020

Following the collapse of the efforts to renegotiate the Towards 2016 transitional agreement in 2009, the government turned to unilateral measures to achieve savings in public sector expenditure, especially the pay bill. A public sector pension levy had already been introduced in 2009 and this was quickly followed in 2010 with public sector wage cuts under the terms of the FEMPI legislation. A universal social charge followed in 2010, which, along with the other tax increases, spelt the end of the low-tax model on which the wage restraint of Irish social partnership had been based. Although the government now legislated in a way that would have been unimaginable at any time since World War II, this did not mean that collective bargaining in the public sector had collapsed. Instead, governments adopted a twin-track approach of legislation and collective agreements. The latter gave a degree of legitimacy to legislation and also influenced it on occasion. Before looking at the collective bargaining arrangements, a list of the main legislative measures is contained in Table 13.9.

The Croke Park Agreement, 2010–2014

The Croke Park Agreement (CPA) was the result of an initiative brokered by the LRC in 2010. It was negotiated during the term of the Fianna Fáil/Green Party coalition but retained subsequently by the Fine Gael/Labour coalition government following the election of 2011. It was approved by a two-thirds majority (1,894 votes to 986) of the Public Sector Committee of ICTU but only after intense internal union debate (Higgins 2010). The agreement provided for voluntary redundancies, cooperation with change, additional unpaid hours for teachers, and restructuring in return for no further reductions in core pay and an implicit acceptance of the pay reductions in the FEMPI legislation. It aimed to achieve reductions in the number of public sector employees of between 18,000 and 22,000. Pension payments for newly recruited workers after 2013 were to be based on average lifetime earnings rather than an average of the final three years. If union members contested any change provided for under the agreement, they had to undertake the work pending the outcome of any appeal. There was a solidaristic provision in the agreement that the pay reductions for those workers earning under €35,000 would be restored if savings were achieved; however, this was only done eventually as part of general pay restoration. Provision was made for monitoring the delivery of the savings through an implementation body and a speedy dispute resolution mechanism, which provided for decisions that were binding in industrial relations terms.

Croke Park Controversy and Renegotiation

Reflecting the febrile atmosphere around economic commentary at the time, the CPA was the subject of much critical commentary, almost all of it outside of the industrial relations arena. The continued payment of increments, the preserved salary for calculating early retirement, the continuation of unparalleled security of employment and the underfunded public sector pension scheme were all condemned. The economist Colm McCarthy described public sector pensions as 'akin to a "Ponzi scheme"' (O'Connell 2012). Much of the commentary was led not by industrial correspondents but by opinion writers and political correspondents, some of whom projected social

Table 13.9

Summary of Main Provisions of the FEMPI Acts 2009–2015 and USC Measures in the Finance Act 2011, Which Applied to All Employees, Both Public and Private

FEMPI 2009: Public sector pension levy introduced, rate as of 1 May 2009 (introduced on 1 March and amended within two months, to lessen impact on lower-paid workers)	• Exempt on the first €15,000 • 5 per cent between €15,000 and €20,000 • 10 per cent between €20,000 and €60,000 • 10.5 per cent above €60,000
FEMPI 2010: Public sector wage reductions	• 5 per cent on the first €30,000 • 7.5 per cent on the next €40,000 • 10 per cent on the next €55,000 • Above €125,000, cuts ranging from 8 to 15 per cent (as recommended by the Review Body on Higher Remuneration in Public Sector) • 20 per cent reduction in the case of the Taoiseach
FEMPI 2010: Reductions to public sector pensions	• Exempt up to €12,000 • 6 per cent over €12,000 to €24,000 • 9 per cent over €24,000 to €60,000 • 12 per cent over €60,000
FEMPI 2013: Additional public sector pay and pension reductions	• Increment freeze of three to twelve months, depending on salary • Further cuts for serving public servants over €65,000 and pensioners over €32,500 • Confined benefits to those unions covered by a collective agreement registered with the Labour Relations Commission (LRC) – the Haddington Road Agreement (HRA)
FEMPI 2015: Gave effect to the pay and pension restoration specified in the Lansdowne Road Agreement (LRA)	• Provided for pay terms of LRA, with some pay restoration, giving priority to those on lower pay, as well as reductions in the pension levy • Special pay restoration terms for those earning €65,001 to €110,000 and those over €110,000 • Equivalent partial restoration of cuts to pensioners • Confined benefits in LRA to those unions covered by a collective agreement registered with the LRC

Source: www.irishstatutebook.ie; www.per.gov.ie; *Industrial Relations News* (2010); www.revenue.ie

partnership as having been a take-over of the political system by the unions. Roche (2012b: 16) considers that such arguments have 'little merit [since] political leaders showed themselves on occasion well capable of standing up to union demands or social partnership commitments, or of ignoring them'. Probably the strongest critic of the agreement was management consultant Eddie Molloy, who described the agreement as 'convoluted, clubby industrial relations machinery' (Molloy 2012: 12). The agreement also gave rise to tensions between Fine Gael and Labour, with the Labour Party seen as protective of the agreement while some elements within Fine Gael were hostile.

Unions seemed bewildered by much of the negative commentary, given the moderate role they had adopted in that time. For them, the crisis arose from the evils of neoliberal policies that allowed the banks and developers to engage in casino capitalism and place the country in peril. Teague and Donaghey (2012: 17) echoed this point, writing that it was 'financialisation' and 'the speculative bubble … causing disorderly economic behaviour' that was responsible for the economic crisis. Unions saw the socialisation of the debts arising from this activity as an affront. The suggestion of a takeover of the political system was particularly galling to them because social partnership had not delivered on greater social equality but 'retained' or 'accentuated' inequality and led to an unequal sharing of the benefits of economic growth.

The CPA also had its defenders. The chairman of the Implementation Body, P. J. Fitzpatrick (2012: 23), described media coverage as 'very often unfair and in some cases factually incorrect'. Roche pointed to the industrial peace the CPA had delivered and the major changes agreed. He noted that international audiences, when told of the agreement, typically responded with: 'We could do with that type of framework here' (Roche 2012c: 1). In its final report in 2013, the CPA Implementation Body noted staff reductions of 8,700 in the public sector by 2013 and an accompanying reduction of the public sector pay bill from €17.5 billion (gross) to €14.4 billion between 2009 and 2012 – a reduction of €3.1 billion, or nearly 18 per cent. Minister for State Brian Hayes TD argued that the CPA was central to managing 'change without street protests' and opposed calls for its renegotiation (Seanad Éireann 2012).

Despite the widespread criticism, the Fine Gael/Labour coalition government remained solidly behind the agreement but distanced itself from the now out of favour 'social partnership', insisting it was engaged in a more modest process of 'social dialogue' (Sheehan 2011c). However, the criticisms had an impact. Faced with troika demands in 2013 and an annual budget deficit of some €15 billion, the government sought to renegotiate the CPA, in spite of previously having rejected calls to do so. It approached the trade unions with demands for (i) productivity and efficiency concessions, (ii) workforce reform and (iii) additional pay and pension bill reductions. The government aimed to deliver savings of €1 billion on the pay bill over the three years of 2013–2015 inclusive. Following what was described as 'difficult negotiations', a Croke Park 2 agreement was concluded. However, it immediately met strong opposition, notably from an alliance of front-line workers, among which were firefighters, prison officers, nurses, midwives, Gardaí and other essential services. As a result, the renegotiated agreement was rejected by a two-thirds majority in a ballot of union members.

The Haddington Road Agreement, 2014–2016

While appearing to represent a victory to those opposed to further union givebacks in the public sector, the rejection of Croke Park 2 presented a problem of 'what to do next' (Sheehan 2013). For unions, neither the legal option of challenging the FEMPI legislation nor industrial action offered any realistic prospect of success (Sheehan 2013). In terms of negotiating theory, the BATNA (best alternative to a negotiated agreement) of the unions opposed to the agreement was limited. On the other hand, the government had the apparently strong BATNA of unilaterally implementing changes through FEMPI legislation (as had been done in 2009–2012). The government indicated its intention to do just that but, without a collective agreement to underpin the legislation, this was considered 'an appalling vista' in government circles (Sheehan 2013). Although industrial action was unlikely to succeed, a campaign of non-cooperation with public sector modernisation and reform was a real prospect. Even unsuccessful strike action would have undermined the gains made in restoring order to the public finances under the original CPA. There was also a potential for significant electoral consequences for the two coalition parties from a go-it-alone policy. In other words, government, unions and their membership faced the very real risks of mutual self-damage.

In the uncertainty prevailing after the rejection of Croke Park 2, the LRC moved quickly to seek to rescue an agreement. It engaged in bilateral discussions with individual unions to explore sectoral adjustments within the envelope of the savings sought by the government. There was a modification of the one-size-fits-all approach and fine-tuning of the proposed measures to different sectors and groups of workers. For example, adjustments to the way the additional hours were to be worked and certain allowances were protected. Allowances comprised a significant part of earnings for many front-line workers and accordingly were of particular concern to them. The result of the LRC's involvement was that agreement was reached with most unions on revised terms within an overall framework of the Public Sector Stability Agreement (PSSA) 2014–2016 or, as it became more commonly known, the HRA. It was an agreement which was reached with individual trade unions and did not involve an aggregate ballot of the unions attached to the Public Sector Committee of ICTU.

The Lansdowne Road Agreement, 2016–2018

By the time the HRA came up for review in early 2015, the economic context had changed, with strong economic growth returning, employment increasing and unemployment in decline (Figures 13.3, 13.4 and 13.5). In 2014–2015 GDP grew by a dramatic 34.4 per cent, causing Nobel-prize-winning economist Paul Krugman to refer

Table 13.10

Outline of Public Sector Collective Bargaining Agreements, 2009–2020

Date/Arrangement/ Savings/Costs	Main Terms
June 2010–2014 Public Sector Agreement (PSA) – Croke Park Agreement €3.8 billion reduction in pay in 2015 as against pay bill in 2009 or less	• Pay freeze with a promise of no further pay reductions beyond those in 2009 and 2010 • Reductions in employee numbers of 18,000–22,000 • Voluntary redundancies • Cooperation with modernisation redeployment • Renegotiated to deliver extra €1 billion savings • Industrial peace with binding dispute resolution • Pension entitlements to be averaged over lifetime earnings, not final years • Teachers to work an extra non-teaching hour per week
2013 Croke Park 2	Rejected by ICTU public sector unions in membership ballots
2014–2016 Public Service Stability Agreement (PSSA) – Haddington Road Agreement (HRA) Additional €1 billion saving over three years, 2014–2016	Pay and pension cuts as in FEMPI Act 2013: • 'Social solidarity' element – pay cuts only to apply to salaries over €65,000 • Working hours increased: 35 to 37 hours a week; 37 to 39 hours a week; those on 39 hours to work a non-paid hour's overtime (subject to sectoral variation) • Increments freeze of between 3–12 months depending on salary, and cuts in overtime pay • Restrictions on outsourcing of jobs • Adjustments made in sectors for unions with a collective agreement registered at the LRC – i.e. the HRA
PSSA 2016–2018 Lansdowne Road Agreement (LRA)	Main pay increases: • 2.5 per cent pay on salaries up to €24,000 from 1 Jan 2016 • 1 per cent pay on salaries €24,001 to €31,000 from 1 Jan 2016 • €1,000 on salaries up to €65,000 (brought forward from September to 1 April 2017 as a result of review) • Earnings under €24,750 (€15,000 previously) to be exempt from pension levy from 1 Jan 2016 • Unions not signed up to a collective agreement registered with the WRC to lose out on increments and some other payments and benefits • Pay restoration dependent on cooperation with change, productivity, public sector reform and industrial peace
PSSA 2018–2020 Lansdowne Road Extensional Agreement, or PSSA	Pay restoration on salaries of up to €70,000 by 2020: • 1 per cent increase from January 2018 • 1 per cent increase October 2018 • 1 per cent increase in salaries of up to €30k from January 2019 • 1.75 per cent from September 2019 • 0.50 per cent increase in salaries of up to €32k from January 2020 • 2 per cent increase from 1 Oct 2020 Additional pay increments for those on lower pay scales to lessen effects of two-tier pay (agreed later in 2018) Pay restoration dependent on delivery on flexibility, change, reform and productivity, and no industrial action on matters in the agreement

Source: Various public sector agreements; *Industrial Relations News*, various editions; and information direct from IRN.

to Irish GDP data as leprechaun economics. This unbelievable GDP growth was due to Apple relocating intellectual property rights to Ireland and, as such, it was not reflective of actual Irish economic performance. Thus, GDP became a largely meaningless term to measure national income. As a result, a modified GNI index was introduced to remove the Apple effect and, in contrast with GDP, it measured a growth rate of 8.6 percent. That represented a healthy growth rate, and over the period 2012–2018 GNI grew by an average of 7.7 per cent, indicating that there was a substantial economic recovery under way. Most significant for industrial relations was the expansion in employment to over two million in 2016 and falling unemployment (Figures 13.3 and 13.4).

Fuelled by this economic resurgence and pay rises in the private sector, pressure was building for public sector pay restoration and a reversal of the two-tier pay system for new entrants. There were also calls for pay increases to address staff shortages, caused by alleged recruitment and retention difficulties in certain sectors, notably in nursing and the defence forces. It had always been envisaged that the FEMPI measures would be unwound, and the 2015 FEMPI Act committed to doing that, but in a gradual and controlled way. Pressures on government included the overhang from the financial crisis of a debt/GNI of 137 per cent in 2014 (Figure 13.2), a requirement under EU budgetary rules to bring the annual deficit to 3 per cent, and the advice of the Irish Fiscal Advisory Council, established in 2011, which called for financial prudence to avoid a repeat of the Celtic Tiger mistakes.

The LRC again coordinated the negotiations within the same model of an over-arching public sector agreement with sectoral adjustments. The LRA was signed in May 2015. On this occasion, unions affiliated to the Public Sector Committee of ICTU accepted the LRA by a majority of approximately 2,300 to 500 delegate votes (figures supplied by *Industrial Relations News*). However, some unions, notably the Association of Secondary Teachers, Ireland (ASTI), opted out of the process. The agreement delivered €840 million in pay restoration. Payment of increments and other allowances was made dependent on cooperation with public sector reform and measures to improve productivity (Table 13.10). Reflecting the commitment to restore pay cuts for lower-paid workers in the CPA, pay restoration to workers earning under €24,000 and €35,000, respectively, was made earlier than to higher earners, and increases were higher in percentage terms (Table 13.10).

Lansdowne Road Extensional Agreement, 2018–2020

In 2017 the formula of gradual pay restoration (prioritising lower-paid workers), cooperation with modernisation and a requirement for industrial peace was again repeated in the Lansdowne Road Extensional Agreement (LREA) – formally known as PSSA 2018–2020. That agreement delivered €877 million in pay restoration (Table 13.10). It abolished the pension levy, converting it into a permanent increase in workers' public sector pension contributions as a contribution to the long-term sustainability of public sector pensions. The Public Sector Committee of ICTU accepted the LREA by a majority of 2,170 to 532 delegate votes (figures supplied by *Industrial Relations News*). As a result, individual unions did not need to sign up to the agreement because ICTU could certify that member unions were covered by it. This arrangement allowed unions opposed, in principle, to certain aspects of the agreement – notably two-tier pay – to benefit from its provisions, provided they did not engage in industrial action. Although voting against the agreement, once ASTI accepted the obligation under the LRA to work the CPA's additional hours in June 2018, it was brought inside the PSSA fold and members became eligible for their increments when due (see Table 10.6).

The Public Service Agreements Considered

The public service agreements after 2014 were not subject to the same level of criticism as the CPA, although there were occasional warnings about the growth in the public sector pay budget. There seemed a general acceptance of the PSA way of doing business, which was given legitimacy by the involvement of the LRC/Workplace Relations Commission (WRC) and, on occasion, the Labour Court. The two agreements spanning 2016–2020 were concluded without the drama surrounding the failed Croke Park 2. This is unsurprising – pay restoration was always going to be an easier sell to union members than pay cuts.

However, the agreements were not without their problems, with disputes in teaching, policing and nursing standing out. While the ASTI strike action against two-tier pay and supervision and substitution remained unresolved as of early 2020 there had only been limited strike action. The garda pay dispute was resolved short of industrial action (see case study in Table 13.11), but the nurses' and midwives' dispute led to strike action by the Irish Nurses and Midwives Organisation and the Psychiatric Nurses Association in early 2019. That dispute involved a demand for a pay increase to tackle a claimed recruitment and retention crisis in nursing. The Public Service Pay Commission (PSPC) had been set up in 2015 with terms of reference 'to advise government on public service remuneration … not [to] take the place of direct negotiations between Government and employee representatives' (PSPC 2015). The commission's 2018 report identified 'specific difficulties in retaining nurses and midwives in specific areas' and recommended that targeted adjustments be made to allowances (PSPC 2018: 111). That report failed to provide a basis for a settlement of the dispute, with the nursing unions seeking general increases, not targeted measures, to address 'the crisis'. Three days of strike action resulted in February 2019, with the dispute eventually being resolved following two Labour Court interventions.

The Garda settlement was regarded as a 'special deal' for the Gardaí, as was the settlement in the nurses' strike action in 2019. The Garda deal cost some €50 million annually, with the cost of the nurses' agreement well in excess of that (Sheehan 2020). Both settlements led to strains on the LRA 2016–2020 agreements but fears that the resentment of other public sector unions would lead to the collapse of the LRA agreements were not borne out. In response to the Garda settlement, a review of the

LRA saw a €1,000 increase (costing €120m) brought forward from September to April 2017 in order to compensate those unions who stayed within the LRA terms (Sheehan 2017). In relation to the nurses' settlement, no immediate adjustment was made to the LREA but several unions saw it as outstanding business to be addressed in a proposed follow-up agreement.

Table 13.11
The Garda Case Study Part 2

In 2016 the Garda Representative Association (GRA) rejected involvement in negotiations on a public sector agreement. In September 2016 a ballot of GRA members was taken, with 95 per cent of those participating indicating a willingness to take industrial action. This action was taken in spite of the immunities in the Industrial Relations Act 1990 not applying to Gardaí (or their representative associations). In addition, it is an offence under the Garda Síochána Act 2005 to encourage industrial action and such action is a criminal offence under the Conspiracy and Protection of Property Act 1875. The GRA asserted that it was not organising the action and it was a matter for individual members to strike or not. With notice of four single days of strike action over four weeks set to commence in early November 2016, the GRA was granted ad hoc access to both the WRC and the Labour Court. Following WRC meetings, the dispute was referred to the Labour Court and its recommendation saw the strike called off. GRA members subsequently accepted the Labour Court's recommendation. It involved pay increases ranging between €3,981 and €5,106, a restoration of a €4,000 per annum rent allowance for post-2012 entrants, the incorporation of the rent allowance into basic pay and other adjustments to allowances. Other garda ranks also benefited, with the Minister for Justice and Equality, Francis Fitzgerald TD, estimating the overall cost at €50 million.

Source: *Industrial Relations News*, various editions; Labour Court Ad Hoc Recommendation, CD/16/321.

A Retrospective View of Collective Bargaining in Ireland, 2010–2020

In evaluating collective bargaining in the period 2010–2020, one can point to its collapse in 2009–2010, the controversy over the CPA, the teachers', nurses' and Gardaí public sector disputes, and the Luas and other transport disputes. However, the dominant impression is the persistence of collective bargaining and how it accommodated to the radically changed economic circumstances. In private and semi-state companies, this adaptation was accomplished without resort to large-scale industrial action. Similarly, in the public sector, what stands out is the extent to which industrial action was limited. None of this was predictable in advance.

Social partnership had previously been regarded as essential to the maintenance of industrial peace and, with its collapse, a return to the previous procyclical nature of strikes was a real prospect. The avoidance of widespread conflict involved consistent and careful effort. Government, employers, trade unions and the state dispute resolution bodies all utilised collective bargaining in a way that adapted to the ever-changing circumstances of the ten years. Their approaches were sophisticated; the agreements that emerged were nuanced and represented a consensual approach to the ever-changing circumstances. This consensus reflected the lack of room for manoeuvre by the actors in the industrial relations system. The restrictions imposed by the troika meant cuts were essential to bridge the public sector deficit but as the cuts were not as severe as those in Greece, there was something to be protected. Excessive government action or strikes, on the other hand, risked self-damage for both government and unions. The consensus was not confined to the public sector but was also evident in the private sector, where the 2 per cent pay deals meshed with employer concerns at the vulnerability of an open economy to competitive pressures. While the industrial relations system limited industrial conflict arising from austerity, it was not eliminated. The fallout from the 'Great Recession' created resentment at austerity and its aftermath. In line with the balloon theory, this resentment found expression elsewhere, on this occasion in the political system. As noted in Chapter 1, Irish politics experienced a realignment with the demise of the two-party system and the rise of Sinn Féin in the 2020 general election, while the Labour Party had borne the main brunt of the blame for the policy adjustments made from 2011 to 2016.

Concluding Comments

Collective bargaining is a nineteenth-century creation that some regard as an undesirable interference with the free market, others see as contributing to democracy and still others see as preserving the status quo in society. Collective bargaining has been an economic and social reality, shaping Irish life most notably since the end of World War II. It is clear that, while so doing, it is greatly influenced by, and responsive to, the underlying economic circumstances of the day. Various forms of collective bargaining have come and gone, changing from a wage round system to national agreements, back to wage rounds, to a long-live partnership era and eventually a twin-track private/public sector model. In this last stage, collective bargaining adapted to a deep recession and a rapid recovery in a way that promoted orderly adjustment, arguably emphasising its conservative nature, as exemplified by its ability to institutionalise conflict.

Bibliography

Abbott, B., Heery, E. and Williams, S. (2011) 'Civil Society Organisations and the Exercise of Power in the Employment Relationship', *Employee Relations*, 34(1), 91–107.

Ackers, P. (2010) 'An Industrial Relations Perspective on Employee Participation', in A. Wilkinson, P.J. Gollan, M. Marchington and D. Lewin (eds), *The Oxford Handbook of Participation in Organizations*. Oxford: Oxford University Press.

Ackers, P. (2019) 'Neo-pluralism as an Approach in Contemporary Employment Relations and HRM: Complexity and Dialogue', in K. Townsend, K. Cafferkey, A.O. McDermott and T. Dundon, *Elgar Introduction to Theories of Human Resources and Employment Relations*. Cheltenham. Elgar Publishing.

Ackers, P. and Black, J. (1992) 'Watching the Detectives: Shop Stewards' Expectations of their Managers in the Age of Human Resource Management', in A. Sturdy, D. Knights and H. Willmott (eds), *Skill and Consent: Contemporary Studies in the Labour Process*. London: Routledge.

Aherne, A. (2010) 'Ireland's Economic Crisis: Implications for the Labour Market', *Eighteenth John Lovett Memorial Lecture*, University of Limerick.

Ahrne, G. and Brunsson, N. (2005) 'Organizations and meta-organizations', *Scandinavian Journal of Management*, 21(4), 429–49.

Allen, K. (1997) *Fianna Fáil and Irish Labour: 1926 to the Present*. London: Pluto Press.

Allen, V. (1971) *The Sociology of Industrial Relations*. London: Longman.

Allred, K.G. (2000) 'Distinguishing Best and Strategic Practices: A Framework for Managing the Dilemma between Creating and Claiming Value', *Negotiation Journal*, October, 16(4), 387–97.

Anthony, A. (2020) 'Thomas Piketty: Why France's "Rock Star Economist" Still Wants to Squeeze the Rich', *The Observer*, 23 February, 46–7.

Armstrong, M. and Stephens, T. (2005) *A Handbook of Employee Reward Management and Practice*. London: Kogan Page.

Arrighi, G. (1990) 'Marxist Century, American Century: The Making and the Remaking of the World's Labour Movement', *New Left Review*, 179, 29–66.

Arvey, R.D. and Ivancevich, J.M. (1980) 'Punishment in Organisations: A Review, Propositions and Research Suggestions', *Academy of Management Review*, 5(1), 123–32.

Association of Secondary Teachers, Ireland (2019) 'Post-2010 Entrants' Pay', accessed 29 November 2019, https://www.asti.ie/news/campaigns/post-2010-entrants-pay/

Auer, P. (2000) *Employment Revival in Europe: Labour Market Success in Austria, Denmark, Ireland and the Netherlands*. Geneva: International Labour Office.

Baccaro, L. and Simoni, M. (2004) *The Irish Social Partnership and the 'Celtic Tiger' Phenomenon* [International Institute for Labour Studies, Discussion Paper (DP/154/2004), Decent Work Research Programme]. Geneva: International Labour Organisation.

Bacon, N. and Storey, J. (2002) 'New Employee Relations Strategies in Britain: Towards Individualism or Partnership?', *British Journal of Industrial Relations*, 38(3), 407–27.

Bain, G.S. and Price, R. (1983) 'Union Growth: Dimensions, Determinants and Destiny', in G.S. Bain (ed.), *Industrial Relations in Britain*. Oxford: Basil Blackwell.

Bambrick, L. (2019) 'The Marriage Bar: A Ban on Employing Married Women', accessed 30 March 2020, www.ictu.ie/blog/2019/10/14/the-marriage-bar-a-ban-on-employing-married-women/

Bank for International Settlements (2019) *Annual Economic Report 2019,* accessed 30 March 2020, https://www.bis.org/publ/arpdf/ar2019e.pdf

Barnard C. (2012) 'A Proportionate Response to Proportionality in the Field of Collective Action', *European Law Review*, 37(2), 117–35.

Barrow, C. (2013) *Industrial Relations and the Law.* London: Cavendish Publishing.

Barry, M. and Wilkinson, A. (2011) 'Reconceptualising Employer Associations Under Evolving Employment Relations: Countervailing Power Revisited', *Work, Employment and Society,* 25, 149–62.

Beale, D. and Hoel, H. (2011) 'Workplace Bullying and the Employment Relationship: Exploring Questions of Prevention, Control and Context', *Work, Employment and Society*, 25(1), 5–18.

Beaumont, P.B. and Harris, R.I.D. (1991) 'Trade Union Recognition and Employment Contraction, 1980–1984', *British Journal of Industrial Relations*, 29(1), 49–58.

Beer, M., Spector, B., Lawrence, P., Quinn-Mills, D. and Walton, R. (1984) *Managing Human Assets: The Groundbreaking Harvard Business School Program.* New York: The Free Press.

Behrens, M. and Pekarek, A. (2016) 'Between Strategy and Unpredictability: Negotiated Decision Making In German Union Mergers', *ILR Review,* 69(3), 579–604.

Belitz, H. (2016) 'Use and Abuse of the Non-Compete: When Employers Utilize Non-Compete Clauses to Undercut Vulnerable Workers', accessed 30 March 2020, https://onlabor.org/2016/05/03/use-and-abuse-of-the-non-compete-when-employers-utilize-non-compete-clauses-to-undercut-vulnerable-workers/

Beynon, H. (1973) *Working for Ford.* Harmondsworth: Penguin.

Blanchflower, D.G. (2006) *Cross-Country Study of Union Membership* [Discussion Paper No. 2016]. Bonn: Institute for the Study of Labor.

Blyton, P. and Turnbull, P. (2004) *The Dynamics of Employee Relations* (3rd edn). London: Red Globe Press.

Bonner, K. (1989) 'Industrial Relations Reform', in Department of Industrial Relations, University College Dublin (eds), *Industrial Relations in Ireland: Contemporary Issues and Developments.* Dublin: University College Dublin.

Boulding, K. (1993) 'The Nature of Power', in R.J. Lewicki, J.A. Litterer, M.D. Saunders and J.W. Minton, *Negotiation Readings, Exercises and Cases* (2nd edn). Boston: Irwin, McGraw-Hill.

Boxall, P. and Purcell, J. (2016), *Strategy and Human Resource Management* (4th edn). London and New York: Palgrave Macmillan.

Boyd, A. (1972) *The Rise of the Irish Trade Unions, 1729–1970.* Tralee: Anvil.

Boyd, A. (1984) *Have Trade Unions Failed the North?* Dublin: Mercier Press.

Boyle, J.W. (1988) *The Irish Labor Movement in the Nineteenth Century.* Washington, DC: The Catholic University of America Press.

Bramel, D. and Friend, R. (1981) 'Hawthorne, the Myth of the Docile Worker, and Class Bias in Psychology', *American Psychologist*, 36(8), 867–78.

Brandl, B. and Lehr, A. (2016) 'The Strange Non-Death of Employer and Business Associations: An Analysis of Their Representativeness and Activities in Western European Countries', *Economic and Industrial Democracy*, DOI: 10.1177/0143831X16669842.

Brannick, T., Doyle, L. and Kelly, A. (1997) 'Industrial Conflict', in T.V. Murphy and W.K. Roche (eds), *Irish Industrial Relations in Practice.* Dublin: Oak Tree Press.

Brannick, T. and Kelly, A. (1982) 'The Reliability and Validity of Irish Strike Data and Statistics', *Economic and Social Review*, 14, 249–58.

Braverman, H. (1974) *Labor and Monopoly Capital: The Degradation of Work in the Twentieth Century*. New York: Monthly Review Press.

Bray, M., Budd, J.W. and Macneil, J. (Forthcoming) 'The Many Meanings of Cooperation in the Employment Relationship and their implications', *British Journal of Industrial Relations*.

Breen, R., Hannon, D., Rottman, D. and Whelan, C. (1990) *Understanding Contemporary Ireland*. Dublin: Gill & Macmillan.

Brown, W. (1981) *The Changing Contours of British Industrial Relations: A Survey of Manufacturing Industry*. Oxford: Blackwell.

Brown, W., Deakin, S. and Ryan, P. (1997) 'The Effect of British Industrial Relations Legislation 1979–97', *National Institute Economic Review*, 161(1), 69–83.

Browne, J. (1994) *The Juridification of the Employment Relationship*. Aldershot: Avebury.

Bruton, R. (2011) *Consultation on the Reform of the State's Employment Rights and Industrial Relations Structures and Procedures*. Dublin: Department of Jobs, Enterprise and Innovation.

Bryson, A., Gomez, R., Kretschmer, T. and Willman, P. (2013) 'Workplace Voice and Civic Engagement: What Theory and Data Tell Us About Unions and their Relationship to the Democratic Process', *Osgoode Hall Law Journal*, 50(4), 965–98.

Budd, J.W., Colvin, A.J.S. and Polhe, D. (Forthcoming) 'Advancing Dispute Resolution by Understanding the Sources of Conflict: Towards an Integrated Framework', *Industrial Relations Journal Review*.

Bullock, Lord (1977) *Report of the Committee of Inquiry on Industrial Democracy*. London: Her Majesty's Stationery Office.

Burchell, B., Ladipo, D. and Wilkinson F. (eds) (2002) *Job Insecurity and Work Intensification*. London: Routledge.

Business & Finance (1990) 'Leaders Try to Sell the New Realism and Tame the Market', *Business & Finance*, 25 October.

Butler, A. (2007) 'Enforcement Issues: Could It Be Me?', Health and Safety Management: Not Just A Slogan – Health and Safety Review Conference, Dublin, 24 May.

Butler, P., Gunnigle, P., Lavelle, J. and O'Sullivan, M. (2018) 'Skating on Thin ICE? A Critical Evaluation of a Decade of Research on the British Information and Consultation Regulations (2004)', *Economic and Industrial Democracy*, 39(1), 173–90.

Cahill, L. (2019) *Forgotten Revolution – The Limerick Soviet 1919*. Orla Kelly Self-Publishing Services.

Carbery, R. and Cross, C. (2019) *Human Resource Management*. Basingstoke: Macmillan International Higher Education.

Carolan, M. (2019) 'Rail Inspector Loses Bid to Have Lawyers Represent Him at Disciplinary Hearing', *The Irish Times* (online), 11 November, accessed 30 March 2020, www.irishtimes.com/news/crime-and-law/courts/supreme-court/rail-inspector-loses-bid-to-have-lawyers-represent-him-at-disciplinary-hearing-1.4079193

Central Bank of Ireland (2020) 'Covid-19 Has Triggered a Severe Negative Shock to the Irish Economy', *Quartely Economic Bulletin*, QB2, April.

Central Statistics Office (2019a) *CSO Statistical Release. Pension Coverage Quarter 3 2018*. Cork: CSO.

Central Statistics Office (2019b) *CSO Statistical Release. LFS Agency Worker Employment Estimates Quarter 1 2019*. Cork: CSO.

Central Statistics Office (2019c) *EHECS Earnings Hours and Employment Costs Survey,* accessed 30 March 2020, https://statbank.cso.ie/px/pxeirestat/Statire/SelectVarVal/Define.asp?maintable=EHQ10&PLanguage=0

Chamberlain, N.W. (1948) *The Union Challenge to Management Control.* New York: Harper.

Chillas, S. and Baluch, A. (2019) 'Cracking Labour Process Theory in Employment Relations and HRM', in K. Townsend, K. Cafferkey, A.O. McDermott and T. Dundon, *Elgar Introduction to Theories of Human Resources and Employment Relations.* Cheltenham. Elgar Publishing.

Cho, S.K. (1985) 'The Labour Process and Capital Mobility: The Limits of the New International Division of Labour', *Politics and Society,* 14(2) 185–222.

Clark, I. and Colling, T. (2018) 'Work in Britain's Informal Economy: Learning from Road-Side Hand Car Washes', *British Journal of Industrial Relations,* 56(2), 320–41.

Clegg, H.A. (1975) 'Pluralism in Industrial Relations', *British Journal of Industrial Relations,* 13(3), 309–16.

Clegg, H.A. (1976) *Trade Unionism Under Collective Bargaining: A Theory Based on Comparisons of Six Countries.* Oxford: Blackwell.

Coates, K. & Topham, T. (1968) *Industrial Democracy in Great Britain.* London: McKibbon & Kee.

Cole, G.D.H. (1913) *The World of Labour: A Discussion of the Present and Future of Trade Unionism.* London: Fabian Research Department.

Colling, T. (2009) *Court in a Trap? Legal Mobilisation by Trade Unions in United Kingdom* [Warwick Papers in Industrial Relations No. 91]. Coventry: University of Warwick.

Collings, D.G., Gunnigle, P. and Morley, M. (2008) 'Between Boston and Berlin: American MNCs and the Shifting Contours of Industrial Relations in Ireland', *The International Journal of Human Resource Management,* 19(2), 242–63.

Collings, D., Wood, G.T. and Szamosi, L.T. (2018) *Human Resource Management: A Critical Approach* (2nd edn). London: Routledge.

Commission of Inquiry on Industrial Relations (1981) *Report of the Commission of Inquiry on Industrial Relations.* Dublin: Stationery Office.

Committee of Ministers of Council of Europe (2018) *Resolution CM/ResChS(2018)2: European Organisation of Military Associations (EUROMIL) v. Ireland, Complaint No. 112/2014.* Strasbourg: Committee of Ministers of Council of Europe.

Conniffe, D. and Kennedy, K.A. (1984) *Employment and Unemployment Policy for Ireland.* Dublin: Economic and Social Research Institute.

Construction Industry Federation (2017) *Submission in Respect of a Sectoral Employment Order in the Construction Sector.* Dublin: Construction Industry Federation.

Coonan, C. (2012) 'Foxconn Workers Threaten Mass Suicide over Pay and Conditions', *The Irish Times* (online), accessed 30 March 2020, https://www.irishtimes.com/news/foxconn-workers-threaten-mass-suicide-over-pay-and-conditions-1.443251

Coser, L. (1956) *The Functions of Social Conflict.* London: Routledge & Kegan Paul.

Cox, B. and Hughes, J. (1989) 'Industrial Relations in the Public Sector', in Department of Industrial Relations, University College Dublin (eds), *Industrial Relations in Ireland: Contemporary Issues and Developments.* Dublin: University College Dublin.

Crouch, C. (1982) *Trade Unions: The Logic of Collective Action.* London: Fontana.

Crouch, C. (2017) 'Membership Density and Trade Union Power', *Transfer,* 23(1), 47–61.

Crouch, C. and Pizzorno, A. (1978) *The Resurgence of Class Conflict in Western Europe Since 1968: Vols I and II*. London: Macmillan.

Cullinane, N. and Dobbins, A. (2014) 'Considering the Impact of the "Right to Bargain" Legislation in Ireland: A Review', *Industrial Law Journal*, 43(1), 52–83.

Cullinane, N., Donaghey, J., Dundon, T. and Hickland, E. (2014) 'Regulating for Mutual Gains? Non-Union Employee Representation and the Information and Consultation Directive', *The International Journal of Human Resource Management*, 25(6), 810–28.

Cullinane, N. and Dundon, T. (2011) Redundancy and Workplace Occupation: The Case of the Republic of Ireland, *Employee Relations*, 33(6), 624–41.

Cullinane, S.J., Bosak, J., Flood, P.C. and Demerouti, E. (2012) 'Job Design Under Lean Manufacturing and its Impact on Employee Outcomes', *Organizational Psychology Review*, 3(1), 41–61.

Cunningham, K. and Marsh, M. (2018) 'Voting Behaviour', in J. Coakley and M. Gallagher (eds), *Politics in the Republic of Ireland* (6th edn). Abingdon: Routledge.

Cush, M. (2016) *Report to the Minister For Education and Skills of the Chairperson of the Expert Group on Fixed-Term and Part-Time Employment in Third Level Education in Ireland*, accessed 20 March 2020, https://www.education.ie/en/Publications/Education-Reports/Report-to-the-Minister-of-Education-and-Skills-of-the-Chairperson-of-the-Expert-Group-on-Fixed-Term-an d-Part-Time-Employment-in-Lecturing-in-Third-Level-Education-in-Ireland.pdf

Cutcher-Gershenfeld, J. and Verma, A. (1994) 'Joint Governance in North American Work-Places: A Glimpse of the Future or the End of an Era', *International Journal of Human Resource Management*, 5(3), 547–80.

Daft, R.L., Murphy, J. and Willmott, H. (2010) *Organization Theory and Design*. Hampshire (UK): Cengage Learning EMEA.

Dahrendorf, R. (1959) *Class and Class Conflict in Industrial Society*. London: Routledge.

Dáil Éireann (1963–2015) *Dáil Debates Collections (various)*. Dublin: Stationery Office.

Daniel, W. and Millward, N. (1983) *Workplace Industrial Relations in Britain: The DE/PSI/SSRC Survey*. London: Heinemann.

Daniels, K. (2006) *Employee Relations in an Organisational Context*. London: Chartered Institute for Personnel and Development.

D'Arcy, F.A. (1994) 'The Irish Trade Union Movement in the Nineteenth Century', in D. Nevin (ed.), *Trade Union Century*. Dublin: ICTU.

D'Art, D. (Forthcoming) 'Freedom of Association and Statutory Union Recognition; A Constitutional Impossibility?', *Irish Jurist*.

D'Art, D. and Turner, T. (2002) 'Corporatism in Ireland: A View from Below', in D. D'Art and T. Turner (eds), *Irish Employment Relations in the New Economy*. Dublin: Blackhall Publishing.

D'Art, D. and Turner, T. (2003) 'Union Recognition in Ireland: One Step Forward or Two Steps Back', *Industrial Relations Journal*, 34(3), 226–40.

D'Art, D. and Turner, T. (2005) 'Union Recognition and Partnership at Work: A New Legitimacy for Irish Trade Unions?' *Industrial Relations Journal*, 36, 121–39.

D'Art, D. and Turner, T. (2006a) 'Profit Sharing and Employee Share Ownership in Ireland: A New Departure?', *Economic and Industrial Democracy*, 27(4), 543–64.

D'Art, D. and Turner, T. (2006b) 'Union Organising, Union Recognition and Employer Opposition: Case Studies of the Irish Experience', *Irish Journal of Management*, 26(2), 165–84.

D'Art, D. and Turner, T. (2007) 'Ireland in Breach of ILO Convention on Freedom of Association', *Industrial Relations News,* 11, 19–21. Available at www.irn.ie

D'Art, D. and Turner, T. (2011) 'Irish Trade Unions under Social Partnership: A Faustian Bargain', *Industrial Relations Journal*, 42(2), 157–73.

Darvall, F.O. (1964) *Popular Disturbances and Public Order in Regency England*. London: Oxford University Press.

D'Cruz, P. and Noronha, E. (2014) 'Workplace Bullying in the Context of Organisational Change: The Significance of Pluralism', *Industrial Relations Journal*, 45(1), 2–21.

Deaton, D. (1985) 'Management Styles and Large Scale Survey Evidence', *Industrial Relations Journal*, 26 (2), 67–71.

Demougin, P., Gooberman, L., Hauptmeier, M. and Heery, E. (2019) 'Employer Organisations Transformed', *Human Resource Management Journal*, 29(1), 1–16.

Department of Finance (2003) *Budgetary and Economic Statistics, January 2003*. Dublin: Department of Finance.

Department of Industry and Commerce (1958) *Programme for Economic Expansion* [Official Publications. Pr. 4796]. Dublin: Stationery Office.

Department of Jobs, Enterprise and Innovation (2016) *First Strategy Statement for the Workplace Relations Commission Embeds Reforms and Targets Improved Services for Users – Minister Bruton*, accessed 30 March 2020, https://merrionstreet.ie/en/News-Room/Releases/First_Strategy_Statement_for_the_Workplace_Relations_Commission_embeds_reforms_and_targets_impro ved_services_for_users_%E2%80%93_Minister_Bruton_.html

Department of Labour (1986) *Outline of Principal Proposals of Proposed New Trade Dispute and Industrial Relations Legislation*. Dublin: Department of Labour.

Department of Labour (1991) *A Speech by the Minister for Labour Prepared for the Seminar on the Industrial Relations Act 1990, Organised by the Irish Society for Labour Law*. Dublin: Department of Labour.

Department of the Taoiseach (1997) *Partnership 2000*. Dublin: Stationery Office.

Dibben, P., Klerck, G. and Wood, G. (2011) *Employment Relations: A Critical and International Approach*.London: Chartered Institute of Personnel and Development.

Dix, G., Forth, J. and Sisson, K. (2009) 'Conflict at Work: The Changing Patterns of Disputes', in W. Brown, A. Bryson, J. Forth and K. Whitfield (eds), *The Evolution of the Modern Workplace*. Cambridge: Cambridge University Press.

Dizikes, P. (2019) 'The Productive Career of Robert Solow', *MIT Technology Review*, 27 December.

Dobbins, A. and Gunnigle, P. (2009) 'Can Voluntary Workplace Partnership Deliver Sustainable Mutual Gains?', *British Journal of Industrial Relations*, 47(3), 546–70.

Dobbins, T. (2008) *Workplace Partnership in Practice: Securing Sustainable Mutual Gains at Waterford Glass and Aughinish Alumina?* Dublin: Liffey Press.

Dobbins, T. (2009) *The Impact of the Information and Consultation Directive on Industrial Relations — Ireland*, accessed 20 March 2020, http://www.eurofound.europa.eu/eiro/studies/tn0710029s/ie0710029q.htm

Dobbins, T. (2010) 'The Case for Beneficial Constraints: Why Permissive Voluntarism Impedes Workplace Cooperation in Ireland', *Economic and Industrial Democracy*, 31(4), 497–519.

Dobbins, T. (2011) *Final Questionnaire for EIRO CAR on 'The Effect of the Information and Consultation Directive on Industrial Relations in the EU Member States Five Years After its Transposition – Ireland'*, accessed 20 March 2020, http://www.eurofound.europa.eu/eiro/studies/tn1009029s/ie1009029q.htm

Dobbins, T. and Dundon, T. (2011) 'Workplace Partnership and the Future Trajectory of Employment Relations Within Liberal Market Economies', in K. Townsend and A. Wilkinson (eds), *The Future of Employment Relations: New Paradigms, New Approaches*. London: Palgrave Macmillan.

Dobbins, T. and Dundon, T. (2017) 'The Chimera of Sustainable Labour–Management Partnership', *British Journal of Management*, 28 (3), 519–33.

Doherty, L. and Teague, P. (2011) 'Building Better Employment Relations: Conflict Management Systems in Subsidiaries of Non-Union Multinational Organisations located in the Republic of Ireland', Labour Relations Commission Symposium, Dublin, 23 February.

Donaghey, J., Cullinane, N., Dundon, T. and Dobbins, T. (2012) 'Non-Union Employee Representation, Union Avoidance and the Managerial Agenda', *Economic and Industrial Democracy*, 33(2), 163–83.

Donaghey, J., Cullinane, N., Dundon, T. and Wilkinson, A. (2011) Re-Conceptualising Employee Silence: Problems and Prognosis, *Work, Employment and Society*, 25(1), 51–67.

Donovan, Lord (1968) *Report on the Royal Commission on Trade Unions and Employers' Associations 1965–1968*. London: Her Majesty's Stationery Office.

Dribbusch, H. and Vandaele, K. (2016) 'Comparing Official Strike Data in Europe – Dealing with Varieties of Strike Recording', *Transfer*, 22(3), 413–18.

Drucker, P.F. (1950) *The New Society: The Anatomy of the Industrial Order*. New York: Harper & Bros.

Dubin, R., Kornhauser, A. and Ross, A.M. (eds) (1954) *Industrial Conflict*. New York: McGraw-Hill.

Duffy, K. (1993) 'Industrial Relations Act 1990 – the Trade Union Experience', *Irish Industrial Relations Review*, January.

Duffy, K. (2010) 'The View of the Labour Court', in A. Kerr (ed.), *The Industrial Relations Act 1990: Twenty Years On*. Dublin: Round Hall.

Duffy, K. (2019) 'Trade Unions and Their Collective Bargaining Conundrum: Where to Next?', *Industrial Relations News*, 18. Available at www.irn.ie

Duffy, K. and Walsh, F. (2011) *Report of Independent Review of Employment Regulation Orders and Registered Employment Agreement Wage Setting Mechanisms*. Dublin: Department for Jobs, Enterprise and Innovation.

Duncan, R. (1979) 'What is the Right Organizational Structure? Decision Tree Analysis provides the Answer', *Organization Dynamics*, Winter, 429–31.

Dundon, T., Cullinane, N. and Wilkinson, A. (2017) *A Very Short, Fairly Interesting and Reasonably Cheap Book about Employment Relations*. London and California: Sage.

Dundon, T., Curran, D., Maloney, M. and Ryan, P. (2008) *The Transposition of the European Employee Information and Consultation Directive Regulations in the Republic of Ireland* [Working Series Research Paper No. 26]. Galway: Centre for Innovation and Structural Change, NUI Galway.

Dundon, T., Curran, D., Ryan, P. and Maloney, M. (2006) 'Conceptualising the Dynamics of Employee Voice: Evidence from the Republic of Ireland', *Industrial Relations Journal*, 37 (5), 492–512.

Dundon, T., Wilkinson, A., Marchington, M. and Ackers, P. (2004) 'The Meanings and Purpose of Employee Voice', *The International Journal of Human Resource Management*, 15(6), 1149–70.

Dunlop, J. (1958) *Industrial Relations Systems*. Carbondale, IL: Southern Illinois University Press.

Ebbinghaus, B. and Visser, J. (1999) 'When Institutions Matter: Union Growth and Decline in Western Europe, 1950–1995', *European Sociological Review*, 15(2), 135–58.

Edwards, P.K. (1977) 'A Critique of Kerr–Siegel Hypothesis of Strikes and the Isolated Mass: A Study of the Falsification of Sociological Knowledge', *The Sociological Review*, 25(3), 551–74.

Edwards, P.K. (1992) 'Industrial Conflict: Themes and Issues in Recent Research', *British Journal of Industrial Relations*, 30(3), 361–404.

Edwards, P.K. (2003) 'The Employment Relationship and the Field of Industrial Relations', in P. Edwards (ed.), *Industrial Relations: Theory and Practice* (2nd edn). Oxford: Blackwell.

Edwards, P.K. (2005) 'Discipline and Attendance: A Murky Aspect of People Management', in S. Bach (ed.), *Managing Human Resources: Personnel Management in Transition*. Oxford: Basil Blackwell.

Edwards, P. and Whitson, C. (1989) 'Industrial Discipline, the Control of Attendance and the Subordination of Labour', *Work Employment and Society*, 3(1), 1–28.

Einarsen, S. and Skogstad, A. (1996) 'Bullying at Work: Epidemiological Findings in Public and Private Organizations', *European Journal of Work and Organizational Psychology*, 5(2), 185–202.

Employment Appeals Tribunal (2019) *Employment Appeals Tribunal Annual Report 2018*. Dublin: Employment Appeals Tribunal.

Equality Authority (2002) *Code of Practice on Sexual Harassment and Harassment at Work*. Dublin: Equality Authority.

Eurofound (2011) *Community Charter of the Fundamental Social Rights of Workers*, accessed 30 March 2020, https://www.eurofound.europa.eu/observatories/eurwork/industrial-relations-dictionary/community-charter-of-the-fundamental-social-rights-of-workers

Ewing, K.D. (2012) 'The Draft Monti II Regulation: An Inadequate Response to Viking and Laval', *The Institute of Employment Rights*, 1–16.

Farnham, D. and Pimlott, J. (1990) *Understanding Industrial Relations*. London: Cassell.

Fenley, A. (1998) 'Models, Styles and Metaphors: Understanding the Management of Discipline', *Employee Relations*, 20(4), 349–64.

Fennell, C. and Lynch, I. (1993) *Labour Law in Ireland*. Dublin: Gill & Macmillan.

Ferner, A. and Hyman, R. (1998) *Changing Industrial Relations in Europe* (2nd edn). Oxford: Blackwell.

Fisher, R. and Ury, W. (1986) *Getting to Yes*. London: Hutchinson.

Fisher, R., Ury, W. and Patton, B. (1997) *Getting to Yes: Negotiating Agreement Without Giving In* (2nd edn). London: Arrow Books.

Fitzgerald, K. (2006) 'Business Leaders Back Social Partnership, Few Plan to Relocate', *Industrial Relations News,* 12. Available at www.irn.ie

Fitzpatrick, P.J. (2012) 'Reflections on the Croke Park Deal', *Countess Markievicz Memorial Lecture Series*, Irish Association for Industrial Relations, 29 November, accessed 20 March 2020, https://www.ul.ie/iair/content/countess-markievicz-lecture

Flanders, A. (1956) 'Collective Bargaining', in A. Flanders and H. Clegg (eds), *The System of Industrial Relations in Great Britain*. Oxford: Basil Blackwell.

Flanders, A. (1965) *Industrial Relations – What's Wrong with the System?* London: Faber and Faber.

Flanders, A. (1968) 'Collective Bargaining: A Theoretical Analysis', *British Journal of Industrial Relations*, 6(1), 1–26.

Flood, P.C. and Toner, B. (1997) 'How do Large Non-union Companies Avoid a Catch 22?', *British Journal of Industrial Relations*, 35 (2), 257–77.

Foa, R.S. and Mounk, Y. (2016) 'The Democratic Disconnect', *Journal of Democracy*, 27(3), 5–17.

Fogarty, M.P., Egan, D. and Ryan, W.J.L. (1981) *Pay Policy for the 1980s*. Dublin: Federated Union of Employers.

Fombrun, C. (1986) 'Structural Dynamics within and Between Organizations', *Administrative Science Quarterly*, 31, 403–21.

Forde, M. (1991) *Industrial Relations Law*. Dublin: Round Hall Press.

Fox, A. (1966) 'Management Ideology and Labour Relations', *British Journal of Industrial Relations*, 4 (1), 366–78.

Fox, A. (1968) *Industrial Sociology and Industrial Relations* [Research Paper no. 3, Royal Commission on Trade Unions and Employers' Associations]. London: Her Majesty's Stationery Office.

Fox, A. (1973) 'Industrial Relations: A Social Critique of Pluralist Ideology', in J. Child (ed.), *Man and Organisation*. London: Allen & Unwin.

Fox, A. (1974) *Beyond Contract: Work, Power and Trust Relations*. London: Faber.

Fox, A. (1975) 'Collective Bargaining, Flanders and the Webbs', *British Journal of Industrial Relations*, 13(2), 151–74.

Fox, A. (1977) 'The Myth of Pluralism and a Radical Alternative', in T. Clarke and L. Clements (eds), *Trade Unions under Capitalism*. London: Faber and Faber.

Franzosi, R. (1989) 'Strike Data in Search of a Theory: The Italian Case in the Post-War Period', *Politics and Society*, 17, 453–87.

Frawley, M. (2002) 'Technology Teachers Latest Group to Switch to LRC, Labour Court', *Industrial Relations News*, 24, 14–5. Available at www.irn.ie

Freeman, R. and Rogers, J. (1999) *What Workers Want*. Ithaca: Cornell University Press and the Russell Sage Foundation.

Freeman, R. B. (2007) 'What Do Unions Do? The 2004 M-Brane Stringtwister Edition', in J. T. Bennett and B. E. Kaufman (eds), *What Do Unions Do? A Twenty-Year Perspective*. New Brunswick, NJ: Transaction.

Frege, C.M. and Kelly, J. (2003) Union Revitalization Strategies in a Comparative Perspective, *European Journal of Industrial Relations*, 9(1), 7–24.

Fuerstenberg, F. (1987) 'The Federal Republic of Germany', in G.J. Bamber and R.D. Lansbury (eds), *International and Comparative Industrial Relations: A Study of Developed Market Economies*. London: Allen & Unwin.

Gall, G. (1999) 'A Review of Strike Activity at the End of the Second Millennium', *Employee Relations*, 23(4), 357–77.

Gall, G. (2017) 'Conflict', in A. Wilkinson and S. Johnston (eds), *Encyclopaedia of Human Resource Management*. Cheltenham: Elgar.

Garavan, T. (2002) *The Irish Health and Safety Handbook* (2nd edn). Dublin: Oak Tree Press.

Gardner, M. and Palmer, G. (1992) *Employment Relations: Industrial Relations and Human Resource Management in Australia*. Sydney: Macmillan.

Geary, J. (1994) 'Task Participation: Employee's Participation – Enabled or Constrained', in K. Sisson (ed.), *Personnel Management: A Comprehensive Guide to Theory and Practice in Britain*. Oxford: Blackwell.

Geary, J. (1996) 'Working at Restructuring Work in Europe: The Case of Team-working', *Irish Business and Administrative Research*, 17, 44–57.

Geary, J. (1998) 'New Work Structures and the Diffusion of Team Working Arrangements in Ireland', *Sixth John Lovett Memorial Lecture*, University of Limerick, 2 April.

Geary, J. (1999) 'The New Workplace: Change at Work in Ireland', *International Journal of Human Resource Management*, 10(5), 870–90.

Geary, J. (2008) 'Do Unions Benefit from Working in Partnership with Employers? Evidence from Ireland', *Industrial Relations: A Journal of Economy and Society*, 47(4), 530–68.

Geary, J. and Roche, W.K. (2001) 'Multinationals and Human Resource Practices in Ireland: A Rejection of the "New Conformance Thesis"', *International Journal of Human Resource Management*, 12(1), 109–27.

Geary, J. and Trif, A. (2011) 'Workplace Partnership and the Balance of Advantage: A Critical Case Analysis', *British Journal of Industrial Relations*, 49(1), 44–69.

Gennard, J. and Judge, G. (2010) *Managing Employment Relations.* London: Chartered Institute of Personnel and Development.

Geoghegan, B. (1996) 'IBEC Expert Defends PCW', *Sunday Business Post*, 30 August.

Gernigon, B., Odero, A. and Guido, H. (2000) 'Principles Concerning Collective Bargaining, *International Labour Review*, 139(1), 33–55.

Godard, J. (2014) 'Labour Management Conflict: Where it Comes from, Why it Varies, and What it Means for Conflict Management Systems', in W.K. Roche, P. Teague and A.J.S. Colvin (eds), *The Oxford Handbook of Conflict Management in Organizations.* Oxford: Oxford University Press.

Goetschy, J. (2000) 'The European Union and National Social Pacts: Employment and Social Protection Put to the Test of Joint Regulation', in G. Fajertag and P. Pochet (eds), *Social Pacts in Europe – New Dynamics.* Brussels: European Trade Union Institute.

Golden, M., Wallerstein, M. and Lange, P. (1999) 'Post-war Trade-Union Organisation and Industrial Relations in Twelve Countries', in H. Kitschelt, P. Lange, G. Marks and J. Stephens (eds), *Continuity and Change in Contemporary Capitalism.* Cambridge: Cambridge University Press.

Goldthorpe, J. (1974) 'Industrial Relations in Great Britain: A Critique of Reformism', *Politics and Society*, 4(4), 419–52.

Goodbody, W. (2019a) 'Ryanair's Injunction Application Granted, Halting Strike Action', *RTÉ News*, 21 August, accessed 20 March 2020, https://www.rte.ie/news/2019/0820/1069983-ryanair/

Goodbody, W. (2019b) 'Up to 500 Jobs Lost as Shannon-based Molex to Close', *RTÉ News*, 22 October, accessed 20 March 2020, www.rte.ie/news/business/2019/1022/1084921-molex-shannon/

Gouldner, A.W. (1954) *Wildcat Strike.* New York: Harper.

Green, F. (1990) 'Trade Union Availability and Trade Union Membership in Britain', *The Manchester School*, 58(4), 378–94.

Griffin, J.I. (1939) *Strikes: A Study in Quantitative Economics.* New York: Colombia University Press.

Grint, K. (1991) *The Sociology of Work: An Introduction.* Oxford: Polity Press.

Grote, J., Lang, A. and Traxler, F. (2007) 'Germany', in F. Traxler and G. Huemer (eds), *Handbook of Business Interest Associations, Firm Size and Governance.* London/New York: Routledge.

Guest, D. (1987) 'Human Resource Management and Industrial Relations', *Journal of Management Studies*, 24 (5), 503–21.

Gunnigle, P. (1995) 'Collectivism and the Management of Industrial Relations in Greenfield Sites', *Human Resource Management Journal* 5(3), 24–40.

Gunnigle, P. (1998a) 'Human Resource Management and the Personnel Function', in W.K. Roche, K. Monks and J. Walsh (eds), *Human Resource Strategies: Policy and Practice in Ireland*. Dublin: Oak Tree Press.

Gunnigle, P. (1998b) 'More Rhetoric than Reality: Industrial Relations Partnerships in Ireland', *Economic and Social Review*, (28)4, 179–200.

Gunnigle, P. and Brady, T. (1984) 'The Management of Industrial Relations in The Small Firm', *Employee Relations*, 6 (5), 21–4.

Gunnigle, P., Foley, K. and Morley, M. (1994) 'A Review of Organisational Reward Practices', in P. Gunnigle, P. Flood, M. Morley and T. Turner (eds), *Continuity and Change in Irish Employee Relations*. Dublin: Oak Tree Press.

Gunnigle, P., Heraty, N. and Morley, M. (2017) *Human Resource Management in Ireland* (5th edn). Dublin: Institute of Public Administration.

Gunnigle, P., Lavelle, J. and McDonnell, A. (2009) 'Subtle but Deadly? Union Avoidance through "Double Breasting" among Multinational Companies', *Advances in Industrial and Labor Relations*, 16, 51–74.

Gunnigle, P., Lavelle, J. and Monaghan, S. (2019) 'Multinational Companies and HRM in Ireland During Recession: A Retrospective from a Highly Globalized Economy', *Thunderbird International Business Review*, 61(3), 481–9.

Gunnigle, P., MacCurtain, S. and Morley, M. (2001) 'Dismantling Pluralism: Industrial Relations in Irish Greenfield Sites', *Personnel Review*, 30(3), 263–79.

Gunnigle, P., Morley, M. and Turner, T. (1997) 'Challenging Collectivist Traditions: Individualism and the Management of Industrial Relations in Greenfield Sites', *Economic and Social Review*, (28)2, 105–34.

Gunnigle, P., O'Sullivan, M. and Kinsella, M. (2002) 'Organised Labour in the New Economy: Trade Unions and Public Policy in the Republic of Ireland', in D. D'Art and T. Turner (eds), *Irish Employment Relations in the New Economy* (222–58). Dublin: Blackhall Publishing.

Hall, P.A. and Soskice, D. (2001) *Varieties of Capitalism: The Institutional Foundations of Comparative Advantage*. Oxford: Oxford University Press.

Hamann, K., Johnston, A. and Kelly, J. (2013) 'Unions Against Governments: Explaining General Strikes in Western Europe, 1980–2006', *Comparative Political Studies*, 46(9), 1030–57.

Hanley, B. (2018) 'The Conscription Crisis 1918: The Nail in the Coffin?', *Countess Markievicz Memorial Lecture Series*, Irish Association for Industrial Relations, 23 November, accessed 30 March 2020, https://www.ul.ie/iair/content/countess-markievicz-lecture

Hardiman, N. (1988) *Pay, Politics and Economic Performance in Ireland 1970–1987*. Oxford: Clarendon.

Hardiman, N. (2000) 'Social Partnership, Wage Bargaining, and Growth', in B. Nolan, J. O'Connell and C. Whelan (eds), *Bust to Boom? The Irish Experience of Growth and Inequality*. Dublin: Institute of Public Administration.

Hardiman, N. (2006) 'Political and Social Partnership: Flexible Network Governance', *Economic and Social Review*, 37(3), 343–74.

Harney, B. (2019) Systems Theory: Forgotten Legacy and Future Prospects, in K. Townsend, K. Cafferkey, A.O. McDermott and T. Dundon, *Elgar Introduction to Theories of Human Resources and Employment Relations*. Cheltenham: Elgar Publishing.

Hastings, T. (2003) *Politics, Management, and Industrial Relations: Semi-State Companies and the Challenges of Marketization*. Dublin: Blackhall Publishing.

Hawkins, K. (1979) *A Handbook of Industrial Relations Practice.* London: Kogan Page.

Hawkins, K. (1982) *Case Studies in Industrial Relations.* London: Kogan Page.

Haynes, P., Vowles, J. and Boxall, P. (2005) 'Explaining the Younger–Older Worker Union Density Gap: Evidence from New Zealand', *British Journal of Industrial Relations* 43(1), 93–116.

Health and Safety Authority (2018) *Health and Safety Authority Summary of Workplace, Injury and Fatality Statistics 2016–17.* Dublin: Health and Safety Authority.

Health and Safety Authority (2019) *Health and Safety Authority Annual Report 2018.* Dublin: Health and Safety Authority.

Hebdon, R.P. and Stern, R.N. (1998) 'Trade-Offs Among Expressions of Industrial Conflict: Public Sector Strike Bans and Arbitrations', *Industrial and Labour Relations Review*, 51(2), 204–21.

Heery, E. (2010) 'Debating Employment Law: Responses to Juridification', in P. Blyton, E. Heery and P. Turnbull (eds), *Reassessing the Employment Relationship.* Basingstoke: Palgrave Macmillan.

Heery, E. (2011) 'Debating Employment Law: Responses to Juridification', in P. Blyton, E. Heery and P.J. Turnbull (eds), *Reassessing the Employment Relationship: Management, Work and Organisations.* London: Palgrave Macmillan.

Heery, E., Simms, M., Simpson, D., Delbridge, R. and Salmon, J. (2000) 'Organising Unionism Comes to the UK', *Employee Relations,* 22(1), 38–57.

Heery, E., Williams, S. and Abbott, B. (2012) 'Civil Society Organisations and Trade Unions: Co-operation, Conflict, Indifference', *Work, Employment & Society*, 26(1), 145–60.

Hepple, B. (2002) 'Introduction', in B. Hepple (ed.), *Social and Labour Rights in a Global Context: International and Comparative Perspectives.* Cambridge: Cambridge University Press.

Hepple, B. (2010) 'Rethinking Laws Against Strikes', *Countess Markievicz Memorial Lecture Series*, Irish Association for Industrial Relations, 11 October, accessed 30 March 2020, https://www.ul.ie/iair/content/countess-markievicz-lecture

Herbert Smith Freehills (2019) *Future of Work. Adapting to the Democratised Workplace,* accessed 30 March 2020, https://www.herbertsmithfreehills.com/futureofwork

Herzberg, F. (1968) *Work and the Nature of Man.* London: Staples Press.

Higgins, C. (2000) 'Train Drivers' Group Not Entitled to Recognition, says High Court', *Industrial Relations News*, 16, 22–3. Available at www.irn.ie

Higgins C. (2010) 'Croke Park Deal "Over the Line" Unions Call for Swift Implementation', *Industrial Relations News*, 23, 9. Available at www.irn.ie

Higgins, C. (2011) 'US Chamber Warns on Collective Bargaining, Agency Working', *Industrial Relations News*, 26. Available at www.irn.ie

Higgins, C. (2019a) 'Officers' Backing for Commission Report, Followed by Moves on Pensions, Promotions', *Industrial Relations News*, 15. Available at www.irn.ie

Higgins, C. (2019b) 'Electrical Contracting Employers and Union Clash at Public Labour Court Hearing', *Industrial Relations News*, 11. Available at www.irn.ie

Higgins, C. (2019c) 'Legal Challenge to Mechanical Craft SEO Considered by Smaller Contractors', *Industrial Relations News*, 41. Available at www.irn.ie

Higgins, C. (2020) 'Private Sector Pay: Wage Settlements Continue to Cluster in 2–3% Range', *Industrial Relations News*, 3. Available at www.irn.ie

Hiltrop, J.M. and Udall, S. (1995) *The Essence of Negotiation.* London: Prentice Hall.

Hirsch, B.T. (2008) 'Sluggish Institutions in a Dynamic World: Can Unions and Industrial Competition Coexist?', *Journal of Economic Perspectives,* 22(1), 153–76.

Hodder, A., Williams, M., Kelly, J. and McCarthy, N. (2017) Does Strike Action Stimulate Trade Union Membership Growth? *British Journal of Industrial Relations,* 55(1), 165–86.

Hodgins, M., MacCurtain, S. and Mannix-McNamara, P. (2014), 'Workplace Bullying and Incivility: A Systematic Review of Interventions', *International Journal of Workplace Health Management,* 7(1), 54–72.

Hoffer, E. (2002) *The True Believer: Thoughts on the Nature of Mass Movements.* New York: Harper Perennial Modern Classics.

Holgate, J., Pollert, A., Keles, J. and Kumarappan, L. (2011) 'Geographies of Isolation: How Workers Don't Access Support for Problems at Work', *Antipode,* 43(4), 1078–101.

Horgan, J. (1989) 'The Future of Collective Bargaining', in Department of Industrial Relations, University College Dublin (eds), *Industrial Relations in Ireland: Contemporary Issues and Developments.* Dublin: University College Dublin.

Horgan, J. (2016) *Review of An Garda Síochána (AGS): Haddington Road Agreement AGS Review Horgan Strand, 12 December,* accessed 20 March 2020, http://www.justice.ie/en/JELR/Horgan%20Review%20(Dec%202016).pdf/Files/Horgan%20Review%20(Dec%202016).pdf

Howell, C. (2005) *Trade Unions and the State.* Princeton, NJ: Princeton University Press.

Huczynski, A.A. and Buchanan, D.A. (1991) *Organizational Behaviour: An Introductory Text.* London: Prentice Hall.

Hug, A. and Tudor, O. (2012) *Single Market, Equal Rights? UK Perspectives on EU Employment and Social Law.* London: The Foreign Policy Centre.

Huselid, M. (1995) 'The Impact of Human Resource Management Practices on Turnover, Productivity, and Corporate Financial Performance', *Academy of Management Journal,* 38(3), 635–72.

Hyman, R. (1975) *Industrial Relations: A Marxist Introduction.* London: Macmillan.

Hyman, R. (1989) *Strikes.* London: Macmillan.

Hyman, R. and Mason, B. (1995) *Managing Employee Involvement and Participation.* London: Sage.

Incomes Data Service/Institute of Personnel and Development (1996) *European Management Guides: Industrial Relations and Collective Bargaining.* London: Institute of Personnel and Development.

Industrial Relations News (2010) 'Private Sector Pay "Marks Time" for 2010, With Some Exceptions', *Industrial Relations News,* 4. Available at www.irn.ie

Industrial Relations News (2012) 'Vita Cortex Update: Workers Vote to Endorse Resolution Proposal', *Industrial Relations News,* 17. Available at www.irn.ie

Industrial Relations News (2019) 'Expert Believes ICTU Hopes for EU Directive on Collective Bargaining Are Slim', *Industrial Relations News,* 27. Available at www.irn.ie

International Labour Organisation (1973) *Collective Bargaining in Industrialised Market Economies.* Geneva: International Labour Organisation.

International Labour Organisation (1975) *Collective Bargaining in Industrialised Market Economies.* Geneva: International Labour Organisation.

International Labour Organisation (1990) *Meeting of Experts on Statistics of Strikes and Lock-outs: Report Prepared by the Bureau of Statistics.* Geneva: International Labour Organisation.

International Labour Organisation (2012) *Report of the Committee on Freedom of Association: 363rd Report of the Committee on Freedom of Association.* Geneva: International Labour Organisation.

Irish Business and Employers Confederation (2019) *Driving Positive Change for Business,* accessed 20 March 2020, https://www.ibec.ie/about-us/our-mission-vision-and-values

Irish Congress of Trade Unions (2018) *Employment Equality Acts 1998–2015. A Guide for Trade Unions*. Dublin: Irish Congress of Trade Unions.

Irish Congress of Trade Unions (2019) *Realising the Transformative Effect of Social Dialogue and Collective Bargaining in Ireland. Route to Reform*. Dublin: Irish Congress of Trade Unions.

Irish Small and Medium Enterprises Association (2019) *About Us*, accessed 3 February 2020, https://isme.ie/about/

Jackson, M.P. (1982) *Industrial Relations: A Textbook*. London: Kogan Page.

Jackson, M.P. (1987) *Strikes: Industrial Conflict in Britain, USA and Australia*. London: Wheatsheaf.

Jackson, M.P. (1991) *An Introduction to Industrial Relations*. London: Routledge.

Jacoby, S.M. (1997) *Modern Manors: Welfare Capitalism Since the New Deal*. New Jersey: Princeton University Press.

Jaumotte, F. and Buitron, C.O. (2015) 'Power from the People', *Finance and Development*, 52(1), 29–31.

Jones, P. and Saundry, R. (2011) 'The Practice of Discipline: Evaluating the Roles and Relationship between Managers and HR Professionals', *Human Resource Management Journal*, 22(3), 252–66.

Kahn-Freund, O. (1977) *Labour and the Law*. London: Stevens.

Kaufman, B.E. (2018) 'Rethinking Industrial Relations, or at Least the British Radical Frame', *Economic and Industrial Democracy*, 39 (4) 577–98.

Kavanagh, R. (1987) *Labour from the Beginning – 75 Years*. Dublin: The Labour Party.

Kelly, A. (1975) 'Changes in the Occupational Structure and Industrial Relations in Ireland', *Management*, 2.

Kelly, A. and Brannick, T. (1983) 'The Pattern of Strike Activity in Ireland, 1960–1979', *Irish Business and Administrative Research*, 5(1), 65–77.

Kelly, A. and Brannick, T. (1988) 'Explaining the Strike Proneness of British Companies in Ireland', *British Journal of Industrial Relation*s, 26(1), 37–57.

Kelly, A. and Brannick, T. (1989) 'Strikes in Ireland: Measurement, Indices and Trends', in Department of Industrial Relations, University College Dublin (eds), *Industrial Relations in Ireland: Contemporary Issues and Developments*. Dublin: University College Dublin.

Kelly, A. and Hourihan, F. (1997) 'Employee Participation', in T.V. Murphy and W.K. Roche (eds), *Irish Industrial Relations in Practice: Revised and Expanded Edition*. Dublin: Oak Tree Press.

Kelly, A. and Roche, W.K. (1983) 'Institutional Reform in Irish Industrial Relations', *Studies: An Irish Quarterly Review*, 72(287), 221–30.

Kelly, D. (2006) 'Workplace Bullying – A Complex Issue Needing IR/HRM Research?', in B. Pocock, C. Provis and E. Willis (eds), *Twenty-first Century Work: Proceedings of the 20th Conference of the Association of Industrial Relations Academics of Australia and New Zealand*. Adelaide: University of South Australia.

Kelly, J. (1998) *Rethinking Industrial Relations: Mobilization, Collectivism and Long Waves*. London: Routledge.

Kelly, J. (2003) 'Labour Movement Revitalization? A Comparative Perspective', *Countess Markievicz Memorial Lecture Series*, Irish Association for Industrial Relations, 7 April, accessed 4 April 2020, https://www.ul.ie/iair/content/countess-markievicz-lecture

Kelly, J. (2015) 'Conflict: Trends and Forms of Collective Action', *Employee Relations* 37(6) 720–73.

Kelly, J. and Hamann, K. (2010) 'General Strikes in Western Europe: 1980–2008', paper presented at the Political Studies Association Annual Conference, Manchester, 7–9 April.

Kennedy, G. (1998) *The New Negotiating Edge: A Behavioural Approach for Results and Relationships*. London: Nicholas Brearly.

Kerr, A. (1989) 'Trade Unions and the Law', in Department of Industrial Relations, University College Dublin (eds), *Industrial Relations in Ireland: Contemporary Issues and Developments*. Dublin: University College Dublin.

Kerr, A. (1991a) 'Consensus not Compulsion', *Industrial Law Journal*, 20(3), 240–57.

Kerr, A. (1992) 'Why Public Sector Workers Join Unions: An Attitude Survey of Workers in the Health Service and Local Government', *Employee Relations*, 14(2), 39–54.

Kerr, A. (2010) 'The Involvement of the Courts', in A. Kerr (ed.), *The Industrial Relations Act Twenty Years On*. Dublin: Round Hall.

Kerr, A. (2015) *The Trade Union and Industrial Relations Acts of Ireland* (5th edn). London: Sweet & Maxwell.

Kerr, A. (2017) 'Industrial Relations Law', in A. Murphy and M. Regan (eds), *Employment Law* (2nd edn). London: Bloomsbury.

Kerr, A. and Whyte, G. (1985) *Irish Trade Union Law*. Abingdon: Professional Books.

Kerr, C., Harbinson, F. and Myers, H. (1962) *Industrialism and Industrial Man*. London: Heineman.

Kerr, C. and Siegel, A. (1954) 'The Interindustry Propensity to Strike – An International Comparison', in A. Kornhauser, R. Dubin and A.M. Ross (eds), *Industrial Conflict*. New York: McGraw-Hill.

Kidner, R. (1982) 'Lessons in Trade Union Reform: The Origins and Passage of the Trade Disputes Act 1906', *Legal Studies*, 2(1), 34–52.

Kitschelt, H. (2013) 'Social Class and the Radical Right: Conceptualizing Political Preference Formation and Partisan Choice', in J. Rydgren (ed.), *Class Politics and the Radical Right* (224–51). London & New York: Routledge.

Klein, J. (1989) 'The Human Cost of Manufacturing Reform', *Harvard Business Review*, March/April.

Kochan, T., Katz, H. and McKersie, R. (1986) *The Transformation of American Industrial Relations*. New York: Basic Books.

Kochan, T.A. and Osterman, P. (1994) *The Mutual Gains Enterprise*. Cambridge, MA: Harvard Business School Press.

Korpi, W. (1983) *The Democratic Class Struggle*. London: Routledge & Kegan Paul.

Labour Court (1948–2019) *Annual Reports* (various). Dublin: Stationery Office.

Labour Party (2020) *Labour Manifesto 2020: Building an Equal Society*, accessed 30 March 2020, https://www.labour.ie/download/pdf/labour_manifesto_web.pdf.

Labour Relations Commission (1992–2015) *Annual Reports* (various). Dublin: Stationery Office.

Labour Relations Commission (2006) *Procedures for Addressing Bullying in The Workplace: Code of Practice No.6*. Dublin: Labour Relations Commission.

Lally, C. (2019) 'Human Traffic: Ireland Part of a Global Trade That Monetises Desperation', *The Irish Times,* 24 October.

Lamare, R., Gunnigle, P., Marginson, P. and Murray, G. (2013) 'Union Status and Double-Breasting at Multinational Companies in Three Liberal Market Economies', *Industrial and Labor Relations Review,* 66(3), 696–722.

Larkin, E. (1965) *James Larkin: 1876–1947 – Irish Labour Leader*. London: Routledge.

Larragy, J. (2010) 'Asymmetric Engagement: The Community and Voluntary Pillar in Irish Social Partnership: A Case Study', Unpublished PhD Thesis, University College Dublin Library.

Lavelle, J. (2008) 'Charting the Contours of Union Recognition in Foreign-Owned MNCs: Survey Evidence from the Republic of Ireland', *Irish Journal of Management*, 29(1), 45–64.

Lavelle, J., Gunnigle, P. and McDonnell, A. (2009) *Human Resource Practices in Multinational Companies in Ireland: A Contemporary Analysis*. Dublin: Stationery Office.

Lavelle, J., Gunnigle, P. and McDonnell, A. (2010) 'Patterning Employee Voice in Multinational Companies, *Human Relations*, 63(3), 395–418.

Law Reform Commission (2008) *Consultation Paper. Alternative Dispute Resolution*. Dublin: Law Reform Commission.

Law Reform Commission (2010) *Report: Alternative Dispute Resolution: Mediation and Conciliation*. Dublin: Law Reform Commission.

Law Reform Commission (2017) *Issues Paper – Suspended Sentences*. Dublin: Law Reform Commission.

Lee, J. (1980) 'Worker and Society since 1945', in D. Nevin (ed.), *Trade Unions and Change in Irish Society*. Dublin: Mercier Press/RTÉ.

Lewicki, R.J., Barry, B. and Saunders, D.M. (2010) *Negotiation*. Boston: McGraw-Hill.

Lewicki, R.J., Saunders, D.M. and Minton, J.W. (1999) *Negotiation* (3rd edn). Boston: McGraw-Hill.

Lewicki, R.J., Saunders, D.M. and Minton, J.W. (2001) *Essentials of Negotiation*. Boston: McGraw-Hill.

Logan, J. (1999) *Teachers' Union: The TUI and its Forerunners 1899–1994*. Dublin: A. & A. Farmer.

Lyddon, D. (2007) 'Strike Statistics and the Problems of International Comparison', in S. van der Velden, H. Dribbusch, D. Lyddon and K. Vandaele (eds), *Strikes Around the World, 1968–2005: Case-studies of 15 countries*. Amsterdam, Netherlands: Aksant.

MacMahon, J. (2019) 'Plus Ça Change? Regulating Zero-Hours Work in Ireland: An Analysis of Provisions of the Employment (Miscellaneous Provisions) Act 2018', *Industrial Law Journal*, 48(3), 447–67.

MacMahon, J., MacCurtain, S. and O'Sullivan, M. (2009) 'Bullying in Healthcare Organizations', in J. Braithwaite, P. Hyde and P. Pope (eds), *Culture, Climate and Teams in Health Care Organizations*. UK: Palgrave Macmillan.

MacMahon, J., O'Sullivan, M., Murphy, C., Ryan, L. and MacCurtain, S. (2018) 'Speaking up or Staying Silent in Bullying Situations: The Significance of Management Control', *Industrial Relations Journal*, 49(5–6), 473–91.

MacSharry, R. and White, P. (2000) *The Making of the Celtic Tiger: The Inside Story of Ireland's Boom Economy*. Cork: Mercier Press.

Madden, D. and Kerr, A. (1996) *Unfair Dismissal: Cases and Commentary* (2nd edn). Dublin: Irish Business and Employers Confederation.

Malhotra, D. and Bazerman, M.H. (2008) 'Psychological Influence in Negotiation: An Introduction Long Overdue', *Journal of Management*, 34(3), 509–31.

Mandate (2019) *Press Release. Mandate Calls for Repeal of Anti-Union Legislation in Ireland*, accessed 20 March 2020, https://mandate.ie/2019/07/mandate-calls-for-repeal-of-anti-union-legislation-in-ireland/

Marchington, M. (1982) *Managing Industrial Relations*. London: McGraw-Hill.

Marchington, M. and Parker, P. (1990) *Changing Patterns of Employee Relations*. Hemel Hempstead: Harvester Wheatsheaf.

Marchington, M. and Wilkinson, A. (2005) 'Direct Participation and Involvement', in S. Bach (ed.), *Managing Human Resources: Personnel Management in Transition*. Blackwell: Oxford.

Marginson, P., Hall, M. and Hoffman, A. (2004) 'The Impact of European Works Councils on Management Decision-Making in the UK and US based Multinationals', *British Journal of Industrial Relations*, 412(2), 209–33.

Maslow, A.H. (1954) *Motivation and Personality*. New York: Harper & Row.

Mayo, E. (1949) *The Social Problems of an Industrial Civilization*. London: Routledge & Kegan Paul.

Mazower, M. (2018) *Dark Continent: Europe's Twentieth Century*. Harmondsworth: Penguin.

McCarthy, C. (1973) *The Decade of Upheaval*. Dublin: Institute of Public Administration.

McCarthy, C. (1977) *Trade Unions in Ireland: 1894–1960*. Dublin: Institute of Public Administration.

McCarthy, C. (1984) *Elements in a Theory of Industrial Relations*. Dublin: Trinity College Dublin.

McCarthy, W.E.J., O'Brien, J.F. and O'Dowd, V.G. (1975) *Wage Inflation and Wage Leadership. Paper No. 79*. Dublin: Economic and Social Research Institute.

McDermott, D. (2019) 'Radical EU change to Irish Legal Framework for Resolution of Employment Disputes', *Industrial Relations News,* 8. Available at www.irn.ie

McDonough, T. and Dundon, T. (2010) 'Thatcherism Delayed? The Irish Crisis and the Paradox of Social Partnership', *Industrial Relations Journal*, 41(6), 544–62.

McDonough, T., Loughrey, J., Klemm, A., Dunne, F. and Pentony, S. (2009) *Hierarchy of Earnings, Attributes and Privilege, Analysis*. Dublin: TASC.

McGinley, M. (1989) 'Pay Increases Between 1981–1987', in Institute of Public Administration, *Personnel and Industrial Relations Directory*. Dublin: Institute of Public Administration.

McGinley, M. (1990) 'Trade Union Law – Look Back in Anguish', *Industrial Relations News*, 16, 19–23.

McGinley, M. (1997) 'Industrial Relations in the Public Sector', in T.V. Murphy and W.K. Roche (eds), *Irish Industrial Relations in Practice*. Dublin: Oak Tree Press.

McGovern, P. (1989) 'Union Recognition and Union Avoidance in the 1980s', in Department of Industrial Relations, University College Dublin (eds), *Industrial Relations in Ireland: Contemporary Issues and Developments*, Dublin: University College Dublin.

McGuinness, S., Redmond, P. and Delaney, J. (2019) *The Prevalence and Effect on Hours Worked of the Minimum Wage In Ireland. A Sectoral and Regional Analysis*. Dublin: Economic and Social Research Institute.

McKersie, R.B. (1996) 'Labour–Management Partnerships: US Evidence and Implications for Ireland', *Irish Business and Administrative Research*, 17(1), 1–16.

McKersie, R.B. (2002) 'Labour–Management Partnerships: US Evidence and the Implications for Ireland', in P. Gunnigle, M. Morley and M. McDonnell (eds), *The Lovett Lectures: A Decade of Developments in Human Resource Management*. Dublin: Liffey Press.

McMahon, G. (1990) 'Multinationals: The Labour Relations Experience in Ireland', *Advances in Business Studies*, 2(2), 86–96.

McMahon, G. (2001) *Recruitment and Selection: How to Get It Right*. Dublin: Oak Tree Press.

McMahon, G. (2009) 'No Place to Hide for Workplace Bullies', *Village Magazine*.

McMahon, G. (2011) 'Pay Cuts and Redundancies – Through the Legal Minefield', *Industrial Relations News*, 14. Available at www.irn.ie

McNamara, G., Williams, K. and West, D. (1988) *Understanding Trade Unions: Yesterday and Today*. Dublin: O'Brien Educational Press in association with the Irish Congress of Trade Unions.

McNamara, G., Williams, K. and West, D. (1994) *Understanding Trade Unions: Yesterday and Today*. Dublin: ELO Publications in association with the Irish Congress of Trade Unions.

McNulty, F. (2019) 'Court Injunctions Against Two Beef Price Protesters to Be Struck Out', *RTÉ News*, 28 November, accessed 20 March 2020, https://www.rte.ie/news/ireland/2019/1128/1095732-beef-farmer-protests/

Mechanical Engineering and Building Services Contracts Association/Construction Industry Federation (2019) *Submission in Respect of a Sectoral Employment Order in the Mechanical Engineering and Building Services Contracting Sector*. Dublin: Construction Industry Federation.

Meenan, F. (1999) *Working within the Law: A Practical Gude for Employers and Employees*. Dublin: Oak Tree Press.

Messersmith, J. G., Patel, P. C., Lepak, D. P. and Gould-Williams, J. S. (2011) 'Unlocking the Black Box: Exploring the Link between High-Performance Work Systems and Performance'. *Journal of Applied Psychology*, 96(6), 1105–18.

Moene, K. and Wallerstein, M. (1999) 'Social Democratic Labour Market Institutions: A Retrospective Analysis', in H. Kitschelt, P. Lange, G. Marks and J. Stephens (eds), *Continuity and Change in Contemporary Capitalism*. Cambridge: Cambridge University Press.

Moffatt, J. (ed.) (2006) *Employment Law*. Dublin/Oxford: Law Society of Ireland/Oxford.

Molloy, E. (2012) 'Breaking Down the Croke Park Monolith', *Sunday Business Post*, 25 November.

Morgan, G. and Doering, H. (2019) 'Varieties of Capitalism', in K. Townsend, K. Cafferkey, A.O. McDermott and T. Dundon, *Elgar Introduction to Theories of Human Resources and Employment Relations*. Cheltenham: Elgar Publishing.

Morley, M., Moore, S., Heraty, N., Linehan, M. and MacCurtain, S. (2004) *Principles of Organisational Behaviour: An Irish Text*. Dublin: Gill & Macmillan.

Morley, M., Moore, S., Heraty, N., Linehan, M. and MacCurtain, S. (2008) *Principles of Organisational Behaviour: An Irish Text*. Dublin: Gill & Macmillan.

Morrissey, T. (1986) *Report of the Advisory Committee on Worker Participation*. Dublin: Stationery Office.

Murphy, C., O'Sullivan, M., Turner, T., McMahon, J., Lavelle, J., Ryan, L. and Gunnigle, P. (2019) 'Trade union responses to zero hours work in Ireland', *Industrial Relations Journal*, 50 (5–6), 468–85.

Murphy, C. and Turner, T. (2016) 'Organising Precarious Workers: Can a Public Campaign Overcome Weak Grassroots Mobilisation at Workplace Level?', *Journal of Industrial Relations*, 58(5), 589–607.

National Centre for Partnership and Performance (2010) *NCPP National Employee Workplace Survey*. Dublin: National Centre for Partnership and Performance.

National Economic and Social Council (1986) *A Strategy for Development 1986–1990*. Dublin: National Economic and Social Council.

National Economic and Social Council (Various years) *Annual Reports*. Dublin: National Economic and Social Council.

Nevin, D. (1994) *Trade Union Century*. Dublin: Irish Congress of Trade Unions and RTÉ.

Nierenberg, G.I. (1968) *The Art of Negotiating*. New York: Cornerstone.

Nolan, J. (2002) 'The Intensification of Everyday Life', in B. Burchell, D. Ladipo and F. Wilkinson (eds), *Job Insecurity and Work Intensification*. London: Routledge.

Nugent, C., Pembroke, S. and Taft, M. (2019) *Precarious Work in the Republic of Ireland. NERI WP 2019/No 64*. Dublin: NERI.

O'Brien, J.F. (1989) 'Pay Determination in Ireland', in Department of Industrial Relations, University College Dublin (eds), *Industrial Relations in Ireland: Contemporary Issues and Developments*. Dublin: University College Dublin.

O'Connell, H. (2012) 'Everything You Need to Know About the Croke Park Agreement', accessed 30 March 2020, https://www.thejournal.ie/everything-you-need-to-know-about-the-croke-park-agreement-509564-Jul2012/

O'Connell, P., Calvert, E. and Watson, D. (2007) *Bullying in the Workplace, Survey Reports*. Dublin: Department of Enterprise, Trade and Employment.

O'Connor, E. (1988) *Syndicalism in Ireland 1917–1923*. Cork: Cork University Press.

O'Donnell, R. and O'Reardon, C. (1996) *Irish Experiment: Social Partnership has Yielded Economic Growth and Social Progress*. Dublin: National Economic and Social Council/Economic and Social Research Institute.

O'Donnell, R. and O'Reardon, C. (2000) 'Social Partnership in Ireland's Economic Transformation', in G. Fajertag and P. Pochett (eds), *Social Pacts in Europe – New Dynamics*. Brussels: ETUI.

O'Donnell, R. and Thomas, D. (2002) 'Ireland in the 1990s', in S. Berger and H. Compston (eds), *Policy Concertation and Social Partnership in Western Europe: Lessons for the Twenty-First Century*. New York/Oxford: Berghann Books.

Oechslin, J.J. (1985) 'Employer Organisations', in R. Blanpain (ed.), *Labour Law and Industrial Relations*. The Hague: Kluwer.

Ó Gráda, C. (1994) *Ireland: A New Economic History 1780–1939*. Oxford: Clarendon Press.

O'Hagan, J.W. (1987) *The Economy of Ireland: Policy and Performance* (5th edn). Dublin: Irish Management Institute.

O'Hara, B. (1981) *The Evolution of Irish Industrial Relations Law and Practice*. Dublin: Folens.

O'Keeffe, S. (1998) 'Industrial Action Ballots in Ireland – Nolan Transport v. Halligan and Others', *Industrial Law Journal*, 28(4), 347–52.

O'Kelly, E. (2020) 'No School for Thousands of Students as TUI Strikes over Equal Pay', *RTÉ News*, 4 February, accessed 30 March, www.rte.ie/news/2020/0204/1112962-teachers/

O'Kelly, K. and Compton P. (2003) 'Workers' Participation at Board Level – The Irish Approach', paper presented to the European Trade Union Institute and the Hans Boeckler Stiftung, Elewijt, Belgium, 27–28 June.

O'Mahony, D. (1958) *Industrial Relations in Ireland*. Dublin: Economic Research Institute.

Organisation for Economic Co-operation and Development (2017) *OECD Employment Outlook 2017*. Paris: OECD Publishing.

Organisation for Economic Co-operation and Development (2018) *OECD Employment Outlook 2018*. Paris: OECD Publishing.

Osigweh, C.A.B. and Hutchison. W.R. (1989) 'Positive Discipline', *Human Resource Management*, 28(3), 367–83.

Osigweh, C.A.B. and Hutchison. W.R. (1990) 'To Punish or Not to Punish? Managing Human Resources through "Positive Discipline"', *Employment Relations*, 12(3) 27–32.

O'Sullivan, M. and Gunnigle, P. (2009) '"Bearing All the Hallmarks of Oppression": Union Avoidance in Europe's Largest Low-cost Airline', *Labour Studies Journal*, 34(2), 252–70.

O'Sullivan, M. and Hartigan, C. (2011) 'The Citizens Information Service in Ireland: Protecting the Non-unionised Employee?' *Journal of Workplace Rights*, 15(1), 65–82.

O'Sullivan, M., Lavelle, J., McMahon, J., Ryan, L., Murphy, C., Turner, T. and Gunnigle, P. (eds) (2019) *Zero Hours and On-call Work in Anglo-Saxon Countries*. Singapore: Springer.

O'Sullivan, M. and Royle, T. (2014) 'Everything and Nothing Changes: The Threat to Minimum Wage Regulation in Ireland', *Economic and Industrial Democracy*, 35(1), 27–47.

O'Sullivan, M., Turner, T., Kennedy, M. and Wallace, J. (2015a) 'Is Individual Employment Law Displacing the Role of Trade Unions?', *Industrial Law Journal*, 44(2): 222–45.

O'Sullivan, M., Turner, T., Lavelle, J., MacMahon, J., Murphy, C., Ryan, L., Gunnigle, P. and O'Brien, M. (2017) 'The Role of the State in Shaping Zero Hours Work in an Atypical Liberal Market Economy', *Economic and Industrial Democracy*, doi.org/10.1177/0143831X17735181.

O'Sullivan, M., Turner, T., McMahon, J., Ryan, L., Lavelle, J., Murphy, C., O'Brien, M. and Gunnigle, P. (2015b) *A Study of the Prevalence of Zero Hours Contracts among Irish Employers and its Impact on Employees*. Dublin: Department of Jobs, Enterprise and Innovation.

Paldam, M. and Pederson, P.J. (1982) 'The Macro-Economic Strike Model: A Study of Seventeen Countries 1948–1975', *Industrial and Labour Relations Review*, 35(4), 504–21.

Palmer, G. (1983) *British Industrial Relations*. London: Allen & Unwin.

Panitch, L. (1979) 'The Development of Corporatism in Liberal Democracies', in P.C. Schmitter and G. Lehmbruch (eds), *Trends Towards Corporatist Intermediation*. London: Sage.

Parker, P.A.L., Hayes, W.R. and Lumb, A.L. (1971) *The Reform of Collective Bargaining at Plant and Company Level*. London: HMSO.

Pateman, C. (1970) *Participation and Democratic Theory*. Cambridge: Cambridge University Press.

Pedaci, M. (2016) 'Flexicurity', in A. Wilkinson and S. Johnston (eds), *Encyclopaedia of Human Resource Management*. Cheltenham: Elgar.

Pedersini, R. (2010) *Trade Union Strategies to Recruit New Groups of Workers*. Dublin: European Foundation for the Improvement of Living and Working Conditions.

Peetz, D. (1997) *Union Membership Trends: Statistics and Selected Analysis*. Melbourne, Australia: Australian Council of Trade Unions.

Pekkarinen, J., Pohjola, M. and Rowthorn, B. (1992) 'Social Corporatism and Economic Performance: Introduction and Conclusions', in J. Pekkarinen, M. Pohjola and B. Rowthorn (eds), *Social Corporatism: A Superior Economic System*. Oxford: Clarendon Press.

Pelling, H. (1976) *A History of British Trade Unionism*. Middlesex: Penguin.

Piazza, J.A. (2005) 'Globalization Quiescence, Globalization, Union Density and Strikes in 15 Industrialised Countries', *Economic and Industrial Democracy*, 26(2) 289–14.

Piketty, T. (2014) *Capital in the Twenty-First Century*. MA: Harvard University Press.

Piketty, T. (2015) 'About Capital in the Twenty-First Century', *American Economic Review: Papers and proceedings*, 105(5), 48–53.

Piketty, T. (2020) *Capital and Ideology*. MA: Harvard University Press.

Pochet, P. and Fajertag, G. (2000) 'A New Era for Social Pacts in Europe', in G. Fajertag and P. Pochet (eds), *Social Pacts in Europe – New Dynamics*. Brussels: European Trade Union Institute.

Poole, M. (1986), 'Managerial Strategies and Styles in Industrial Relations: A Comparative Analysis', *Journal of General Management*, 12 (1), 40–53.

Poutsma, E., Blasi, R. and Kruse, D.L. (2012) 'Employee Share Ownership and Profit Sharing in Different Institutional Contexts', *The International Journal of Human Resource Management*, 23(8), 1513–8.

Prendergast, A. (2016) 'Sharp End Experience and Lawyers' Tricks: A Conversation with Kevin Duffy and Alan Neal', *Industrial Relations News*, 36. Available at www.irn.ie

Prendergast, A. (2017) 'Failure to Prevent Sexual Harassment of Retail Worker Leads to Award', *Industrial Relations News*, 14. Available at www.irn.ie

Prendergast, A. (2019a) 'Interview: Liam Kelly, Director General of the WRC', *Industrial Relations News*, 40. Available at www.irn.ie

Prendergast, A. (2019b) 'Supreme Court Agrees that Lawyers May Not [be] Necessary in Internal Discipline Cases', *Industrial Relations News*, 41. Available at www.irn.ie

Prendergast A. (2019c) 'SIPTU to Ballot on Strike at Coca Cola Plant over Recognition', *Industrial Relations News*, 17. Available at www.irn.ie

Public Service Pay Commission (2015) *Terms of Reference,* accessed 20 March 2020, www.paycommission.gov.ie/work-of-the-commission/phase-1/terms-of-reference/

Public Service Pay Commission (2018) *Report of the Public Service Pay Commission: Recruitment and Retention Module 1.* Dublin: Public Service Pay Commission.

Purcell, J. (1987) 'Mapping Management Styles in Employee Relations', *Journal of Management Studies,* 24 (5), 533–48.

Purcell, J. (1992) 'The Impact of Corporate Strategy on Human Resource Management', in G. Salamon (ed.), *Human Resource Strategies.* London: Sage/Open University.

Purcell, J. and Sisson, K. (1983) 'Strategies and Practice in the Management of Industrial Relations', in G. Bain (ed.), *Industrial Relations in Britain.* Oxford: Blackwell

Rabbitte, P. and Gilmore, E. (1990) *Bertie's Bill.* Dublin: The Workers' Party.

Rackham, N. (1993) 'The Behaviour of Successful Negotiators', in R. J. Lewicki, J.A. Litterer, M.D. Saunders and J.W. Minton, *Negotiation Readings, Exercises and Cases* (2nd edn). Boston: Irwin, McGraw-Hill.

Reed, M. (1989) *The Sociology of Management: Themes, Perspectives and Prospects.* London: Harvester Wheatsheaf.

Registry of Friendly Societies (2019a) *Registry of Friendly Societies Annual Report 2018.* Dublin: Registry of Friendly Societies.

Registry of Friendly Societies (2019b) *Trade Union Acts 1871–1990. Annual Return Prescribed by the Registrar of Friendly Societies for a Registered Trade Union.* Dublin: Registry of Friendly Societies.

Reynaud, J.P. (1978) *Problems and Prospects for Collective Bargaining in the EEC Member States* [Document No. V/394/78-EN]. Brussels: Commission of the European Community.

Rhodes, M. (1998) 'Globalisation, Labour Markets and Welfare States: A Future of Competitive Corporatism', in M. Rhodes and Y. Meny (eds), *The Future of European Welfare: A New Social Contract.* London: Macmillan.

Riccucci, N.M. (1988) 'Nonpunitive Discipline in the Public Sector', *International Journal of Public Administration,* 11(1), 117–34.

Rigby, M. and Aledo, M.L.M. (2001) 'The Worst Record in Europe? A Comparative Analysis of Industrial Conflict in Spain', *European Journal of Industrial Relations,* 7(3), 287–305.

Roche, W.K. (1989) 'State Strategies and the Politics of Industrial Relations in Ireland', in Department of Industrial Relations, University College Dublin (eds), *Industrial Relations in Ireland: Contemporary Issues and Developments.* Dublin: University College Dublin.

Roche, W.K. (1995) 'The New Competitive Order and Employee Relations in Ireland', paper presented to the IBEC conference on Human Resources in the Global Market, Dublin, November.

Roche, W.K. (1997) 'The Trend of Unionisation', in W.K. Roche and T.V. Murphy (eds), *Irish Industrial Relations in Practice, Revised and Expanded Edition.* Dublin: Oak Tree Press.

Roche, W.K. (2001) 'Accounting for the Trend in Trade Union Recognition in Ireland', *Industrial Relations Journal* 32(1), 37–54.

Roche, W.K. (2007a) 'Social Partnership and Workplace Regimes in Ireland', *Industrial Relations Journal*, 38(3), 188–209.

Roche, W.K. (2007b) 'Developments in Industrial Relations and Human Resource Management in Ireland', *Economic and Social Research Institute*, Quarterly Economic Commentary (March), 62–77.

Roche, W.K. (2008) 'Social Partnership in Ireland and New Social Pacts', *Industrial Relations*, 46(3), 395–425.

Roche, W.K. (2009) 'Social Partnership from Lemass to Cowen', *Economic and Social Review*, 40(10), 183–205.

Roche, W.K. (2011) 'Irish Research Throws Light on HR's Recession', *People Management* (July), 32–5.

Roche, W.K. (2012a) 'Austerity Without Solidarity: Industrial Relations, Employment and Welfare in the Irish Crisis', paper presented at Varieties of Capitalism and Responses to the European Employment Crisis Research Conference, Centre for the Study of Europe and the World, University of Denver, Colorado, 1–2 June.

Roche, W.K. (2012b) '"After the Ball Is Over": Accounts of the Functioning and Demise of Social Partnership', in B. Sheehan (ed.), *The Labour Relations Commission: Recalling 21 Years: 1999– 2012* (114–49). Dublin: Labour Relations Commission.

Roche, W.K. (2012c) 'The Future of HR in the Public Sector', Contribution to Panel Session on the Croke Park Agreement: Performance to Date and Future, Public Affairs Ireland Annual Conference, Dublin, 27 September.

Roche, W.K. (2016) 'Turning Third-Party Intervention on its Head: Assisted Bargaining and the Prevention of Workplace Conflict in Ireland', in R. Saundry, P. Latreille and I. Ashman (eds), *Reframing Resolution: Innovation and Change in the Management of Workplace Conflict*. London Palgrave: Macmillan.

Roche, W.K. and Ashmore, J. (2001) 'Irish Unions in the 1990s: Testing the Limits of Social Partnership', in G. Griffin (ed.), *Changing Patterns of Trade Unionism: A Comparison of English Speaking Countries*. London: Mansell.

Roche, W.K. and Geary, J.F. (2002) 'Collaborative Production and the Irish Boom: Work Organisation, Partnership and Direct Involvement in Irish Workplaces', in D. D'Art and T. Turner (eds), *Irish Employment Relations in the New Economy*. Dublin: Blackhall Publishing.

Roche, W.K. and Gormley, T. (2017a) 'The Advent of Pattern Bargaining in Irish Industrial Relations', *Industrial Relations Journal*, 48(5/6), 442–62.

Roche, W.K. and Gormley, T. (2017b) 'The Durability of Coordinated Bargaining: Crisis, Recovery and Pay Fixing in Ireland', *Economic and Industrial Democracy*, accessed 20 March 2020, https://doi.org/10.1177/0143831X17718067

Roche, W. and Gunnigle, P. (1997) 'Competition and the New Industrial Relations Agenda', in T. Murphy and W. Roche (eds), *Irish Industrial Relations in Practice*. Dublin: Oak Tree Press.

Roche, W.K. and Larragy, J. (1986) *The Formation of the Irish Trade Union Movement and Organisational Developments since 1945* [Working Paper]. Dublin: Department of Industrial Relations, University College Dublin.

Roche, W.K. and Larragy, J. (1989) *The Determinants of the Annual Rate of Trade Union Growth and Decline in the Irish Republic: Evidence from the DUES Membership Series*. Dublin: University College Dublin.

Roche, W.K. and Teague, P. (2011) 'Firms and Innovative Conflict Management Systems in Ireland', *British Journal of Industrial Relations*, 49(3), 436–59.

Roche, W.K., Teague, P., Coughlan, A. and Fahy, M. (2011) *Human Resources in the Recession: Managing and Representing People at Work in Ireland*. Dublin: Labour Relations Commission.

Roche, W.K. and Turner, T. (1998) 'Human Resource Management and Industrial Relations: Substitution, Dualism and Partnership', in W.K. Roche, K. Monks and J. Walsh (eds), *Human Resource Strategies: Policy and Practice in Ireland*. Dublin: Oak Tree Press.

Rollinson, D. (1993) *Understanding Employee Relations: A Behavioural Approach*. Wokingham: Addison-Wesley.

Rose, M. (1977) *Industrial Behaviour: Theoretical Development since Taylor*. Middlesex: Penguin.

Ross, A.M. and Hartman, P. (1960) *Changing Patterns of Industrial Conflict*. New York: Wiley.

Royle, T. and Towers, B. (2002) *Labour Relations in the Global Fast-Food Industry*. London: Routledge.

RTÉ (1985) 'Dunnes Stores Workers Strike Against Apartheid', *The Womens Programme, RTÉ*, accessed 30 March 2020, www.rte.ie/archives/exhibitions/1861-strikes-pickets-and-protests/469917-dunnes-stores-strike/

RTÉ (2012a) 'Gilmore Warns Against "Season of Kite-Flying"', 12 September, accessed 30 March 2020, www.rte.ie/news/2012/0912/gilmore-says-croke-park-deal-will-be-honoured.html.

RTÉ (2012b) 'Vita Cortex Staff Accept Outstanding Redundancy Payments Proposal', 3 May, accessed 30 March 2020, https://www.rte.ie/news/2012/0502/319420-vita-cortex-staff-vote-to-accept-wages-proposal/

RTÉ (2019) 'France's Orange and ex-CEO Found Guilty over Workers' Suicides', 20 December, accessed 30 March 2020, www.rte.ie/news/business/2019/1220/1102379-orange-moral-harassment-finding/

Ryan, L. and Wallace, J. (2016), 'Annual Hours, Workplace Partnership and Mutual Gains: Exploring the Links', *Employee Relations*, 38 (2), 248–66.

Salamon, M. (1998) *Industrial Relations: Theory and Practice* (3rd edn). London: Prentice Hall.

Salamon, M. (2000) *Industrial Relations: Theory and Practice* (4th edn). Harlow: Financial Times/Prentice Hall.

Salin, D. (2003) 'Ways of Explaining Workplace Bullying: A Review of Enabling, Motivating and Precipitating Structures and Processes in the Work Environment', *Human Relations*, 56(12), 13–32.

Salin, D. (2008) 'The Prevention of Workplace Bullying as a Question of Human Resource Management: Measures Adopted and Underlying Organizational Factors', *Scandinavian Journal of Management*, 24(3), 221–31.

Saundry, R. (2016) 'Conceptualising Workplace Conflict and Conflict Management', in R. Saundry, P. Latreille and I. Ashman, *Reframing Resolution: Innovation and Change in the Management of Workplace Conflict*. London: Palgrave Macmillan.

Saundry, R., Jones, C. and Antcliff V. (2011) 'Discipline, Representation and Dispute Resolution – Exploring the Role of Trade Unions and Employee Companions in Workplace Discipline', *Industrial Relations Journal*, 42(2), 195–211.

Saville, J. (1967) 'Trade Unions and Free Labour: The Background to the Taff Vale Decision', in A. Briggs and J. Saville (eds), *Essays in Labour History*. London: Macmillan.

Schmitt, J. and Mitukiewicz, A. (2011) *Politics Matter: Changes in Unionization Rates in Rich Countries, 1960–2010*. Washington: Center for Economic and Policy Research.

Schmitter, P.C. (1979) 'Introduction', in P.C. Schmitter and G. Lehmbruch (eds), *Trends Towards Corporatist Intermediation*. London: Sage.

Schmitter, P.C. and Lehmbruch, G. (eds) (1979) *Trends Towards Corporatist Intermediation*. London: Sage.

Schmitter, P.C. and Streeck, W. (1999) *The Organization of Business Interests: Studying the Associative Action of Business in Advanced Industrial Societies* [Discussion Paper 99/1]. Cologne: Max-Planck Institut für Gesellschaftsforschung.

Scott, J.F. and Homans, G.C. (1947) 'Reflections on the Wildcat Strikes', *American Sociological Review*, 12, 278–87.

Seanad Éireann (2012) 'Croke Park Agreement: Statements, Seanad Debates', 213(6), 9 February, accessed 20 March 2020, https://www.oireachtas.ie/en/debates/debate/seanad/2012-02-09/

Sebenius, J.K. (2001) 'Six Habits of Merely Effective Negotiators', *Harvard Business Review*, 79(4), 89–95.

Shalev, M. (1992) 'The Resurgence of Labour Quiescence', in M. Regini (ed.), *The Future of Labour Movements*. London: Sage.

Sheehan, B. (2004) 'Looking Forward – "Stage Two" of National Pay Deal in Prospect', *Industrial Relations News*, 1 & 2, 16–17. Available at www.irn.ie

Sheehan, B. (2010) 'Employer Body Withdraws from National Pay Deal', accessed 30 March 2020, www.eurofound.europa.eu/publications/article/2010/employer-body-withdraws-from-national-pay-deal

Sheehan, B. (2011a) 'Dáil Answers Reveal Fees Paid to IBEC by Some State Agencies', *Industrial Relations News*, 20. Available at www.irn.ie

Sheehan, B. (2011b), 'Bruton's Plan to Change "Haphazard" Employment Rights System', *Industrial Relations News,* 30. Available at www.irn.ie

Sheehan, B. (2011c), 'Government's Policy Continues Shift Towards "Social Dialogue", Away from Partnership', *Industrial Relations News*, 14, 1–3. Available at www.irn.ie

Sheehan, B. (2011d) 'Social Partnership Gets Mixed Reviews from Consultants', *Industrial Relations News,* 9, 17–18. Available at www.irn.ie

Sheehan, B. (2012) 'Bruton's Plan Will Limit Right to a "Fair Trial", says EAT Committee', *Industrial Relations News,* 23. Available at www.irn.ie

Sheehan, B. (2013) 'Skill, and Some Luck, sees Haddington Road in Place for Vast Majority', *Industrial Relations News,* 24. Available at www.irn.ie

Sheehan, B. (2015) 'IBEC Rejects "Lazy Narrative" on Costs and Incomes, Rules Out National Deal', *Industrial Relations News*, 1. Available at www.irn.ie

Sheehan, B. (2017) 'Feared "Winter of Discontent" in Public Service Fails to Materialise', *Industrial Relations News*, 10. Available at www.irn.ie

Sheehan, B. (2018a) 'GE Healthcare – Pay Harmonisation for SIPTU Operators is Framework's Latest Dividend', *Industrial Relations News*, 33. Available at www.irn.ie

Sheehan, B. (2018b) 'New Style Stability Agreements –A New Form of Collective Bargaining', *Industrial Relations News*, 15. Available at www.irn.ie

Sheehan, B. (2018c) 'Unions Accused of Adopting "A la Carte" Approach on Collective Bargaining', *Industrial Relations News*, 31. Available at www.irn.ie

Sheehan, B. (2019a) 'SIPTU Says No to National Pay Trade-off, but Yes to More Dialogue', *Industrial Relations News*, 37. Available at www.irn.ie

Sheehan, B. (2019b) 'New ICTU Policy on Collective Bargaining Aspires to EU Directive', *Industrial Relations News*, 25. Available at www.irn.ie

Sheehan, B. (2019c) 'The Journey Towards a "World Class" Workplace Relations System – Where Are We?', *Industrial Relations News*, 43. Available at www.irn.ie

Sheehan, B. (2019d) 'Debate on IR Highlights Pros and Cons of the Dispute Resolution System', *Industrial Relations News*, 44. Available at www.irn.ie

Sheehan, B., Sheehan, Z. and Higgins, C. (2020) 'LCR Review: Unions Still Favour "Section 20" Route to "Recognition"', *Industrial Relations News*. Available at www.irn.ie

Sheldon, P., Della Torre, E. and Nacamulli, R. (2019) 'When Territory Matters: Employer Associations and Changing Collective Goods Strategies', *Human Resource Management Journal*, 29(1), 17–35.

Sheldon, P., Nacamulli, R., Paoletti, F. and Morgan, D. E. (2016) 'Employer Association Responses to the Effects of Bargaining Decentralization in Australia and Italy: Seeking Explanations from Organizational Theory', *British Journal of Industrial Relations*, 54(1), 160–91.

Sheldon, P. and Thornthwaite, L. (2005) 'Members or Clients? Employer Associations, the Decentralization of Bargaining, and the Reorientation of Service Provision: Evidence from Europe and Australia', *Business and Economic History*, 3, 1–21.

Sherman, M. and Lucia, A. (1992) 'Option: Positive Discipline and Labor Arbitration', *Arbitration Journal*, June, 56–8.

Silverman, J. (1970) *The Theory of Organisations*. London: Heinemann.

Silvia, S. and Schroeder, W. (2007) 'Why are German Employer Associations Declining? Arguments and Evidence', *Comparative Political Studies*, 40(12), 1433–59.

Simms, M., Eversberg, D., Dupuy, C. and Hipp, L. (2018) 'Organizing Young Workers Under Precarious Conditions: What Hinders or Facilitates Union Success', *Work and Occupations*, 45(4), 420–50.

Sisson, K. (1994) 'Workplace Europe. Direct Participation in Organisational Change: Introducing the EPOC Project', paper presented to the International Industrial Relations Association 4th European Regional Congress on 'Transformation of European Industrial Relations: Consequences of Integration and Disintegration', Helsinki.

Skogstad, A., Einarsen, S., Torsheim, T. Aasland, M.S. and Hetland, H. (2007) 'The Destructiveness of Laissez-Faire Leadership Behavior', *Journal of Occupational Health Psychology*, 12(1), 80–92.

Smith, S. (2003) *Labour Economics* (2nd edn). London: Routledge.

Social Justice Ireland (2009) *Income and Poverty.* Dublin: Social Justice Ireland.

Sparrow, P. and Hiltrop, J. (1994) *European Human Resource Management in Transition*. London: Prentice Hall.

Stafford, P. (2011) 'The Rise and Fall of Social Partnership: Its Impact on Interest Group Lobbying in Ireland', *Journal of Public Affairs*, 11(2), 74–9.

Stokke, T.A. and Thörnqvist, C. (2001) 'Strikes and Collective Bargaining in the Nordic Countries', *European Journal of Industrial Relations*, 7(3), 245–67.

Stratis Consulting (2019) *White Paper on The Journey Towards a 'World Class' Workplace Relations System – Where Are We?*, accessed 30 March 2020, https://bc6a1feb-3c9d-4101-97e5-07f0cdef797.filesusr.com/ugd/c048a5_068395f93e0d4a52a8e64029a562ef04.pdf

Strauss, G. and Sayles, L. R. (1980) *Personnel: Human Problems of Management* (4th edn). New Jersey: Prentice-Hall.

Sturdy, A., Knights, D. and Willmott, H. (1992) 'Introduction: Skill and Consent in the Labour Process', in A. Sturdy, D. Knights and H. Willmott (eds), *Skill and Consent: Contemporary Studies in the Labour Process*. London: Routledge.

Tailby, S. and Pollert, A. (2011) 'Non-unionized Young Workers and Organizing the Unorganized', *Economic and Industrial Democracy*, 32(3), 499–522.

Taras, D.G. and Bennett, J.T. (2002) 'Technological Change and Industrial Relations', *Journal of Labor Research,* 23 (3), 335–8.

Teague, P. (2009) 'Path Dependency and Comparative Industrial Relations Conflict Management Systems in Sweden and the Republic of Ireland', *British Journal of Industrial Relations*, 47(3), 499–520.

Teague, P. and Doherty, L. (2009) 'Reforming our IR Institutions – A Snip in the Wrong Direction?', *Industrial Relations News*, 28. Available at www.irn.ie

Teague, P. and Donaghey, J. (2009) 'Why Has Irish Social Partnership Survived?', *British Journal of Industrial Relations*, 47(1), 55–78.

Teague, P. and Donaghey, J. (2012) 'The Death of Irish Social Partnership: Should We Care?' [Working Paper Supplied by the Authors].

Teague, P., Roche, W.K. and Hann, D. (2012) 'The Diffusion of Workplace ADR in Ireland', *Economic and Industrial Democracy*, 33(4), 581–604.

Teague, P. and Thomas, D. (2008) *Employment Dispute Resolution and Standard Setting in the Republic of Ireland*. Dublin: Oak Tree Press.

Thelen, H. and Withall, J. (1949) 'Three Frames of Reference: The Description of Climate', *Human Relations*, 2(2), 159–76.

Thelen, K. and van Wijnbergen, C. (2003) 'The Paradox of Globalization: Labor Relations in Germany and Beyond', *Comparative Political Studies*, 36(8), 859–80.

Thomas, D., Brannick, T. and Kelly, A. (2003) 'Social Partnership and Industrial Conflict in Ireland: Securing the Peace Dividend?' [Working Paper]. Dublin: University College Dublin.

Thomason, G. (1984) *A Textbook of Industrial Relations Management*. London: Institute of Personnel Management.

Thompson, L. (2009) *The Mind and Heart of the Negotiator* (5th edn). New Jersey: Prentice Hall.

Thompson, P. (2016) 'Labour Process Theory', in A. Wilkinson and S. Johnston (eds), *Encyclopaedia of Human Resource Management*. Cheltenham: Elgar.

Thornthwaite, L. and Sheldon, P. (1997) 'Employer Associations, Dual Membership and the Problem of Conflicting Policies', in T. Bramble *et al.* (eds), *Current Research in Industrial Relations, Proceedings of the 11th AIRAANZ Conference*. Brisbane: January.

Tiernan, S. and Morley, M. J. (2019) *Modern Management* (5th edn). Dublin: Institute for Public Administration.

Tolich, P. and Harcourt, M. (1999) 'Why Do People Join Unions? A Case Study of the New Zealand Engineering, Printing and Manufacturing Union', *New Zealand Journal of Industrial Relations*, 24(1), 63–74.

Tolliday, S. and Zeitlin, J. (1991) 'Employers and Industrial Relations between Theory and History', in S. Tolliday and J. Zeitlin (eds), *The Power to Manage? Employers and Industrial Relations in Comparative-Historical Perspective*. London: Routledge.

Torrington, D. and Hall, L. (1998) *Human Resource Management*. London: Prentice Hall.

Torrington, D., Hall, L., Taylor, S. and Atkinson, C. (2011) *Human Resource Management* (8th edn). Harlow, UK: Pearson Education.

Toubøl, J. and Strøby Jensen, C. (2014) 'Why do People Join Trade Unions? The Impact of Workplace Union Density on Union Recruitment', *Transfer*, 20(1), 135–54.

Traxler, F. (2004) 'Employer Associations, Institutions and Economic Change: A Crossnational Comparison', *Industrielle Beziehungen*, 11(2), 42–60.

Turner, H. (1969) *Is Britain Really Strike Prone? A Review of the Incidence, Character and Costs of Industrial Conflict* [Occasional Paper No. 20]. Cambridge: Cambridge University Press.

Turner, T. (2006) 'Industrial Relations Systems, Economic Efficiency and Social Equity in the 1990s', *Review of Social Economy*, 64(1), 93–108.

Turner, T., Cross, C. and O'Sullivan, M. (2014) 'Does Union Membership Benefit Immigrant Workers in Hard Times?', *Journal of Industrial Relations*, 56(5): 611–30.

Turner, T. and D'Art, D. (2000) 'A Review of Centralised Wage Agreements in Ireland 1987–2000', *Croner's Employee Relations Review*, 12, 16–9.

Turner, T. and D'Art, D. (2003) 'The Feminization of Irish Trade Unions: Involvement, Solidarity and the Relevance of Gender', *Women in Management Review*, 18(5), 228–35.

Turner, T. and D'Art, D. (2012) 'Public Perceptions of Trade Unions in Countries of the European Union: A Causal Analysis', *Labor Studies Journal*, 37(1), 33–55.

Turner, T., D'Art, D. and O'Sullivan, M. (2008) 'Union Availability, Union Membership and Immigrant Workers: An Empirical Investigation of the Irish Case', *Employee Relations*, 30(5): 479–93.

Turner, T. and O'Sullivan, M. (2013) 'The Economic Crisis and the Restructuring of Wage Setting Mechanisms for Vulnerable Workers in Ireland', *Economic and Social Review*, 44(2): 197–219.

Turner, T., Ryan, L. and O'Sullivan, M. (2019) 'Does Union Membership Matter? Political Participation, Attachment to Democracy and Generational Change', *European Journal of Industrial Relations*.

Turner, T. and Wallace, J. (2000) 'The Irish Model of Social Partnership: Achievements and Limitations', paper presented to the European Congress of the International Industrial Relations Association, Oslo, 25–9 June.

Tyson, S. and Fell, A. (1986) *Evaluating the Personnel Function*. London: Hutchinson.

Undy, R. (2008) *Trade Union Merger Strategies*. Oxford: Oxford University Press.

UNI Global Union (2019) *Connective Action. Digital Tools for Trade Unions: 2019,* accessed 30 March 2020, http://www.thefutureworldofwork.org/media/35630/fwowconnectiveaction _2019.pdf

Ury, W. (1992) *Getting Past NO: Negotiating with Difficult People*. London: Century Business.

Vahabi, M. (2011) 'The Economics of Destructive Power', in D.L. Braddon and K. Hartley, *Handbook on the Economics of Conflict*. Cheltenham: Edward Elgar Publishing.

Vandaele, K. (2019) *Bleak Prospects: Mapping Trade Union Membership in Europe Since 2000*. Brussels: ETUI.

Visser, J. (2019a) *Trade Unions in the Balance. ILO ACTRAV Working Paper*. Geneva: International Labour Office.

Visser, J. (2019b) *ICTWSS Data Base. Version 6.1*. Amsterdam: Amsterdam Institute for Advanced Labour Studies.

von Prondzynski, F. (1989) 'Collective Labour Law', in Department of Industrial Relations, University College Dublin (eds), *Industrial Relations in Ireland: Contemporary Issues and Developments*. Dublin: University College Dublin.

von Prondzynski, F. (1992) 'Ireland Between Centralism and the Market', in A. Ferner and R. Hyman (eds), *Industrial Relations in the New Europe*. Oxford: Blackwell.

von Prondzynski, F. (1998) 'Ireland: Corporatism Revived', in A. Ferner and R. Hyman (eds), *Changing Industrial Relations in Europe*. Oxford: Blackwell.

von Prondzynski, F. and McCarthy, C. (1984) *Employment Law*. London: Sweet and Maxwell.

Waddington, J. (2005) 'Trade Union Membership in Europe: The Extent of the Problem and the Range of Trade Union Responses'. Background Paper for the ETUC/ETUI-REHS Top-Level Summer School, Florence, July.

Waddington, J. and Whitson, C. (1997) 'Why Do People Join Unions in a Period of Membership Decline?', *British Journal of Industrial Relations,* 35(4), 515–46.

Wall, M. (2012) 'Bruton Stands by His Dispute Reform Plans', *The Irish Times*, 6 July.

Wallace, J. (1982) *Industrial Relations in Limerick City and Environs. Employment Research Programme.* Limerick: University of Limerick.

Wallace, J. (1989) 'Procedure Agreements and their Place in Workplace Industrial Relations', in Department of Industrial Relations, University College Dublin (eds), *Industrial Relations in Ireland: Contemporary Issues and Developments.* Dublin: University College Dublin.

Wallace, J. and Clifford, N. (1998) *Collective Bargaining and Flexibility in Ireland.* Geneva: International Labour Office.

Wallace, J. and Delany, B. (1997) 'Back to the Future? The Irish Industrial Relations Act 1990', in F. Meenan (ed.), *Legal Perspectives – The Juridification of the Employment Relationship.* Dublin: Oak Tree Press.

Wallace, J. and McDonnell, C. (2000) 'The Institutional Provisions of the Industrial Relations Act 1990 in Operation', *Irish Business and Administrative Research*, (21)1, 169–88.

Wallace, J. and O'Shea, F. (1987) *A Study of Unofficial Strikes in Ireland.* Dublin: Government Publications Office.

Wallace, J. and O'Sullivan, M. (2002) 'The Industrial Relations Act 1990: A Critical Review', in D. D'Art and T. Turner (eds), *Irish Employment Relations in the New Economy.* Dublin: Blackhall Publishing.

Wallace, J. and O'Sullivan, M. (2006) 'Contemporary Strike Trends Since 1980: Peering Through the Wrong End of a Telescope', in M. Morley, P. Gunnigle and D.G. Collins (eds), *Global Industrial Relations.* London: Routledge.

Wallace, J., Turner, T. and McCarthy, A. (1998) 'EMU and the Impact on Irish Industrial Relations', in T. Kauppinen (ed.), *The Impact of EMU on Industrial Relations in Europe. Publication No. 9.* Helsinki: Finnish Labour Relations Association.

Walsh, F. (2019) 'Symposium on the Labour Market. Union Membership in Ireland Since 2003', *Journal of the Statistical and Social Inquiry Statistical Society of Ireland*, 44, 86–100.

Walton, R.E. McKersie, R.B. (1965) *A Behavioural Theory of Labour Negotiations: An Analysis of a Social Interaction System.* New York: McGraw-Hill.

Ward, P. (2014) *Report to the Minister for Education and Skills of the Chairperson of the Expert Group on Fixed-Term and Part-Time Employment in Primary and Second Level Education in Ireland*, accessed 30 March 2020, https://www.ictu.ie/download/pdf/ward_report.pdf

Webb, S. and Webb, B. (1897) *Industrial Democracy: Vol. I.* London: Longman.

Webb, S. and Webb, B. (1920) *The History of Trade Unionism.* London: Longman.

Wedderburn, W.K. (1965) *The Worker and the Law.* London: Penguin.

Wedderburn, W.K. (1986) *The Worker and the Law* (3rd edn). London: Penguin.

Wheeler, H.N. (1976) 'Punishment Theory and Industrial Discipline', *Industrial Relations*, 15(2), 235–43.

Wheeler, H.N. and McClendon, J.A. (1991) 'The Individual Decision to Unionize', in G. Strauss, D. G. Gallagher and J. Fiorito (eds), *The State of the Unions.* Madison, WI: Industrial Relations Research Association.

Whelan, C. (1982) *Worker Priorities, Trust in Management and Prospects for Worker Participation, Paper III.* Dublin: Economic and Social Research Institute.

Whyte, W.F. (1951) *Pattern for Industrial Peace.* New York: Harper.

Wichert, I. (2002) 'Stress Intervention', in B. Burchell, D. Lapido and F. Wilkinson (eds), *Job Insecurity and Work Intensification.* London: Routlidge.

Wilkinson, A. (2002) 'Empowerment', in M. Poole and M. Warner (eds), *International Encyclopaedia of Business and Management Handbook of Human Resource Management.* London: ITB Press.

Wilkinson, A., Dundon, T., Marchington, M. and Ackers, P. (2004) 'Changing Patterns of Employee Voice: Case Studies from the UK and Republic of Ireland', *Journal of Industrial Relations*, 46(3), 298–322.

Wilkinson, R. and Pickett, K. (2009) *The Spirit Level: Why More Equal Societies Almost Always Do Better*. London: Allen Lane.

Wilkinson, R. and Pickett, K. (2019) 'The Health and Social Costs of Inequality', *Countess Markievicz Memorial Lecture Series*, Irish Association for Industrial Relations, 22 November, accessed 4 April 2020, https://www.ul.ie/iair/content/countess-markievicz-lecture

Williams, S., Abbott, B. and Heery, E. (2011) 'Non-Union Worker Representation Through Civil Society Organisations: Evidence from the United Kingdom', *Industrial Relations Journal* 42(1), 69–85.

Williams, S., Abbott, B. and Heery, E. (2017) 'Civil Governance in Work and Employment Relations: How Civil Society Organizations Contribute to Systems of Labour Governance', *Journal of Business Ethics*, 144, 103–19.

Wilthagen, T. and Tros, F. (2004) 'The Concept of "Flexicurity": A New Approach to Regulating Employment and Labour Markets', *Transfer: European Review of Labour and Research*, 10(2), 166–86.

Wood, G. and Allen, M.M.C. (2019) 'Institutional Theory, Business Systems and Employment Relations', in K. Townsend, K. Cafferkey, A.O. McDermott and T. Dundon, *Elgar Introduction to Theories of Human Resources and Employment Relations*. Cheltenham: Elgar Publishing.

Wood, S. & Peccei, R. (1990) 'Preparing For 1992? Business-Led Versus Strategic Human Resource Management', *Human Resource Management Journal*, 1(1), 63-88.

Workplace Relations Commission (2015–2019) *Workplace Relations Commission Annual Reports*. Dublin: Workplace Relations Commission.

Wright Mills, C. (1948) *The New Men of Power*. New York: Harcourt Brace.

Yeates, P. (2000) *Lockout: Dublin 1913*. Dublin: Gill & Macmillan.

Yeates, P. (2003) '1913 Lockout', *The Irish Times*, 25 August.

Yeates, P. (2013) 'Class War Versus Social Compact? A Contemporary Analysis of the 1913 Lockout, John Lovett Memorial Lecture', *Industrial Relations News*, 10. Available at www.irn.ie

You, K. (2016) Varieties of Capitalism, in A. Wilkinson and S. Johnston (eds), *Encyclopaedia of Human Resource Management*. Cheltenham: Elgar.

Index